GOVERNING THE EXTRACTIVE SECTOR

This book considers, and offers solutions to, the problems faced by local communities and the environment with respect to global mining.

The author explores the idea of grievance mechanisms in the home states of the major mining conglomerates. These grievance mechanisms should be functional, pragmatic and effective at resolving disputes between mining enterprises and impacted communities. The key to this provocative solution is twofold: the proposal harnesses the power of industry-sponsored dispute mechanisms to reduce the costs and other burdens on home state governments and judicial systems. Critically, civil society actors will be given a role as both advocates and mediators in order to achieve a fair result for those impacted abroad by extractive enterprises.

Compelling, engaging and timely, this book presents an innovative approach for regulating the foreign conduct of the extractive sector.

Global Energy Law and Policy: Volume 5

Global Energy Law and Policy

Series Editors
Peter D Cameron
Pieter Bekker
Volker Roeben

Energy policy and energy law are undergoing rapid global transformation, characterised by the push in favour of decarbonisation. The 2015 Sustainable Development Goals and the 2015 Paris Agreement on international climate action have forged a consensus for a pathway to a universal just transition towards a low-carbon economy for all states and all societies.

This series publishes conceptual work that help academics, legal practitioners and decision-makers to make sense of these transformational changes. The perspective of the series is global. It welcomes contributions on international law, regional law (for example, from the EU, US and ASEAN regions), and the domestic law of all states with emphasis on comparative works that identify horizontal trends, and including transnational law. The series' scope is comprehensive, embracing both public and commercial law on energy in all forms and sources and throughout the energy life-cycle from extraction, production, operation, consumption and waste management/decommissioning. The series is a forum for innovative interdisciplinary work that uses the insights of cognate disciplines to achieve a better understanding of energy law and policy in the 21st century.

Recent titles in this series:

Decarbonisation and the Energy Industry
edited by Tade Oyewumni, Penelope Crossley, Frédéric Gilles Sourgens and Kim Talus

The Global Energy Transition: Law, Policy and Economics for Energy in the 21st Century
edited by Peter D Cameron, Xiaoyi Mu and Volker Roeben

The Law and Governance of Mining and Minerals: A Global Perspective
by Ana Elizabeth Bastida

National Climate Change Acts: The Emergence, Form and Nature of National Framework Climate Legislation
edited by Thomas L Muinzer

Governing the Extractive Sector: Regulating the Foreign Conduct of International Mining Firms
by Jeffrey Bone

Governing the Extractive Sector

Regulating the Foreign Conduct of International Mining Firms

Jeffrey Bone

•HART•
OXFORD • LONDON • NEW YORK • NEW DELHI • SYDNEY

HART PUBLISHING

Bloomsbury Publishing Plc

Kemp House, Chawley Park, Cumnor Hill, Oxford, OX2 9PH, UK

1385 Broadway, New York, NY 10018, USA

29 Earlsfort Terrace, Dublin 2, Ireland

HART PUBLISHING, the Hart/Stag logo, BLOOMSBURY and the Diana logo are trademarks of Bloomsbury Publishing Plc

First published in Great Britain 2021

A catalogue record for this book is available from the British Library.

Library of Congress Cataloging-in-Publication data

Names: Bone, Jeffrey (Writer on international mining firms), author.

Title: Governing the extractive sector : regulating the foreign conduct of international mining firms / Jeffrey Bone.

Description: Oxford, UK ; New York, NY : Hart Publishing, an imprint of Bloomsbury Publishing, 2021. | Series: Global energy law and policy ; volume 5 | Includes bibliographical references and index.

Identifiers: LCCN 2020048486 (print) | LCCN 2020048487 (ebook) | ISBN 9781509941872 (hardback) | ISBN 9781509944750 (paperback) | ISBN 9781509941896 (pdf) | ISBN 9781509941889 (Epub)

Subjects: LCSH: Mining law. | Mineral industries—Law and legislation. | Mines and mineral resources.

Classification: LCC K3904 .B66 2021 (print) | LCC K3904 (ebook) | DDC 343.07/7—dc23

LC record available at https://lccn.loc.gov/2020048486

LC ebook record available at https://lccn.loc.gov/2020048487

ISBN: HB: 978-1-50994-187-2
ePDF: 978-1-50994-189-6
ePub: 978-1-50994-188-9

Typeset by Compuscript Ltd, Shannon

ACKNOWLEDGEMENTS

This book is the product of my doctoral studies at the University of Connecticut School of Law. I am tremendously fortunate to have had Mark Weston Janis as my supervisor, who went beyond what I would have expected him to offer in terms of guidance and support. He is the person who encouraged me to turn this project into a book.

I benefitted greatly from having two extremely dedicated dissertation examination committee members, Peter Lindseth and Joseph MacDougald. The arguments in the book have also benefitted from thorough feedback from the members of my prospectus examination committee, Stephen Utz, Mathilde Cohen and Jessica Rubin. I would also like to thank Will Randall for his helpful advice on chapter seven.

I also received valuable feedback from audiences at the University of Connecticut School of Law, Cornell Law School, University of Alberta Faculty of Law and the Canadian Academy of Legal Studies in Business. As some of the arguments contained in this book are now published in the *McGill International Journal of Sustainable Development Law*, I would also like to acknowledge the comments and critiques offered by its external reviewers.

Thank you to Hart Publishing, whose dedicated and professional staff were supportive and helpful throughout the publishing process.

To Shaun Fluker at the University of Calgary, thank you for believing in my abilities as a legal academic and future professor. I cannot imagine being on this path were it not for your encouragement during and after my LLM.

I would also like to mention Development and Peace, a civil society organisation of the Catholic Church in Canada. The idea for this book began when I came across a 2013 bulletin from Development and Peace outlining the graphic experiences of communities living near Canadian-owned mines in Africa, Asia and Latin America. These experiences included conflict, pollution, forced displacements and other negative impacts. Whenever working on this project proved frustrating, I reminded myself that the issues I was addressing impacted vulnerable people in significant ways.

Finally, thank you to my friends and family for their unwavering support.

Jeff Bone
Philadelphia, PA
July 2020

CONTENTS

LIST OF ABBREVIATIONS

Alien Tort Statute (ATS)

Australia Mining Ombudsman (AMO)

Canada Energy Regulator (CER)

Canada's Export Development Compliance Officer (EDC Officer)

Canadian Network on Corporate Accountability (CNCA)

Canadian Ombudsperson for Responsible Enterprise (CORE)

Corporate Social Responsibility (CSR)

Democratic Republic of the Congo (Congo)

Export Development Compliance Officer (EDC Officer)

Foreign Corrupt Practices Act (FCPA)

Global Reporting Initiative (GRI)

International Criminal Court (ICC)

International Finance Corporation (IFC)

International Finance Corporation Performance Standards on Environmental and Social Sustainability (Performance Standards)

International Finance Corporation Policy on Environmental and Social Sustainability (IFC Policy)

International Petroleum Industry Environmental Conservation Association (IPIECA)

Key Performance Indicators (KPIs)

Multinational Investment Guarantee Agency (MIGA)

Newmont Mining Corporation (Newmont)

Non-Governmental Organisation (NGO)

North American Free Trade Agreement (NAFTA)

Office of the Extractive Sector Corporate Social Responsibility Counsellor (CSR Counsellor)

Organisation for Economic Co-operation and Development (OECD)

OECD Due Diligence Guidance on Responsible Supply Chains of Minerals from Conflict-Affected and High-Risk Areas (OECD Minerals Policy)

OECD Guidelines for Multinational Enterprises (OECD Guidelines)

OECD National Contact Point (NCP)

Oxfam Australia Mining Ombudsman (AMO)

Quebec Civil Code (CCQ)

Restatement (Fourth) of the Foreign Relations Law (Restatement)

UN Commission on International Trade Law Model Law on International Commercial Arbitration (Model Law)

UN Guiding Principles on Business and Human Rights (UN Guiding Principles)

UN Norms on the Responsibilities of Transnational Corporations and Other Business Enterprises with Regards to Human Rights (UN Norms)

US Drug Enforcement Administration (DEA)

US Securities and Exchange Commission (SEC)

Voluntary Principles on Security and Human Rights (Voluntary Principles)

*Note that other key terms are provided at the beginning of chapter seven that are only applicable to the proposal presented in chapters seven, eight and the Appendix.

Introduction

There is a copper mine in the Democratic Republic of Congo (Congo). Initially, the mine was operated by the Canadian mining company First Quantum Minerals. Though located in the Congo, the mine has deeply impacted a community in Zambia, which sits on the southern border of the country. Having settled in a particular area on account of its rich soil, an area ideal for farming, the community was forced to relocate after First Quantum moved in, paving over the location and using it as an entrance to the copper mine.

In 2018, a civil society group in Zambia wrote a letter to the president of First Quantum Minerals.[1] The group, the Network for Community Resources Governance, is a youth-led network of mining communities in Zambia. The subject line of the letter is simply 'Community Grievance' and it details how First Quantum Minerals' resettlement programme has negatively impacted local residents, laying out a fervent plea for support from the company that is responsible for their resettlement.

When the community first learned that they would be resettled, meetings were held with the company's representatives. As a result, the company made several commitments as part of the resettlement, including the provision of new homes. A picture of one of these homes is included in the letter. It is a tiny, unwelcoming structure. The door is a cloth sheet.

All of the homes provided by First Quantum have one bedroom regardless of the size of the family. One relocated family has 12 members. Out of necessity they have constructed an additional dwelling made with a grass roof to accommodate everyone.

The resettled land is also less fertile than where community members had originally lived and cultivated crops. They can no longer harvest enough to feed themselves, let alone sell at market as they had in the past to support their families.

Another picture is contained within the letter. It shows some of the yield of corn grown at the resettlement. What should be yellow is off-white. It is misshapen and marked with spoiled kernels. The letter ends: 'Your kind attention to this matter will be highly appreciated. We stand ready to work with you to address the local community's plight.'

[1] Letter from Mutinta Hadunka Governance and Community Liaison Officer at the Network for Community Resource Governance to Clive Newall, President of First Quantum Minerals (30 July 2018).

…

This story is not unique and similar scenarios can be found all over the world. One need only look to the litany of troubling complaints against the international extractive sector: the forced relocation of Indigenous peoples, violent quashing of protests and the insensate poisoning of the environment. Are these alleged actions the result of deliberate malfeasance by greedy and rapacious mining executives? The problem is not that straightforward.

Many of the companies accused of wrongdoing have good intentions for the communities they operate in overseas. They truly believe that they can be good corporate citizens towards the people that their activities impact at the same time as they seek a hefty return on value for shareholders. Be that as it may, it does not usually turn out this way.

Finding a feasible strategy to protect social and environmental rights is not easy. This problem could potentially be resolved with the imposition of new regulations aimed at creating liability for the international conduct of western mining empires.

While noble in theory, there are costs for exacting rules on business in a home state when those rules are not present in other jurisdictions. Creating legal requirements that do not exist elsewhere could lead to a dramatic flight of capital out of a country.

While this indictment of the global extractive sector is not directed to any particular jurisdiction, this book develops the proposed framework for regulation in the context of the Canadian mining industry.

Canada presents a particularly compelling example on which to construct a theory of regulating the foreign conduct of the extractive sector because its Federal Government has taken recent regulatory action to address the problem. In addition, there are attempts underway in the Canadian judicial system to hold Canadian companies to account for their actions overseas. As this book will reveal, similar attempts to regulate the mining sector through a home state judicial process have also been brought in the US, UK and Australia.

Many Canadians do not realise that their country is a major player in the extractive sector, with nearly 75 per cent of the world's mining companies listed on the Toronto Stock Exchange. In 2017, Canadian mining companies' international assets were estimated to be worth $168.7 billion.[2] With this kind of investment at stake, caution should be heeded before implementing strict legal requirements that will impact Canada's mining sector. Mass relocation of businesses headquartered in Canada may occur, along with the delisting of multinational extractive sector corporations from the Toronto Stock Exchange.

The time for reshaping Canada's policy towards the foreign conduct of the extractive sector is now. The initial political thrust to strengthen Canadian

[2] Natural Resources Canada, 'Canadian Mining Assets' (*Government of Canada*, February 2019), www.nrcan.gc.ca/mining-materials/publications/19323.

performance on these issues was raised by the now governing Liberal party when they were in opposition in 2009. A leading Canadian politician on these concerns, Liberal Member of Parliament John McKay, unsuccessfully tabled Bill C-300 that called for comprehensive regulation of Canada's extractive sector abroad. He attempted again in 2014. Current Prime Minister Justin Trudeau, an opposition MP in 2014, voted for that Bill, but to no avail. These actions occurred prior to the Liberal Party of Canada forming government in 2015.

Since their ascension into power, the Liberals have taken steps to govern the foreign conduct of the Canadian extractive sector. However, the most recent developments raise questions about their authenticity towards the cause and their commitment to the original policy. These developments include the formation of a new ombudsperson office aimed at governing the conduct of businesses abroad. The concern is that its proposed powers are flat and inadequate.

In 2018, the Minister of International Trade announced the creation of the Canadian Ombudsperson for Responsible Enterprise (CORE).[3] The CORE's mandate is to investigate human rights incidents involving Canadian companies operating in the mining, oil and gas and garment sectors. The office is empowered to compel documents and witnesses, issue independent reports and recommend remedies to be implemented by various arms of the Government. This includes the withdrawal of government advocacy and financial assistance.

Entities equivalent to the CORE do not currently exist in other countries. In this way, the CORE may be without precedent, but it lacks the power to affect any meaningful sanctions. For instance, the CORE's mandate is to independently investigate complaints but the only real power it has is to recommend the withdrawal of government services and support. On top of this, the recommendation for denial of government services affects very few public agencies. It has no effect on provincial governments and does not impact the investment decisions of the Canada Pension Plan Investment Board.

As a comparison, the authority of the CORE is strikingly similar to the National Contact Point (NCP) in Canada. The Canadian NCP is a venue for dispute resolution concerning foreign operations of Canadian companies. The implementation of an NCP is compulsory for Member States of the Organisation for Economic Co-operation and Development (OECD) that adhere to the OECD Guidelines for Multinational Enterprises (OECD Guidelines).[4] The purpose of an NCP is to provide a process for dealing with complaints against multinational corporations from that particular Member State.

Much like the CORE, Canada's NCP also has the power to recommend the withdrawal of government support and services to multinational Canadian enterprises. Also much like the CORE, the utility of Canada's NCP is highly questionable.

[3] Government of Canada, 'Office of the Canadian Ombudsperson for Responsible Enterprise' (2020), core-ombuds.canada.ca/core_ombuds-ocre_ombuds/index.aspx?lang=eng.

[4] OECD, 'The OECD Guidelines for Multinational Enterprises' (2011), www.oecd.org/dataoecd/56/36/1922428.pdf.

Take one notable example from 2014 where Canada's NCP attempted to impose sanctions against China Gold International Resources Corp Ltd, a subsidiary of a Chinese state-owned mining company.

China Gold is headquartered in British Columbia and listed on the Toronto Stock Exchange, giving it a firm Canadian presence. A Canadian civil society group alleged that China Gold's labour, health and safety practices were below the standards expected by the OECD. The complaint asserted that these deficiencies in China Gold's practices resulted in the deaths of 83 mine workers living in a camp in the Gyama Valley of Tibet. The sanctions were levied, not for findings of wrongdoing, but on account of China Gold's refusal to participate in Canada's NCP process regarding the company's mining activities in Tibet.[5]

The only impact of the sanctions was that China Gold became ineligible for official letters of support, commercial advocacy in foreign markets and participation in Canadian Government trade missions. Canada's NCP did not have any power beyond issuing these anaemic sanctions to compel China Gold to partake in their dispute resolution process.

In this case, the sanctions were especially useless, as the parent company was a state-owned enterprise. It did not need any Canadian Government support and thus the sanctions were meaningless.[6] This was the first and only decision in which Canada's NCP imposed such consequences.[7] Beyond this example, there are no other cases demonstrating the Canadian NCP's willingness to sanction extractive sector corporations.[8]

Given the ineffectual nature of Canada's NCP at resolving disputes, one could ask why the Canadian Government believes the CORE will produce different results with similar powers as Canada's NCP?

A more fundamental question is: why grant the CORE similar powers as an existing government agency? The Government suggests that the CORE and NCP are complementary as the NCP focuses on mediation. In turn, the CORE focuses on investigations, informal resolution and public recommendations.[9]

[5] Global Affairs Canada, 'Final Statement on the Request for Review Regarding the Operations of China Gold International Resources Corp. Ltd., at the Copper Polymetallic Mine at the Gyama Valley, Tibet Autonomous Region' (2015), www.international.gc.ca/trade-agreements-accords-commerciaux/ncp-pcn/statement-gyama-valley.aspx?lang=eng.

[6] S Imai, L Gardner and S Weinberger, '"The Canada Brand": Violence and Canadian Mining Companies in Latin America' (2017) Osgoode Legal Studies Research Paper No 17/2017, dx.doi.org/10.2139/ssrn.2886584, 39.

[7] M Torrance, 'Remedying Human Rights: From the International, Regional and Domestic Status Quo to Future Innovations' (Human Rights Law and the Extractive Industries, Rocky Mountain Mineral Law Foundation, February 2016) 7–8.

[8] Global Affairs Canada, 'Closed National Contact Point Specific Instances' (*Government of Canada*, 2019), www.international.gc.ca/trade-agreements-accords-commerciaux/ncp-pcn/specific-specifique.aspx?lang=eng.

[9] Global Affairs Canada, 'Responsible Business Conduct Abroad – Questions and Answers' (*Government of Canada*, 2019), www.international.gc.ca/trade-agreements-accords-commerciaux/topics-domaines/other-autre/faq.aspx?lang=eng.

The jurisdictional bounds within which these two entities operate are opaque, to say the least.

In sum, the reality is that the CORE as a non-judicial grievance mechanism ultimately does not have the power to impose any meaningful sanctions. Despite this, the notion of an office charged with a mandate to protect communities and individuals impacted abroad by home state mining corporations is an intriguing concept that has merit. Building on Canada's effort in developing the CORE, this book proposes a novel proposal. The thrust of the proposal calls for the development of a more robust home state grievance mechanism than the CORE offers.

The intent of this proposal is to be functional, pragmatic and effective. There are two objectives in this proposal. The first is to help mining operators understand how to protect the environmental and human rights of the foreign communities impacted by their extraction activities. The second objective is to minimise the costs and other burdens on home state governments and judicial systems in regulating the foreign operations of their extractive sectors. Backing up these ideas in the proposal is the assertion that the involvement of civil society organisations is beneficial in resolving disputes between impacted communities and mining companies.

While many aspects of the proposal are intended for Canada, the findings of the book will also be applicable towards the design of similarly purposed grievance mechanisms in other countries. In particular, the proposal will be of assistance for other common law jurisdictions that seek to regulate the foreign conduct of the extractive sector such as the US, UK and Australia.

Part I is intended to introduce the reader to the historical and contemporary concerns and opportunities for potential regulation of the international extractive sector. In chapter one, I address the historical context of the extractive industry dating back to the sixteenth century with the global ascent of Spanish colonisation in the Americas. Injustices against local populations that are outlined include enslavement, environmental damage as well as other social, cultural and economic impacts.

As the chapter progresses, I explore similar situations in Africa and India as well as colonial activities undertaken on behalf of the French, Portuguese and British Crown. This chronical continues into the modern era with wrongdoing caused by US and Canadian mining interests. Ultimately, I argue that the foreign operations of Canada's extractive sector has created its own legacy of colonialism.

Turning the focus on theory in more detail, chapter two explores the history and theoretical foundations of civil society. Further, it provides a background on the role of civil society actors in facilitating a remedy for communities and individuals impacted by the extractive sector. It suggests that with the erosion of public control, civil society organisations have attempted to fill the governance gap by entering the regulatory sphere as dominant players.

Themes that are addressed throughout the chapter include corporate social responsibility (CSR) and social licence. To this end, I review the concept of corporate self-governance. This analysis does not lead to the conclusion that corporations should govern themselves. Rather, it indicates that there is an important role for the global community of corporations to insist that its members adhere to internationally-recognised voluntary commitments aimed at protecting the environment and human rights.

Part II provides a comprehensive overview of the US, Canadian, UK and Australian approaches for regulating the overseas conduct of the extractive sector. Chapters three, four and five set out relevant case law from these countries concerning regulating parent corporations in their home state courts. This research covers how doctrines and rules such as *forum non conveniens*, international comity and limitation of jurisdiction operate with different effects in these legal systems.

The US, Australia and Canada are common law legal systems, related in history and origin as they were all once colonies under the British Crown. In this way, their legal systems are inextricably related. Their court systems all utilise some form of *forum non conveniens*. For these reasons, among others, it will be fruitful to compare the differences and similarities of how these somewhat parallel legal systems treat foreign wrongdoing by their respective extractive sectors.

The findings of this book suggest that UK and Australian case law is preferable for those who believe that foreigners should have access to judicial restitution in the home state of a corporation that has negatively impacted their community abroad. In contrast, US and Canadian courts have a track record of preventing extraterritorial litigation against multinational corporations from proceeding in the home state based on procedural grounds. These results will be discussed and used to form the proposal for a home state grievance mechanism developed with the purpose of regulating the foreign activities of the extractive sector.

Part II also examines state-based and civil society-sponsored mechanisms for holding the extractive sector to account for extraterritorial conduct. In chapter six, I explore various strands of home state regulation aimed at governing the extractive sector's international conduct. These chapters examine state-based and civil society sponsored mechanisms for holding the extractive sector to account for extraterritorial conduct.

Chapter six compares home state legislation directed at regulating the extractive sector's human rights performance in Australia, the UK, Canada and the US. The laws and mechanisms that will be reviewed in this chapter include legislative attempts aimed at curbing overseas human rights and environmental violations caused by the extractive sector. This includes regulation that has been implemented as well as unsuccessful or on-going attempts at regulation.

The findings demonstrate that state-based grievance mechanisms have not provided an effective remedy in preventing abuses caused by extractive enterprises and serve as an indictment of the regulatory attempts in the US, UK, Canada and Australia. In each case, there has been consistent opposition to home state regulation.

Chapter six also reviews the involvement of civil society actors. The analysis highlights the prominent role of civil society actors in facilitating a remedy for communities and individuals impacted by the extraterritorial conduct of the extractive sector. This leads to the consideration of whether effective state-based regulation should include an expansive role for civil society actors in representing or mediating between impacted parties and extractive enterprises.

The final two chapters flesh out the contours of a proposal for regulating corporate conduct abroad in the extractive sector. This proposal is based on the premise that the capacity of foreigners to access dispute resolution in the home state of a corporation that has negatively impacted their community or environment is the optimal outcome.

Chapter seven proposes a new system that supersedes and replaces existing mechanisms for dispute resolution. The proposal creates an agency with regulatory jurisdiction over disputes between the extractive sector and foreign communities. It is premised on the assertion that the involvement of civil society is beneficial in resolving disputes, and that enforcement, accountability, compliance and judicial review must feature prominently in a state-based grievance mechanism.

The proposal envisions a quasi-judicial institution that can review complaints and conduct hearings into the foreign conduct of the extractive sector. This grievance mechanism will have powers to examine parties and evidence, to inspect property and to assess monetary penalties and issue costs. It will also be able to set its own procedural rules and to enforce its own orders. Importantly, it will harness the power of industry-sponsored dispute mechanisms and civil society for efficiency and practicality in achieving a fair result for those impacted abroad by extractive enterprises.

Chapter eight provides an assessment of the proposal in accordance with the United Nations Guiding Principles on Business and Human Rights (UN Guiding Principles).[10] Criterion that defines effectiveness in the context of non-judicial grievance mechanisms is set out in the UN Guiding Principles. These key performance indicators (KPIs) in UN Guiding Principle 31 stipulate that grievance mechanisms should be legitimate, accessible, equitable, predictable, transparent, rights-compatible, a source of continuous learning and based on engagement and dialogue. The home state grievance mechanism advanced in the book embraces all of these KPIs, demonstrating its merits.

Chapter eight also examines and contrasts various other proposals put forward for reforming the human rights performance of the extractive sector. The conclusion reiterates the book's overall arguments and contributions. It ends with a

[10] United Nations Special Representative on Business and Human Rights, 'United Nations Guiding Principles on Business and Human Rights: Implementing the United Nations "Protect, Respect and Remedy" Framework' (United Nations, 2011), www.ohchr.org/documents/publications/guidingprinciplesbusinesshr_en.pdf.

positive and hopeful note on the prospect for enduring reform and regulation in this area.

This book makes three major contributions to the field. First, it is one of the first to set out a detailed proposal specifically tailored for a home state government and its extractive industry to achieve and exceed the obligations set out in the UN Guiding Principles. This area of research is a novel and evolving topic of legal regulation that is important to explore because it gives further insight on the question of corporate accountability in a globalised world.

Second, the book is one of the first on this subject of international mining regulation to address as a leading theme the involvement of civil society actors. The book demonstrates that civil society groups have taken on various roles from representing plaintiffs, mediating disputes to advocating for home state regulation over the extraterritorial conduct of the extractive sector. It includes a literature review on the role of civil society actors within the regulatory regimes of the global extractive sector. A major contribution of the book is extensive coverage on the under-reported work of Oxfam Australia, a civil society organisation that considered complaints from local communities concerning environmental and human rights abuses by the extractive sector. This approach predates the UN Guiding Principles and proved rather effective in Australia.

Third, the book is unique in promoting the untapped potential of site-level grievance mechanisms for resolving disputes between local communities and the foreign extractive sector. A site-level grievance mechanism is a company sponsored and financed process. They assist companies in addressing disputes in a non-judicial manner. Corporations and industry groups have promoted site-level grievance mechanisms,[11] while the topic has been largely underdeveloped in academic literature.[12] Several benefits of implementing a site-level grievance mechanism are suggested in the book.

Reliance on industry-led site-level grievance mechanisms is a form of corporate self-regulation over foreign extractive activities as opposed to government oversight. Corporate self-regulation is linked to the concept of CSR where it is the responsibility of businesses to increase the public good.[13] CSR is a

[11] International Petroleum Industry Environmental Conservation Association, 'Community Grievance Mechanisms in the Oil and Gas Industry. A Manual for Implementing Operational-Level Grievance Mechanisms and Designing Corporate Frameworks' (2015), www.ipieca.org/resources/good-practice/community-grievance-mechanisms-in-the-oil-and-gas-industry-a-manual-for-implementing-operational-level-grievance-mechanisms-and-designing-corporate-frameworks; Mining Association of Canada, 'Site-Level Grievance and Community Response Mechanisms: A Practical Design and Implementation Guide for the Resource Development Industry' (2015), mining.ca/site-level-grievance-mechanisms-guide.

[12] As one exception, see E Wilson and E Blackmore (eds), *Dispute or Dialogue: Community Perspectives on Company-Led Grievance Mechanisms* (London, International Institute for Environment and Development, 2013).

[13] M Ararat, AM Colpan and D Matten, 'Business Groups and Corporate Responsibility for the Public Good' (2018) 153 *Journal of Business Ethics* 911, 914.

voluntary practice that has been associated with 'soft law',[14] 'social enterprise law',[15] 'enlightened self-interest'[16] and 'public-regarding theory',[17] among others concepts.

Some commentators have suggested that self-regulation through CSR is a compulsory requirement that has led to the rise of a new 'customary global law'[18] or '*Lex Mercatoria*'[19] where corporations must follow social norms and or risk exclusion from capitalistic endeavours by investors, consumers, civil society and governments.

Corporations are also intrinsically motivated to embrace CSR, for example, in the event of an unfavourable incident. Demonstrating past and current commitments to CSR may buffer reputational damage or buy goodwill from stakeholders.[20] Taking a more cynical approach, it has also been suggested that CSR has become a mere exercise in public relations and that companies are checking boxes and producing glossy CSR reports as a way to avoid regulations and being spotlighted by civil society groups.[21]

Transnational corporations are exposed to diverse pressures and demands across countries that lead them to follow an array of CSR practices.[22] Embracing CSR principles is also pragmatic for transnationals that are appearing to operate outside the bounds of home state governance. It is possible that the increasing concentration of corporate power has resulted in tyrannical organisations that are beyond regulatory control.[23] Some commentators have even predicted the progression towards a dystopian world order, where transnational corporations align with multinational military forces such as NATO to form a 'supranational nexus' that rivals the power of any particular state, or alliance of states which seek to govern them.[24] According to this ideology, corporations are cunningly espousing CSR

[14] M Kerr, C Pitts and R Janda, *Corporate Social Responsibility: A Legal Analysis* (Markham, LexisNexis Canada Inc, 2009) 153.

[15] B Means and J Yockey (eds), *The Cambridge Handbook of Social Enterprise Law* (Cambridge, Cambridge University Press, 2019).

[16] A Crane and D Matten, *Business Ethics: Managing Corporate Citizenship and Sustainability in the Age of Globalization*, 4th edn (Oxford, Oxford University Press, 2007) 47.

[17] C Williams, 'Corporate Compliance with the Law in the Era of Efficiency' (1998) 76 *North Carolina Law Review* 1265, 1382–83.

[18] C Pitts, 'Business, Human Rights, and the Environment: The Role of the Lawyer in CSR & Ethical Globalization' (2008) 26 *Berkeley Journal of International Law* 479, 488.

[19] R Steinhardt, 'Soft Law, Hard Markets: Competitive Responsibilities for Multinational Corporations' (2008) 33 *Brooklyn Journal of International Law* 933, 937.

[20] Y Shiu and S Yang, 'Does Engagement in Corporate Social Responsibility Provide Strategic Insurance-like Effects' (2017) 38 *Strategic Management Journal* 455.

[21] S Sethi and D Schepers, 'United Nations Global Compact: The Promise-Performance Gap' (2014) 122 *Journal of Business Ethics* 193.

[22] D Crilly, N Ni and Y Jiang, 'Do-No-Harm Versus Do-Good Social Responsibility: Attributional Thinking and the Liability of Foreignness' (2016) 37 *Strategic Management Journal* 1316.

[23] D Korten, *When Corporations Rule the World*, 3rd edn (Oakland, Berrett-Koehler Publications, 2015) 19.

[24] A McCoy, *In the Shadows of the American Century: The Rise and Decline of US Power* (Chicago, Haymarket Books, 2017) 254. This concept is similar to the compelling book by M Hardt and A Negri, *Empire* (Cambridge, Harvard University Press, 2000).

initiatives in order to placate those who seek public scrutiny over their precipitous powers as their powers continue to incubate and grow.

Even if this prediction of colossal corporate power is exaggerated, it is clear that corporations are currently operating outside the reach of home state governance and accounting for their activities abroad may require some form of corporate self-regulation. There is reason to suggest that voluntary corporate initiatives such as CSR programmes may achieve morally defensible results, as those who champion this pathway of regulation view it as efficient and effective in practice.[25]

While the chief concern of corporations is increasing profits, the concepts of self-regulation and CSR rely on a belief that corporate activity is also guided by other factors beyond immediate financial compensation. In Adam Smith's *The Wealth of Nations*, corporations are characterised as instruments that supress competitive forces as opposed to expanding unfettered free market economies.[26] If this is true, corporations may be unleashed from the pursuit of profit-making activities in its purest form in order to achieve other objectives that are not wholly economic.[27] Under these conditions, corporations may moderate social and environmental impacts without the introduction of external regulatory requirements.

In this conception, are multinationals potential agents of change in producing meaningful contributions to the livelihood of foreign communities and mitigating environmental effects abroad? Or have corporations effectively escaped the authority of home states which have failed, either by choice or inability, to regulate the foreign activities of business? If so, does this lead inexorably to sinister outcomes on account of insatiable corporate greed? These are some of the questions this book seeks to answer.

What is particularly fascinating about posing these questions as related to the extractive sector is that the industry is progressing through an extraordinary epoch of change. The world is rapidly shifting towards cleaner forms of energy. This is having a significant impact on the mining sector, as several metals markets have been redefined by emerging technologies. For example, the need for batteries in electric vehicles is growing at an unprecedented rate, and battery metals such as cobalt, cooper and nickel are becoming of greater necessity and value.[28] In contrast, the reliance on coal as a source of power production is waning in most countries.[29]

[25] S Rose-Ackerman, 'Comment: Consensus Versus Incentives: A Skeptical Look at Regulatory Negotiation' (1994) 43 *Duke Law Journal* 1206, 1220.

[26] A Smith, *An Inquiry into the Nature and Causes of the Wealth of Nations* (New York, Modern Library, 1937 edn, first published 1776) 123.

[27] WT Allen, 'Our Schizophrenic Conception of the Business Corporation' (1992) 14 *Cardozo Law Review* 280.

[28] J Kettle, 'Mining Sector Faces Energy Transition Conundrum' *Financial Times* (18 February 2020), www.ft.com/content/36ef7ab2-4f44-11ea-95a0-43d18ec715f5.

[29] S Carley, TP Evans and DM Konisky, 'Adaptation, Culture, and the Energy Transition in American Coal Country' (2018) 37 *Energy Research and Social Science* 133.

Mining activities are a significant generator of carbon, and the increasing regulation of pollution in countries around the world will no doubt impact the industry. For instance, actions such as the UN Paris Agreement on climate change are fueling growth in the renewable energy sector.[30] For mining operators, this will inevitably lead to an increase in the cost of production, slow the speed of extraction and effect demand at the consumer level.

Moreover, investors are changing their expectations regarding social and environmental concerns. This, in turn, has caused many financial institutions, such as largescale pension funds, to consider the carbon footprint and supply chains of the business operations they invest in. These trends will impact the ability of the traditional mining sector to raise capital in the future. As such, these disruptions pose significant challenges when it comes to the CSR practices of the extractive sector.

Another layer of complexity involving the extractive industry is the impact of evolving forms of mining. Take, for example, the experimental field of deep sea mining, which involves extracting submerged minerals and deposits from the sea floor. This emerging mining practice is raising concerns about its impacts on marine and coastal ecosystems. As a result, there is a growth in relevant regulations developing as a novel field of international law. This is another area of uncertainty for the commercial interests involved in deep sea mining as discussed in chapter three.

The primary contribution of the book is the development of a vision of how extractive sector corporations can do better when it comes to minimising the human and environmental impacts of their operations abroad. Despite the fact that some aspects of the proposal are intended for Canada, the findings of the book will also be applicable to other countries that seek to govern the foreign conduct of the extractive sector. In particular, the UK, the US and Australia are places where the comparative analytical research in this book applies. Readers will come to understand that the implementation of these proposed reforms will remedy many of the weaknesses in the judicial systems, government institutions and international organisations that have struggled and failed to address these concerns.

[30] United Nations, 'Paris Agreement' (2015), unfccc.int/files/essential_background/convention/application/pdf/english_paris_agreement.pdf.

PART I

The Problem Persists

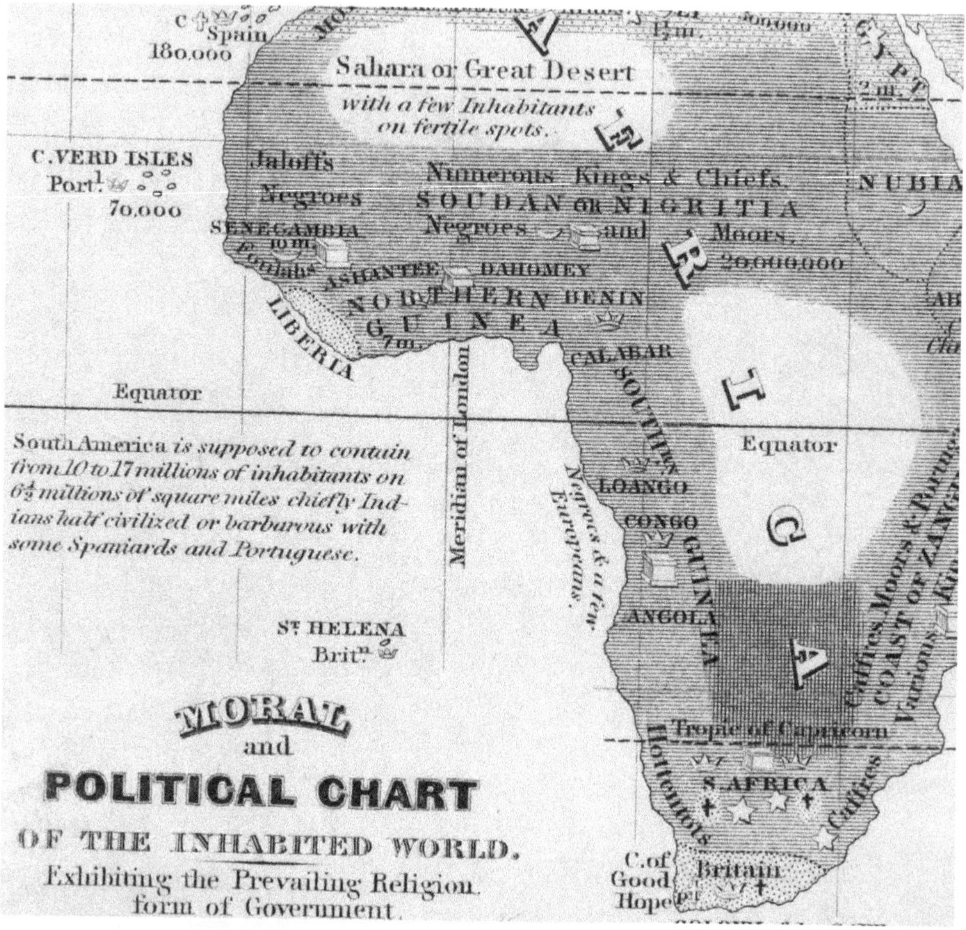

Moral and Political Chart of the Inhabited World (1845)

Creator: William Channing Woodbridge

Source: The Cornell University PJ Mode Collection of Persuasive Cartography.

1

Dark History

Men also, and by his suggestion taught,
Ransacked the centre, and with impious hands
Rifled the bowels of their mother Earth
For treasures better hid. Soon had his crew
Opened into the hill a spacious wound,
And digged out ribs of gold. Let none admire

Paradise Lost[1]

This quote from Milton's *Paradise Lost* describes the fallen angel Mammon, who values earthly treasure over all other things. Milton is not subtle in describing a doomed and evil character as the original miner who passes the practice on to man. This is an early portrayal of mining and its association with sin.

Mining and conflict often run together. The extractive industry is filled with significant human rights disputes, environmental concerns and, in some cases, has even led to warfare. These concerns date back to at least the sixteenth century with the global ascent of the Spanish Empire. Prior to the Spanish conquest of New Spain, primitive mining techniques had been used on a small scale by the Indigenous peoples of the Americas since 1500 BC.[2] The Spanish began mining precious metals on a commercial scale after the conquest of the Aztec and Tarascan states in the sixteenth century, enslaving large numbers of Indigenous people to work in their mines, including men, women and children.[3] These slaves were branded on their cheek to demonstrate that they were the property of the Spanish Crown.[4]

Beyond the practice of forced labour, the Spanish looted palaces, graves and other sacred places for precious ceremonial artifacts.[5] Large tracts of forests were

[1] J Milton, *Paradise Lost* (W Kerrigan, J Rumrich and SM Fallon, eds, 2008 edn, New York, The Modern Library, first published 1667) book I, 42.

[2] R Burger, *Chavin and the Origins of Andean Civilization* (London, Thames and Hudson, 1992) 127.

[3] R West, 'Early Silver Mining in New Spain, 1531–1555' in A Criag and R West (eds), *In Quest of Mineral Wealth: Aboriginal and Colonial Mining and Metallurgy in Spanish America* (Baton Rouge, Geoscience Publication, 1994) 119.

[4] *Ibid* 127.

[5] *Ibid* 120.

cut to make charcoal for fueling smelters as part of the mining operations. This led to the significant depletion of vegetation surrounding the mines. A special mining ordinance was enacted in 1542 for one mine in modern day Mexico to prevent any further logging.[6]

Enslavement and environmental damage were not the only injustices the Spanish inflicted on the local Indigenous population. Aggressive missionary activities, the occupation of lands to block foreign aggression and the cultivation of crops on the most fertile soil for European markets were also the effects of Spanish colonisation in the Americas.[7]

The 'New Laws' of 1542 abolished slavery in New Spain partially on account of the advocacy of the Dominican friar, Bartolomé de las Casas.[8] However, the abolition was not enforced effectively and the institution of slavery continued into the 1550s.[9] During this period, Spain endured difficult economic times on account of a shortage of silver within its boundaries due in part to its exportation by Genoese and German merchants. The diminishing volume of precious metal imports and the rise of illegal exporting negatively impacted the prosperity of Spain.[10] Believing there was a link between their economic misfortune and the exportation of silver, the Spanish Crown began to embrace a form of mercantilism known as bullionism, a concept based on the notion that wealth is ultimately bound up in precious metals.[11]

This belief led to a growing demand for silver in Spain during the seventeenth century. For example, from 1621 to 1631, spending on silver doubled every year by the Spanish Crown.[12] In order to meet the growing demand for precious metals, the Spanish devised various methods for ramping up production and output from their mines in New Spain.[13]

Given that slavery was now abolished, the Spanish needed to create a new method to exploit the local Indigenous population as a source of labour. They did so through a system known as the *mit'a* in what is now modern day Peru. The *mit'a* is considered an ancient version of mandatory state service. Before the arrival of the Spanish, the majority of Inca subjects performed their *mit'a* obligations

[6] SA Zavala, *Libros de Asientos de La Gobernación de La Nueva España: Período Del Virrey Don Luis de Velasco, 1550–1552* (Mexico, Archivo General de la Nación, 1982) 180.

[7] R West, *Colonial Placer Mining in Columbia* (Baton Rouge, Louisiana State University Press, 1952) 1.

[8] H Wagner and H Parish, *The Life and Writings of Bartolomé de Las Casas* (Albuquerque, University of New Mexico Press, 1967) 109–13.

[9] LB Simpson, *Studies in the Administration of the Indians in New Spain* (Berkeley, University of California Press, 1940).

[10] D Studnicki-Gizbert, *A Nation upon the Ocean Sea: Portugal's Atlantic Diaspora and the Crisis of the Spanish Empire, 1492–1640* (Oxford, Oxford University Press, 2007) 92.

[11] *Ibid* 161.

[12] *Ibid* 214.

[13] I use the term Spanish to refer to Spaniards born in Spain as opposed to *Criollo* people born in the Americas.

in local agricultural settings near their homes.[14] The original Inca version of the *mit'a* provided public goods and services, such as the maintenance of roads, irrigation and other agricultural systems.[15]

In contrast, the Spanish used the *mit'a* to service their vast silver mines. This created a subsidy for private mining interests and the Spanish Empire, which used the revenues to finance wars in Europe.[16] Under Spanish rule, the use of the *mit'a* became increasingly abusive as miners were taxed and forced to purchase their own food while they participated in the *mit'a*. On account of these costs, the miners were persistently in debt, a burden they passed down to the next generation. This oppressive practice permitted the rapid expansion of silver mining by the Spanish who exploited tens of thousands of miners under the *mit'a* system. The system also severely impacted the Inca population by reducing the amount of healthy workers capable of producing food sources. This led to famine in the local communities and was further exacerbated by fleeing workers who evaded the Spanish *mit'a*.[17] Little changed into the eighteenth century as the Spanish exploitation of the *mit'a* continued.[18]

The disparity between the miners and those who conquered them was stark. While the miners toiled away in slavery, the mine owners received wine and clothing from foreign merchants.[19] It was not only the local inhabitants near these mines who were forced into these repressive conditions by the Spanish. For example, in the gold fields of the New Kingdom of Granada, Spanish mine owners relied on the importation of African slaves to form the bulk of their labour force.[20] Thus, the Spanish Empire's pursuit of precious metals was an example of a global human rights catastrophe centred in the Americas.

This practice of exporting slaves from Africa was also utilised for copper mining in the mountains of Cuba. Since the sixteenth century, the copper mining industry has continuously operated in Cuba and control has passed from the Spanish Crown, to private contractors, foreign companies and eventually to the socialist state. In 1670, the Spanish Crown confiscated a neglected mine, El Cobre, from a former contractor that failed to abide by the terms of its licence. In doing so, 270 slaves originally from Africa became the property of the Spanish Crown

[14] J Rowe, 'Inca Culture at the Time of the Spanish Conquest' in J Steward (ed), *Handbook of South American Indians*, 2nd vol (Washington, Smithsonian Institution, 1946) 267–69.

[15] TN D'Altroy, *The Incas* (Oxford, Blackwell Publishing, 2003) 266.

[16] J Cole, *The Potosí Mita, 1573–1700: Compulsory Indian Labor in the Andes* (Palo Alto, Stanford University Press, 1985) 20.

[17] ND Cook, *Demographic Collapse, Indian Perú, 1520–1620* (Cambridge, Cambridge University Press, 1981) 237.

[18] E Tandeter, *Coercion and Market: Silver Mining in Colonial Potosi 1692–1826* (Albuquerque, University of New Mexico Press, 1992) 3.

[19] Studnicki-Gizbert, *A Nation upon the Ocean Sea* 108.

[20] JC Boyajian, *Portuguese Bankers at the Court of Spain, 1626–1650* (New Brunswick, Rutgers University Press, 1983) 54.

and the mines' production level began to increase.[21] In the 1830s, a British corporation took over the mine and continued to rely on African slave labour well into the nineteenth century.[22]

A similar history can be found in Brazil in which the Portuguese Crown began to exploit the colonised land for minerals in the early seventeenth century.[23] It has been suggested that news of gold strikes in Brazil during the 1690s set off the first significant gold rush in Western history that was unparalleled until the gold rush in California 150 years later.[24] As in the Spanish American Empire, the Portuguese Crown owned all subsurface rights but granted use and benefit to local miners in return for a concession payment.[25] Soon after Brazilian independence was declared in 1822, the Constitution was amended to allow foreign investment into the nation.[26] This produced a flood of British investment into Brazilian mining.[27]

By the nineteenth century, corporations became the predominant vehicle that British investors used to manage their Brazilian extractive operations. As one example, the Saint John d'el Rey Mining Company was formed in London in 1830. The first acquisition made by the company was a 25-year lease of a Brazilian gold mine. The stockholders purchased these rights from three British merchants and a German physician who obtained an imperial decree to the resources located at the mine in 1828.[28] The company's reliance on slave labour to operate the mine had some commercial complexities. For instance, the costs of purchasing healthy African slaves nearly tripled from the 1850s to the 1870s.[29] Therefore, the company began to rely on rented slaves at a reduced cost. These slaves were often rented from failed mining ventures.[30] The management of the Saint John d'el Rey Mining Company created an elaborate rating system to evaluate rented slaves based on age, health, demeanor and gender.[31] Thus, slave labour was commoditised so that the company directors could ensure the mine's operations were sufficiently profitable. This continued even after the British Parliament passed the Aberdeen Act of 1845, which prohibited British citizens from purchasing slaves.[32] Subsequent to 1845,

[21] ME Diaz, 'Mining Women, Royal Slave: Copper Mining in Colonial Cuba, 1670–1780' in L Mercer and J Gier (eds), *Mining Women: Gender in the Development of a Global Industry, 1670 to the Present* (New York, St Martin's Press, 2006) 22.

[22] *Ibid* 23.

[23] MC Eakin, *British Enterprise in Brazil: The St, John d'el Rey Mining Company and the Morro Velho Gold Mine, 1830–1960* (Durham, Duke University Press, 1989) 7–8.

[24] CR Boxer, *The Golden Age of Brazil, 1695–1750: Growing Pains of a Colonial Society* (Berkeley, University of California Press, 1962).

[25] Eakin, *British Enterprise in Brazil* 14.

[26] Eakin (n 23).

[27] I Stone, 'British Direct and Portfolio Investment in Latin America Before 1914' (1977) 37 *Journal of Economic History* 690.

[28] Eakin (n 23) 22.

[29] E Viotti da Costa, *The Brazilian Empire: Myths and Histories* (Chicago, Chicago Dorsey Press, 1988) 144.

[30] Eakin (n 23) 32.

[31] Eakin (n 23) 33.

[32] Eakin (n 23) 33.

the company's board of directors lobbied successfully to allow for the continued renting of slaves and to keep slaves purchased before the commencement of the Aberdeen Act.[33] The company continued to rely on slave labour until shortly before abolition took effect in Brazil in 1888.[34]

Since at least the colonial period, similar abuses caused by the extractive sector have occurred in Africa. The expropriation of resources was just one way colonial powers acted despotically toward the local African populations. In the Gold Coast (modern Ghana), the British colonial state removed the local chieftain King Amba N'kroma and imprisoned him from 1867 to 1889. This removed local regulations and opened the door for corporations to operate within the lucrative gold mining company.[35]

Angola provides another example of the disenfranchising effects of colonisation in Africa. Under Portuguese rule in the twentieth century, corporations operated prodigious diamond mines that used forcible recruitment practices up until the country gained its independence in 1975. These mines became known in both Europe and Africa as 'a state within the state'.[36]

I. Germs of Empires

The Congo has a history of at least 150 years of resource exploitation that has included brutality and neglect of local populations by foreigners.[37] This brutality was fictionalised in Joseph Conrad's *Heart of Darkness* wherein he described the Belgian dominated ivory plunder of the Congo during the nineteenth century. In the novella, as the narrator Charles Marlow begins his journey up the River Congo, he speaks romantically of the voyages of great captains and admirals. He describes these as the 'seed of commonwealths, the germs of empires'.[38] It is only later that he witnesses the cruel reality and abject terror of the colonial project in the territory that became the Congo.

The country has had persistent political unrest and turmoil for at least 100years. In the 1990s, the Congo was plagued by war-related mineral plunder. A UN report of these incidents notes that the opportunistic behaviour of some

[33] DB Davies, *The Problem of Slavery in the Age of Revolution, 1770–1823* (Ithaca, Cornell University Press, 1975) 419; Eakin (n 23) 33.

[34] Eakin (n 23); L Bethall, *The Abolition of the Brazilian Slave Trade* (Cambridge, Cambridge University Press, 1970).

[35] K Akurang-Parry, 'Making a Difference in Colonial Intervention in Gold Mining in Wassa Fiase, Gold Coast (Ghana): The Activism of Two Women, 1874–1893' in Gier and Mercer (eds), *Mining Women* 40.

[36] T Cleveland, *Diamonds in the Rough: Corporate Paternalism and the Mines of Colonial Angola, 1917–1975* (Athens, Ohio University Press, 2015) 3.

[37] A Hochschild, *King Lepold's Ghost: A Story of Greed, Terror, and Heroism in Colonial Africa* (Boston, Houghton Mifflin, 1998).

[38] J Conrad, *Heart of Darkness* (Waiheke Island, The Floating Press, 2008) 7.

private companies was a contributing factor.[39] The Congo's extensive resource wealth has not benefited the majority of Congolese citizens in terms of infrastructure developments or living standards.[40] The Government has been accused of failing to act as a competent trustee of natural resources. One study found that between 2010 and 2012 state-owned mining concessions were sold off at one-sixth of their commercial value.[41] African countries such as the Congo provide mining operators with an excessive return on investment as compared with other regions in the world.[42]

Despite paying inadequate royalties, there is evidence to suggest that the extractive sector has advanced social welfare through the development of infrastructure in the African countries in which they operate. For instance, in Ghana, there are reports that local communities near mining operations do benefit in some respects, through the construction of roads, schools and health facilities.[43] However, these benefits need to be weighed against the negative impacts such as the loss of agricultural land, harmful environmental impacts, crime and socio-economic deprivation.[44]

As one example, a Canadian-Australian company, Anvil Mining, listed on the Toronto Stock Exchange, operated a copper and silver mine in Ghana's eastern region. A community near the mine had a high mortality rate among children, many of whom died from malaria, dysentery and conditions related to malnutrition. These diseases are directly linked to socio-economic deprivation and a lack of medical facilities to service the community.[45] In one year, the company earned a profit of US $6.85 million yet failed to voluntarily provide support for the development of medical amenities or social programmes to ameliorate the high mortality rate among children.[46]

A Ghanaian civil society group reported another case concerning a Canadian gold mining company that abruptly closed, leaving 400 employees out of work and without their contractually agreed upon severance pay.[47] Additionally, the company owed US $18 million in outstanding debts to the Government and

[39] Panel of Experts on the Democratic Republic of the Congo, 'Final Report of the Panel of Experts on Illegal Exploitation of Natural Resources and Other Forms of Wealth of the Democratic Republic of Congo' (2002) 7–8, repositories.lib.utexas.edu/bitstream/handle/2152/5170/2477.pdf?sequence=1.

[40] M Lamer, A Laudati and J Clark, 'Neither War nor Peace in the Democratic Republic of Congo (DRC): Profiting and Coping amid Violence and Disorder' (2013) 40 *Review of African Political Economy* 1, 1.

[41] Africa Progress Panel, 'Equity in Extractives: Stewarding Africa's Natural Resources for All' (2013) 100.

[42] *Ibid* 64.

[43] T Garvin et al, 'Community–Company Relations in Gold Mining in Ghana' (2009) 90 *Journal of Environmental Management* 571.

[44] *Ibid* 571.

[45] Panel of Experts, 'Final Report' (n 39) 13–14.

[46] P Butler, *Colonial Extraction: Race and Canadian Mining in Contemporary Africa* (Toronto, University of Toronto Press, 2015) 99.

[47] A Darimani, 'Canadian Company Plunders Ghana' *Modern Ghana* (8 April 2004), www.modernghana.com/news/62859/canadian-company-plunders-ghana.html.

private entities in Ghana. The site of the mine was left in an environmentally hazardous state and the company failed to provide any support for the reclamation costs. Local farmers who had been seeking compensation for lost land were left with little prospect of recovery. A Chinese firm subsequently acquired the mine and the company has not been forthcoming with information on the condition of either the local village or the mine.

South Africa has also seen abuses as a result of the foreign extractive sector. In one example, workers at a Canadian-owned uranium mine alleged poor working conditions and a lack of protective clothing from radiation exposure.[48] They reported various other work-related health concerns such as chronic headaches, tuberculosis and nausea. In 2007, a civil society group claimed that a government office instructed the mine to halt operations until health and safety standards were met. When the changes were not implemented, the workers went on strike and the company issued an unlawful dismissal notice to the majority of its staff. Over 1,000 workers were fired without severance pay. A small core of employees remained to maintain the mine, yet the health and safety concerns were not addressed. Subsequently, a child trespassed on the mine property, slipped into a sinkhole and was seriously injured. The company refused to apologise or implement any changes.[49] Eventually, the mine was sold to a Russian state-owned firm.[50]

These examples from the Congo, Ghana and South Africa demonstrate the problematic impacts experienced by the communities' neighbouring foreign-owned mines in Africa. A conclusion drawn from these examples is that the Canadian extractive sector is a major source of the concern. This is troubling for Canadians who are used to thinking of their country as a humane global actor.[51]

According to a 2009 study, Canadian companies cause one-third of corporate social responsibility violations in the global mining sector.[52] Canada is itself a nation where Europeans came in search of natural resources and property rights to those resources. During the nineteenth century, the pre-confederation British Government simply claimed these rights without recognising any entitlements of the Indigenous populations of Canada.[53] It has been suggested that, through the foreign operations of its extractive sector, Canada has created its own legacy of colonialism.[54]

[48] International Women and Mining Network, 'Women from Mining Affected Communities Speak Out: Defending Land, Life & Dignity' (*Academia.edu*, 2010) 21, www.academia.edu/4195877/Women_from_Mining_Affected_Communities_Speak_Out_Defending_Land_Life_and_Dignity.

[49] *Ibid* 22.

[50] 'Uranium One to Delist Shares as Russia's State Nuclear Firm Takes Control' (*Reuters*, 19 October 2013), www.reuters.com/article/uranium-one-private-idUSL5N0I902T20131019.

[51] Butler, *Colonial Extraction* 6.

[52] Canadian Centre for the Study of Resource Conflict, 'Corporate Social Responsibility: Movement and Footprints of Canadian Mining and Exploration Firms in the Developing World' (October 2009) 7, caid.ca/CSRRep2009.pdf.

[53] Butler (n 46) 65.

[54] Butler (n 46) 6.

Indeed, the results of colonialism are present in the modern day legal systems of countries such as Canada, Australia and the United States, among others. Despite the grave injustices brought by colonialism in these countries, the rules that provided for the alienation of rights and land from Indigenous peoples were largely encouraged by their legal systems. For instance, colonialism is in part a product of pernicious legal premises such as the Discovery Doctrine. The Discovery Doctrine, also known as the Right of Discovery or the Doctrine of Discovery, is a concept of public international law that was formulated during the fifteenth and sixteenth centuries.[55] Two of the most important sources of this principle are the Papal Bulls of *Romanus Pontifex* (1455) and *Inter Caetera* (1493).[56] These decrees embodied the Catholic conceptualisation of the rights of non-Christian peoples, which were regarded as inferior to Christians, if they were regarded at all.[57] Natural law theories suggesting that Christians have rights over the lands and resources of non-Christians have existed since at least the thirteenth century.[58]

The Discovery Doctrine played a central role in the Spanish and Portuguese conquest of the New World.[59] In this conception of property law, the rights of those already in possession of minerals are diminished, as these groups do not have the legal capacity to transfer or hold mineral rights.[60]

The French and British monarchs also used the doctrine to lay claims to land based on discovery.[61] Consider the examples of Australia, Canada and the United States which have similar historical narratives concerning the expropriation of the lands and rights of Indigenous peoples.[62] This is not surprising given that their legal systems are founded upon English law and they trace their cultural and social norms back to Britain. The Doctrine of Discovery justified these countries' claims to sovereignty and property rights in the native lands they colonised. Further, the colonisers immediately and automatically acquired governmental, political and commercial rights without the consent of the Indigenous peoples. The doctrine served as the primary legal tool for accomplishing these tasks.[63]

In effect, the doctrine became the basis of all European claims in the Americas as well as the foundation for the United States' western expansion. By the early

[55] R Miller et al, *Discovering Indigenous Lands: The Doctrine of Discovery in the English Colonies* (Oxford, Oxford University Press, 2010) 1.

[56] The Gilder Lehrman Institute of American History, 'The Doctrine of Discovery, 1493' (2012), www.gilderlehrman.org/sites/default/files/inline-pdfs/04093_FPS.pdf.

[57] K Worthen, 'Sword or Shield: The Past and Future Impact of Western Legal Thought on American Indian Sovereignty (Book Review)' (1991) 104 *Harvard Law Review* 1372, 1375.

[58] B Watson, 'John Marshall and Indian Land Rights: A Historical Rejoinder to the Claim of "Universal Recognition" of the Doctrine of Discovery' (2006) 36 *Seaton Hall Law Review* 481, 499.

[59] S Luk, 'Ditching the Doctrine of Discovery (and What That Means for Canadian Law)' (*Olthuis Kleer Townshend LLP*, 30 November 2015), oktlaw.com/ditching-doctrine-discovery-means-canadian-law.

[60] N Mickenberg and P Cumming (eds), *Native Rights in Canada*, 2nd edn (Toronto, The Indian-Eskimo Association in Canada and General Publishing, 1970) 18–19.

[61] Luk, 'Ditching the Doctrine of Discovery'.

[62] Miller et al, *Discovering Indigenous Lands* 1.

[63] Miller et al (n 55) 1–2.

nineteenth century, the Discovery Doctrine was also the governing concept among European imperial powers with a presence in Africa.

The concept has appeared in litigation that stripped Indigenous peoples of legal rights in favour of colonial powers. Most notably, the doctrine was central to the 1823 US Supreme Court case of *Johnson v M'Intosh*.[64] In the decision, authored by Chief Justice John Marshall, the Court held that European discovery of America 'gave exclusive title to those who made it'.[65] In the 1984 case of *Guerin v The Queen*,[66] the Supreme Court of Canada referred to *Johnson v M'Intosh*, holding that European claims to sovereignty in North America were justified by the Discovery Doctrine.[67]

In recent times, legal scholars have argued that the doctrine should be abandoned.[68] Further, religious institutions and other non-governmental organisations have called for its repudiation.[69] Nonetheless, the Discovery Doctrine remains a foundational legal principle in the United States, Australia, Canada and elsewhere.[70]

II. The Extractive Sector at the Gates

A. Yanacocha

In 1532, the last Inca Emperor, Atahualpa was captured by the Spanish conquistadors in Cajamarca, Peru.[71] Understanding the conquistador's lust for precious metals, Atahualpa agreed to fill a large room with gold and silver to secure his freedom.[72] Instead, the conquistadors kept the gold and killed Atahualpa.[73]

We see the same level of exploitation of the local populations of Central and South America today, only now, rather than Spanish conquistadors leading the way, it is the large corporations that dominate the foreign extractive sector. The apparent inability and limited access for these exploited populations to seek a remedy against the foreign extractive sector is iniquitous. Consider, for example, the Yanacocha mine in Northwestern Peru, South America's largest gold mine.

[64] *Johnson v M'Intosh* 21 US (8 Wheat) 543 (1823).
[65] *Ibid* 574.
[66] *Guerin v The Queen* [1984] 2 SCR 335.
[67] *Ibid* 378. Note the doctrine was called in this case the 'principle of discovery'.
[68] Miller et al (n 55) vii (in Foreword by J Borrows); B Watson, 'The Doctrine of Discovery and the Elusive Definition of Indian Title' (2012) 15 *Lewis & Clark Review* 995, 1023.
[69] A Forget, 'Church's Knowledge of Doctrine of Discovery "Woefully Inadequate"' *Anglican Journal* (28 August 2015), www.anglicanjournal.com/articles/church-s-knowledge-of-doctrine-of-discovery-woefully-inadequate.
[70] Miller et al (n 55) 2–3.
[71] J Hemming, *The Conquest of the Incas* (London, Macmillan Publishers Ltd, 1993) 45–46.
[72] *Ibid* 48.
[73] *Ibid* 84.

Fittingly, the Yanacocha mine is located 48 kilometers north of the city of Cajamarca where Atahualpa was held for ransom and killed almost 500 years earlier.[74]

One of the major shareholders of the Yanacocha mine is a US-based company, Newmont Mining Corporation (Newmont). The mine is owned through a joint venture between Newmont Mining of Denver and Compania de Minas Buenaventura, a Peruvian company. The World Bank has also provided partial funding for Yanacocha and has a five per cent equity investment.[75]

In 2000, contractors of the mine were responsible for spilling over 300 pounds of mercury that poisoned approximately 900 nearby villagers. While being transported by a contracted truck from Yanococha to the Pacific coast, 151 kilograms of the toxic metal was spilt, contaminating the town of Choropampa and two neighbouring villages. Impacted residents of the spill were able to bring complaints to the World Bank ombudsman. This ombudsman office considers disputes between impacted communities and projects led by multinational corporations that are subject to World Bank financing. The ombudsman convened a series of public workshops that grew into an ongoing dialogue between the mine operators and the community. These efforts resulted in mixed success in terms of satisfying the nearby residents of Yanacocha.[76] For instance, the ombudsman ordered an independent water study in the region and a more comprehensive health study was planned to evaluate the effects of the mercury spill. According to a report made by the ombudsman, the health study was not completed due in part to 'on-going litigation in host state courts in Peruvian and home state US courts, community divisions and lack of government support for the study'.[77]

Some of the host state litigation the ombudsman referred to includes a group of several hundred plaintiffs who took action against Newmont for the mercury spill incident. In 2002, they filed claims against Newmont in the local courts of Cajamarca. Some of these individuals had accepted monetary offers to settle their claims and to release the company from further liability. One plaintiff, Giovanna Angélica Quiroz, received US $14,000 for damages caused by mercury poisoning to her and her two children.[78] Victims such as Ms Quiroz attempted to have their settlement agreements with Newmont overturned so they could bring a lawsuit to

[74] M Whellams, 'The Role of CSR in Development: A Case Study Involving the Mining Industry in South America' (Masters Theses, Saint Mary's University, 2007) 51.

[75] *Ibid* 51–52.

[76] In its 2006 exit report, the ombudsman office notes that: 'Over the past four years, the Mesa [roundtable for dialogue] has addressed various issues and concerns raised at Mesa assembly meetings and workshops. There are also issues of community concern that the Mesa has not addressed.' Office of the Compliance Advisor/Ombudsman, 'Regarding Two Complaints Filed with the CAO in Relation to Minera Yanacocha, Cajamarca, Peru' (February 2006) 2, www.cao-ombudsman.org/cases/document-links/documents/Exitreportenglish02-7-06-final.pdf.

[77] *Ibid*. Further: 'The CAO agreed to commission an independent health study at the request of affected communities and the Mesa. Due to lack of cooperation from government authorities and desire by some complainants to seek remedies through litigation, the health study was not implemented.' *Ibid* 3.

[78] Environmental Justice Organisations, Liabilities and Trade (EJOLT), 'The Yanacocha Mine Case' (5 August 2015) 7, www.ejolt.org/wordpress/wp-content/uploads/2015/08/FS-43.pdf.

claim further financial damages; however, the Peruvian Supreme Court upheld the validity of their settlement agreements.[79] The Supreme Court did not find a legal reason to interfere in these agreements between the plaintiffs and Newmont.[80]

Those plaintiffs who failed to sign a settlement agreement with Newmont also did not receive a remedy from host state courts. Some commentators have suggested that this case demonstrates the institutional weakness of the Peruvian judiciary in dealing with settlements that have been unfairly procured from victims of the foreign extractive sector.[81]

In 2004, over 1,000 alleged Peruvian victims of the mercury spill filed lawsuits in Denver District Court for the State of Colorado where Newmont's parent company is headquartered. In 2004, Newmont lost the fight to keep these lawsuits out of US home state courts. Subsequently, Newmont offered the possibility of a settlement with all the plaintiffs.[82] The parties agreed to submit their grievances to binding arbitration with retired Colorado judges serving as arbitrators.[83] In 2007, a court-approved agreement was reached, though it is not clear how much compensation was paid to the plaintiffs as the terms were kept confidential. Some have speculated that in the aftermath of the spill, Newmont paid no more than US $6,000 apiece[84] in compensation to the individuals whose health was affected by the spill, including those who were blinded as a result of mercury poisoning.[85]

It is important to underscore the substantial economic disparity between the plaintiffs, mostly poor peasants, and the defendant, one of the world's largest gold mining enterprises. Despite the power imbalance, the US and Peruvian courts were equally hesitant to have a trial on the merits until settlement options were exhausted. The US lawsuits were either sent to arbitration or settled. By 2009, all remaining US legal actions associated with the spill were settled.[86] Fresh litigation attempts against Newmont continue to be launched in US courts concerning their past activities in Peru, however.[87]

[79] United States Securities and Exchange Commission (SEC), 'Form 10-Q' (30 September 2009) 43, www.sec.gov/Archives/edgar/data/1164727/000095012309054293/c91265e10vq.htm.

[80] *Decision on Cassation Appeal (Cajamarca)* 1465–2007 (Supreme Court of Peru).

[81] A Pigrau, S Borras and A Cardesa-Salzmann, 'The Interplay of National, Transnational and International Litigation for Environmental Justice: Seeking Effective Means of Redress for Grave Environmental Damage' (ISEE Conference – Ecological Economics and Rio+ 20: Challenges and Contributions for a Green Economy, 2012) 8, www.isecoeco.org/conferences/isee2012-versao3/pdf/p751.pdf.

[82] EJOLT, 'The Yanacocha Mine Case' 7.

[83] EJOLT (n 78) 8.

[84] P Hecht, 'Andean Villagers Seek American Justice: Mercury Contamination near Peru Mine Leads to Legal Showdown in Denver Court' (*Chronicle Foreign Service*, 14 March 2015), www.sfgate.com/news/article/Andean-villagers-seek-American-justice-Mercury-2723416.php.

[85] As one commentator observed: 'Most residents said the compensation was paltry, especially from a firm that is, quite literally, sitting on a gold mine and whose annual output is worth some $514 million.' M Ryan, 'Plight of Peru Town Dim after Mine's Mercury Spill' *Reuters* (3 July 2002, www.business-humanrights.org/en/plight-of-peru-town-dim-after-mines-mercury-spill.

[86] SEC, 'Form 10-Q' 43.

[87] EarthRights International, 'Peruvian Farmers Appeal in Fight to Hold Newmont Accountable in U.S. Court' (4 May 2018), earthrights.org/media/peruvian-farmers-appeal-fight-hold-newmont-accountable-u-s-court/.

The Yanacocha example highlights the obstacles that an impacted community may face when attempting to seek compensation for wrongdoing caused by a multinational corporation. In this example, the victims and local residents utilised the World Bank as well as home and host state courts in order to seek restitution from Newmont. After receiving a complaint, the World Bank ombudsman attempted to mitigate the mercury spill by conducting a health study. However, Peru's government officials were partially responsible for preventing the health study from occurring. Lawsuits were filed in both the home and host state against Newmont, but these continued for almost a decade without a trial on the question of compensation.

These outcomes were also ruinous for Newmont's planned expansion for mining operations in Peru. In 2004, Newmont and its partners announced plans to exploit mineral reserves on the mountain Cerro Quilish. The mountain supplies the area with fresh water and is considered sacred by the local Indigenous population. The proposed expansion resulted in violent protests outside of Newmont's Yanacocha mine by over 10,000 people.[88] Protestors faced tear gas and other forms of police violence when they refused to back down from blocking access to the mine.[89]

During the siege, the company continued the gold production at Yanacocha by helicoptering the workers in and out in order to avoid confrontation with the protestors.[90] A Catholic priest, Father Arana, was a formidable figure in representing the protestors. Father Arana was devoted to social activism for the poor and to this end founded a civil society organisation that received financial assistance from Oxfam.[91] In 2010, he was defrocked when he ran as a candidate for public office in Peru.[92] As the protest went on, Arana became a key negotiator between Newmont, the peasants and the Peruvian Government. Eventually, the company determined that prospects for any expansion to Cerro Quilish were significantly dire and the project was formally halted.

B. Bhopal

Another leading case demonstrating the inability of local communities to seek a remedy against multinational corporations resulted from a 1984 gas leak at a Union Carbide pesticide plant in Bhopal, India. It is not an extractive case, yet it is indicative of the problems faced when multinational organisations cause serious injury and death abroad.

[88] JG Ruggie, *Just Business: Multinational Corporations and Human Rights* (New York, W. W. Norton & Company, 2013) xxxvii.

[89] Earthworks, 'Yanacocha' (2017), earthworksaction.org/stories/yanacocha/.

[90] J Perlez and L Bergman, 'Tangled Strands in Fight Over Peru Gold Mine' *New York Times* (25 October 2005).

[91] *Ibid.*

[92] Ruggie, *Just Business* xl.

Bhopal remains one of the world's largest industrial accidents and took the lives of thousands of local residents.[93] Over 500,000 people, mostly impoverished residents of shanty towns, were exposed to poisonous methyl isocyanate gas and other chemicals.[94] Hundreds of thousands of the survivors suffered partial to severe long-term injuries.

Union Carbide, an American corporation, had a 50 per cent ownership interest in the plant through an Indian subsidiary. Numerous violations were caused directly by the Indian subsidiary and at the direction of Union Carbide. Beyond claims of negligence in the plant's operations, the Indian Government was also implicated for failing to set adequate safety standards and ensuring that the standards were enforced. Thus, it was not clear how to allocate legal liability among the parent corporation, subsidiary and the Indian Government for the disaster and resulting injuries and deaths.[95] Equally as vexing was determining which legal forums would assert jurisdiction. Immediately after the accident, there was contemplation by US class action lawyers about the possibility of bringing an action in home state courts despite the clear connections of the disaster to the host state.[96] The plant was constructed and managed by Indian nationals and Americans were not employed on site, nor had they visited the plant for over five years before the accident. Furthermore, most of the evidence was located in India.

Bringing lawsuits in home state courts would be advantageous for injured parties from Bhopal, given that US tort law is friendlier toward victims and there is the option of seeking jury-awarded damages. This prospect would also be beneficial for American lawyers retained and compensated through lucrative contingency fees.[97]

Ultimately, US class action lawyers would not benefit financially from the disaster. In 1985 the Indian Government passed the Bhopal Gas Leak Act, allowing the Government of India to act as the sole legal representative for victims of the disaster in India and elsewhere. Pursuant to this legislation, the Indian Government brought a claim against Union Carbide in an American court on behalf of the victims.[98] A federal district court judge suggested that 'fundamental human decency' required Union Carbide to provide between US $5 to $10 million to immediately help the injured. The company offered US $5 million which the Indian Government promptly rejected. On the question of whether a US court should adjudicate an event that occurred in India, the Indian Government made the somewhat unusual argument that its own courts were insufficient to deal with

[93] MW Janis, 'The Doctrine of Forum Non Conveniens and the Bhopal Case' (1987) 34 *Netherlands International Law Review* 192.

[94] R Varma and D Varma, 'The Bhopal Disaster of 1984' (2005) 25 *Bulletin of Science, Technology and Society* 37.

[95] Janis, 'The Doctrine of Forum Non Conveniens' 198.

[96] Janis (n 93) 199.

[97] C Frank, 'Bhopal Blowup: Are Some Lawyers Vultures?' (1985) 71 *American Bar Association Journal* 17.

[98] Janis (n 93) 199.

this complex matter. For this reason, the claim was brought forth under American federal jurisdiction. The United States Court of Appeals for the Second Circuit upheld a dismissal because the presiding judges considered the Indian courts adequate to hear the claim.[99]

The Supreme Court of India ultimately upheld a 1989 US $470 million settlement reached between the parent company and Indian Government for all criminal and civil liability.[100] It was the responsibility of the Indian Government to distribute these settlement funds to victims of the disaster.

Reflecting the dissatisfaction of the victims, the Indian Supreme Court's decision has been challenged a number of times.[101] In 2006, the Second Circuit Court of Appeals dismissed claims filed in the United States seeking redress for property damages linked to the disaster. These claims were not time-barred in the same way as personal injury actions.

Dow Chemical purchased Union Carbide in 2001. In 2013, a group of Dow investors submitted a shareholder proposal requesting a report assessing the financial, reputational and operational impacts that the legacy of the Bhopal disaster had on Dow's Indian and global business opportunities. However, the Securities Exchange Commission (SEC) found that Dow was not required to go forward with the proposal.[102] This activity occurred almost 20 years after the initial events, which suggests that the fallout from Bhopal remains controversial. In 2017, the issue came up again amidst the merger of Dow Chemical and the American mega-conglomerate, DuPont. As Dow Chemical still faces the prospect of liability associated with Bhopal, some commenters have speculated that the merger creates another layer with which to deprive victims of an effective remedy.[103]

There have also been attempts by shareholders to table resolutions to force Dow to accept responsibility for the Bhopal disaster. They argue that, from an investor's point of view, this is a lost business opportunity, given that it has resulted in Dow being excluded from India's economic market.[104]

An underlying trend between the events at Yanacocha and Bhopal is that the implicated corporate entities were not able to prevent, or ultimately deal with, the damages they inflicted on local individuals in the host state. I suggest that

[99] *In re Union Carbide Corp Gas Plan Disaster at Bhopal, India in Dec 1984* 634 F Supp 842 SDN 1986.

[100] I Eckerman, *The Bhopal Saga – Causes and Consequences of the World's Largest Industrial Disaster* (Hyderabad, Universities Press, 2005) s 8.3.3.1 on p 3.

[101] *Ibid.*

[102] SEC, 'Division of Corporate Finance Letter' (18 March 2014), www.sec.gov/divisions/corpfin/cf-noaction/14a-8/2014/amnestyinternational031814-14a8.pdf.

[103] E Goodard, 'Bhopal Disaster Victims May Never Get Compensation Following Dow-DuPont Merger, Fears UN Official' *Independent* (14 September 2017), www.independent.co.uk/news/business/news/bhopal-disaster-victims-dow-dupont-merger-un-india-official-gas-leak-chemical-industrial-a7946346.html.

[104] F Bermingham, 'Exclusive: 30 Years on from Bhopal Gas Tragedy, Dow Chemical Shareholders Demand Justice' *International Business Times* (19 November 2014), www.ibtimes.co.uk/exclusive-30-years-bhopal-gas-tragedy-thousands-victims-still-wait-justice-1475466.

these impacted individuals were not compensated in an appropriate fashion. One could only imagine if these events unfolded in the location of Union Carbide or Newmont's parent corporations in the United States, or in Canada, the United Kingdom or Australia. These home state jurisdictions have enforcement measures embedded in their legal systems to prevent these types of injustices from playing out.

The US, Canada, UK and Australia do not rely on corporations to regulate themselves. As outlined in the next chapter, corporate self-regulation is a voluntary practice that, when linked to the concept of corporate social responsibility, has been described as 'soft law'.[105] Soft law does not employ criminal or even public regulation over the environment, labour and human rights practices. Instead, it relies on corporations fearing potential legal punishment as a deterrent.[106] It depends on corporations acting with self-interest to avoid shame, moral condemnation, bad publicity and general dissatisfaction with the corporation.[107] In the examples of Yanacocha and Bhopal, such voluntary measures were either not considered by these corporations or, if they were, they were not properly implemented. Quite simply, these examples show that the extractive sector will not bring about compelling changes to prevent future wrongdoing on their own accord.

These examples also raise timely questions: Are resource-rich countries with underdeveloped legal systems equipped to regulate multinational companies? What is the role of civil society and non-binding complaint mechanisms such as the World Bank ombudsman when intervening in disputes between local communities and foreign-owned corporations? Can a domestic court govern the extraterritorial conduct of a locally incorporated business enterprise? Do individuals have the ability to seek compensation against a multinational corporation that negatively impacts their local environment, means of livelihood or way of life? These questions are about legal power and whether the law permits impacted communities to exercise that power against multinational corporations.

As we have seen throughout this chapter, there has been a long history of abuses inflicted on local communities on account of mining activities, a history dating back to at least the invasion of the Americas by the Spanish and Portuguese Empires, and later expanded to Africa during the colonial period. These abuses were perpetrated by a variety of European powers in pursuit of precious metals and other natural resources within the African continent. This represents nascent human rights and environmental violations caused by the extractive sector that

[105] R Steinhardt, 'Soft Law, Hard Markets: Competitive Responsibilities for Multinational Corporations' (2008) 33 *Brooklyn Journal of International Law* 933.

[106] F Pearce and S Tombs, 'Ideology, Hegemony and Empiricism: Compliance Theories of Regulation' (1990) 30 *British Journal of Criminology* 423.

[107] E Oshionebo, *Regulating Transnational Corporations in Domestic and International Regimes: An African Case Study* (Toronto, University of Toronto Press, 2009) 32.

persist to the present day. Canadian extractive sector companies have been implicated in human rights and environmental violations in Ghana, the Congo and South Africa.

The Bhopal and Yanacocha events, among others involving US parent companies, provide context in demonstrating the inability of local communities to seek a remedy in judicial and non-judicial proceedings for abuses by multinational corporations. To date, civil society actors, domestic courts and international mechanisms have not been able to provide a sufficient remedy for communities impacted by the foreign extractive sector.

2

The Case for Civil Society and Corporate Actors

Extractive sector corporations have to go where resources are physically located. These areas are often remote, environmentally delicate, and inhabited by Indigenous people who will not share equally in the economic benefits of development. Civil society organisations and human rights groups have taken notice of these concerns and prompted action on behalf of the UN with the activities of UN Special Representative of the Secretary-General for Business and Human Rights, John Ruggie. This cumulated with the development of the UN Guiding Principles.[1] Such initiatives have value, but are designed to be voluntary and aspirational in effect as the UN approach consistently relies on home and host states to regulate the conduct of multinational corporations.

Since the 1990s, civil society organisations have been attempting to develop internal solutions that monitor multinational corporate activity. In one example, Oxfam Australia operated an independent ombudsman office that reviewed environmental and human rights complaints from 2000–2009. Some countries have crafted regulatory solutions to prevent abuse by multinational enterprises. In 2009, the Canadian Government established the Office of the Extractive Sector Corporate Social Responsibility Counsellor (CSR Counsellor). The mandate of the CSR Counsellor was to review complaints brought forward against Canadian mining companies operating abroad. The process was contingent on voluntary participation by both parties as simply a form of mediation between mining companies and foreign complainants.

Comprehensive legislation aimed at regulating the extractive sector's human rights performance has been attempted without success in some countries. For instance, failed legislative initiatives have been tried in Australia, the United Kingdom, United States and Canada.[2] In the case of the United States, there

[1] Special Representative on Business and Human Rights (SRBHR), 'United Nations Guiding Principles on Business and Human Rights: Implementing the United Nations "Protect, Respect and Remedy" Framework' (United Nations, 2011), www.ohchr.org/documents/publications/guidingprinciplesbusinesshr_en.pdf.

[2] For more information on these failed pieces of legislation, see Australia: Corporate Code of Conduct Bill 2000 (C2004B01333), s 4.3; UK: J Lux, SS Thorsen and A Meisling, 'The European Initiatives' in R Mullerat (ed), *Corporate Social Responsibility: The Corporate Governance of the 21st Century*, 2nd edn (Alphen aan den Rijn, Kluwer Law International, 2011) 346; US: Corporate

exists a curious centuries old law that has ripened in the last 30 years into a civil (as opposed to criminal) tool to sanction corporate conduct, including wrongdoing by the extractive sector. The US Alien Tort Statute 1789 (ATS) has been used by foreign nationals against large companies for alleged human rights violations occurring outside the United States.[3] However, a 2013 Supreme Court decision severely limited the utility of the statute.[4]

Canadian, Australian and UK courts have also been the forums to hear cases alleging human rights abuses by corporations in their foreign operations. Currently, these three countries do not have a statutory framework such as the ATS. Thus, claims have been left to tort and negligence.

Lawsuits have been brought in Canada alleging human rights abuses by multinational corporations against local populations in foreign countries. The probability of the victims receiving a remedy in these cases is doubtful given numerous procedural and substantive limitations. For instance, the limited liability concept of a corporate enterprise protects parent corporations from the negligent activities of its subsidiaries.

In sum, the various international initiatives, common law judicial systems, civil society organisations and individual states concerned with corporate conduct abroad have not produced effective models for regulating multinational enterprises. Further, it does not appear that these forms of regulation will, without substantial modification, become effective methods of regulating the foreign operations of the extractive sector.

The UN Guiding Principles outline several mechanisms to hold multinational corporations to account for environmental and human rights violations.[5] These include judicial, non-judicial, state-based and non-state-based remedies of various proportions. It is challenging to compartmentalise each mechanism into only a few categories. However, there are at least four possibilities for holding multinational corporations responsible for environmental and human rights abuses that occur in foreign operations:

1) domestic courts of the host state where the subsidiary operates;
2) domestic courts of the home state where the parent corporation is domiciled;
3) international regulations; and
4) non-judicial grievance mechanisms.

Options one and two focus on liability enforced by a legal system in a home or host state. Option three envisions an international instrument that governs the conduct of multinationals, whereas option four foresees the possibility of state-based or non-state-based dispute resolution mechanisms. Two actors transcend

Code of Conduct Act 2006 [5377]; Canada: An Act Respecting Corporate Accountability for the Activities of Mining, Oil or Gas Corporations in Developing Countries Canada 2009 [C–300].

[3] Alien Tort Statute 1789 (28 USC § 1350).

[4] *Kiobel v Royal Dutch Petroleum Co* [2013] 133 S Ct 1659.

[5] SRBHR, 'United Nations Guiding Principles'.

these options as possible change agents in holding multinational corporations to account.

Civil society organisations have played a prominent role in judicial and non-judicial processes dealing with allegations of environmental and human rights abuses that occur internationally. This chapter provides a background on the role of civil society organisations as important players in providing a remedy for victims of the extractive sector.

Another important actor in regulating the foreign conduct of the extractive sector is corporations. This is not to suggest that corporations should govern themselves. Rather, there is an important role for the global community of corporations to insist that its members adhere to internationally-recognised voluntary commitments aimed at protecting the environment and human rights.

The proposal presented at the end of this book employs a significant role for corporations and civil society actors in remedying disputes between the foreign extractive sector and impacted communities. For instance, the proposal relies on corporations establishing consequential site-level grievance mechanisms for resolving disputes with local communities. Such grievance mechanisms can provide compensation to impacted communities. They can also provide a user-friendly dispute process to prevent issues from escalating into litigation.

In this way, the proposal is centred on ensuring that corporations are responsive to possible conflict with local communities without the requirement of significant judicial or otherwise legal intervention. A best practice is for corporations to include civil society groups as representatives or even to serve mediators in these business-run dispute resolution processes.

I. Civil Society: Origins and Impact

The history of civil society is a rich and fascinating one. Classical Greek and Roman writers described concepts related to civil society as mechanisms to establish a geometry of human relations.[6] Civil society was associated with the common good and responsible citizenship. For instance, to Plato, civil society warned against the danger of private interests. For him, this danger came in the form of 'Athenian military defeat, economic chaos, political instability and ethical confusion' that transferred power from public authority to private self-interested actors.[7] In some of his writings, Plato developed a framework of a principled government to counter these uncertainties. He describes a civil society based on truth, beauty and goodness with knowledge, power and the state.[8]

[6] J Ehrenberg, 'The History of Civil Society Ideas' in M Edwards (ed), *The Oxford Handbook of Civil Society* (Oxford, Oxford University Press, 2011).

[7] J Ehrenberg, *Civil Society: The Critical History of an Idea* (New York, New York University Press, 1999) 4.

[8] *Ibid* 7.

It should be noted, Plato was opining on a civil society in the form of political society as opposed to non-government institutions. It is only later that civil society becomes associated with organisations outside the apparatus of the state. It has been suggested that this critical moment of transformation came after the French Revolution.[9] That event partly inspired the development of communist philosophy, which invoked new ideas on civil society. This new model focused on the growing power of the independent bourgeois class that emerged with the industrial revolution. That concept was central to understanding civil society outside the traditional political power structures of the state. According to this theory, the writings of Hegel, Marx and Lenin directly created social movements based on the belief that government institutions were incapable of serving the objectives of a civil society. Thus, notions of civil society were to be found autonomous to the state, replacing the older concepts of civil society being linked to the government that trace back to antiquity.[10]

No discussion on the origins of civil society would be complete without reference to Alexis de Tocqueville's *Democracy in America*.[11] Written in the nineteenth century, Tocqueville emphasised equality, localism and association in his expression of civil society. He asserted it was voluntary activity that connected individual Americans to a common good and protected freedom.[12] Tocqueville's optimistic impression of civic engagement has been challenged with more recent arguments that suggest voluntary associations in America are in decline.[13]

Whether voluntary associations are in decline or not, Tocqueville believed these local associations have the capacity to mitigate the inherent friction between private power and notions of equality. It is possible that Tocqueville's theory does not apply when it comes to the imposing power structures of today's transnational corporations.

One of the objectives of this book is to explore whether civil society organisations have a quasi-regulatory role concerning the human rights performance of extractive sector corporations. Modern international relations scholarship contains a foundational body of work directed at the changing role of civil society in global affairs. Indeed, compelling pieces on the changing role of civil society have been written by Risse and Sikkink,[14] Finnemore and Sikkink,[15]

[9] L Kolakowski, *Main Currents of Marxism: The Founders, the Golden Age, the Breakdown* (New York, W. W. Norton & Company, 2005 edn, first published in 1978) 90–91, 150 and 152–53.

[10] B Dewiel, 'A Conceptual History of Civil Society: From Greek Beginnings to the End of Marx' (1997) 6 *Past Imperfect* 3, 6.

[11] A Tocqueville, *Democracy in America* (Birmingham, The Legal Classics Library, 1988 edn, first published in 1838).

[12] Ehrenberg, 'The History of Civil Society Ideas' 24.

[13] R Putnam, *Bowling Alone: The Collapse and Revival of American Community* (New York, Simon & Schuster, 2000).

[14] T Risse and K Sikkink, 'The Socialization of International Human Rights Norms into Domestic Practices: Introduction' in S Ropp, K Sikkink and T Risse (eds), *The Power of Human Rights: International Norms and Domestic Change* (Cambridge, Cambridge University Press, 1999).

[15] M Finnemore and K Sikkink, 'International Norm Dynamics and Political Change' (1998) 52 *International Organization* 887.

Hudson,[16] Carpenter[17] and other notable commentators addressed below. This book builds on the contributions made by these authors and aims to use their foundational work to conceptualise a role for civil society organisations in resolving extractive industry disputes.

Before proceeding, a more thorough definition of a civil society actor is in order. Civil society includes non-governmental organisations and other institutions that manifest the will of citizens. Among them are grassroots groups, religious organisations, think tanks, scientific associations, online activists and even filmmakers.[18] As Larry Catá Backer put it succinctly when commenting on civil society's involvement in disputes between individuals and business enterprises:

> Civil society, in effect, represents the individual in their aggregate manifestation, and their role ensures that all three major stakeholders in the human rights arena – states, corporations and individuals – are reified in equivalent form, as aggregations of political, economic and mass power.[19]

According to Backer, civil society actors serve as a representative for a collective of individuals, and in doing so, equalise the power dynamic of all parties including corporations, the state and individuals.

The intent in this book is not to demonstrate that the global empowerment of civil society actors is a trend that is challenging the power of the state or business. Rather, the purpose is to highlight the increasing involvement of civil society actors in using judicial and non-judicial mechanisms to hold extractive sector corporations to account for human rights abuses.

Specifically, I focus on what has been described as humanitarian organisations that protect universal as well as local human interests.[20] For this reason, the civil society organisations addressed in this book represent both the major global players, as well as diminutive, less formidable civil society members in the extractive sector. Some commentators have argued that global organisations such as Amnesty International tend to dominate the discourse when a civil society perspective is sought.[21] I agree that global civil society, albeit effective in different endeavours, cannot make up for the perceived lack of voice of local groups. Smaller civil society organisations located near, and connected with, a community

[16] A Hudson, 'NGO's Transnational Advocacy Network: From Legitimacy to Political Responsibility?' (2002) 1 *Global Networks* 331.

[17] RC Carpenter, 'Setting the Advocacy Agenda: Theorizing Issue Emergence and Nonemergence in Transnational Advocacy' (2007) 51 *International Studies Quarterly* 99.

[18] C Rodríguez-Garavito, 'The Future of Human Rights: From Gatekeeping to Symbiosis' (2014) 11 *International Journal on Human Rights* 499, 504.

[19] LC Backer, 'An Institutional Role for Civil Society Within the U.N. Guiding Principles?: Comments on César Rodríguez-Garavito and Tatiana Andia "Business and Human Rights: Beyond the End of the Beginning"' (Workshop on Implementing the UN's Guiding Principles on Business and Human Rights: A South-Initiated North-South Dialogue, Brown University, February 2014) 5.

[20] M Hardt and A Negri, *Empire* (Cambridge, Harvard University Press, 2000) 313.

[21] Backer, 'Institutional Role for Civil Society' 8.

impacted by an extractive sector project will likely prove more effective at representing that community's interest in resolving disputes than larger global civil society organisations. This book addresses this issue by carving out a role for local civil society organisations in the proposals for reform.

A. A Potential New Form of Medievalism

The traditional view is that human rights law is created and governed by individual states and applies to its citizens. Some commentators argue that this understanding has changed significantly since the Second World War.[22] For instance, a primary issue at stake in the notorious Hart-Fuller debate of the 1950s was how the German legal system should respond to heinous acts committed by individuals associated with the Nazi regime.[23] Hart argued that such acts were lawful at the time they were committed. Further, any reasoning that suggested Nazi laws were not valid laws because they were morally wrong would confuse what the law 'is' with what the law 'ought to be'.[24] In contrast, Fuller argued that post-Nazi German courts could legitimately punish individuals for heinous acts even though they were not specifically invalid according to Nazi rules. Fuller contended that the Nazi legal system seriously departed from fundamental principles of fairness and justice. As such, these Nazi rules could not be characterised as legal, or as Fuller referred to the concept elsewhere, these rules were outside the 'morality of law'.[25] In this way, Fuller's position suggested that the conduct of individual citizens was governed by rules outside the apparatus of the existing state's legal system.

As part of this transformation away from the perspective of exclusive state rule, some commentators argue that civil society organisations, among other groups, threaten the authority of the state as a singular force in the regulation of multinational business enterprises.[26] As one example, Parag Khanna suggests the world is increasingly reflecting a new form of medievalism with less reliance on government institutions to resolve disputes around the globe.[27] He calls this emerging structure 'mega-diplomacy' which is based on dialogue between governments, corporations and civil society.[28]

[22] J Donnelly, 'Human Rights and International Organizations: States, Sovereignty, and the International Community' in F Kratochwil and E Mansfield (eds), *International Organization: A Reader* (New York, HarperCollins Publishers, 1994) 191.

[23] HLA Hart, 'Positivism and the Separation of Law and Morals' (1957) 71 *Harvard Law Review* 593; L Fuller, 'Positivism and Fidelity to Law-A Reply to Professor Hart' (1957) 71 *Harvard Law Review* 630.

[24] S Rehaag, 'The Hart-Fuller Debate in the Twenty-First Century' (2010) 48 *Osgoode Hall Law Journal* 691, 691.

[25] L Fuller, *The Morality of Law* (New Haven, Yale University Press, 1964).

[26] D Held et al, *Global Transformations: Politics, Economics, and Culture* (Redwood City, Stanford University Press, 1999); K Ohmae, *The End of the Nation State* (New York, Simon and Schuster Inc, 1995).

[27] P Khanna, *How to Run the World: Charting a Course to the Next Renaissance* (New York, Random House, 2011) 20.

[28] *Ibid* 22.

Similarly, another commentator has argued that there is a legitimacy crisis in the global political economy caused by a disconnect between the theory and practice of the Westphalian system.[29] The Peace of Westphalia in 1648 brought about an end to the Thirty Years War which effectively ended religious warfare in Europe.[30] The Peace of Westphalia is generally regarded as the beginning of an emerging state-centric system that transitioned away from religious and dynastic authority in European affairs. It has been suggested that this theory dominates international relations theory and international law.[31] The theory is rooted in legal positivism which suggests that international law applies only to states.[32] Some commentators suggest that the traditional notion that states are subjects of the law, while individuals and corporations are objects, has become anachronistic, assuming it was ever a proper historical interpretation.[33] For instance, commentary as far back as William Blackstone did not draw this distinction that is outlined in legal positivism.[34] This alternative view to legal positivism dismisses the Westphalian-inspired notions of state-centrality and lends support to the argument that there is a decidedly greater role for civil society actors in setting expectations and standards concerning the impacts of business enterprises on human rights.

Whether one believes that civil society organisations have a role to play in regulating corporate activity abroad depends in part on whether one prescribes to the functionalist or realist approach of international relations theory. In the realist tradition, the state is the only actor with power and authority, whereas the functionalists view the state as the most important actor, but other actors have roles, including transnational interest groups. The realist position focuses on self-interest of nation-states. Functionalists focus on common interests and needs shared by states (and non-state actors) in a process of global integration.[35] The functionalist concept is grounded in an idealist model that traces back to Kant and arose during the period between the First and Second World War.[36]

Functionalism is similar to the theory of constructivism in political science that focuses on the socially constructed nature of international politics.[37]

[29] AC Cutler, *Private Power and Global Authority: Transnational Merchant Law in the Global Political Economy* (Cambridge, Cambridge University Press, 2003) 241.

[30] R Cavendish, 'The Treaty of Westphalia' (1998) 48 *History Today*, www.historytoday.com/richard-cavendish/treaty-westphalia.

[31] R Falk and S Kim (eds), *Towards a Just World Order* (Boulder, Westview Press, 1982).

[32] J Austin, *The Province of Jurisprudence Determined, and the Uses of the Study of Jurisprudence* (London, Weidenfeld and Nicolson, 1832).

[33] Cutler, *Private Power and Global Authority* 247–49.

[34] MW Janis, 'Individuals as Subjects of International Law' (1984) 17 *Cornell International Law Journal* 61, 61.

[35] P Wolf, 'International Organization and Attitude Change: A Re-examination of the Functionalist Approach' (1973) 27 *International Organization* 347.

[36] D Mitrany, *A Working Peace System* (London, Royal Institute of International Affairs, 1943).

[37] PL Berger and T Luckmann, *The Social Construction of Reality: A Treatise in the Sociology of Knowledge* (New York, Doubleday, 1966).

Functionalism and constructivism theories on the prominence of non-state actors suggest that civil society organisations have a role in regulating multinational corporate activity.

There is also support for empowering civil society actors drawn from social movement theory. Noted sociologist Jürgen Habermas suggested that social movements emerge when individuals are colonised by threatening forces they are unable to control which could include extractive sector operations in the developing world.[38] Social movement theory is based in part on the view that civil society has an important role in empowering marginalised groups impacted by the mining sector. Some commentators have argued civil society organisations are a vehicle to promote democracy and hold states and corporations to account for abuses by the mining sector.[39]

The importance of civil society actors in providing a quasi-regulatory role concerning the human rights performance of extractive sector corporations is underscored by emerging social norms – the customary rules that govern behaviour in groups and societies – that are shifting the expectations placed on businesses in terms of protecting human rights. Social norms may be preferable to standard legal rules, as they internalise negative externalities and provide efficient signaling mechanisms.[40]

B. Social Licence for Business: Bestowed by Civil Society

One of the novel expectations on account of emerging social norms is that business enterprises will earn 'social licence' before proceeding with the development of extractive sector projects. Social licence is a nebulous concept that generally means that a business receives its privilege to operate from society at large. Other commentators have labeled this concept a 'license to operate' to refer to the idea that industrial facilities must conform to expectations of local communities impacted by their operations and the public.[41]

One way among others to achieve social licence or licence to operate is to ensure the social benefits of a business activity exceed its social costs.[42] This form of social licence draws on the work of Larry Catá Backer, who uses a legal pluralism theory to argue that various international mechanisms such as those influenced by

[38] J Habermas, *The Theory of Communicative Action Volume 2: System and Lifeworld* (Boston, Beacon Press, 1987).

[39] A Bebbington et al, 'Mining and Social Movements: Struggles Over Livelihood and Rural Territorial Development in the Andes' (2008) 36 *World Development* 2888.

[40] E Posner, *Law and Social Norms* (Cambridge, Harvard University Press, 2000).

[41] J Howard-Grenville, J Nash and C Coglianese, 'Constructing the License to Operate: Internal Factors and Their Influence on Corporate Environmental Decisions' (2008) 30 *Law & Policy* 73.

[42] R Jeurissen, 'Institutional Conditions of Corporate Citizenship' (2004) 53 *Journal of Business Ethics* 87, 89.

civil society organisations are collectively creating non-legal standards that corporations are expected to follow.[43]

Obtaining social licence is not mandatory, and represents a merging of legal compliance and standards of appropriate business conduct.[44] Civil society and communities, rather than formal legal authority, grants social licence as credibility, trust and authenticity are central themes of the concept. In this way, the noted international law expert Harold Koh explained that civil society organisations can be 'transnational norm entrepreneurs'.[45] Similarly, in their influential article on the link between business strategy and CSR, Mark Kramer and Michael Porter argue that 'social entrepreneurs' such as civil society organisations 'create shared value' between business and society.[46]

Similarly, as Michael Ignatieff observed, a result of globalisation is the clash between the global North and global South.[47] As a result of this clash, the moral entrepreneurs in our post-imperial world primarily include multinational corporations with reaches across the globe. Another agent of moral globalisation is civil society organisations that serve as the bearers of 'universal values'.[48]

Civil society groups understand the injustices brought about by rapacious extractive sector companies. At the same time, multinational corporations are being pressured by social norms to partake in an ethical international economy where there are consequences for environmental and social harm. I advocate that there is a potent role for civil society organisations and multinational corporations in creating moral operating systems for business. Further, effective moral operating systems will nurture an enduring social licence for businesses to operate within.

In sum, the necessity of achieving social licence as an emerging business model has elevated the role of civil society organisations in setting informal standards of corporate accountability. The work of civil society organisations has proved challenging and frequently does not result in substantive accountability for the impacts of business enterprises on human rights. However, it is clear that civil society actors will have a crucial role as states develop strategies for aligning with

[43] LC Backer, 'The Structure of Global Law: Fracture, Fluidity, Permeability, and Polycentricity' (2012) 17 *Tilburg Law Review* 177.

[44] L Edelman, 'The Endogeneity of Legal Regulation: Grievance Procedures as Rational Myth' (1999) 105 *American Journal of Sociology* 406.

[45] HH Koh, 'The 1998 Frankel Lecturer: Bringing International Human Rights Home' (1998) 35 *Houston Law Review* 647; HH Koh, 'The 1994 Roscoe Pound Lecture: Transnational Legal Process' (1996) 75 *Nebraska Law Review* 181.

[46] M Kramer and M Porter, 'Creating Shared Value: Redefining Capitalism and the Role of the Corporation in Society' (2011) 89 *Harvard Business Review* 62, 70. Further: 'Forward-thinking foundations can also serve as honest brokers and allay fears by mitigating power imbalances between small local enterprises, NGOs, governments, and companies.' *Ibid* 73.

[47] M Ignatieff, *The Ordinary Virtues: Moral Order in a Divided World* (Cambridge, Harvard University Press, 2017) 16.

[48] *Ibid* 15.

the internationally-recognised standards of human rights and environmental protection and as the extractive sector begins to take seriously its responsibility to respect human rights.

II. Corporate Accountability, Responsibilities and Self-Governance

Corporations are social actors capable of generating public benefits through the creation of employment opportunities, the payment of taxes and the manufacturing of necessary goods, to name just a few. Yet they remain an artificial creation of law that serves the interests of shareholders and executives, as their primary aim is to amass wealth and externalise costs. There are two traditional theories of corporate accountability.[49] I adopt the labels of the shareholder primacy and the stakeholder model.[50]

Included among the shareholder primacy theorists is the late Nobel Prize winning economist Milton Friedman who argued that the socially responsible objective for corporations is to increase profits.[51] More recent proponents of shareholder primacy have been extraordinarily confident in the inevitable success of this model, so much so that two noted experts in 2001 declared the 'end of corporate law' as consensus was forming in 'leading jurisdictions' around shareholder primacy.[52]

The shareholder primacy model is challenged by the stakeholder conception. Stakeholder theory of corporate accountability extends the concept of corporate managers' obligations to several stakeholders including shareholders, creditors, employees, suppliers, customers, the public and the environment.[53] In terms of corporate structure, stakeholder theory does not question that corporate managers should be responsible for the running of a corporation. However, proponents of this theory question the various stakeholder interests that should be regarded and promote a more community-based decision-making process. In this way, shareholder wealth is seen as one of many competing interests and not the dominant constituent.

[49] A Dhir, 'Realigning the Corporate Building Blocks: Shareholder Proposals as a Vehicle for Achieving Corporate Social and Human Rights Accountability' (2006) 43 *American Business Law Journal* 365, 369.

[50] RE Freeman, *Strategic Management. A Stakeholder Approach* (Cambridge, Cambridge University Press, 2010).

[51] M Friedman, 'The Social Responsibility of the Corporation Is to Increase Its Profits' (*New York Times Magazine*, 13 September 1970).

[52] H Hansmann and R Kraakman, 'The End of History for Corporate Law' (2001) 89 *Georgetown Law Journal* 439, 441.

[53] C Fiesel, 'Fiduciary Duties of Directors, Corporate Governance and the End of Shareholder Primacy' in P Puri (ed), *Corporate Governance and Securities Regulation in the 21st Century* (Toronto, Butterworths, 2004) 77.

In the international mining arena, it is important to draw a distinction between large, junior and state operated corporations. Of particular importance is that smaller industry players may have more risk tolerance in their mining practices because they are less concerned with their corporate reputation and brand. These entities will be more likely to focus on short-term gains for shareholders, as they do not have the resources or motivation to consider the environment or human rights. In contrast, larger companies or state owned enterprises may have more invested in satisfying the needs of various stakeholders by implementing a long-term and risk-adverse approach to avoid controversy.

An emerging concept in corporate accountability closely linked to the stakeholder model is the various frameworks developed on CSR.[54] An early and dominant theory on CSR was forwarded by Archie Carroll who broke down the topic into economic, legal, ethical and philanthropic corporate responsibilities.[55] Today, CSR is about maximising corporate profit along with the public good in all its forms.[56]

CSR has been described as voluntary, market-based and 'soft law'.[57] Soft law is based in the belief that strict enforcement of rules is not necessarily the most effective tool for corporate compliance.[58] Soft law is distinguished from the public law approach of regulation, often referred to as 'hard law' or command-and-control, which is based on legally binding obligations.[59] Hard law includes criminal regulation over the environment, labour and human rights practices in the belief that fear of legal sanctions will act as an effective deterrent.[60]

As a middle ground between hard and soft law, some commentators have called for 'responsive regulation', in which policy makers should seek to promote private market governance.[61] It has been suggested that responsive regulation encourages corporations to be virtuous.[62] A primary objective of responsive

[54] For a review of the early literature on corporate social responsibility see D Matten et al, 'Behind the Mask: Revealing the True Face of Corporate Citizenship' (2003) 45 *Journal of Business Ethics* 109, 110; A Carroll, 'A Three Dimensional Model of Corporate Social Performance' (1979) 4 *Academy of Management Review* 497.

[55] A Carroll, 'The Pyramid of Corporate Social Responsibility: Toward the Moral Management of Organizational Stakeholders' (1991) 34 *Business Horizons* 39.

[56] M Ararat, AM Colpan and D Matten, 'Business Groups and Corporate Responsibility for the Public Good' (2018) 153 *Journal of Business Ethics* 911, 914.

[57] R Steinhardt, 'Soft Law, Hard Markets: Competitive Responsibilities for Multinational Corporations' (2008) 33 *Brooklyn Journal of International Law* 933; M Kerr, C Pitts and R Janda, *Corporate Social Responsibility: A Legal Analysis* (Markham, LexisNexis Canada Inc, 2009) 153.

[58] K Hawkins, 'Compliance Strategy, Prosecution Policy, and Aunt Sally: A Comment on Pearce and Tombs' (1990) 30 *British Journal of Criminology* 444, 461.

[59] E Oshionebo, *Regulating Transnational Corporations in Domestic and International Regimes: An African Case Study* (Toronto, University of Toronto Press, 2009) 32–35.

[60] F Pearce and S Tombs, 'Ideology, Hegemony and Empiricism: Compliance Theories of Regulation' (1990) 30 *British Journal of Criminology* 423.

[61] I Ayres and J Braithwaite, *Responsive Regulation: Transcending the Deregulation Debate* (Oxford, Oxford University Press, 1992).

[62] J Braithwaite, 'Responsive Business Regulatory Institutions' in CAJ Coady and CJG Sampford (eds), *Business Ethics and the Law* (Leichardt, The Federation Press, 1993) 85.

regulation is to compel corporations to cooperate with regulators.[63] This promotes cognisance of legal trends as corporations are persuaded by regulators to be reactive to changes in the public's expectations.

CSR in the environmental context can involve at least two types of instruments: 1) corporate policies and pledges such as voluntary codes of conduct that are adopted by business enterprises; and 2) incentive schemes that provide an economic benefit for compliance, or a penalty for lack of adherence to the programme.[64] These voluntary environmental codes are commitments undertaken by corporate polluters in the absence of an express legal requirement.[65] In the human rights context, several commentators have attempted to outline frameworks of corporate responsibility for human rights violations where the protection of human rights is regarded as an explicit corporate objective.[66]

Those who advocate for CSR initiatives argue that these programmes are effective and efficient in achieving regulatory outcomes.[67] Other commentators predict that corporations will seek to follow best practices on account of 'enlightened self-interest', that is, the corporation embraces social responsibilities in promoting its own self-interest.[68] This idea has also been called 'public-regarding theory' which requires corporate managers to focus on the underlying ethical quality of corporate action and the effects of that action on other people.[69] CSR has also been associated with 'social enterprise law' where corporate stakeholders consciously seek lower economic returns in order to support sustainability, fair wages and fair trade.[70]

CSR is appealing because perceived socially responsible businesses may attract more customers or talented employees, create better communities which generate a stable context in which to do business, and by adopting a voluntary commitment

[63] J Braithwaite, *Restorative Justice & Responsive Regulation* (Oxford, Oxford University Press, 2002) 30.

[64] For an overview of economic instruments for regulating multinational corporations, see W Oates, *The Economics of Environmental Regulation* (Cheltenham, Edward Elgar Publishing, 1996).

[65] S Wood, 'Voluntary Environmental Codes and Sustainability' in B Richardson and S Wood (eds), *Environmental Law for Sustainability* (Oxford, Hart Publishing, 2006) 230.

[66] R Steinhardt, 'The New Lex Mercatoria' in P Alston (ed), *Non-State Actors and Human Rights* (Oxford, Oxford University Press, 2005) 177; B Frey, 'The Legal and Ethical Responsibilities of Transnational Corporations in the Protection of International Human Rights' (1997) 6 *Minnesota Journal of Global Trade* 153; D Weissbrodt and M Kruger, 'Norms on the Responsibilities of Transnational Corporations and Other Business Enterprises with Regard to Human Rights' (2003) 97 *American Journal of International Law* 901; D Kinley and J Tadaki, 'From Talk to Walk: The Emergence of Human Rights Responsibilities of Transnational Corporations at International Law' (2004) 44 *Virginia Journal of International Law* 931.

[67] S Rose-Ackerman, 'Comment: Consensus Versus Incentives: A Skeptical Look at Regulatory Negotiation' (1994) 43 *Duke Law Journal* 1206, 1220.

[68] A Crane and D Matten, *Business Ethics: Managing Corporate Citizenship and Sustainability in the Age of Globalization*, 2nd edn (Oxford, Oxford University Press, 2007) 47.

[69] C Williams, 'Corporate Compliance with the Law in the Era of Efficiency' (1998) 76 *North Carolina Law Review* 1265, 1382–83.

[70] B Means and J Yockey (eds), *The Cambridge Handbook of Social Enterprise Law* (Cambridge, Cambridge University Press, 2019).

to social goals, a corporation may 'forestall legislation and ensure greater corporate independence from government'.[71] Implementing CSR programmes also has the ability to protect a corporation's reputation in the event the corporation is cast in a negative light. For instance, highlighting past and current commitments to CSR may cushion reputational harm or buy goodwill from consumers, shareholders, civil society and the public.[72]

As a critique, it has also been suggested that CSR has become a mere exercise in public relations and that corporations are creating glowing CSR reports as a way to avoid government oversight.[73] Other commentators have suggested that CSR activities may increase corporate executives' ability to opportunistically exploit corporate resources through unnecessary increased spending outside the primary activities of the business such as through charitable donations.[74]

CSR is based partly on the notion that corporations are able to self-regulate and achieve positive ends for society and the environment. An early form of corporate self-governance grew with the *Lex Mercatoria*, an ancient merchant law that filled the gaps of Roman civil law in the medieval period. The development of the *Lex Mercatoria* was pivotal in the creation of private law norms concerning the regulation of commercial activity.

In the eleventh and twelfth centuries, Europe experienced a revival in trade in the East as Crusades had freed up the Mediterranean Sea and fueled the commercial growth of certain Italian cities. Trading between these Italian cities and northern ports, known at the time as the Hanseatic League, is where the *Lex Mercatoria* began.[75] The *Lex Mercatoria* thrived from the thirteenth to the seventeenth century. During this period, there was no distinction between public and private international law, but the merchant community provided an early notion of what was to become the private realm with the development of capitalism and the privatisation of commercial relations.[76] The *Lex Mercatoria* has been characterised by one commentator as the private international law of the Middle Ages.[77] It mainly drew upon ancient Greek maritime customs, Roman law of sales,

[71] Crane and Matten, *Business Ethics* 47.

[72] Y Shiu and S Yang, 'Does Engagement in Corporate Social Responsibility Provide Strategic Insurance-like Effects' (2017) 38 *Strategic Management Journal* 455.

[73] S Sethi and D Schepers, 'United Nations Global Compact: The Promise-Performance Gap' (2014) 122 *Journal of Business Ethics* 193.

[74] RW Masulis and SW Reza, 'Agency Problems of Corporate Philanthropy' (2015) 28 *Review of Financial Studies* 592.

[75] Cutler (n 29) 113.

[76] Cutler (n 29) 111.

[77] One commentator wrote that the 'international nature of the sources from which it drew its rules and of the persons over whom it exercised jurisdiction, combined with the universality of its guiding principles, fairly entitle the Law Merchant to be called "the private international law of the Middle Ages"'. W Mitchell, *An Essay on the Early History of the Law Merchant* (Cambridge, Cambridge University Press, 1904) 21. Note that Mitchell is quoting from FW Maitland's *Select Pleas in Manorial and Other Seignorial Courts* (London, B. Quaritch, 1889) 133.

debt and civil obligations, as well as Roman *jus gentium*.[78] This includes the ancient Rhodian Maritime Law that dates from somewhere between 300 and 900 BCE.[79] The *Lex Mercatoria* was also based upon the best practices of merchants of this era in determining trustworthiness and business reputation.[80]

Some commentators suggest that current developments in corporate self-governance represent the emergence of a new *Lex Mercatoria* that expands beyond purely commercial concerns to incorporate hard law with voluntary initiatives.[81] There are various theories suggesting that cross-listings on international stock markets have raised corporate governance standards on an international level, impacting all large-scale public corporations. As one example, John Coffee used the term 'bonding hypothesis' to describe when corporations raise governance standards by agreeing to follow robust compliance rules as a condition of selling their stock on public markets.[82]

It has even been suggested that by following best practices through self-governance tied to CSR, corporations may be creating a new 'customary global law' as opposed to a voluntary regime.[83] For example, concerning the international context of regulating transnational corporations, John Ruggie envisions the development of a 'slow and gradual accretion of customary international law standards'.[84]

From a private law perspective, a similar concept can be seen in the growth of ubiquitous modern corporate compliance programmes. There are indications that directors' fiduciary duties require corporation to have adequate compliance programmes.[85] The whistleblower provisions of the Dodd-Frank Act, the Sarbanes–Oxley Act, the Federal Criminal Sentencing Guidelines and the New York Stock Exchange listing requirements further buttress this argument for the raising of corporate governance standards on an international level by, among other things, requiring disclosure on whether a corporation has a Code of Conduct.[86]

[78] Cutler (n 29) 112–13.

[79] R Benedict, 'The Historical Position of the Rhodian Law' (1909) 18 *Yale Law Journal* 223.

[80] Kerr et al, *Corporate Social Responsibility* 329–30, 546.

[81] Steinhardt, 'Soft Law, Hard Markets' 936–37, 947.

[82] J Coffee, 'The Future as History: The Prospects of Global Convergence in Corporate Governance and Its Implications' (1999) 93 *Northwestern University Law Review* 641, 652; J Coffee, 'Racing Towards the Top?: The Impact of Cross-Listings and Stock Market Competition on International Corporate Governance' (2002) 102 *Columbia Law Review* 1757.

[83] It is a global law rather than international law because it involves not just countries but non-state actors as well. C Pitts, 'Business, Human Rights, and the Environment: The Role of the Lawyer in CSR & Ethical Globalization' (2008) 26 *Berkeley Journal of International Law* 479, 488.

[84] JG Ruggie, *Just Business: Multinational Corporations and Human Rights* (New York, W. W. Norton & Company, 2013) xxii.

[85] See, eg, Chancellor Allen's comments in *Re Caremark International Inc Derivative Litigation* [1996] 698 A 2d 959 (Del Ch).

[86] Dodd-Frank Wall Street Reform and Consumer Protection Act Pub L No 111-203, 124 Stat 1376 (2010); s 406(a) Sarbanes–Oxley Act (US), 15 USC s 7264, codified at 17 CFR s 228.406(a) and (b); United States Sentencing Commission, 'USSC Guideline Manual' (2018) c 8, www.ussc.gov/guidelines/2018-guidelines-manual/2018-chapter-8; New York Stock Exchange Listed Company Manual, s 303A.10 and Marketplace Rule 4350(n).

All of this leads to one of the primary arguments made in this book, that corporations may potentially govern their relations with impacted individuals through the implementation of an operational-level grievance mechanism. A prescient example of this is the situation that occurred at the Porgera gold mine in Papua New Guinea. The majority owner between 2006 and 2015 was a Canadian-based company, Barrick Gold. Barrick's operational-grievance mechanism at the mine was one of the first to be implemented in accordance with the UN Guiding Principles. For this reason, it serves as a valuable learning tool for understanding approaches to designing future remedy mechanisms involving the extractive sector.

The Porgera mine has a controversial human rights record. Like many international mining operators, Barrick employed its own security force of between 400 and 500 local individuals. In 2011, Human Rights Watch reported a history of serious cases of sexual violence against local women by security personnel at the mine.[87] In 2012, Barrick launched an operational-level grievance mechanism to offer reparations to women who were sexually assaulted by these security officials. Ultimately, 119 women were awarded financial compensation, medical care, counselling, school fees and business training if there was a sexual violence committed against them between 1990 and 2010.[88] As part of these agreements, the women had to waive their right to sue Barrick.

Some victims did not accept the settlement offer and sought legal representation from Earth Rights International, a US-based civil society organisation. To these individuals, Barrick offered confidential settlement packages believed to be more than the amounts offered to the other victims.[89] Subsequently, in 2015, Barrick offered each of the 119 women an additional payment.[90] This suggests that the involvement of a civil society actor as a representative for victims can be advantageous and effective in terms of obtaining a greater financial remedy.

A 2015 report prepared jointly by researchers from Columbia and Harvard Law School provided key lessons for corporations, civil society groups and affected communities about the benefits, challenges and limitations of Barrick's operational-level grievance mechanism. The report noted the significant barriers to justice resulting from Papua New Guinea's weak judicial system, the remote location of the mine and other disadvantages that specifically impacted women. For instance, the victims that experienced sexual violence faced challenges in

[87] Human Rights Watch, 'Human Rights Impacts of Papua New Guinea's Porgera Gold Mine' (February 2011), www.hrw.org/report/2011/02/01/golds-costly-dividend/human-rights-impacts-papua-new-guineas-porgera-gold-mine.

[88] Enodo Rights, 'Pillar III on the Ground: An Independent Assessment of the Porgera Remedy Framework' (2016) 1, barrick.q4cdn.com/788666289/files/porgera/Enodo-Rights-Porgera-Remedy-Framework-Independent-Assessment.pdf.

[89] Human Rights Clinic (Columbia Law School) & International Human Rights Clinic (Harvard Law School), 'Righting Wrongs? Barrick Gold's Remedy Mechanism for Sexual Violence in Papua New Guinea: Key Concerns and Lessons Learned' (2015) 1.

[90] Enodo Rights, 'Pillar III' 15.

speaking out about their attacks and seeking a remedy due in part to lack of education, the social stigma of sexual assault and the potential for violence from family members.[91] This highlights the particularly acute issues surrounding gender and resource extraction that are social as well as economic in nature.[92]

As a positive feature, the report noted that in contrast to Papua New Guinea's weak judicial system, Barrick's operational-level grievance mechanism offered an accessible path for victims to articulate their accounts of abuse and seek compensation. Further, the company took encouraging steps towards transparency by publishing the procedures governing the remedy mechanism.

The report also criticised Barrick for some deficiencies in the programme.[93] These include Barrick's failure to address the power imbalance between themselves as a multinational corporation that can wield enormous power over host states, and individuals affected by their operations. According to the report, these power imbalances can impact the remedy a multinational corporation is willing to offer victims of human rights abuses. To mitigate this risk, the report recommended that strict safeguards should be put in place to address the balance of bargaining power between corporations and local individuals.

A key to addressing this concern is to deeply involve legitimate local and international civil society actors as representatives for the interests of impacted individuals throughout the course of designing and implementing an operational-level grievance mechanism. To a limited degree, Barrick did consult with civil society groups and other experts in designing the programme. However, as opposed to simply consulting these groups, the entire grievance process should be built around the centrality of civil society as representatives for victims. That is precisely the thrust of the proposal as presented in this book for remedying the impacts of formidable international mining companies.

In conclusion, the customary models for creating legal liability, such as through home state legislation and judicial systems, have not adequately resolved international disputes between impacted communities and the extractive sector. Two actors potentially overlooked in creating obligations on businesses operating abroad are civil society organisations and the corporate sector.

Civil society organisations have a rich history and more recently have played a prominent role in judicial and non-judicial processes dealing with allegations of corporate wrongdoing abroad. Further, social norms and expectations of business have begun to compel multinational corporations to adhere to internationally-recognised covenants of business conduct.

The proposal advanced in this book encourages businesses to operate meaningful site-level grievance processes without the necessity of government

[91] S Seck and P Simons, 'Resource Extraction and the Human Rights of Women and Girls' (2019) 31 *Canadian Journal of Women and the Law* i, ii–iii.

[92] S Hertel, *Tethered Fates: Companies, Communities, and Rights at Stake* (New York, Oxford University Press, 2019) 152.

[93] Human Rights Clinic, 'Righting Wrongs?' 2.

or judicial oversight. The proposal further encourages businesses to utilise civil society actors as representatives or even to serve as mediators in these business-run dispute resolution mechanisms.

An underlying tenet of this proposal is that there are persuasive and substantial reasons to utilise both corporate self-regulation techniques, as well as to promote a dominant role for civil society actors in regulating the foreign conduct of the extractive sector.

PART II

The Judicial and Non-Judicial Approach

3

Obstacles in Holding Corporations to Account

The history of human rights and environmental abuses in the extractive sector suggests that it is difficult for victims to obtain an adequate remedy. The need for a legal solution to provide redress to injured parties is long-standing.

Part II of this book addresses important questions: what are the obstacles in holding parent corporations to account for extraterritorial conduct in the courts of their home states? Taking into account that there are only so many effective legal systems, does it make sense to use the legal apparatus of a progressive judicial institution when a host state court fails to provide an adequate remedy to victims?

The next two chapters provide an overview of the case law concerning the ability of foreign nationals to hold extractive sector corporations to account in the US, UK, Canada and Australia. The primary focus is on *forum non conveniens* in testing the efficacy of domestic judicial systems. *Forum non conveniens* is a key legal doctrine in holding corporations accountable for overseas misconduct. It is a procedural doctrine rooted in the common law system. The doctrine permits a court to dismiss a claim if an alternative forum is more appropriate to consider the matter. While the concept is similar across the US, UK, Canada and Australia, some UK jurists have preferred the term 'appropriate forum' to describe *forum non conveniens*.[1] Regardless of how the doctrine is phrased, it is crucial to consider because it limits the ability of plaintiffs to bring lawsuits for actions that occur outside of the forum's legal system.

The US, Australia and Canada are common law legal systems, related in history and origin as they were all once colonies under the British Crown. In this way, their legal systems are inextricably related. Their court systems all utilise some form of *forum non conveniens*. For these reasons, among others, it will be fruitful to compare the differences and similarities of how these somewhat parallel legal systems treat foreign wrongdoing by their extractive sectors. However, there are drawbacks to reducing the comparative analysis to just these jurisdictions. For one, comparing jurisdictions with a civil legal system, or other types of approaches

[1] *Spiliada Maritime Corp v Cansulex Ltd* [1987] AC 460 (HL).

may provide greater context and possibilities for understanding how to effectively regulate in this area.

As such, this work is cognisant of the many limitations posed by analysing legal systems that are effectively counterparts of each other. A rich discussion on these issues would be had by factoring in civil law countries such as France, Germany, the Netherlands, Russia, China and Japan, among many others. That work is left to other researchers to address in time. However, the material within this book contrasting these four legal systems is a cogent analysis with illuminating results. For instance, One aim of this chapter is to highlight Canadian and Australian efforts, which are under-accounted for in the literature compared to the US and UK models. These results are instructive in forming a proposal for regulating the foreign activities of the Canadian extractive sector.

The US legal system has been used extensively by claimants seeking redress for human rights abuses committed overseas. The US is home to some of the world's largest extractive sector corporations. Exxon Mobil, Chevron and Conoco Phillips all have significant operations with a global reach. The market capitalisation and production capacity of these companies make the US a formidable actor in the extractive sector. Further, the US is considered a world stage for civil society organisations to generate public attention for wrongdoing committed by US corporations and non-US corporations.[2]

Cases applying the US Alien Tort Statute 1789 (ATS) are also reviewed.[3] The ATS is considered as a special statute that has been utilised by foreign nationals against the extractive sector for alleged human rights violations occurring outside the United States. The ATS is a distinctive creation.[4] Such a statutory framework for litigating activities overseas is not provided in other countries.[5]

The UK, Canada and Australia are also major players in the international extractive sector. For instance, the UK is the headquarters of many prominent mining companies. According to a Financial Times Global 500 list, of the top ten mining corporations in the world, seven are headquartered in the UK.[6]

[2] For a report comparing the importance of non-governmental organisations (NGOs) in Europe and the US, see J Lee, 'Brief: Comparing NGO Influence in the EU and the U.S.' (CASIN, September 2006), www.files.ethz.ch/isn/25102/ngoinfluenceinuandusa.pdf.

[3] Alien Tort Statute 1789 (28 USC § 1350).

[4] In the US Court of Appeals for the Second Circuit decision of *Kiobel*, Justice Cabranes wrote that the ATS is 'of a kind apparently unknown to any other legal system in the world'. *Kiobel v Royal Dutch Petroleum Co* [2010] 621 F3d 111 (2d Cir) 115.

[5] A close example of a similar statute is in Belgium. The 1993 *Act Concerning the Punishment of Grave Breaches of International Humanitarian Law* grants 'universal jurisdiction' to the Belgian courts for dealing with human rights breaches by Belgium citizens regardless of the place where the offence was committed. S Smis and K Van der Borght, 'Belgium: Act Concerning the Punishment of Grave Breaches of International Humanitarian Law: A Contested Law with Uncontested Objectives' (American Society of International Law, 2003), www.asil.org/insights/volume/8/issue/18/belgian-law-concerning-punishment-grave-breaches-international.

[6] 'FT Global 500' *Financial Times* (2014), www.ft.com/content/988051be-fdee-11e3-bd0e-00144feab7de.

Australia is another mining powerhouse driven by export demands from China, among other things.[7] Canada is also a dominant player with almost three quarters of the world's extractive sector listed on the Toronto Stock Exchange.

Increasingly over the past two decades, US, UK, Canadian and Australian extractive sector corporations have been accused of human rights abuses and environmental violations in foreign operations. Lawsuits arising out of these allegations have predominantly been brought against the parent corporations in their countries of domicile, and consequently these lawsuits run into procedural bars such as *forum non conveniens* and limitation of jurisdiction.

The findings suggest that UK and Australian courts are rather willing to consider lawsuits against extractive sector corporations for conduct that occurs abroad. Comparatively, courts in the US have provided mixed results, with the more recent decisions indicating a reticence in allowing such claims to proceed.

I. Justification for Home State Regulation

There are several options to hold multinational corporations responsible for environmental and human rights abuses that occur in foreign operations, including:

1) international mechanisms such as the United Nations, World Bank or Organisation for Economic Co-operation and Development (OECD);
2) domestic courts of the host state where the subsidiary operates;
3) domestic courts of the home state where the parent corporation is domiciled; and
4) comprehensive home state legislation.

The last two options are backed by the weight of a domestic home state legal system.

Ideally, local courts of both subsidiary and parent corporations should be seized of these matters and able to apportion liability in cases of wrongdoing. Moreover, one or several of these options should offer a venue for redress and remedy to impacted individuals. Unfortunately, the prospects concerning all of these options are dire and inadequate.

A. Limitations of International Regulation

Multinational corporations are not regulated internationally. With no central regulator, they are instead subject to the laws of the state in which they operate,

[7] One report states that 'Australia is among the top ten mining countries in the world'. Mining Technology.com, 'Australian Mining Industry Forecast to 2015' (2011), www.mining-technology.com/features/featureaustralian-mining-industry-forecast-to-2015.

even if that state is unable or unwilling to address corporate human rights abuses. An international solution would avoid these problems and ensure a harmonised approach in determining corporate liability for extraterritorial abuses.

There have been efforts by international organisations to develop a harmonised approach. Looking at the United Nations, three initiatives stand out as noteworthy. In a 1999 speech, former UN Secretary-General, Kofi Annan challenged business leaders to adopt practices aimed at achieving a sustainable global market.[8] This was the beginning of what would develop into the UN Global Compact. The Global Compact invites businesses to embrace ten principles relating to human rights, labour standards, environmental practices and anti-corruption policies.[9] However, there are a number of shortcomings regarding the effectiveness of the Global Compact. Critics have argued that it is vague and does not set clear standards for companies to meet.[10]

A more precise proposal in terms of regulating corporate conduct was contained in the 2003 United Nations Norms on the Responsibilities of Transnational Corporations and Other Business Enterprises with Regards to Human Rights (UN Norms).[11] The UN Norms would have placed the same human rights responsibilities on multinational businesses that countries have accepted under treaties. As such, the enforcement of the UN Norms would have transferred to corporations the responsibilities of those countries. The UN Norms faced significant opposition by the business community. For this reason, among others, the UN Norms were effectively abandoned, but they set the stage for the 2011 UN Guiding Principles.[12]

The UN Guiding Principles rely heavily on existing standards of international law and do not create fresh regulation to mitigate the concern over human rights abuses by multinational corporations. This is problematic for those who desire more robust regulation, as states are often reluctant to rein in multinational corporations.[13]

The OECD also maintains guidelines for recommended business conduct. Although a key aspect of the OECD Guidelines is that as they are voluntary,

[8] United Nations, 'Secretary-General Proposes Global Compact on Human Rights, Labour, Environment, in Address to World Economic Forum in Davos' (1999), www.un.org/press/en/1999/19990201.sgsm6881.html.

[9] The United Nations Global Compact website is accessible at www.unglobalcompact.org.

[10] E Oshionebo, 'The U.N. Global Compact and Accountability of Transnational Corporations: Separating Myth from Realities' (2007) 19 *Florida Journal of International Law* 1, 22–23.

[11] Subcommission on the Promotion and Protection of Human Rights, 'Norms on the Responsibilities of Transnational Corporations and Other Business Enterprises with Regard to Human Rights' (*United Nations Digital Library*, 2003), digitallibrary.un.org/record/501576?ln=en.

[12] Special Representative on Business and Human Rights (SRBHR), 'United Nations Guiding Principles on Business and Human Rights: Implementing the United Nations "Protect, Respect and Remedy" Framework' (United Nations, 2011), www.ohchr.org/documents/publications/guidingprinciplesbusinesshr_en.pdf.

[13] RE Rauxloh, 'A Call for the End of Impunity for Multinational Corporations' (2008) 14 *Texas Wesleyan Law Review* 297, 305.

they are not legally enforceable.[14] Other examples of approaches taken by international organisations to regulate the conduct of multinational corporations include the Voluntary Principles on Security and Human Rights (Voluntary Principles),[15] the World Bank's International Finance Corporation Performance Standards (Performance Standards),[16] Equator Principles,[17] Global Reporting Initiative (GRI),[18] and Extractive Industries Transparency Initiative.[19] Of these instruments, only the Extractive Industries Transparency Initiative and the Voluntary Principles are specifically designed to target the unique concerns of the extractive sector. These concerns include the hazards of arming local security, police and military to protect mining assets and voluntary disclosure of payments made to foreign governments.

Finally, another alternative that has been suggested for regulating multinational corporations is international criminal law. The Rome Statute is a 1998 Treaty that established the International Criminal Court (ICC) and recognises the core international crimes of genocide, murder, torture and kidnapping.[20] It was adopted by an overwhelming majority of countries, with the notable exception of the US. Article 25 of the Rome Statute limits criminal responsibility to individual natural persons, and negates the ability to put corporations and other business entities on trial. However, one commentator has argued that the structure and textual language of the Rome Statute makes it possible to extend the jurisdiction of the ICC to corporations.[21] Even if jurisdiction is extended to corporations, the chief limitation of the ICC as a means of ensuring corporate accountability is the lack of US participation, which likely exempts all US corporations. Moreover, the expertise of the ICC is in criminal law and it may be overstepping and potentially inappropriate to introduce commercial law into the realm of the ICC.

In sum, these international mechanisms tend to be voluntary and do not exhibit binding authority. The failure of these mechanisms to provide an effective remedy for those impacted by the extractive sector is one reason victims may seek a home state judicial solution.

[14] OECD, 'The OECD Guidelines for Multinational Enterprises' (2011) 17, www.oecd.org/dataoecd/56/36/1922428.pdf.

[15] The content of the Voluntary Principles can be accessed at www.voluntaryprinciples.org/what-are-the-voluntary-principles.

[16] International Finance Corporation World Bank Group, 'IFC Performance Standards on Environmental and Social Sustainability – Effective January 1, 2012'.

[17] 'The Equator Principles July 2020' (2020), www.equator-principles.com.

[18] The GRI website is accessible at www.globalreporting.org.

[19] The Extractive Industries Transparency Initiative website is accessible at www.eiti.org.

[20] Rome Statute of the International Criminal Court 1998 (2187 UNTS 90).

[21] B Choudhury, 'Beyond the Alien Tort Claims Act: Alternative Approaches to Attributing Liability to Corporations for Extraterritorial Abuses' (2005) 26 *Northwestern Journal of International Law and Business* 41, 57, 59–61.

B. Concerns with Host State Judicial Systems

The option of using host state courts to hold a subsidiary accountable in the jurisdiction of operation has many proven limitations. For one, the domestic legal system in the host state may be a weak venue to provide a legal remedy for victims impacted by the operations of a multinational enterprise. Resource-rich countries are often plagued with underdeveloped legal systems that are not equipped to deal with lawsuits against multinational companies. For example, the host state's judicial system may be inefficient, or susceptible to bribes or political influence that has a vested interested in protecting foreign investment. Even when laws exist in the host state to prevent abusive conduct, the states may fail to implement them because of a lack of capacity, or the fear of creating an unfriendly business environment to foreign investors.[22] Even if a plaintiff is successful in obtaining a judgment, the subsidiary may deliberately hold insufficient capital or insurance to satisfy a successful damage award.

As outlined in chapter one, examples of failed host state litigation include the victims from Yanacocha and Bhopal who attempted to hold the corporate defendants properly to account in Peruvian and Indian courts, respectively. There are several other cases that demonstrate the difficulty of holding the foreign extractive sector to account for wrongdoing in extraterritorial courts. Consider the case of *Ngcobo v Thor Chemicals Holdings Ltd*.[23]

In *Ngcobo*, injured workers in South Africa attempted to hold a UK extractive sector corporation responsible in their host state domestic courts. In the 1980s, Thor was a chemical manufacturer in the UK and around the world. Their UK operations came under scrutiny by health and safety regulators due to the substantiated discovery of elevated levels of mercury in one of their chemical plants. This led to the closure of the plant.[24]

Thor also had operations in South Africa with similarly high levels of mercury as those in the UK plant. It was alleged that the South African plant relied extensively on an untrained labour force.[25] In 1992, mercury poisoning of South African workers came to light. Three workers were hospitalised for mercury poisoning and one died as a result.[26]

In 1993, a criminal inquiry concerning manslaughter was launched by the Attorney General's office in South Africa against Thor and three of its top officials in South Africa. However, in 1995 the Attorney General expressed concern that

[22] JG Ruggie, *Just Business: Multinational Corporations and Human Rights* (New York, W. W. Norton & Company, 2013) xvi.

[23] *Ngcobo v Thor Chemicals Holdings Ltd* [1995] TLR 10 (Eng CA).

[24] M Butler, 'Lessons from Thor Chemicals' in L Bethlehem and M Goldblatt (eds), *The Bottom Line: Industry and the Environment in South Africa* (Cape Town, University of Cape Town Press, 1997) 195.

[25] R Meeran, 'Liability of Multinational Corporations: A Critical Stage' (1999), www.labournet.net/images/cape/campanal.htm.

[26] Butler, 'Lessons from Thor Chemicals' 200–201.

there were no prospects for a successful prosecution. Evidentially, Thor had been given a permit from the South African Department of Water Affairs and Forestry to store exposed mercury in its plant close to the workers. Thus, according to the Attorney General, the permit potentially served as an adequate defence to any alleged crimes or violations of occupational health and safety laws. Of more concern in the Attorney General's office, the prosecution team assigned to the case was under-resourced. Although offers came from international organisations to fund the prosecution, they were surprisingly rejected by the Attorney General. This led some to speculate that the Government of South Africa did not wish to have a vigorous prosecution against Thor.[27]

A trial proceeded before the Pietermaritzburg Magistrate Court. In 1995, a plea agreement was reached and Thor was fined 13,500 rand (the South African currency) for contravening occupational health and safety legislation which was approximately US $5,000 at the time.[28] The manslaughter charges against the company and the three executives were all withdrawn.

As a consequence of the ineffective prosecution in the host state of South Africa, litigation was commenced in the home state of the UK. That litigation resulted in a settlement agreement for 9.1 million rand, which was approximately $2.1 million in US currency at the time.[29]

Another example highlighting the difficulty of holding the foreign extractive sector to account for wrongdoing in host state courts is *Aguinda v Texaco*.[30] This case was a class action lawsuit against Texaco (now Chevron). The class group included approximately 30,000 Ecuadoreans claiming that Texaco caused extensive destruction to the Amazon rainforest prior to formally leaving Ecuador in 1992.[31] It was alleged that this environmental damage harmed the traditional lifestyles of local Indigenous tribes and contributed to an increase in cancer and other various health issues. In the US District Court, Judge Rakoff dismissed the case on *forum non conveniens* and international comity grounds. The dismissal was conditional upon the corporate defendant consenting to jurisdiction in Ecuador. Judge Rakoff determined Ecuador had suitable experience dealing with multinational corporations without any evidence of corruption. Ecuador had taken significant steps to secure the independence of its judiciary and numerous US courts have found Ecuador adequate for the resolution of civil disputes involving US companies.[32]

[27] Butler (n 24) 202.

[28] At the time, this equated to approximately £3,000. Meeran, 'Liability of Multinational Corporations'. Using a conversion formula, the author of this book found that £3,000 was approximately US $5,000 in 1995 (citation omitted).

[29] ICIS Chemical Business, 'Thor Chemicals Settles out of Court for $2.1m' (20 April 1997), www.icis.com/resources/news/1997/04/21/30350/thor-chemicals-settles-out-of-court-for-2-1m/.

[30] *Aguinda v Texaco, Inc* [2001] 142 FSupp2d 534.

[31] C Gillis, 'Ecuador vs. Chevron-Texaco: A Brief History' (*Counterspill*, 27 April 2011).

[32] *Aguinda v Texaco* (n 30) 544–46. There were many appeals on several issues. The second circuit upheld the dismissal and found there was 'no merit in plaintiffs' further argument that Ecuadorian courts are unreceptive to tort claims'. See *Aguinda v Texaco, Inc* 303 F.3d 470 (2002) 477.

After a trial in 2011, an Ecuadorian court ordered Chevron to pay $8 billion in compensation. The Ecuadorian plaintiffs have not attempted to have the judgment enforced in the home state of the US, however Chevron brought a case to invalidate the Ecuadorian judgment.[33] Justice Kaplan of the US District Court held that the Ecuadorian judgment was procured by fraud, and thus was unenforceable.[34] In his comprehensive and lengthy opinion, Justice Kaplan described the case as 'extraordinary' and outlined his concerns with the judgment, including judicial incompetence, and that the judgment was obtained through bribery and coercion.[35]

This case is somewhat ironic. The US home state declined to consider the matter on *forum non conveniens* grounds and ruled that the host state judicial system was the preferable forum. Ten years later the same Court firmly denied the legitimacy of the host state legal decision in this matter and prevented the plaintiffs from enforcing the judgment in the home state. This reveals the concern when a foreign legal system is considered the appropriate forum for the purposes of *forum non conveniens*, and yet when it comes to the enforcement of judgments, the court applies a different standard that invalidates a foreign judicial process. The concern is that it leads to an inability for alleged victims to seek redress against a foreign corporation given perceived weaknesses in the host state judicial system. This case is particularly notable given that Judge Rakoff upheld the reputation of the Ecuadorian judicial system as a factor in dismissing the original case in 2001.

The South African case of *Ngcobo*, along with the Ecuadorian case of *Aguinda*, demonstrates the difficulty of holding the extractive sector to account for wrongdoing in host state courts. As outlined in chapter one, the same concern was raised in Peru with the Yanacocha example and in India as highlighted by the case in Bhopal.

Finally, there have also been cases where extractive sector corporations attempt to use multilateral free trade agreements as mechanisms to curtail and obfuscate host state regulation. Take, for example, the circumstances surrounding Odyssey Marine Exploration, a US company engaged in the practice of deep sea mining. This innovative form of mining requires intensive processes to retrieve mineral deposits underwater. Some civil society groups have argued that the science around the environmental impact of deep sea mining is incomplete and unproven.[36]

As of 2020, there is an ongoing investment dispute under the North American Free Trade Agreement (NAFTA) being pursued in relation to Odyssey's planned

[33] The plaintiffs have attempted to have the judgment enforced in Canada. See *Chevron Corp v Yaiguaje* [2015] SCC 42.

[34] *Chevron Corp v Donziger* [2014] 974 FSupp2d 362.

[35] *Ibid* 556–59.

[36] German NGO Working Group on Deep Sea Mining, 'Position Paper of German Civil Society Organizations on Deep Sea Mining: Stop the Exploitation of the Deep Sea!' (April 2018), www.asienhaus.de/archiv/asienhaus/erklaerungen/Position_paper_on_Deep_Sea_Mining-web.pdf.

phosphate project in Mexico. The claim arises out of a decision by Mexico's Ministry of the Environment and Natural Resources to deny necessary environmental permits for Odyssey's project. In declining the permit, the Ministry cited an environmental impact study associated with the project, which claims that it will generate risk for biodiversity and sea life.[37] Odyssey alleges that the Ministry's decision is arbitrary and disregards the applicable scientific evidence.

In 2019, the company began the process of filing this claim under NAFTA. It is seeking US $3.5 billion in damages from the Mexican Government. As of the time of writing, the claim has not yet to be arbitrated as set out under the NAFTA process for dispute settlement.

This action demonstrates how a company may attempt to utilise multilateral free trade agreements against host state governments, and represents another challenge to host state regulation over the conduct of the foreign extractive sector.

As opposed to proceeding in a local court or using free trade mechanisms, injured parties may instead bring an action against the parent corporation in that company's forum in order to benefit from the legal system. There are several barriers a claimant will face in attempting to bring an action against the parent corporation in its home state jurisdiction.

II. Substantive and Procedural Hurdles

Multinational business enterprises are often composed of a number of operating, financing and concession-holding subsidiary corporations. Several of these subsidiaries may be incorporated under the domestic law of the home state, while others are foreign subsidiaries incorporated under the domestic law of the host state in which they operate. Corporations that operate overseas through subsidiaries or affiliates will generally be protected from sharing liability with these entities because corporations have separate personhood. This is despite the fact that in most cases the subsidiary is fully owned and controlled by the parent corporation. Given these advantages, the use of a subsidiary is a common practice for corporations operating abroad.

Not all subsidiaries are wholly owned by parent corporations. They may be entities where the parent company holds a majority or minority position. These arrangements raise a host of liability issues such as contributory negligence that are beyond the scope of this book.

[37] D Pastrana, 'US Mining Company Demands $3.5 Billion Dollars from the Mexican Government for Stopping Project' (*stopesmining.org*, 24 September 2019), www.stopesmining.org/news/89-free-trade-agreements-news/576-us-mining-company-demands-3-5-billion-dollars-from-the-mexican-government-for-stopping-project.

A. Limited Liability of Corporations

Limited liability as a feature of corporate personhood is a relatively modern development in the long history of the corporation as a legal institution. In order to fully understand the importance of protecting the limited liability between a parent and a subsidiary corporation, one must consider some of its history in the UK and US.

Limited liability was of little importance before the nineteenth century and there is a paucity of literature or cases on the subject. As one example, the Court of Kings Bench held in 1668 that the creditors of a dissolved corporation could not assert corporate debts directly against the former shareholders.[38]

Following the South Sea Bubble in 1720,[39] corporations played a declining role as joint stock companies were more popular forms of conducting business. A joint stock company is an unincorporated association organised through a deed of settlement. Trustees own the stock and hold it for members. The question of limited liability revolved around the proliferated use of these devices, and not the more rare form of corporations that required charters from government and were difficult to obtain.[40]

Limited liability became a central theme to the traditional view of the corporation in the nineteenth century. Limited liability of shareholders was introduced in England in 1855 with the Limited Liability Act.[41] The landmark 1897 *Salomon* case in the House of Lords firmly established the doctrine as a durable attribute of the modern corporation.[42] This traditional view of corporate law has been unable to prompt the development of an effective mechanism to ensure that multinational corporations are held accountable for wrongdoing abroad, particularly where the extraterritorial state is unable or unwilling to address human rights and environmental concerns.

Some commentators have characterised the traditional law approach as the entity conception, which presupposes that corporations are individual, distinct and unitary.[43] Given the rise of multinational corporations, which operate through complex partnerships and subsidiaries across the globe, the entity theory is being

[38] *Edmonds v Brown* [1668] 83 Eng Rep 385.

[39] The South Sea Company was a British joint-stock company that was granted a monopoly to trade with South America. When the company was created, Britain was involved in the War of the Spanish Succession and Spain controlled South America. There was no practical foreseeability that trade would take place between South America and the company never realised any profit. The company stock vastly rose in price, peaking in 1720 before collapsing. The economic bubble became known as the South Sea Bubble (citation omitted).

[40] P Blumberg, *The Multinational Challenge to Corporation Law: The Search for a New Corporate Personality* (Oxford, Oxford University Press, 1993) 14–15.

[41] Limited Liability Act (18 & 19 Vict c 133).

[42] *Salomon v A Salomon & Co Ltd* [1897] AC 22.

[43] P Blumberg, 'The Transformation of Modem Corporation Law: The Law of Corporate Groups' (2005) 37 *Connecticut Law Review* 605, 605.

supplemented by the enterprise conception that focuses on the business enterprise collectively. However, this view has not permeated into regulation of the extractive sector operating abroad through the use of subsidiaries.[44]

In the late twentieth century, the American jurisprudence term 'alter ego' began to be used to represent the concurrent liability of a parent company and a subsidiary corporation.[45] This concept grew into the doctrine of 'piercing the corporate veil'.[46] This occurs when a court puts aside limited liability to hold corporate shareholders or directors personally liable for the corporation's actions or debts. It can also apply to make parent corporations directly responsible for the acts and omissions of its subsidiary. By the 1920s, piercing the corporate veil became a fully formed legal principle. Today, corporations' separate existence should not be disregarded lightly under common law legal systems.[47]

In the US, the doctrine of piercing the corporate veil varies from state to state and in the federal system. However, it is generally understood that the doctrine should only be implemented in 'exceptional' cases.[48] Those exceptional cases exist when the parent corporation dominates a subsidiary in a way that the court concludes it is a 'conduit',[49] or 'mere department'[50] of the parent corporation. Further, some courts still insist that piercing the corporate veil requires fraud as an essential element. One case even went so far as to require that the subsidiary be a 'shell' that is used for 'fraudulent or illegal purposes so as to avoid a legal obligation'.[51] However, most courts permit the less severe requirement of 'injustice' or 'fundamental unfairness' in the absence of fraud.[52] For these reasons, very few US cases have attempted to pierce the corporate veil of a subsidiary or parent corporation in the context of human rights abuses emanating from abroad.

Even if a plaintiff overcomes the argument of limited liability, the court may refuse to hear the matter because of *forum non conveniens*. Many cases brought in the UK, US, Australia and Canada have been dismissed under the doctrine of *forum non conveniens*.[53] International comity may also block an attempt to

[44] *Ibid* 606.

[45] *Harris v Youngtown Bridge Co* [1898] 90 F 322 (6th Cir).

[46] For an outline of this doctrine, see J Macey, 'The Three Justifications for Piercing the Corporate Veil' (*Harvard Law School Forum on Corporate Governance*, 27 March 2014), corpgov.law.harvard.edu/2014/03/27/the-three-justifications-for-piercing-the-corporate-veil/.

[47] For instance, in the following two cases the Court holds 'piercing the corporate veil' should be done with 'great caution'. *Rhodes v Veith* [2003] 96 SW3d 734, 737; *Yukon Partners Inc v Lodge Keeper Group, Inc* [2002] 572 SE2d 647, 651.

[48] For an example of two Connecticut cases using the term 'exceptional' to describe 'piercing the corporate veil', see *KLM Industries Inc v Tylutki* [2003] 31815 A2d 688, 691; *Hersey v Lonrho Inc* [2002] 723 Conn App 78, 105–16.

[49] *Larson v Western Underwriters Inc* [1958] 87 NW2d 883 (SD) 886.

[50] *Mondello v Dun & Bradstreet Corp* [1995] US Dist LEXIS 7419 (SDNY).

[51] *Hamilton v Carrell* [2001] 243 F3d 992 (6th Cir), 1003–1004; *Culbreth v Amosa (Pty) Ltd* [1990] 898 F 2d 13 (3rd Cir) 14.

[52] *Cunningham v Rendezvous Inc* 699 F2d 676 680.

[53] M Eroglu, *Multinational Enterprises and Tort Liabilities* (Cheltenham, Edward Elgar Publishing Limited, 2008) 97.

litigate matters that occur in a separate country if the litigation interferes with the legitimate authority of that country to regulate conduct in its own territory. Moreover, a court may simply refuse to hear a matter if the activity occurred outside the court's territorial and subject-matter jurisdiction and if the parties involved do not have a connection that requires or permits a court to assert personal jurisdiction.

It should be noted that an attractive option for those interested in bringing claims resulting from foreign activity would be the removal of these procedural barriers. This would be an impractical and imprudent solution. Procedural deterrents prevent the clogging of court systems with litigation that belongs elsewhere, or does not impact the country and its citizens in such a way that it warrants the expense of limited judicial resources.[54] Further, these rules prevent plaintiffs from forum shopping by picking a judicial system merely to gain an advantage in the proceeding. Finally, litigation that commences in a distant legal system outside of where the dispute occurred can often result in an unnecessary and harsh burden on defendants and witnesses, especially when these individuals are not trying to avoid their obligations but simply prefer that the matter be handled by local courts for convenience.[55]

[54] EL Barrett, 'The Doctrine of Forum Non Conveniens' (1947) 35 *California Law Review* 380, 384.
[55] *Ibid* 381.

4

The United States

The concept of *forum non conveniens* is a flexible doctrine that is applied in a discretionary fashion in the United States.[1] In assessing whether *forum non conveniens* dismissal is appropriate, courts engage in a two-step process. The first step is to determine if an adequate alternative forum exists. If so, courts must then balance a series of factors involving the private interests of the parties in maintaining the litigation in another forum and any public interests at stake. The defendant has the burden to establish that an adequate alternative forum exists and then to demonstrate that the private and public factors are in favour of a trial in the foreign forum.

In the 1947 case of *Gulf Oil Corp v Gilbert*, the US Supreme Court held that the balancing test provided in *Gilbert* would rarely displace the plaintiff's choice of forum.[2] However, if another forum exists to hear the matter, the court may exercise discretion to dismiss the action based on a series of private interest factors affecting the convenience of the litigants and a list of public interest factors affecting the convenience of the forum. Private interest factors include access to evidence, witnesses and the power of subpoena.[3] Public interest factors include court congestion, conflict of laws and the unfairness of burdening citizens in an unrelated forum with jury duty.[4]

A leading case on the application of *forum non conveniens* involving human rights and environmental concerns resulted from a poisonous gas leak at a pesticide plant in Bhopal, India. As referenced in chapter one, it remains one of the world's largest industrial accidents as it took the lives of thousands of local residents.[5]

An American corporation, Union Carbide, had a shared interest in the plant through a wholly owned Indian subsidiary. Several violations were caused by

[1] *Forum non conveniens* is Latin for 'forum not agreeing' (citation omitted). The traditional doctrine of *forum non conveniens* originated in Scotland in the 19th century and was eventually adopted by the English courts. As a note on methodology, I have focused on the major US Supreme Court cases and other federal court cases where the facts are germane to the issue of a US corporation accused of wrongdoing in a foreign jurisdiction.

[2] *Gulf Oil Corp v Gilbert* [1947] 330 US 501.

[3] *Ibid* 508.

[4] *Ibid* 509.

[5] MW Janis, 'The Doctrine of Forum Non Conveniens and the Bhopal Case' (1987) 34 *Netherlands International Law Review* 192.

the Indian subsidiary at the express direction of Union Carbide. In 1985, the Indian Government brought a claim against Union Carbide in American courts on behalf of the victims. On the question of dismissing the claim for *forum non conveniens*, the Indian Government argued that its own courts were insufficient to deal with the complexities of this matter. Therefore, they brought the claim in US federal court.

This issue of whether a foreign court was insufficient to deal with a claim was not considered in *Gilbert*. The United States Court of Appeals for the Second Circuit upheld a dismissal based on *forum non conveniens* because it considered the Indian courts adequate to hear the claim upon review of expert testimony.[6] In weighing the private and public interests, both the US District Court and the Second Circuit determined that since the plaintiffs were foreigners, their claim in American courts was less credible compared to whether they had been US citizens. Justice Keenan of the Second Circuit held that Indian courts were the proper forum because the plant had been constructed and managed by Indian nationals. Americans were not employed on site, nor had they visited the plant for over five years before the accident. Most, if not all, evidence was located in India. In balancing the public interest, the Court held that the litigation mattered a great deal to India in terms of determining liability and compensating victims. Comparatively, Americans had relatively little public interest in the outcome of the case. The US Supreme Court chose not to review this decision.[7]

In contrast to the finding in *Bhopal*, consider the case of *Bhatnager v Surrendra Overseas Ltd* where an Indian national was injured on an Indian ship that was operated by an Indian company.[8] The only connection to the United States was that the injured party boarded the ship at a US port. In allowing the claim to proceed, the US District Court held that the potential for a significant delay in the Indian judicial system was a relevant factor in a motion for *forum non conveniens*. The finding was upheld on appeal. The case did not unleash a torrent of similar cases brought by foreigners in the US court. In fact, the Circuit Court called the facts of the case 'narrow and unusual'.[9]

In 2000, *Wiwa v Royal Dutch Petroleum Co* was an important case for those desiring US federal courts to consider claims against corporations for overseas conduct.[10] The plaintiffs were three Nigerian nationals who alleged suffering human rights abuses at the hands of the Nigerian authorities with the participation of the Royal Dutch Shell group of companies. The Second Circuit reversed the trial

[6] *In re Union Carbide Corp Gas Plan Disaster at Bhopal, India in Dec 1984* 634 F Supp 842 SDNY 1986.

[7] In India, the Supreme Court ultimately upheld a US $470 million settlement against Union Carbide (citation omitted).

[8] *Bhatnager v Surrendra Overseas Ltd* 52 F3d 1220 3d Circ 1995.

[9] *Ibid* 1236.

[10] *Wiwa v Royal Dutch Petroleum Co* 226 F3d 88 2d Cir 2000.

court's dismissal of the claim based on *forum non conveniens*, and instead allowed the case to proceed in the United States. The successful appeal was surprising as the application of *forum non conveniens* was widely understood to be in the discretion of the District Court. This case highlights that US citizenship or residency is an important factor as two of the plaintiffs were United States residents and the Second Circuit held this as a consideration favouring the plaintiff's choice of forum.[11] For these reasons the case was permitted to proceed and eventually settled out-of-court for US $15.5 million.[12]

The 2006 case of *Bigio v Coca Cola Company* continued this trend towards allowing plaintiffs to overcome dismissals based on *forum non conveniens* when the incident giving rise to the claim occurs in another country. The case involved the wrongful expropriation of vast commercial holdings from a Jewish family that was expelled from Egypt in the 1950s under the Nasser regime. The family then fled to Canada, but, after Nasser died, the Egyptian Government ordered the property to be returned. However, the family had been unable to obtain relief in the Egyptian courts. For this reason, the family brought suit in the United States. The family's assets were subsequently taken over by the Coca Cola Company.[13]

In denying Coca Cola's motion for *forum non conveniens*, the Second Circuit held that:

1) international comity was not a concern as it was strictly a commercial matter and unlikely to offend US relations with Egypt;[14]
2) the US District Court failed to accord proper deference to the plaintiffs' choice of forum;[15] and
3) the plaintiffs chose a US court for legitimate reasons as the key witnesses and legal counsel all resided in North America.[16]

The fact that Coca Cola was a US corporation only bolstered the argument in favour of US courts asserting jurisdiction.

The doctrine of *forum non conveniens* was also a central factor in *Aguinda v Texaco*.[17] In that case, thousands of Ecuadoreans claimed that Texaco caused destruction to the Amazon rainforest.[18] A US District Court dismissed the case based on *forum non conveniens* and international comity grounds. However, the dismissal was conditional upon the defendant consenting to jurisdiction in Ecuador.[19]

[11] *Ibid* 24.
[12] J Mouwad, 'Shell to Pay $15.5 Million to Settle Nigerian Case' *New York Times* (8 June 2009).
[13] *Bigio v Coca Cola Company* 448 F3d 176 2d Cir 2006.
[14] *Ibid* 178.
[15] *Ibid* 176.
[16] *Ibid* 179.
[17] *Aguinda v Texaco Inc* [2001] 142 F Supp 2nd 534.
[18] C Gillis, 'Ecuador vs. Chevron-Texaco: A Brief History' (*Counterspill*, 27 April 2011).
[19] *Aguinda* (n 17) 544–46; *Aguinda v Texaco Inc* 303 F 3d 470 (2002).

In 2011, an Ecuadorian court ordered the defendant to pay US $8 billion in compensation to the plaintiffs. When the plaintiffs attempted to have that order enforcement in the US, the defendant successfully invalidated the Ecuadorian judgment, arguing that it was procured by fraud, and thus was unenforceable.[20]

These cases demonstrate a relatively malleable application of *forum non conveniens*. In early decisions the second circuit appeared to have a preference for dismissal of actions that mainly arose from activity in foreign jurisdictions based on *forum non conveniens*. Subsequent cases to the US Bhopal litigation offer a variety of exceptions regarding when *forum non conveniens* will not result in dismissal such as in *Bhatnager*, *Wiwa* and *Coca Cola*. The latter case was a commercial matter in which the plaintiffs were unable to obtain relief in the Egyptian court. Further, the key witnesses and legal representatives either resided in the United States or Canada. Thus, the United States was the appropriate forum according to the Second Circuit. The *Wiwa* case proceeded because two of the plaintiffs were US residents at the time of the claim. The *Bhatnager* case was a personal injury matter and took place in international waters as opposed to within a particular country.

It does not appear that these cases concerning *forum non conveniens* have opened the floodgates to foreign applicants; nor does it appear that it has restricted them from US courts. Arguably, the more recent cases provide promise for foreigners to bring claims against US corporations in US courts. The major exception is in *Aguinda v Texaco* where the Court considered the Ecuadorian legal system the appropriate forum for the purposes of *forum non conveniens* and yet failed to enforce its judgment given the insufficiency of its judicial process.

Before moving beyond *forum non conveniens*, it is important to consider similar litigation that has taken place in US state court. States have their own authority for rules of *forum non conveniens*. Most notably, Texas has a very limited version of *forum non conveniens*.[21] At least one case has been tried in US state court against an extractive sector company that raised issues of *forum non conveniens*. In 2005, a provincial government of the Philippines, Marinduque island, brought a claim seeking damages for environmental harm caused by a local mining operation on the island. The defendant, Placer Dome Inc, owned and operated the mine for over three decades. In 2006, Canadian mining company Barrick Gold Corp acquired Placer Dome and became a party to the lawsuit. Barrick's connection to Nevada was that it owned five mines in the state among other assets.

In 2011, a Nevada district court judge dismissed the case on the basis of *forum non conveniens*. As part of the ruling, the Court held that the case should be based in Canada where Barrick Gold is domiciled. Further, Barrick was required to formally waive its personal jurisdiction, statute of limitations, and

[20] The plaintiffs unsuccessfully attempted to have the judgment enforced in Canada. See *Yaiguaje v Chevron Corporation* 2018 ONCA 472.

[21] LE Teitz, *Transnational Litigation* (Charlottesville, Michie, 1996) 27 and 35.

forum non conveniens arguments in Canadian courts and agree that both monetary and injunctive relief could be awarded against them. Barrick agreed to these conditions and the District Court dismissed the suit without prejudice.[22]

At the Nevada Supreme Court, the plaintiff argued that the case should remain in Nevada, or, if it is dismissed, that it be dismissed to the Philippines with conditions similar to those imposed on Barrick by the District Court in 2011. Prior to the case being elevated to the State Supreme Court, the parties agreed to stay in Nevada and attempted mediation to seek a settlement. Between 2011 and 2014, mediated settlement negotiations took place that ultimately failed to produce a resolution between the parties.[23] In 2015, the Nevada Supreme Court held that the case did not have a strong enough association to the state of Nevada to proceed.[24]

In its ruling, the Court noted that there were no parties, witnesses or documents related to the case in Nevada. Thus, the District Court imposed appropriate conditions to ensure the existence of an adequate alternative forum in Canada.[25] The Court did not extend the conditions placed on Barrick in the 2011 ruling to the courts in the Philippines. They reasoned that by the District Court ensuring that there was an alternate forum in Canada was enough to satisfy the condition that another forum is available for the dispute. As a result of this decision, the plaintiff now has the opportunity to re-file the lawsuit in Canada. At the time of writing, it is unclear whether the case will proceed with a claim in Canada.[26]

Beyond the doctrine of *forum non conveniens*, there are other factors that hinder foreigners from bringing international legal disputes to US courts. These include issues of international comity and limitations of jurisdiction.[27] In one high profile case, a Canadian company was sued in US Federal Court despite the fact the activity giving rise to the lawsuit occurred in Sudan. In 2001, the Presbyterian Church of Sudan, as well as a number of Sudanese individuals, filed suit in federal court against Talisman Energy Inc, a Canadian company which operated in South Sudan with a consortium of multinational oil companies. They alleged that Talisman acted with complicity in the Sudanese Government's human rights abuses during the country's second civil war. Given that Talisman is incorporated outside of the US, they initially argued that the Court did not

[22] S Newman, 'Summary of Provincial Gov't of Marinduque v. Placer Dome, Inc., 131 Nev. Adv. Op. 63076 (11 June 2015) Paper 878' *Nevada Supreme Court Summaries*, (2015), scholars.law.unlv.edu/nvscs/878.

[23] C Coumans, 'Marinduque vs. Barrick Gold: The Province at a Crossroads. Handout to Facilitate Discussion of Options' (*MiningWatch Canada*, 13 August 2014).

[24] *Provincial Gov't of Marinduque v Placer Dome, Inc* [2015] 131 Nev Adv Op 63076.

[25] Newman, 'Marinduque v. Placer Dome, Inc'.

[26] N Dizon, 'The Marcopper Disaster: A Tragedy that Continues in People's Veins' (*MiningWatch Canada*, 3 April 2019).

[27] An early case providing a definition of international comity is *Hilton v Guyot* where Justice Grey described comity as the 'recognition which one nation allows within its territory to the legislative, executive or judicial acts of another nation, having due regard both to international duty and convenience, and to the rights of its own citizens or of other person who are under the protection of its laws'. *Hilton v Guyot* [1895] 159 US 113, 164.

have personal jurisdiction over the claim.[28] This is similar to the circumstances in *Wiwa* involving a UK and Dutch corporate defendant and alleged activities that occurred outside the United States. As with *Wiwa*, the Court in Talisman asserted jurisdiction.

The Court found that Talisman had numerous links to New York including a listing on the New York Stock Exchange, and at least two US based Talisman subsidiaries were found to have 'significant operations in New York'.[29] The issue of international comity was also raised given that the case may interfere with US-Canadian relations. For instance, Talisman argued that the lawsuit obstructs Canada's policy of supporting development and ending the civil war. However, the Court was not persuaded that the case impacted Canadian efforts in Sudan.[30]

The concerns with international comity and personal jurisdiction over Talisman were not overturned in the several subsequent proceedings. For unrelated reasons, the case was eventually dismissed on the grounds that the plaintiffs failed to establish purposeful complicity by Talisman in the human rights abuses.[31]

The case is a noteworthy example of foreign plaintiffs litigating a dispute that occurred not only outside the United States, but between foreign parties. This was despite the principles of international comity and limitations on jurisdiction that was carefully considered by the Second Circuit.

Daimler AG v Bauman is a US Supreme Court case concerning the limitations of jurisdiction.[32] In the 2014 decision, the Supreme Court imposed strict jurisdictional requirements on the ability of plaintiffs to bring actions in US courts against foreign parent corporations. In 2017, the US Supreme Court upheld the jurisdictional limitations set out in *Daimler* in *BNSF Railway Co v Tyrrell*[33] and *Bristol-Myers Squibb Co v Superior Court*.[34]

A group of Argentinian plaintiffs brought a lawsuit against Daimler AG, a German corporation. The plaintiffs alleged that Daimler's Argentinean subsidiary worked with state security forces in committing human rights abuses against local

[28] Under the Federal Rules of Civil Procedure, a court may exercise jurisdiction over any defendant who 'could be subjected to the jurisdiction of a court of general jurisdiction in the state in which the district court is located'. Federal Rules of Civil Procedure 4(k)(1)(A). Further, that exercise of jurisdiction must meet the due process requirements of the Fifth Amendment of the US Constitution. Under New York law, a foreign corporation is subject to general personal jurisdiction if it is doing business in the state. The US Court of Appeals for the Second Circuit analysed the concept of 'doing business' in *Wiwa* and held that '[i]n order to establish that this standard is met, a plaintiff must show that a defendant engaged in "continuous, permanent, and substantial activity in New York"' *Landoil Resources Corp v Alexander & Alexander Servs Inc* 918 F2d 1039, 1043 (2d Cir 1990). *Wiwa v Royal Dutch Petroleum Co* (n 10) 95.

[29] *Presbyterian Church of Sudan v Talisman Energy Inc* [2003] 244 FSupp2d 289, 330.

[30] *Ibid* 300 and 344.

[31] *Presbyterian Church of Sudan v Talisman Energy Inc* 582 F3d 244 (2nd Cir 2009) 259. For a fascinating case study on Talisman in Sudan, see P Simons and A Macklin, *The Governance Gap: Extractive Industries, Human Rights, and the Home State Advantage* (Toronto, Routledge, 2014) Ch 2.

[32] *Daimler AG v Bauman* [2014] 134 S Ct 746.

[33] *BNSF Railway Co v Tyrrell* [2017] 137 S Ct 1549.

[34] *Bristol-Myers Squibb Co v Superior Court* [2017] 137 S Ct 1773.

Daimler employees during the 1976–1983 Dirty War, in which the military and security forces perpetrated violence against political dissidents.

The parent corporation moved to dismiss the suit for lack of personal jurisdiction. Personal jurisdiction over Daimler in California was grounded on the notion of another Daimler subsidiary incorporated in Delaware with its primary place of business in New Jersey. The plaintiffs argued that Daimler was the exclusive importer in the United States and had significant operations in California, and therefore, under an agency theory, the Court could exercise general personal jurisdiction over Daimler. California was likely chosen as the forum by the plaintiffs because, as noted by Justice Ginsburg's opinion, California's long-arm statute allows the exercise of personal jurisdiction to the full extent permissible under the US Constitution.[35]

The Supreme Court disagreed and held that Daimler's California presence was insufficient to support general personal jurisdiction and the subsidiary had not acted as Daimler's agent. In Justice Ginsburg's opinion for the majority, she warned about the risks to international comity posed by an expansive view of general personal jurisdiction. The opinion relied heavily on the 2011 *Goodyear* decision, which stated that a corporate defendant or its subsidiary must be 'essentially at home' in that forum in order to exercise general personal jurisdiction.[36] There is a distinction between general or all-purpose jurisdiction compared to specific or conduct-linked jurisdiction. In *Goodyear*, there was not a sufficient connection of facts to North Carolina.

In *Daimler*, the only basis for California jurisdiction over the parent corporation was the subsidiary's activities in selling Mercedes products in the United States. However, the jurisdiction over the parent through its US subsidiary was specific jurisdiction only. Thus, the claim had to be connected to what the parent company, either itself or through another entity, did in California for there to be general jurisdiction.

The Supreme Court reversed the earlier Ninth Circuit Court of Appeals decision and held that Daimler's subsidiary does not ordinarily act as an agent for the parent corporation. The Ninth Circuit's interpretation would have effectively ended the limited liability between parent and subsidiary corporations. The Supreme Court rejected this notion because it 'would sweep beyond even the sprawling view of general jurisdiction' that had previously been rejected in *Goodyear*.[37]

On account of its decision in *Daimler*, it is clear the Supreme Court is committed to limiting the ability of plaintiffs to use US courts to target non-US corporations for conduct occurring outside of the United States. It is worth noting that had the parent company been a US corporation, the California Court would

[35] *Daimler AG* (n 32) 753.
[36] *Goodyear Dunlop Tires Operations, SA v Brown* 131 S Ct 2846 (2011) 2851.
[37] *Ibid* 2856.

have had general jurisdiction over it and, subject to *forum non conveniens*, that jurisdiction would extend to wrongs committed anywhere. As such, the door was left open for future claims in US courts alleging extraterritorial environmental and human rights violations by US multinationals on account of general jurisdiction. However, these claims would have to overcome the hurdles presented by the doctrine of *forum non conveniens*.

As a final analysis, it is necessary to explore whether a foreign subsidiary acquires the nationality of its parent corporation, and therefore, is subject to extraterritorial jurisdiction of US law. If so, this would be an intriguing opportunity for foreign claimants to seek legal recourse against US corporations based on the nationality principle.

The nationality principle is a development of international law to avoid clashes of countries asserting jurisdiction over the same matter.[38] The nationality of a corporation is generally considered the state of incorporation in common law legal systems.[39] The nationality of investors or base of operation is irrelevant.[40] Under US law, a foreign subsidiary does not acquire the nationality of the parent corporation.[41] The Restatement (Fourth) of the Foreign Relations Law (Restatement)[42] suggests that US legislation may have extraterritorial application that captures the parent corporation and foreign subsidiaries for very limited purposes, such as accounting and corporate disclosure requirements.[43] The Restatement further provides for the exercise of extraterritorial jurisdiction over the parent company or even directly over a foreign subsidiary in 'exceptional circumstances'.[44] The listed exceptions are broadly categorised and lack clear guidance in determining when extraterritorial regulation is appropriate. The burden is higher when the regulation is aimed at the foreign subsidiary compared to regulation of the domestic parent corporation.

[38] For a classic example on the treatment of the nationality principle in US law, see *Blackmer v United States* [1932] 52 S Ct 252.

[39] Concepts such as siege social, domicile and economic control are different models for determining corporate nationality under civil law legal systems. See MJ Matheson and S Bickler, 'The Fifty-Fifth Session of the International Law Commission' (2004) 98 *American Journal of International Law* 309, 318.

[40] For example, see *Barcelona Traction Co (Belgium v Spain)* [1970] ICJ 3.

[41] For an example of the application of this principle, see *Sumitomo Shoji Am Inc Avagliano* [1982] 457 US 176.

[42] Restatement (Fourth) of the Foreign Relations Law of the United States Jurisdiction (Philadelphia, American Law Institute, 2017).

[43] For example, under s 403 and subject to s 441, 'it may not be unreasonable for a state to exercise jurisdiction for limited purposes with respect to activities of affiliated foreign entities by direction to the parent corporation in respect of such matters as uniform accounting, disclosure to investors, or preparation of consolidated tax returns of multinational enterprises'. Note that I cite below from the previous 3rd edition of the Restatement. The 4th edition expressly states that it addresses 'categories of jurisdiction in similar terms' *ibid* 9. Restatement (Third) of the Foreign Relations Law of the United States (Philadelphia, American Law Institute, 1987).

[44] *Ibid* s 414(2)(b). See this section of the 3rd Restatement for the list of factors that should be considered in determining if the matter is an exceptional circumstance.

Moreover, the regulation of a foreign subsidiary through the application of extraterritorial jurisdiction should not interfere with local activities, such as it would impact labour law, health and safety, or the preservation of the local environment.[45] These so-called 'local activities' are directly related to human rights and environmental matters, and are outside the scope of what may be regulated through extraterritorial application under the Restatement. As a consequence, the Restatement does not support the notion that US legislation may apply extraterritorially to regulate foreign subsidiary corporations for human rights or environmental purposes. Thus, this limits the nationality principle's effectiveness under American law for those seeking the ability to bring US corporations to account for wrongdoing abroad. Arguably, if a host state has investment-friendly laws that are harmful to the local environment or do not protect the human rights of its citizens, this alone does not justify the extraterritorial application of US law. Further, the Restatement itself provides interpretation on American law and, as such, is not mandatory in its guidance.

Lastly, the Restatement speaks to the concept of the territorial principle and effects doctrine under US law. Under the territorial principle, the state has jurisdiction over activity that substantially takes place in its territory.[46] Conversely, the effects doctrine extends territorial jurisdiction to include activities outside of the home state when that activity has a substantial impact on the home state. It is difficult to apply the effects doctrine to human rights and environmental concerns abroad, as these alleged violations do not generally impact activity in the home state in an obvious or measurable way.[47] Taken together, these concepts support limited, if any, extraterritorial jurisdiction by home states for environmental and human rights abuses that occur abroad.

I. The Alien Tort Statute

One of the most robust frameworks concerning legal liability for foreign conduct is found in the United States under the US Alien Tort Statute 1789 (ATS). This statute permits foreign nationals to bring a claim in US court for conduct that violates the *law of nations*. The *law of nations* concept predates the 1789 ATS and

[45] The 3rd edition of the Restatement states that jurisdiction may be exercised 'over activities of a branch or subsidiary related to international transactions, such as export and import, foreign exchange and credits, and transborder investment; but not generally over predominantly local activities, such as industrial and labor relations, health and safety practices, or conduct related to preservation or control of the local environment'. *Ibid* s 414.

[46] For a classic review of the territorial principle, see *American Banana Co v United Fruit Co* [1909] 29 S Ct 511 in which Justice Holmes held that the territorial principle limits the application of the Sherman Antitrust Act 15 USC ss 1–38 against a corporate defendant for activities occurring in foreign countries.

[47] For an overview on the application of the effects doctrine, see *United States v Aluminum Co of America* 148 F2d 416 (2nd Cir).

was addressed by Blackstone in reference to three specific offences in the criminal law of England: violation of safe conducts; infringement of the rights of ambassadors; and piracy.[48] It is important to understand the obscure origin of the ATS and how it eventually became a statutory device used to litigate foreign conduct of multinationals.

A. Elusive History

The ATS was included in the 1789 Judiciary Act of the First Congress and provides that '[t]he district courts shall have original jurisdiction of any civil action by an alien for a tort only, committed in violation of the *law of nations* or a treaty of the United States'.[49] Originally, the provision stated that the federal court 'shall have cognizance, concurrent with the courts of several States, or the circuit courts, as the case may be, of all causes where an alien sues for a tort in violation of the *law of nations* or a treaty of the United States'.[50]

The initial purpose of the ATS was once the subject of controversy, as the Act has no formal legislative history. Judge Friendly of the Second Circuit commented that the ATS is a 'legal Lohengrin' and that 'no one seems to know whence it came'.[51] In the case of *Tel-Oren v Libyan Arab Republic*, Judge Edwards suggested that given the international implications, the statute was originally motivated by a desire to ensure that claims brought by foreigners against US citizens were litigated in federal court rather than state court.[52] Another commentator suggested that the exclusive purpose of the ATS may have been intended to control the conduct of ships and their crews in the course of blocking and boarding vessels suspected of supporting an enemy in wartime.[53]

Today, there is much more information available concerning the origins of the ATS. The statute was based in part on a 1782 Connecticut law providing criminal sanctions and a civil remedy for violations of the *law of nations*.[54] Other states, such as Pennsylvania, supported a common law basis to prosecute violations of the *law of nations*.[55] The drafter of the 1789 Judiciary Act, who was a member of the

[48] See W Blackstone, *Commentaries on the Laws of England* (Chicago, University of Chicago Press, 1979 edn, first published in 1765) at 68 as cited in A Bellia and B Clark, 'The Alien Tort Statute and the Law of Nations' (2011) 78 *University Chicago Law Review* 445, 448, fn 9.

[49] Alien Tort Statute 1789 (28 USC § 1350).

[50] Judiciary Act 1789 ch 20 s 9 1 Stat 73, 77.

[51] *IIT v Vencap, Ltd* [1975] 519 F 2d 1001 (2d Cir) 1015.

[52] *Tel-Oren v Libyan Arab Republic* [1984] 726 F2d 782–83.

[53] JM Sweeney, 'A Tort Only in Violation of the Law of Nations' (1995) 18 *Hastings International and Comparative Law Review* 445.

[54] W Casto, 'SOSA v. Alvarez-Machain and the End of History' (2012) 43 *Georgetown Journal of International Law* 1001, 1001.

[55] An early US case concerning these offences is *Respublica v De Longchamps* 1 LEd 59 (1784). The case predates the US Constitution and the federal court system. The facts of the case are historically compelling. Francis Barbe Marbois, a French minister, was threatened by Charles Julian De Longchamps, in front of a coffee house on Market Street in Philadelphia. Longchamps struck the cane

Connecticut legislature, likely had this Connecticut law in mind when he included the ATS.[56]

After 200 years of relative dormancy, the ATS became a central issue in *Filartiga v Pena-Irala*, when the US District Court dismissed a claim brought by the relative of a Paraguayan national who was allegedly tortured and killed by a Paraguayan police officer.[57] At the time of the case, both the plaintiff and defendant were living in the United States. Upon appeal, Justice Kaufman held that ATS claims may be brought for violations of modern international law as opposed to only claims recognised at the time of enactment in 1789 to combat piracy. Thus, torture was recognised as a violation of the *law of nations*, and US courts had jurisdiction over this claim given that both parties resided in the United States.

The reach of the ATS gradually expanded after *Filartiga*, and one federal judge remarked that the case was a 'watershed opinion'.[58] Not only would claims be recognised against non-state individual actors,[59] but also against non-state corporate actors starting in the late 1990s.

In *Doe I v Unocal Corp*, Burmese villagers sued Unocal for alleged conduct that occurred during the construction of the Yadana gas pipeline to Thailand. Unocal was accused of partaking in human rights abuses with the ruling military junta of Myanmar. *Unocal* was the first case in which the federal court analysed corporate liability under the ATS. The Court ruled that Unocal and its corporate officers could be held legally responsible for the alleged human rights abuses.[60] The case eventually settled for an undisclosed amount. In subsequent cases, civil society organisations became integral to ATS litigation against extractive sector corporations such as ExxonMobil, Texaco, Occidental and Chevron.[61]

Given that most ATS cases either settle or are dismissed, only a few cases concerning corporate activity abroad have proceeded to trial under the ATS. *Bowoto v Chevron* is one of the few cases to reach a jury verdict under the ATS.[62] In the case the plaintiffs alleged that Chevron was indirectly liable for attacks by the local military officials near Chevron operations in Nigeria. The trial ended with a jury verdict acquitting Chevron.

of Monsieur Marbois after becoming frustrated by his refusal to authenticate Longchamps' alleged service in the French military. Evidently, several publications had been made injuring Longchamps' character about his military service which inspired Longchamps' failed request of Marbois. The French Crown demanded Longchamps be returned to France to stand trial. Chief Justice McKean of the Court of Oyer and Terminer in Philadelphia sentenced Longchamps to two years in prison for a violation of the 'principles of the law of nations, which formed part of the municipal law of Pennsylvania'. *Ibid.*

56 Casto, 'SOSA' 1001.

57 *Filartiga v Pena-Irala* [1980] 630 F 2d 876 (2nd Cir).

58 *Presbyterian Church of Sudan v Talisman Energy, Inc* (n 31) 304.

59 As one example, see *Kadic v Karadzic* [1995] 70 F3d 232 (2nd Cir).

60 *Doe I v Unocal Corp* [2002] 395 F3d 932 (9th Cir).

61 J Davis, *Justice Across Borders: The Struggle for Human Rights in U.S. Courts* (Cambridge, Cambridge University Press, 2008) 58.

62 *Bowoto v Chevron* [2004] 312 F Supp 2d 1229 (ND Cal).

Estate of Rodriguez v Drummond Co is another example of a case cumulating in a jury verdict. In this case, it was alleged that the local management of Drummond, a US coal producer, had financially supported the paramilitary units of the Columbian Government to intimidate and in some cases even murder local union leaders.[63] The trial ended with a jury verdict acquitting Drummond.

B. Sosa

The framework of the ATS as utilised in *Filartiga* was left standing by the US Supreme Court in *Sosa v Alvarez-Machain*.[64] The facts of the case were equally as gruesome as *Filartiga*. A US Drug Enforcement Administration (DEA) agent was tortured and killed in Mexico. Alvarez-Machain is alleged to have participated in the torture, as a doctor was employed to assist in keeping the informant conscious so that members of a drug cartel could continue the torture. The Mexican authorities refused to deport Alvarez-Machain to the United States to face charges. The DEA kidnapped Alverez-Machain without legal authority, despite the fact that an extradition treaty existed between Mexico and the US Government. The US Government's position in Alvarez-Machain's criminal trial was that the treaty did not preclude kidnapping. The charges were eventually dismissed and Alvarez-Machain returned to Mexico. He brought a civil suit against the US Government and an DEA agent (Sosa) allegedly involved in the kidnapping.

In this case, one of the questions was whether Alvarez–Machain's allegation that the DEA instigated his abduction from Mexico for a criminal trial in the United States supports a claim against the US Government under the Federal Tort Claims Act.[65] Alvarez–Machain was unsuccessful in this claim. Another issue was whether he could be compensated based on a civil claim against Sosa and other Mexican citizens under the ATS. It was argued that the statute did not authorise lawsuits in US federal court on matters of international law. The American Petroleum Institute and the administration of former US President George W Bush joined Sosa in presenting this argument.

The Supreme Court did not allow Alverez-Machain to bring his claim under the ATS given that kidnapping is not a definite violation of the *law of nations*; however, the Supreme Court upheld the principles and validity of the ATS. Justice Souter gave the opinion on behalf of the majority. His opinion explored the 'historical paradigms' that informs ATS inquiries under 'the present-day law of nations'.[66] He analysed with careful precision the differences between the 1789

[63] *Estate of Rodriguez v Drummond Co* [2003] 256 F Supp 2d 1250 (ND Ala).
[64] *Sosa v Alvarez-Machain* [2004] 542 US 692.
[65] Federal Tort Claims Act (28 USC § 1346(b)(1)).
[66] *Sosa* (n 64) 724.

ATS and the modern interpretation of the statute, and in doing so enumerated the appropriate sources of international law.

According to Justice Souter, the ATS as a statute is jurisdictional in nature. It does not confer an independent cause of action and instead requires that judges look to the *law of nations* to carve out a 'modest number' of specific violations.[67] This includes customary international law, which as explained in *Sosa* rests on a 'norm of international character accepted by the civilized world'.[68]

The threshold question in the ATS is whether the conduct alleged violates the *law of nations*. Concerning the original 1789 statute, Justice Souter looked to Blackstone and found at least three violations of the *law of nations*: 1) offences against ambassadors; 2) violations against safe conduct; and 3) piracy.[69] In reviewing piracy, Justice Souter notes the 1820 case of *United States v Smith*, in which Justice Story asserts that the *law of nations* is found in 'jurist; writing professedly on the public law; or by the general usage and practice of nations; or by judicial decisions recognising and enforcing that law'.[70]

In finding sources for the *law of nations*, Justice Souter relied on legislative history in congress, the First Congress,[71] the founding fathers drafting the Constitution, and writers on the *law of nations*. Justice Souter supported the contention that the *law of nations* can be found in 'ancient usage among civilized nations',[72] and that new violations may become 'sufficiently definite'[73] in modern international law to qualify for protection. As a condition of acceptance, the new violations must have comparable 'specificity' as the original violations as described by Blackstone.[74] Thus, the decision in *Sosa* breathes life into the ATS by expanding upon *Filartiga*, and opening the door to new violations of the *law of nations* that were not contemplated in 1789.

The Supreme Court did not revisit the ATS for nine years until the case of *Kiobel v Royal Dutch Petroleum Co*.[75] During that period there were several other cases concerning the ATS and corporate wrongdoing abroad at the district and circuit level, the vast majority of which did not result in a judicially awarded remedy against the defendants.[76]

[67] *Sosa* (n 64) 724.

[68] *Sosa* (n 64) 725.

[69] *Sosa* (n 64) 715.

[70] *United States v Smith* [1820] 18 US 5 Wheat 160–61.

[71] Justice Souter wrote: '[T]here is every reason to suppose that the First Congress did not pass the ATS as a jurisdictional convenience to be placed on the shelf for use by a future Congress or state legislature that might, someday, authorize the creation of causes of action or itself decide to make some element of the law of nations actionable for the benefit of foreigners'. *Sosa* (n 64) 719.

[72] *The Paquete Habana* [1900] 20 S Ct 290; *The Paquete Habana* is cited in *Sosa* (n 64) 715.

[73] *Sosa* (n 64) 732.

[74] Justice Souter wrote 'we think courts should require any claim … [be] defined with specificity comparable to the features of the 18-century paradigms we have recognized'. *Sosa* (n 64) 725.

[75] *Kiobel v Royal Dutch Petroleum Co* [2013] 133 S Ct 1659.

[76] See, eg, *Khulumani v Barclay National Bank* 504 F3d 254 (2d Cir 2007); *Doe v Exxon Mobil* 654 F3d 11 (DC Cir 2011); and *Flomo v Firestone Natural Rubber Co* 643 F3d 1013 (7th Cir 2011).

C. Kiobel

The Supreme Court's decision in *Kiobel* addressed the issue of whether the 1789 statute provides the necessary jurisdiction for a court to review matters that occur outside the United States. The facts in *Kiobel* concerned alleged environmental damage to lands occupied by the Ogoni people in the Niger delta region. The alleged damage was caused by energy projects operated by Royal Dutch Shell. A protest by the Ogoni people over this environmental damage was brutally suppressed by Nigerian military forces. During the suppression, the military was accused of murder, rape, plundering and looting in the region. A class action lawsuit was brought under the ATS, claiming that the Dutch and UK parent companies and the Nigerian subsidiaries aided and abetted the criminal actions of the Nigerian military forces by providing them transportation, food and funding.

The second circuit dismissed the case on the basis that while international law recognises individuals as offenders of certain human rights abuses, it does not recognise corporate defendants.[77] Upon appeal, the Supreme Court decided that the more important question was the extent to which the ATS could be applied to conduct outside the United States. They ordered re-argument over whether the ATS allows US courts to recognise a cause of action for violations of the *law of nations* occurring outside the territory of the United States.[78] In the majority opinion, Chief Justice Roberts dismissed the claim given a lack of sufficient connection to the United States.[79] The decision to dismiss the claim was based on the history and purpose of the ATS, rather than as a consequence of restrictions under international law.

In contrast to the finding in *Kiobel*, it should be noted that it is not uncommon for US courts to assert jurisdiction based on conduct occurring outside of the United States. Some case law examples include the extraterritorial application of securities laws,[80] civil claims under racketeering and corruption laws,[81] and extending US anti-discrimination laws to protect US citizens overseas.[82] More generally, extraterritorial jurisdiction as a topic of debate has deep roots and traces back to at least the 1600s.[83]

In the case of *Kiobel*, the Supreme Court limited the ATS by the presumption against extraterritoriality, which courts do in the ordinary course of business unless the statute expressly has an extension in the legislation.

[77] *Kiobel v Royal Dutch Petroleum Co* [2010] 621 F3d 111 (2d Cir).

[78] *Kiobel v Royal Dutch Petroleum Co* [2012] 132 S Ct 1738.

[79] *Kiobel* (n 75).

[80] *United States v Vilar* [2013] 729 F3d 62 (2nd Cir).

[81] Organized Crime Control Act, Pub L No. 91-452 84 Stat 941 (1970); *Norex Petroleum Ltd v Access Industries Inc* [2010] 631 F3d 29 (2nd Cir).

[82] *EEOC v Arbian American Oil Co* [1991] 111 S Ct 1227.

[83] H Grotius, *De Jure Beli Ac Pacis Libri* (translated by FW Kelsey) (Oxford, Clarendon Press, 1925 edn, first published 1625).

The presumption against extraterritoriality is a canon of statutory construction that asserts that statutes do not apply outside US territory unless Congress affirmatively indicates extraterritorial application.[84] Thus, only claims that 'touch and concern' the US will be considered actionable under the ATS and 'they must do so with sufficient force to displace the presumption against extraterritorial application'.[85]

The majority did not pass specific judgment on the Second Circuit's holding that while international law recognises individuals as potential offenders of human rights abuses, it does not recognise corporate defendants. The majority concluded that '[c]orporations are often present in many countries, and it would reach too far to say that mere corporate presence suffices'.[86] This left the question of holding corporations to account under the ATS in an ambiguous state.

Between 1990 and 2009 the federal courts did not question whether the ATS was applicable to corporations.[87] There have been cases, before and after *Kiobel*, which illustrate that the issue has not been clearly decided among various federal courts.[88]

In 2017, the Supreme Court agreed to hear *Jesner v Arab Bank, PLC*.[89] The sole question for consideration is whether the ATS permits corporate liability. *Jesner* involves a claim against Arab Bank, a bank based in Jordan for injuries allegedly caused by the Palestinian Sunni-Islamic fundamentalist organisation known as Hamas. Hamas is located primarily in Israel and Palestine. Arab Bank is alleged to have provided financial services to Hamas affiliates. The only connection to the US is that some of these financial services are claimed to have been provided through one of Arab Bank's US offices.

In a closely spilt decision, the Supreme Court held that foreign corporations cannot be sued under the ATS. In the decision, Justice Kennedy reasoned that to do otherwise will create diplomatic problems that only political branches of government, as opposed to the judiciary, are well equipped to handle.[90] As such, foreign corporations may not be defendants in ATS suits.

Back to the findings in *Kiobel*, Justice Breyer wrote a concurring opinion joined by Justices Ginsburg, Sotomayor and Kagan. This concurring opinion

[84] As one example, in this case the Supreme Court held that US securities laws do not apply extraterritorially. *Morrison v Nat'l Austl Bank Ltd* [2010] 130 S Ct 2869, 2878.

[85] *Kiobel* (n 75) 1669.

[86] *Kiobel* (n 75) 1669.

[87] D Scheffer, 'The Impact of War Crimes Tribunals on Corporate Liability for Atrocity Crimes under US Law' in C Walker-Said and JD Kelly (eds), *Corporate Social Responsibility? Human Rights in the New Global Economy* (Chicago, University of Chicago Press, 2015) 154.

[88] As one example, in *John Doe, I v Nestle*, the District Court in California followed the *Kiobel* Second Circuit ruling on corporate liability. *John Doe, I v Nestle SA* 748 FSupp2d 1057. However, the Ninth Circuit rejected the notion that corporations cannot be held liable under the ATS. *Doe I v Nestle USA Inc* 766 F.3d 1013 (9th Cir 2014). At the time of writing this litigation remains ongoing. *John Doe I v Nestle SA* 929 F3d 623 (9th Cir 2019).

[89] *Jesner v Arab Bank, PLC* 2nd Cir 16–49.

[90] *Jesner v Arab Bank PLC* [2018] 138 S Ct 1401.

was concerned with minimising 'international friction' that may result from the ATS reaching into activities that occur in foreign states. After considering the Restatement, Justice Breyer would have set aside the presumption against extraterritorial application and instead interpreted the ATS as providing jurisdiction 'only where distinct American interests are at issue'.[91] This condition would have been in addition to the restrictive principles of exhaustion of local remedies, *forum non conveniens* and comity. In any event, this concurring opinion concluded that the role played by Royal Dutch Shell in the suppression of the Ogoni peoples' protest by the Nigerian military was outside the territory of the US and therefore outside the jurisdiction of the ATS.

Kiobel does not displace the findings in *Sosa* concerning a court's ability to find new violations of the *law of nations* under the ATS. Rather, *Kiobel* introduces a 'touch and concern' requirement to demonstrate a sufficient connection to the United States. This is a limitation on legislative jurisdiction.[92] In effect, most foreign claims arising from activity occurring outside the United States will not be considered given the reasoning in *Kiobel*. The decision goes against 30 years of US case law that increased the role of the ATS as a civil remedy. These cases were the fruits of civil society organisations, such as various US-based advocacy groups, that initially developed the idea of the ATS as a tool to protect human rights in US courts.

On account of *Kiobel* and *Jesner*, it appears that the Supreme Court is committed to limiting the ability of plaintiffs to target non-US corporations for conduct occurring outside of the United States using the ATS. The case calls into question the effectiveness of the ATS in providing legal recourse to foreign citizens. For instance, the *Kiobel* decision led to the dismissal of the majority of the ATS cases that were pending in US federal courts.[93] In one of those cases the District Court compared *Kiobel* to 'an earthquake that has shaken the very foundation of Plaintiffs' claims against Defendants'.[94]

Comparatively, courts considering other ATS cases have permitted plaintiffs to amend their complaints subsequent to *Kiobel* in order to articulate a stronger

[91] Further, such interests arise where: '(1) the alleged tort occurs on American soil, (2) the defendant is an American national, or (3) the defendant's conduct substantially and adversely affects an important American national interest, and that includes a distinct interest in preventing the United States from becoming a safe harbor (free of civil as well as criminal liability) for a torturer or other common enemy of mankind'. *Kiobel* (n 75) 1674.

[92] In *Kiobel*, Chief Justice Roberts and Justice Breyer on behalf of the minority, borrow from Justice Story in *The La Jeune Eugenie* case (citation omitted) from 1822: 'No nation has ever yet pretended to be the *custos morum* of the whole world.' *Kiobel* (n 75) 1668.

[93] Cases dismissed include two related actions, *Cardona v Chiquita Brands Intern Inc* 760 F3d 1185 (2014); and *Doe v Chiquita Brands* (2014) No. 12-14898. The Eleventh Circuit ruled that the Court did not have jurisdiction to hear the two matters because all the relevant conduct occurred in Columbia. In 2015, the US Supreme Court declined to hear both cases. There are other post-*Kiobel* decisions that were dismissed such as *Mujica v AirScan Inc*, F3d (9th Cir 2014).

[94] *Giraldo v Drummond Co, Inc* [2013] WL 3873960 1.

connection to the United States.[95] Thus far, two cases have overcome the narrower standard on extraterritoriality established in *Kiobel*. One case involved a US based military contractor whose employees allegedly tortured military combatants on behalf of the US armed forces at the Abu Ghraib prison near Baghdad, Iraq. In June of 2017, a district court judge ruled that the plaintiffs' claims were actionable under the ATS and could proceed to trial.[96] The defendant entered a motion to dismiss. In 2018, another district court judge dismissed the plaintiffs' direct liability claims on the grounds that the complaint failed to establish direct contact between CACI employees and the plaintiffs. However, the Court allowed the claims based on conspiracy and aiding and abetting war crimes and torture to proceed pursuant to the ATS. A motion by the defendant was also dismissed that was filed in light of the 2018 US Supreme Court decision in *Jesner*. It was dismissed because *Jenser* applies to foreign corporations and does not foreclose plaintiffs' claims against domestic corporations concerning their actions abroad.[97] The case was subject to several complicated motions throughout 2019. These include motions to dismiss for lack of jurisdiction, a claim of immunity by the CACI and the dismissal of the US Government as a party to the suit. In 2020, the Supreme Court is considering whether to hear an appeal by CACI requesting that the case be dismissed based on an intricate claim of derivative sovereign immunity. At the time of this writing, the Supreme Court has not yet decided whether they will proceed with CACI's appeal.

In *Mastafa v Chevron Corp*,[98] the plaintiffs were victims of human rights abuses committed by the Iraqi regime of Saddam Hussein. They alleged that the defendants aided Hussein in obtaining illegal payments through financial transactions that occurred in the United States. The United States Court of Appeals for the Second Circuit held that this conduct touched and concerned the US with sufficient force to displace the presumption against extraterritoriality. However, the Court ultimately concluded that the allegations of the complainants were insufficient to demonstrate that the defendants acted with the purpose of violating the *law of nations*, and the complaint was dismissed.[99]

These cases demonstrate that following *Kiobel*, the extraterritorial use of the ATS by US courts continues to evolve and may prove beneficial for foreign claimants if the circumstances provide a clear US connection to the alleged wrongdoing. On the other hand, at least two other cases following *Kiobel* have been dismissed on the basis that the alleged conduct did not touch and concern the United States sufficiently to rebut the presumption against extraterritoriality.[100] Based on

[95] For example, see *Al Shimari v CACI Premier Technology, Inc* [2014] 758 F3d 516.
[96] *Al Shimari v CACI et al* [2017] 108-Cv-827 ED Va.
[97] *Al Shimari v CACI Premier Tech Inc* [2018] ED Va No 08-827 WL 3118183.
[98] *Mastafa v Chevron Corp* [2014] 770 F3d 170 (2nd Cir).
[99] *Ibid* 194.
[100] *Adhikari v Kellogg Brown & Root Inc* [2017] 845 F3d 184 (5th Cir); *Sexual Minorities Uganda v Scott Lively* [2017] Mass Dist Ct No. 12-cv-30051.

these results, it is unclear exactly what conduct will give rise to overcoming the presumption against extraterritoriality in future cases.[101]

D. Involvement of Civil Society

When it comes to international mining, civil society groups have taken on various roles. Advocacy is traditionally seen as the primary function of civil society organisations that focus on mining. This typically takes the form of calling for regulatory changes and greater social awareness.[102] However, civil society groups have also appeared as legal representatives in several cases.

An underreported aspect of the ATS is that many of these cases have been led almost exclusively by counsel at non-profit advocacy groups such as the Center for Constitutional Rights, the Center for Justice and Accountability, EarthRights International and the International Labor Rights Fund. Even when civil society organisations such as these groups are not acting as direct counsel, they often participate by filing *amicus curiae* briefs as 'friends of the court'. According to one review, the involvement of civil society organisations in ATS cases indicates a 34 per cent increased chance that the case will succeed at trial than if the plaintiff is not assisted by a civil society organisation. Further, involvement at the appellate level indicates a 41 per cent more likely chance of success.[103]

Arguably, civil society actors have utilised the ATS to harness the law as a system of social power that goes beyond success in individual cases. For instance, ATS cases typically occur in the context of class action lawsuits or group litigation where there are several plaintiffs in the suit. It has been suggested that group litigation promotes desirable ends such as citizen empowerment and deliberation.[104] Group litigation is also powerful as a historical record, where victims have an opportunity to tell their story in a public proceeding.[105]

The idea of using the ATS in *Filartiga* was first conceived by lawyers with the Center for Constitutional Rights which was assisting the plaintiff.[106]

[101] The ATS has also been used regarding climate change. It has been suggested that there is an emerging international norm of limiting contributions to climate change as a recognised form of customary international law under the ATS. As such, the plaintiffs bringing ATS claims regarding climate change may be successful. This is even in light of the restrictions in *Kiobel*. J Lopez, 'The New Normal: Climate Change Victims in Post-Kiobel United States Federal Courts' (2013) 8 *Charleston Law Review* 113.

[102] A good example are the evolving concerns presented by deep sea mining and its impacts on marine and coastal ecosystems. As a result of these concerns, a collection of civil society groups has emerged to advocate for increased regulation and study. These groups include the Deep Sea Mining Campaign, Deep Sea Conservation Coalition and the Ocean Foundation, among others.

[103] Davis, *Justice Across Borders* 275.

[104] A Lahav, 'The Political Justification for Group Litigation' 81 *Fordham Law Review* 3193.

[105] L Bilsky, 'The Judge and the Historian: Transnational Holocaust Litigation as the New Model' (2012) 24 *History & Memory* 117, 129–30.

[106] Davis (n 61) 19.

The *Doe I v Unocal Corp* case was initially launched by the Center for Constitutional Rights and EarthRights International on behalf of Burmese villagers.[107] *Bowoto v Chevron* was also filed by EarthRights International on behalf of the plaintiffs.

The framework of the ATS as first proposed by lawyers at the Center for Constitutional Rights in the 1980 *Filartiga* case was left standing by the US Supreme Court in *Sosa v Alvarez-Machain*. The 2004 case generated significant interest with civil society organisations and several filed amicus briefs with the Court.[108]

Due in part to the work of non-profit advocacy groups, the last 30 years has seen a growing wave of ATS cases against US and non-US corporations accused of human rights abuses. Most, if not all, of these cases were led by civil society organisations as either direct counsel, friends of the court or they were responsible for providing other forms of advocacy and support. The involvement of civil society in the ATS cases suggests that there is a role for these groups in protecting those impacted abroad by the activities of multinational corporations.

[107] *Doe v Unocal* [1997] 936 F Supp 880 (CD Cal); Davis (n 61) 120; B Stephens, *International Human Rights Litigation in U.S. Courts*, 2nd edn (Leiden, Martinus Nijhoff Publishers, 2008) 312; M Koebele, *Corporate Responsibility under the Alien Tort Statute: Enforcement of International Law through US Torts Law* (Leiden, Martinus Nijhoff Publishers, 2009) 131–32.

[108] Davis (n 61) 25.

5

Canada, the UK and Australia

Lawsuits have been brought in Canada alleging human rights abuses by multinational corporations against local populations in foreign countries. The probability of the victims receiving a remedy in these cases is doubtful given numerous procedural and substantive limitations. For instance, the limited liability concept of a corporate enterprise protects parent corporations from the negligent activities of its subsidiaries.

Assuming a plaintiff overcomes this hurdle, a Canadian court may be unwilling to act if a connection to its legal system is lacking or if another court is the preferable forum under the doctrine of *forum non conveniens*. For this reason, Canadian courts may not consider a case if the central activities have occurred in another jurisdiction.

Similarly, the doctrine of *forum non conveniens* operates with different effects in other common law legal systems such as the UK and Australia. Beyond the doctrine of *forum non conveniens*, there are additional hurdles such as international comity and limitation of jurisdiction among others. As such, the blockades for litigating the international activities of multinational enterprises in their home state are substantial and numerous.

I. Canada

The test for determining whether a Canadian court should take jurisdiction over an international private law action has three parts. The plaintiff must first satisfy the legal requirement that has come to be known as the 'real and substantial connection' test. Assuming that the plaintiff meets this requirement, the court retains the discretion to decline jurisdiction if there is another forum more appropriate to consider the claim using the doctrine of *forum non conveniens*. Finally, there may be issues concerning choice of law in a Canadian forum.[1]

The 2012 case of *Club Resorts Ltd v Van Breda* is the most recent decision in which the Supreme Court of Canada addressed the 'real and substantial

[1] This three-part approach was outlined in *Bouzari v Iran* [2004] 71 OR3d 675, para 23.

connection' test and *forum non conveniens*.[2] The case combines two separate actions in which both plaintiffs were injured while on vacation in Cuba. Lawsuits were brought in Ontario against a company incorporated in the Cayman Islands that managed the two hotels where the accidents occurred. The Supreme Court of Canada allowed the claims to proceed, holding that a real and substantial connection to Canada existed, and in considering *forum non conveniens*, it was clear that Canadian courts were the most appropriate forum.

As outlined in *Van Breda*, the important factors that a court considers under the 'real and substantial connection' test include: where the defendant is domiciled or maintains residency, where the defendant carries on business, where the tort is allegedly committed or where the contract is executed.[3] Only one of the presumptive factors is required to satisfy the 'real and substantial connection' test.[4] Thus, it is relatively clear when a claim has a real and substantial connection to Canada, given the test is based on factual circumstances such as residency.[5]

Forum non conveniens has a more discretionary application than the 'real and substantial' connection test and is only considered once a connection to Canada has been established. The burden is on the defendant to demonstrate why the court should decline to exercise its jurisdiction and displace the forum chosen by the plaintiff. The relevant factors include, among other issues, the location of the parties and witnesses, the cost of transferring the case to another jurisdiction and the impact of a transfer upon the prospects of the litigation.[6] International comity was also cited as a relevant factor in the decision.[7] The Supreme Court cautioned against placing too much weight on assuming that another legal system is inadequate where it differs from Canadian law, as doing so would be inconsistent with international comity.[8]

In sum, corporations that reside, conduct business or enter into agreements in Canada may be subject to its jurisdiction, unless they can rebut the presumption of a real and substantial connection. If jurisdiction is established under the

[2] *Club Resorts Ltd v Van Breda* [2012] 1 SCR 572.

[3] *Ibid* para 90; *Muscutt v Courcelles* [2002] 60 3d 20 213 DLR 4th 577 CA, paras 76–102.

[4] *Van Breda* (n 2) para 99.

[5] In *Beals v Saldanha* [2003] 3 SCR 416, the Supreme Court of Canada applied the 'real and substantial connection' test in the international context for the first time. The doctrine had already been developed in earlier decisions, including a case from the House of Lords. In *Beals*, the Supreme Court adopts the test from *Moran v Pyle National (Canada) Ltd* [1975] 1 SCR 393 and *Indyka v Indyka* [1969] 1 AC 33 (HL). In considering the last factor on the principle of international comity, the Supreme Court relied on the reasons it had previously outlined in the 1990 case of *Morguard Investments Ltd v De Savoye* [1990] 3 SCR 1077. In *Morguard*, Justice La Forest wrote that international comity is the acceptance by states of the legitimacy and authority of other states acting within its own territory. For this reason, the decision in *Beals* restricts the possibility of bringing lawsuits in Canada that concerns activity occurring within another country.

[6] *Van Breda* (n 2) para 110.

[7] *Van Breda* (n 2) para 92.

[8] For more information on the *Van Breda* case, see generally E Edinger, 'Club Resorts Ltd. v. Van Breda: Extraterritoriality Revisited Papers from the 43rd Annual Workshop on Commercial and Consumer Law' (2014) 55 *Canadian Business Law Journal* 263.

'real and substantial connection' test, the doctrine of *forum non conveniens* may be raised by the defendant to dismiss the claim. Under this framework, a foreign plaintiff will have difficulty overcoming *forum non conveniens* in a case in which they are suing a Canadian corporation for the activities of its foreign subsidiary. First, the activity will have primarily occurred in the host state and the majority of parties and their witnesses will be in that country. Second, foreign corporate activity is normally undertaken by a subsidiary incorporated in the host state, and therefore, the parent corporation will be protected from the subsidiaries' liabilities. Third, the issue of comity will restrict the court's willingness to assert jurisdiction over a matter that takes place primarily in another country. For these reasons, Canada is comparatively restrictive in its approach towards extending extraterritorial jurisdiction over the foreign activities of its business enterprises. Some commentators have suggested that provincial legislatures may be inclined to codify the *forum non conveniens* test in a way that allows greater access to Canadian courts for victims of the extractive sector.[9] To date, only a handful of provinces have codified *forum non conveniens*, and generally speaking those statutes largely reflect the common law principles provided in *Van Breda*.[10]

Procedural hurdles other than the 'real and substantial connection' test and *forum non conveniens* may bar plaintiffs from bringing claims in Canadian courts. In *Tolofson v Jensen*, the Supreme Court of Canada enacted a choice of law rule for torts committed in a jurisdiction other than that in which the action was being brought.[11] The Court held that the primary factor in determining the jurisdiction of a tort claim should be the *lex loci* rule (the location where the tort occurred) as opposed to the *lex fori* rule (the law of the forum). The Court considered the approach in the United Kingdom where if the wrong is 'unjusticiable' in the state in which the wrong is committed, UK law will then apply in adjudicating the wrong despite the fact that it was committed in another state.[12]

[9] G Skinner, R McCorquodale and O De Schutter, 'The Third Pillar: Access to Judicial Remedies for Human Rights Violations by Transnational Business' (The International Corporate Accountability Roundtable, 2013) 84; P Simons and A Macklin, *The Governance Gap: Extractive Industries, Human Rights, and the Home State Advantage* (Toronto, Routledge, 2014) 286.

[10] The Uniform Law Conference of Canada provided provincial legislatures a template to codify the application of *forum non conveniens* through the Court Jurisdiction and Proceedings Transfer Act (CJPTA), which has been modified and adopted in Saskatchewan, British Columbia, Nova Scotia and Yukon. The Court Jurisdiction and Proceedings Transfer Act SS 1997 c C-41.1; Court Jurisdiction and Proceedings Transfer Act SBC 2003 c 28; Court Jurisdiction and Proceedings Transfer Act SNS 2003 (2d Sess) c 2; Court Jurisdiction and Proceedings Transfer Act SY 2000 c 7. The provincial law reform bodies in Alberta and Manitoba have recommended the enactment of the CJPTA, without any progression by the respective legislatures. The CJPTA largely reflects the common law principles provided in *Van Breda*. There are differences between the provinces that have adopted the CJPTA. For example, Saskatchewan has not enacted the provision on forum of necessity, while British Columbia and Nova Scotia did. For more information on the CJPTA, see V Black, S Pitel and M Sobkin, *Statutory Jurisdiction: An Analysis of the Court Jurisdiction and Proceedings Transfer Act* (Toronto, Carswell, 2012).

[11] *Tolofson v Jensen* [1994] 3 SCR 1022.

[12] *Ibid* 1052.

In writing for the majority, Justice La Forest had two primary concerns with this approach. First, judicial consideration of activities in other states carries the risk of overriding the territoriality principle, which provides that a state should have jurisdiction over conduct substantially taking part within its territory. Second, if adopted widely, this approach would have the effect of allowing courts of different countries to address the same incident and apply conflicting legal rules. This practice potentially invites forum shopping by claimants in search of the most beneficial place to litigate an issue. For these reasons, Justice La Forest declined to follow the UK approach and instead set a high threshold in limiting cases from Canadian courts for extraterritorial conduct.

The Supreme Court held that if the legal system where the tort was committed does not recognise the act as wrongful, that action could not be brought in Canadian courts under Canadian law. However, one exception was carved out. The Court noted that exemptions would be made in a 'few' international cases to avoid injustice at the discretion of the court.[13]

Despite this exception seeming to open the door to foreign litigants, the *Tolofson* exception has limited utility when it comes to extraterritorial claims. First, plaintiffs would still need to meet the requirements of the 'real and substantial connection' test, which is difficult when the alleged wrongdoing has occurred outside of Canada. Second, the exception appears to be designed for circumstances where residents of Canada have been harmed outside of the country. For instance, the Ontario Court of Appeal upheld the application of the *Tolofson* exception in a case involving a car accident in Minnesota between two Canadians, both insured under a contract in Canada. The reason for the exception was that the specific claim was not permitted under Minnesota law.[14] Thus, *Tolofson* is not particularly effective for foreign nationals seeking legal recourse in Canadian courts for wrongdoing that occurred abroad.

In sum, the precedents from the Supreme Court of Canada concerning the 'real and substantial connection' test, *forum non conveniens* and choice of law have not provided a framework allowing foreign litigants to hold Canadian companies to account for human rights abuses and environmental violations abroad.

Some recent cases have departed from this narrow approach and partially align with UK decisions that recognise parent corporations may be directly liable for harm caused by a subsidiary.[15] The *Choc v Hudbay* trilogy is three related actions against Hudbay Minerals Inc for alleged human rights abuses in Guatemala.[16] The allegations include rape of Indigenous women and the murder of a community

[13] *Ibid* 1054.

[14] In *Hanlan v Sernesky* the Ontario Court of Appeal upheld an exercise of discretion for an international case under the *Tolofson* precedent. *Hanlan v Sernesky* [1998] 38 OR (3d) 479 (Ont CA).

[15] M Conway, 'A New Duty of Care? Tort Liability from Voluntary Human Rights Due Diligence in Global Supply Chains' (2015) 40 *Queen's Law Journal* 741, 766–67.

[16] *Angelica Choc et al v Hudbay Minerals Inc et al* 2013 ONSC 414.

leader who advocated against Hudbay's mining project. Both crimes are alleged to have occurred in the course of an ongoing dispute over land rights at the site of a mine owned by Hudbay's Guatemalan subsidiary.[17] The Ontario Superior Court of Justice ruled that a Canadian parent corporation may be liable for the actions of its subsidiary operating in another country through agency law.[18] The Court rejected Hudbay's argument for dismissal based on the limited liability of its Guatemala subsidiary, which most of the allegations were directed towards. The Court found that the plaintiffs properly alleged that the subsidiary was acting as an authorised agent of Hudbay, and if plaintiffs could establish this at trial, they may pierce the corporate veil. The Court also found that the plaintiffs had properly alleged Hudbay's direct involvement in some of the wrongful conduct, and could be liable for its own actions.[19] Prior to the hearing, Hudbay withdrew part of their motion relating to *forum non conveniens*. It has been reported that Hudbay possibly withdrew this portion of their motion because they believed the position was untenable.[20] In 2015, the company was compelled by a plaintiff's motion to disclose internal corporate documents.[21]

In 2020, Hudbay was unsuccessful in an application to block the plaintiffs from amending their lawsuit. The plaintiffs added new details about the alleged assaults perpetrated by mine company private security forces, military and police in Guatemala.[22] At the time of writing, lawyers for the plaintiffs continue the examination for discovery process in anticipation of trial.

These pre-trial *Hudbay* rulings are not a substantive precedent, although similar cases are emerging. For example, in 2014 three Eritreans filed a lawsuit against Nevsun Resources in British Columbia where the corporation is located. Nevsun operates the Bisha gold, copper and zinc mine in western Eritrea. The Eritreans, now refugees in Canada, allege that they were conscripted under Eritrea's national service programme to work at the mine which has become the country's largest source of revenue. The plaintiffs allege that they were forced to work in unbearable heat and were subjected to physical assault, threats and torture if they attempted to take breaks.[23]

The plaintiffs believe that Nevsun was complicit in this use of forced labour by Nevsun's contractor in Eritrea, whereas Nevsun suggests that use of that particular contractor was required by the Eritrean Government as a condition of the licence to operate the mine. This case demonstrates the moral hazards of attempting to

[17] S Imai, 'Will Canadian Companies Be Held Responsible for Their Actions Abroad?' (*Globe and Mail*, 31 July 2013).
[18] *Hudbay* (n 16) para 49.
[19] *Hudbay* (n 16) para 54.
[20] Skinner et al, 'The Third Pillar' 37.
[21] *Angelica Choc et al HudDay Minerals Inc et al* CV-lO-4111-59 (2015).
[22] *Caal Caal v Hudbay Minerals Inc* 2020 ONSC 415.
[23] A Coletta, 'A Canadian Company Is Accused of Human Rights Abuses Overseas. Can It Be Sued in Canada?' *The Washington Post* (24 January 2019).

work in a developing country that sets unconventional conditions, such as the use of a particular vendor, as a stipulation of operating.

This lawsuit is the first in Canada where claims are based directly on violations of international law in the context of holding an extractive sector corporation to account for foreign conduct. The plaintiffs argue that the complicit conduct of the company in acquiescing to torture and the use of slave labour is a violation of customary international norms.

Nevsun filed several motions to challenge the jurisdiction of these suits.[24] However, the Supreme Court of British Colombia (BC) dismissed Nevsun's motions,[25] and the dismissal was upheld by the BC Court of Appeal.[26] The Court stated that there was a real risk of corruption and unfairness in the Eritrean legal system, while also conveying the considerable practical difficulties of hearing the claims in British Columbia.[27]

In 2018, the Canadian Supreme Court granted Nevsun leave to appeal. Arguments and submissions were presented in early 2019 along with the involvement of several civil society intervenors such as EarthRights International, Mining Watch Canada, Amnesty International Canada, as well as industry-supported intervenors such as the Canadian Mining Association.

Similar to *Hudbay*, Nevsun was not arguing for an appeal based on *forum non conveniens*. Instead, Nevsun argued that the case should be dismissed based on the act of state doctrine, which is complementary to the principle of international comity. The act of state doctrine precludes adjudication of a foreign state's sovereign conduct within its own territory. The act of state doctrine had not been applied in Canadian courts. Therefore, both litigates were relying on US and UK cases that contain different applications of the concept.[28] The plaintiffs argued that the doctrine does not apply in this case as, for one, the activities involved were commercial in nature as opposed to sovereign acts. Beyond the act of state doctrine, Nevsun also argued it could not be sued for violating customary international law in Canadian courts. The basis of this argument is that a breach of customary international law is not a cause of action in the Canadian legal system. For this reason, Nevsun argued that the claims based on customary international law should be struck because they have no reasonable prospect of success at trial.

In 2020, the Supreme Court released its decision dismissing the pre-trial motion by Nevsun to have the plaintiffs' claims struck.[29] In dismissing the motion, a seven-judge majority of the nine-member Court held that the act of state

[24] J Gray, 'Nevsun Resources Faces Lawsuit over "Forced Labour" in Eritrea' (*The Globe and Mail*, 20 November 2014).

[25] *Araya v Nevsun Resources Ltd* [2016] BCSC 1856.

[26] *Araya v Nevsun Resources Ltd* [2017] 401 (BCCA).

[27] MiningWatch Canada, 'Can Slave Labour Charges Against Canadian Company Be Heard in Court in Canada? Supreme Court of Canada Hears Arguments Today' (23 January 2019).

[28] *WS Kirkpatrick & Co Inc v Environmental Tectonics Corporation International* [1990] USC 493 US 400; *Belhaj v Straw* [2017] UKSC 3.

[29] *Nevsun Resources Ltd v Araya*, 2020 SCC 5.

doctrine was not part of Canadian law. This is an interesting development, as it makes Canada an outlier amongst most other common law jurisdictions including Australia, the UK and the US, which have some form of the act of state doctrine.

On the second issue of customary international law, a narrow five-judge majority held that slavery, torture and crimes against humanity are enforceable norms in Canada. In so doing, the Court held that the plaintiffs may proceed with their claims of alleged breaches of customary international law against the company.

What is novel about the second issue is that traditionally, customary international law is understood as creating obligations upon states only, and not private actors such as corporations. In this case, the Court advanced the traditional understanding by holding that customary international law is potentially applicable against private actors as well.

It is possible that this decision will open the floodgates to similar litigation in Canada. However, the *Nevsun* ruling is procedural in nature and not a decision on the merits. The Supreme Court did not decide whether Nevsun was responsible for violating the plaintiffs' rights; rather it simply allowed the plaintiffs' lawsuit to proceed. Thus, if the case moves forward, a trial judge will have to decide whether Nevsun breached customary international law, and if so, how it should be held responsible.

It should also be noted that in 2018, it was announced that Nevsun was purchased by a Chinese mining company. Some commentators have suggested that this may result in the plaintiffs being unable to collect on any eventual award or settlement regardless of the outcome.[30]

As another example of a similar case to *Nevsun*, in 2014 several Guatemalans sued Tahoe Resources in British Columbia, alleging that Tahoe security personnel fired weapons at them as they were protesting against a local mine.[31] Tahoe Resources is a Canadian mining company and its prime asset is the Escobal mine where the shootings took place.[32] The plaintiffs alleged that Tahoe authorised the use of excessive force by its security personnel or was negligent in preventing it. The plaintiffs also alleged that Tahoe failed to adhere to its corporate social responsibility policies and internationally accepted standards for the use of private security personnel.

In 2015, the BC Supreme Court declined jurisdiction over the lawsuit.[33] In its ruling, the Court focused on the procedural hurdles, expenses and general

[30] MiningWatch Canada, 'Slave Labour'.

[31] S Fairley and A Sumakova, 'Tort Liability at Home for Alleged Wrongs Abroad: The Common Law Goes Extraterritorial?' (*WeirFoulds LLP*, November 2014), www.mondaq.com/canada/international-trade-investment/357576/tort-liability-at-home-for-alleged-wrongs-abroad-the-common-law-goes-extraterritorial.

[32] J Bone, 'Do Mining Companies Adequately Value Corporate Social Responsibility?' (*Mining.com*, 4 March 2015), www.mining.com/web/mining-companies-adequately-value-corporate-social-responsibility/.

[33] *Garcia v Tahoe Resources Inc* [2015] BCSC 2045, 5.

inconvenience of bringing the lawsuit in Canada.[34] However, in 2017, the BC Court of Appeal reversed the order and held that the possibility of corruption in the Guatemalan legal system made Canadian courts a more appropriate forum.[35]

The Court of Appeal held that the trial judge failed to give adequate consideration to:

1) the inadequate discovery process under Guatemalan civil procedure to obtain documents in the possession of a foreign corporation;
2) the expiry of the one-year limitation period in the Guatemalan legal system; and
3) the possibility of corruption in the Guatemalan justice system.[36]

The Court of Appeal also found that the trial judge had not applied the correct test for *forum non conveniens* factors. One of the factors the trial judge used in assessing the risk of corruption was whether the foreign forum was 'capable of providing justice'.[37] The Court of Appeal held that the correct test is whether there is a 'real risk' that the proposed alternative forum would not provide adequate justice.[38]

The Court of Appeal held that there was a measurable risk that the plaintiffs would encounter difficulty in receiving a fair trial against a powerful mining corporation whose interests aligned with the political interests of the Guatemalan Government. Most recently, Tahoe's application for leave to appeal to the Supreme Court was denied.[39] Thus, the claim was allowed to be pursued in Canada for damages relating to alleged human rights violations.

On a different legal front, a Guatemalan court suspended two of Tahoe's licences to operate the Escobal silver mine in the summer of 2017. This particular litigation involved an action brought by an anti-mining organisation that alleged violation of Indigenous people's rights to be consulted prior to the development of the mine.[40] The ruling was upheld by the Guatemalan Constitutional Court. The suspension will remain in effect as the Guatemalan Ministry of Energy and Mines consults with Indigenous populations that are impacted by the mine.[41] As of the time of writing, the mine remains closed pending the outcome of this consultation.

Beyond the attribution of any legal liability, it is possible that this lawsuit has resulted in economic loss for Tahoe. For instance in 2015 Goldcorp, one of

[34] *Ibid* 43 and 99.
[35] *Garcia v Tahoe Resources Inc* [2017] 39 (BCCA).
[36] *Ibid* para 127.
[37] *Ibid* para 34.
[38] *Ibid* para 124.
[39] MiningWatch Canada, 'The Lawsuit (Tahoe on Trial)' (2019), tahoeontrial.net/the-lawsuit/.
[40] S Menchu, 'Guatemala Court Confirms Suspension of Tahoe Mining Licenses' *Reuters* (6 July 2017), www.reuters.com/article/us-guatemala-mining/guatemala-court-confirms-suspension-of-tahoe-mining-licenses-idUSKCN1LK074.
[41] MiningWatch Canada, 'Guatemala's Highest Court Orders Tahoe's Escobal Mine to Remain Suspended' (4 September 2018), https://miningwatch.ca/news/2018/9/4/guatemala-s-highest-court-orders-tahoe-s-escobal-mine-remain-suspended?.

the world's largest gold companies, divested from Tahoe, along with Norway's Government Pension Fund.[42] It is unclear whether the lawsuit over the Escobal mine played any factor in this decision. Further, a proposed securities class action lawsuit against Tahoe relating to their activities in Guatemala was filed in 2018 by a Canadian law firm.[43]

In 2018, Pan American Silver announced the purchase of all of the outstanding shares of Tahoe. In a joint effort, two civil society groups sent notices to investors and securities regulators alleging that Tahoe had not properly disclosed relevant information on social conflict surrounding the Escobal mine as part of the acquisition.[44] In 2019, Pan American Silver completed the acquisition of Tahoe and agreed to settle the outstanding Canadian lawsuits under terms that remain confidential. The company did publicly acknowledge that human rights had been violated. For this reason, the *Tahoe* litigation represents a successful example of foreign individuals using the Canadian legal system to seek recourse for the actions of the extractive sector that occurred abroad. Despite this, the success is attributable to the defendant corporation deciding to settle the suit, as opposed to a finding based on law and evidence presented at trial. Thus, it is not clear whether the Canadian judicial system will reliably provide an effective remedy for those seeking redress for human rights abuses against Canadian mining operators.

Despite the outcome in *Tahoe*, given that litigation in *Hudbay* and *Nevsun* is ongoing, it is increasingly likely that one or both of these cases may face a trial on the merits of these issues in Canadian courts. However, it is clear that the pre-trial rulings allowing these claims to proceed are not a substantive precedent.[45] At least two Courts of Appeal and two trial courts in Canada have dismissed similar claims. For instance, in *Recherches Internationales Québec v Cambior Inc*, a judge of the Québec Superior Court dismissed a class action brought by a public interest group against a Québec corporation. The proceedings were initiated on behalf of victims of an environmental spill of cyanide-contaminated tailings from a gold mine in Guyana.[46] The judge considered the doctrine of *forum non conveniens* and found that while the courts of Québec had joint jurisdiction with the courts

[42] S Vergara and U Gneiting, 'Why Did Goldcorp Really Pull out of Tahoe Resources' Troubled Guatemalan Mining Project?' (*Oxfam America*, 7 July 2015), https://politicsofpoverty.oxfamamerica.org/why-did-goldcorp-really-pull-out-of-tahoe-resourcess-troubled-guatemalan-mining-project/.

[43] Siskinds LLP, 'Siskinds LLP Announces Filing of Proposed Securities Class Action against Tahoe Resources Inc.' (*CISION*, 19 November 2018), www.newswire.ca/news-releases/siskinds-llp-announces-filing-of-proposed-securities-class-action-against-tahoe-resources-inc-700827921.html.

[44] Letter from the Justice and Corporate Accountability Project to the British Columbia Securities Commission (3 January 2019).

[45] The decisions are simply a precedent that these claims can survive a dispositive motion to strike. As one commentator said: 'It's not a ruling that tells us anything definitive about how the law is going to shake out when the case goes to trial.' P Koven, 'HudBay Case Raises Litigation Risk for Canadian Resource Companies' *Financial Post* (30 October 2013), https://financialpost.com/legal-post/hudbay-case-raises-class-action-risk-for-canadian-resource-companies.

[46] *Recherches Internationales Québec v Cambior Inc* [1998] QJ No 2554 JE 98-1905.

of Guyana, neither the victims nor their action had any real connection with Québec.[47] However, Cambior had to commit to an undertaking that if the Court dismissed Recherches Internationales' Québec's motion and the victims started proceedings in Guyana, Cambior could not argue in Guyana that the case should be heard in Québec. Such a complaint was eventually brought, but it was dismissed by the Guyanese Court and the plaintiffs were ordered to pay for Cambior's legal expenses.[48]

In *Anvil Mining Ltd c Association canadienne contre l'impunité*, an Australian mining corporation was accused of supporting the army of the Congo that raped, murdered and brutalised citizens. The only connection Anvil had with Québec was that it had an investor relations representative office in the jurisdiction. However, that office was opened after the events that gave rise to the plaintiffs' claim for what Anvil's agents allegedly did in the Congo.

The Québec Court of Appeal held that the province did not have jurisdiction to hear the matter.[49] Leave to appeal to the Supreme Court of Canada was subsequently denied. Compared to the other Canadian provinces based in the common law, Québec has a civil law tradition, and therefore the Québec Civil Code was considered for the purpose of determining *forum non conveniens* in the *Anvil* case.[50]

At trial Anvil argued that there was no basis for jurisdiction under Article 3148 of the Québec Civil Code, which defines the circumstances in which a non-resident defendant can be sued in Québec.[51] Simply put, Anvil argued that Québec courts did not have jurisdiction as a matter of the Civil Code, not *forum non conveniens*. The trial Court held that the case should be heard in Québec because it was impossible for the parties to commence a hearing elsewhere based on the forum of necessity doctrine. Therefore, Anvil's motion was dismissed.

The forum of necessity doctrine first developed in Europe and is present in both common and civil law legal systems including France, Germany, Netherlands, Ireland, Portugal and Switzerland.[52] The doctrine is included in the Québec Civil Code, and permits Québec courts to consider cases if they have sufficient connections with Québec and where proceedings cannot be instituted in another forum.[53]

[47] Stikeman Elliott, 'Global Mining Update: Québec Court Decides to Dismiss Proceedings: Tailings Dam Collapse to Be Litigated in Guyana' (1999).

[48] A Mocle, 'Corporate Human Rights Risk' in L Rayman-Bacchus and P Walsh (eds), *Corporate Responsibility and Sustainable Development: Exploring the Nexus of Private and Public Interests* (New York, Routledge, 2016) 57, fn 9.

[49] *Anvil Mining Ltd c Association canadienne contre l'impunité* [2012] QCCA 117.

[50] Article 3135 of the Québec Civil Code (CCQ) allows the court to decline jurisdiction if another forum is more appropriate. Civil Code of Québec SQ 1991 c 64, art 3135.

[51] *Ibid* Art 3148.

[52] M Goldhaber, 'Corporate Human Rights Litigation in Non-U.S. Courts: A Comparative Scorecard' (2013) 3 *UC Irvine Law Review* 127, 135.

[53] CCQ (n 50) Art 3136.

In *Anvil*, the Québec Court of Appeal overturned the trial Court's decision. The forum of necessity finding was rejected because the plaintiffs had failed to demonstrate the requisite condition that they could not sue Anvil in Australia. The plaintiffs only established that they had not found Australian counsel willing to act for them. On account of this ruling, the Québec Court of Appeal did not address the issue of *forum non conveniens*.

In *Piedra v Copper Mesa Mining Corporation*, which included the Toronto Stock Exchange as a co-defendant, the Court of Appeal for Ontario dismissed a claim by Ecuadorian peasants who alleged that they were assaulted by security forces hired on behalf of a Canadian mining company.[54] In dismissing the claim for lack of jurisdiction, the Court also confirmed that the Toronto Stock Exchange does not have a legal duty to consider corporate human rights records when deciding to list corporations on its stock exchange.[55]

Anvil Mining Ltd and *Piedra* demonstrate the hesitance of Canadian Courts of Appeal to intervene with alleged human rights abuses arising from international Canadian mining operations. In sum, as noted by former Supreme Court Justice Ian Binnie, historically Canadian courts have an 'undistinguished record' in dealing with global human rights concerns attributed to the Canadian extractive sector.[56] However, there are promising recent developments in Canadian case law that demonstrate a willingness to adjudicate extractive sector corporations for their overseas conduct.

Finally, unlike the United States and the United Kingdom, Canada's highest courts have not considered a direct case involving the extraterritorial human rights track record of an extractive sector corporation. However, Canada's highest court has permitted foreign claimants to bring an action for recognition and enforcement of an \$8 billion Ecuadorian judgment in *Chevron Corp v Yaiguaje*.[57] Although, for the reasons explained below, the judgment cannot be enforced in Canada.

This case is a result of a trial in a class action lawsuit claiming that the corporation caused significant destruction to the Amazon rainforest, which harmed the health and traditional lifestyles of local Indigenous groups. In 2014, a US district court held that the Ecuadorian judgment was procured by fraud, and thus was unenforceable in the United States.[58]

In Canada, the Supreme Court took a generous and liberal approach to the recognition of foreign judgments and stressed the importance of international comity. The Court determined that the enforcement proceedings may continue

[54] *Piedra v Copper Mesa Mining Corporation* [2011] 332 DLR 4th 118.
[55] *Ibid* 16–17.
[56] Simons and Macklin, *The Governance Gap* xi.
[57] *Chevron Corp v Yaiguaje* [2015] SCC 42.
[58] *Chevron Corp v Donziger* [2014] 974 FSupp2d 362.

as there is no need to demonstrate a real and substantial connection between the dispute and the Canadian forum. However, the Supreme Court confined itself to the procedural question of whether Canadian courts had jurisdiction over Chevron for the purpose of enforcing a foreign judgment.[59]

The Court did not comment on potential defences to the enforcement action based on natural justice, fraud and public policy as had been utilised successfully by Chevron in the US District Court.[60] It also did not address the merits of the claimant's action or assess the Ecuadorian judgment to determine whether it can be enforced in Canada.

The Court made its findings despite the fact that Chevron was not a party to the Ecuadorian case and was only an indirect subsidiary of Chevron Corp. The Court noted in its decisions that the recognition of a judgment against a parent company does not automatically capture the assets of a subsidiary.[61] Thus, the principle of limited liability of a corporation was upheld in the decision.

In 2017, the plaintiffs attempted to enforce the judgment. The Ontario Superior Court of Justice ruled that Chevron's Canadian subsidiary is a separate entity from its parent corporation, and is thus not a debtor under the Ecuadorian judgment. The Ecuadorian plaintiffs subsequently appealed that decision to the Ontario Court of Appeal. In response, Chevron brought a motion for security for costs, which was granted in Chevron's favour.[62]

In 2018, the Ontario Court of Appeal upheld the Ontario Superior Court's ruling that Chevron Canada cannot be held liable for the international activities of its parent corporation.[63] In 2019, the plaintiffs leave to appeal application was denied by the Supreme Court. Thus, these enforcement proceedings were ultimately terminated in Canada.

Also in 2018, the Permanent Court of Arbitration in The Hague held Ecuador liable for denying justice to Chevron and violating the company's procedural rights. The panel held that the Ecuadorian judgment should not be recognised or enforced in any jurisdiction.[64]

Unlike in *Hudbay*, *Tahoe* and *Nevsun*, the Chevron case before the Supreme Court turned on the issue of enforcement of a foreign judgment, not an issue of direct liability between a parent corporation and a foreign subsidiary or on the doctrine of *forum non conveniens*. As such, there was no need for the plaintiffs to establish parent company liability, vicarious liability, negligence or that the foreign court had a real and substantial connection either with the litigants or the underlying dispute.

[59] *Chevron Corp v Yaiguaje* (n 57) para 42.
[60] *Chevron Corp v Yaiguaje* (n 57) para 77.
[61] *Chevron Corp v Yaiguaje* (n 57) para 95.
[62] *Yaiguaje v Chevron Corporation* 2017 ONCA 741.
[63] *Yaiguaje v Chevron Corporation* 2018 ONCA 472.
[64] *Chevron v The Republic of Ecuador* UNCITRAL, PCA Case No 2009-23.

II. United Kingdom

The concept of *forum non conveniens* is a flexible doctrine that is liberally applied in English courts. In assessing whether *forum non conveniens* dismissal is appropriate, courts engage in a two-step process. The first step is to determine if English courts are the natural forum. If so, in seeking a dismissal the defendant must establish that another available forum is clearly more appropriate to consider the matter. This test was outlined in the 1987 case of *Spiliada Maritime Corp v Cansulex Ltd*.[65]

The Spiliada was a Liberian vessel that sustained significant damages while in a Canadian port. By the time litigation was contemplated the owner had missed the relevant limitation period under Canadian law. An action was brought in England on the basis that the Spiliada was insured through an English corporation. The House of Lords allowed the case to proceed in England given that it was the 'natural forum' with the 'most real and substantial connection'.[66] In determining the natural forum, the House of Lords considered a variety of factors including the availability of witnesses, the applicable law, the location of the parties and the possibility for the plaintiff to obtain a fair and expedient hearing in the foreign jurisdiction. The House of Lords held that the burden rested on the defendant to demonstrate that England was not the natural forum for the trial and that another available forum was clearly more appropriate than English courts. This is the application of *forum non conveniens* that the House of Lords adopted from Scots law.[67]

As a result of the recognition of *forum non conveniens*, English courts are willing to adjudicate if the defendant cannot prove that a more appropriate forum exists to consider the matter. Subsequent to the *Spiliada* decision, several cases concerning corporate wrongdoing committed abroad have proceeded in English courts. These cases generally arose from injured workers in Africa who attempted to attribute liability to UK parent corporations.

As one example, in the case of *Ngcobo v Thor Chemicals Holdings Ltd*,[68] South African workers were injured due to mercury poisoning at an English-owned mine. The plaintiffs were employed in South Africa by a subsidiary of Thor, a British company. The plaintiffs alleged that they were exposed to hazardous quantities of mercury over the course of their employment. As previously addressed in chapter three, they recovered limited compensation in South Africa from the subsidiary, and brought a claim in English courts against the parent corporation. The Court of Appeal ruled the claim could proceed in English court.

[65] *Spiliada Maritime Corp v Cansulex Ltd* [1987] AC 460 (HL) 476.
[66] *Ibid* 478.
[67] *Ibid* 476. Scots law is the legal system of Scotland. It is a mixed legal system, containing both civil law and common law features.
[68] *Ngcobo v Thor Chemicals Holdings Ltd* [1995] TLR 10 Eng CA.

It was not considered whether South Africa was the more appropriate jurisdiction, thus leaving the question of *forum non conveniens* unaddressed by the Court of Appeal.

In *Connelly v RTZ Corp Plc*, the plaintiff developed a work-related illness while employed by an English subsidiary corporation in Namibia.[69] The employer's insurers denied liability, leaving the plaintiff without compensation. In its 1997 decision, the House of Lords held that England was not the most appropriate jurisdiction. Namibia was considered the proper forum with which the action had the closest connection. Nevertheless, the House of Lords allowed the case to proceed in English court. The House of Lords decided that the case was complex and warranted legal aid or a contingency fee arrangement that could only be provided to the plaintiff in England. As a result of the plaintiff's financial circumstances, the case could not proceed in Namibia. The House of Lords was persuaded that 'substantial' justice could not be done in the appropriate forum but could be done in the jurisdiction where resources were available. Thus, 'substantial justice' required that English courts become the proper forum.[70]

The effect of the *Connelly* decision potentially overrides the limited liability concept of corporations established in the historic *Salomon* case of 1897.[71] The House of Lords was clear in asserting an increasing willingness to overlook the separate legal personality issue and recognise liability for UK parent corporations towards employees of its foreign subsidiaries. This case represents a rare occasion in the common law when courts reached backwards in time to when limited liability was not a central driver in the purpose and utility of the corporate form.

Following *Connelly*, the Court of Appeal considered *Sithole v Thor Chemicals Holdings Ltd*,[72] a similar case to *Ngcobo*. The claim was brought by miners alleging injuries from mercury poisoning at an English-owned mine in South Africa. The case was filed in England, due in part to a South African statute that prohibited employees from directly suing their employer. Surprisingly, the subsidiary corporation in South Africa was not even a party in this action.

Applying the test in *Connelly*, the Court of Appeal held that the action should proceed in English courts. The finding was based primarily on three factors. First, the defendant had not satisfied their burden of showing that South Africa was a more appropriate jurisdiction. Second, under the circumstances at hand, justice could not be done in South Africa given the complex scientific testimony and expert witness who would have to travel to South Africa. Third, given the unavailability of legal aid, contingency fees or other financial arrangements in

[69] *Connelly v RTZ Corp Plc* [1997] 3 WLR 373 (HL).

[70] Connelly's claim was subsequently struck down by the courts on limitation grounds. See *Connelly v Rio Tinto Zinc Corp Plc* [1998] AC 584 (QB).

[71] *Salomon* was one of the first UK cases to firmly uphold the doctrine of separate corporate personality. *Salomon v A Salomon & Co Ltd* [1897] AC 22.

[72] *Sithole v Thor Chemicals Holdings Ltd* [1999] TLR 110 Eng CA.

South Africa, the case would not proceed as a result of the plaintiff's financial circumstances.[73]

The *Connelly* decision was again reinforced in *Lubbe and others v Cape Industries Plc*.[74] The *Lubbe* decision is a high point for those who advocate for extraterritorial litigation as it involved thousands of plaintiffs in one class action lawsuit. The plaintiffs were afflicted with an asbestos-related disease, some as a result of working at a mine in South Africa owned by an English corporation, Cape Plc. Other plaintiffs were exposed to asbestos as a result of living in a contaminated area near Cape's South African operations. The plaintiffs argued that the parent corporation owed a direct duty of care to the employees of its foreign subsidiaries and nearby residents living in contaminated areas. The parent corporation was applying to stay the action on the basis of *forum non conveniens*.

Although South Africa was the more appropriate forum, the plaintiffs were not able to obtain the professional representation and expert evidence essential to their cases without legal aid or contingency fee arrangements that was only available in England. Further, the transformation of the lawsuit into a class action complicated the proceedings and it was clear to the House of Lords that South Africa did not have the resources necessary for such complex litigation. On this basis, the House of Lords held that England was the appropriate forum for the dispute. However, the issue of whether a UK parent corporation owes a direct duty to local communities impacted by a foreign subsidiary, as compared to employees of the foreign subsidiary, was not addressed.[75] The case went back to the High Court and eventually the parent corporation settled with the plaintiffs for a total of £21 million.[76]

A subsequent case confirmed the finding in *Connelly* and *Lubbe* on 'piercing the corporate veil' between parent and subsidiary corporations. In *Chandler v Cape Plc*, an employee of a subsidiary corporation had been exposed to asbestos resulting in injury, and the subsidiary no longer existed and had no policy of insurance covering the employee. The Court of Appeal upheld a duty of care directly between employees of the subsidiary and the parent corporation.[77]

Taken together, the *Connelly* and *Lubbe* decisions have potentially wide implications for international corporations as UK courts are increasingly willing to overlook the separate legal personality issue and recognise liability for parent corporations resulting from the actions of its foreign subsidiaries. It is noteworthy, however, that these cases involved employee plaintiffs, which limits the utility of the case law for impacted communities who do not have an employment or contractual arrangement with a foreign corporation. Therefore, the question

[73] *Ibid.*
[74] *Lubbe and others v Cape Industries Plc* [2000] 1 WLR 1545.
[75] *Ibid* 1556–62.
[76] A Dignam and J Lowry, *Company Law*, 7th edn (Oxford, Oxford University Press, 2012) 45.
[77] *Chandler v Cape Plc* [2012] PIQR P17.

remains whether UK courts will distinguish between the legal duties of a parent corporation towards the employees of its foreign subsidiary, compared to the legal duties owed to local communities impacted by a foreign subsidiary.

Subsequent UK courts have exercised jurisdiction in respect of events that have taken place overseas.[78] For example, in *Guerrero v Monterrico Metals Plc*, the High Court of Justice allowed an injunction to proceed against a parent corporation even though the primary activities giving rise to the lawsuit were of its subsidiary, the Peruvian police, and an independent security contractor in Peru.[79] In the case, several Peruvians commenced legal proceedings against Monterrico Metals, a UK mining company and its Peruvian subsidiary. The claim alleged abuse by police towards protesters who were rallying against a proposed mining development.[80] In 2011, the company settled the case out of court without admitting liability. Thus, a final judicial determination on parent-subsidiary liability was not made in this case.

In a 2016 decision, the UK High Court rejected claims by a group of local farmers in relation to construction of the Ocensa pipeline in Colombia during the mid-1990s.[81] The class action lawsuit alleged negligence by British Petroleum's subsidiary that caused environmental damage to over 73 farmlands.

The trial lasted 62 days over a two-year period with extensive evidence provided by witnesses, many of whom appeared by video link from Colombia. In the 648-page judgment, the Court focused its decision on insufficient factual evidence as opposed to issues surrounding UK jurisdiction or *forum non conveniens*. This case is distinguishable from the cases above as it was brought directly against a former UK-based subsidiary of BP and not in relation to the operations of a Columbian-based subsidiary. This was the basis for UK jurisdiction as held by the High Court.

More recently, a group of Zambian residents brought a lawsuit against UK-based Vedanta Resources Plc and its Zambian subsidiary in UK court over water pollution caused by the subsidiary's copper mining operations. The plaintiffs claimed that the pollution caused damage to property and loss of income for local residents. The claims were grounded in negligence in a similar fashion to Canadian cases such as *Hudbay*.[82]

[78] S Baughen, *Human Rights and Corporate Wrongs: Closing the Governance Gap* (Cheltenham, Edward Elgar Publishing, 2015) 175.

[79] In 2009, an interim worldwide freezing injunction was granted to the claimants by the English High Court. Monterrico argued that there was no justification for freezing its assets, as the claimants did not have an arguable case against Monterrico. Justice Gloster confirmed that the claimants had a good arguable case against Monterrico and that company assets should remain frozen. *Guerrero v Monterrico Metals Plc* [2009] EWHC 2475; and *Guerrero v Monterrico Metals Plc* [2010] EWHC 3228.

[80] For a detailed review on the facts of the case, see C Kamphuis, 'Foreign Investment and the Privatization of Coercion: A Case Study of the Forza Security Company in Peru' (2012) 37 *Brooklyn Journal of International Law* 529, 542–48.

[81] *Pedro Emiro Florez Arroyo and others v Equion Energia Limited (formerly known as BP Exploration Company (Colombia) Limited* [2016] EWHC 1699 TCC.

[82] *Hudbay* (n 16).

The companies challenged the English courts' jurisdiction to hear this case given that the events occurred in Zambia. In 2016, the High Court ruled that the lawsuit may proceed, which gave rise to an application for appeal by the companies. In 2017, the Court of Appeal allowed the case to proceed in the UK, acknowledging that a duty of care may exist because Vedanta provided safety and environmental training, financially supported and exercised control over its Zambian subsidiary.[83] In 2019, the UK Supreme Court allowed the case to proceed to trial.

A similar case involves two communities in Nigeria that have filed lawsuits in the UK against Royal Dutch Shell and its Nigerian subsidiary. The lawsuits allege that oil spills from a subsidiary-operated pipeline caused water and land pollution. Royal Dutch Shell filed an application challenging UK jurisdiction over the lawsuits. The High Court of Justice declined jurisdiction over both lawsuits, ruling that the plaintiffs failed to demonstrate that the company had sufficient control over its Nigerian subsidiary.[84]

In 2018, the Court of Appeal upheld the High Court's judgment. The plaintiffs appealed to the Supreme Court which granted permission to appeal.[85] The plaintiffs formally filed their appeal in 2020. At the time of writing, the case has yet to be heard before the Supreme Court. This leaves open the question on whether UK courts will recognise legal responsibility of a parent corporation towards those impacted abroad by their foreign subsidiaries.

In 2020, the UK Court of Appeal did not recognise a legal responsibility of a parent corporation towards individuals overseas.[86] The case of *Kadie Kalma v African Minerals Ltd* arose out of two episodes of police brutality against civilians in Sierra Leone. The defendant was a UK-based corporation, African Minerals Ltd. They had significant iron ore operations in Sierra Leone and had given various support to the local police, such as vehicles and cash. The company argued that they had legitimate reasons to provide this support because without it, operating in the area would have been extremely perilous.

The Court of Appeal dismissed the case by agreeing with the trial judge that the required elements in negligence law of duty of care and causation were not established by the plaintiffs. The Court of Appeal decision confirms that companies engaging with local authorities to support their operations do not necessarily assume responsibility for the actions of those authorities.

[83] *Lungowe and Ors v Vedanta Resources Plc and Konkola Copper Mines Plc* [2017] EWCA Civ 1528.

[84] *Okpabi and others v Royal Dutch Shell Plc and Shell Petroleum Development Company of Nigeria Ltd* [2017] EWHC 89 (TCC); and *AAA and others v Unilever Plc and another* [2017] EWHC 371 (QB).

[85] Business & Human Rights Resource Centre, 'Shell Lawsuit (Re Oil Spills & Ogale & Bille Communities in Nigeria – Okpabi v Shell)' (2020), www.business-humanrights.org/en/shell-lawsuit-re-oil-spills-ogale-bille-communities-in-nigeria-okpabi-v-shell.

[86] *Kadie Kalma & Ors v (1) African Minerals Ltd. (2) African Minerals (SL) Ltd. (3) Tonkolili Iron Ore (SL) Ltd* [2020] EWCA Civ 144.

Finally, UK courts may assert jurisdiction over extraterritorial human rights abuses under the Brussels I Regulation, which makes it necessary for European Union Member States to accept jurisdiction in civil liability cases.[87] The Regulation specifically confers jurisdiction to member countries over corporate misconduct that occurs abroad, provided that the corporate defendant is domiciled in the forum jurisdiction.[88]

Currently, its import is uncertain given that at the time of writing, the UK is transitioning to exit from the European Union.[89] This leaves the future legal landscape for civil jurisdiction and the application of *forum non conveniens* quite unclear. The question of whether the application of *forum non conveniens* would be in conflict with the Brussels I Regulation has generated considerable debate.[90]

In the past, the European Court of Justice rejected *forum non conveniens* in *Group Josi Reinsurance Company SA v Universal General Insurance Company*.[91] Comparatively, the majority opinion in *Lubbe* did not address whether *forum non conveniens* has been swept aside. Subsequent UK case law has followed the Brussels I Regulation and not applied the *forum non conveniens* doctrine.[92] Some commentators have suggested that the doctrine of *forum non conveniens* is unlikely to be applied in the United Kingdom even in cases falling outside the Brussels I Regulation.[93] Thus, it is likely foreign citizens can bring claims against UK extractive sector companies in UK courts concerning conduct that occurs abroad. As the UK continues its transition to exit from the European Union, it will become clearer what effect Brussels I Regulation will have in the UK court system in the future.

[87] Council Regulation (EC) No 44/2001 of 22 December 2000 on jurisdiction and the recognition and enforcement of judgments in civil and commercial matters (Brussels I Regulation) [2001] OJ L12/1).

[88] *Ibid* Art 2(1). The Civil Jurisdiction and Judgments Act 1982 (c 27) implemented the Brussels Convention into UK law. Brussels Convention (1982) OJ L388/1. As one example in which a UK court applied the Brussels I Regulation relating to the overseas activity by a UK business enterprise, see *Yao Essaie Motto v Trafigura Ltd* [2011] EWHC 90206.

[89] Regulation (EU) No 1215/2012 of the European Parliament and of the Council of 12 December 2012 on jurisdiction and the recognition and enforcement of judgments in civil and commercial matters (recast) [2012] OJ L351/1. See also A Pertoldi and M McIntosh, 'Brexit under the Withdrawal Agreement: The Implications for Disputes' *Herbert Smith Freehills LLP* (22 January 2020).

[90] Skinner et al (n 9) 28; R Fentiman, 'Jurisdiction, Discretion and the Brussels Convention' (1993) 26 *Cornell International Law Journal* 59, 73; TC Hartley, 'The Brussels Convention and Forum Non Conveniens' (1992) 17 *European Law Review* 6; W Kennett, 'Forum non conveniens in Europe' (1995) 54 *Cambridge Law Journal* 552, 555.

[91] *Group Josi Reinsurance Company SA v Universal General Insurance Company* (Case C – 412/98) [2000] ECR I-5925. See also P Muchlinski, 'Corporations in International Litigation: Problems of Jurisdiction and the United Kingdom Asbestos Cases' (2001) 50 *International & Comparative Law Quarterly* 1, 12–13.

[92] See, eg, *Bodo Cmty v Shell Petroleum Dev Co of Nigeria* [2012] EWHC (QB) HQ11X01280 (Eng); *Motto & Others v Trafigura Ltd* [2011] EWHC 90201 (Costs) (Eng).

[93] Skinner et al (n 9) 40.

III. Australia

Australian courts have adopted a rather lenient approach in applying *forum non conveniens*. For example, in *Oceanic Sun Line Special Shipping Co v Fay*, an Australian citizen brought a negligence claim in Australian court for injuries sustained while he was a passenger on a cruise ship in Greek waters.[94] There was a strong case that the matter should be heard by Greek courts. Greece is where the defendant was incorporated, the vessel was registered, and both the port of destination and departure. Further, an exclusive jurisdiction clause was found in the ticket issued in Athens. However, the contract had been made before the clause was inserted, thus the clause was held to be inoperable as it did not form part of the contract. For these reasons, the defendant corporation moved to stay the proceedings on the grounds that Greece was the appropriate forum.

The High Court of Australia did not adopt the UK approach from *Spiliada* and instead devised its own test in which a claim will only be dismissed if the plaintiff is using the forum 'vexatiously, oppressively or in abuse of process'.[95] On account of this narrow standard, only claims brought to Australian court for abusive or oppressive reasons would be dismissed on the grounds of *forum non conveniens*. That was not found to be the case in *Oceanic Sun*, and thus the action proceeded in Australian court. In the minority decision, those justices disagreed, and wrote that the UK *Spiliada* decision should be followed, with the consequence that a stay should be granted and that Greece was the natural and most appropriate forum.

In *Voth v Manildra Flour Mills Pty, Ltd*, the plaintiffs brought a claim of professional negligence against an accountant in the United States.[96] Even though the High Court held that the United States was the most appropriate forum, they upheld the standard applied in *Oceanic Sun*.[97] The case was dismissed because Missouri was found to be the more appropriate forum. However, Australian courts kept the wide discretion granted in *Oceanic Sun* when it came to *forum non conveniens*. For instance, the rule in *Oceanic Sun* was again confirmed in *Regie Nationale des Usines Renault SA v Zhang*, in which the High Court confirmed that an action will only be dismissed on account of *forum non conveniens* if the Australian forum will bring about an injustice that is oppressive, prejudicial, or vexatious in terms of serious trouble and harassment.[98]

The above cases indicate that the plaintiff's choice of forum is given deference unless the plaintiff is bringing the suit in an oppressive or vexatious manner. Accordingly, it is very difficult for a defendant in Australia to have a claim against them dismissed for reasons of *forum non conveniens*.

[94] *Oceanic Sun Line Special Shipping Co v Fay* [1988] 165 CLR 197.
[95] *Ibid* 24.
[96] *Voth v Manildra Flour Mills Pty, Ltd* [1990] HCA 55.
[97] *Ibid* 26.
[98] *Regie Nationale des Usines Renault SA v Zhang* [2002] 210 CLR 491 521.

The Australian court's interpretation of *forum non conveniens* directly impacted at least one case pertaining to the extraterritorial conduct of an Australian mining enterprise. *Dagi v BHP Billiton* concerned an open-pit mine in Papua New Guinea, an archipelagic state located in the Western Pacific Ocean, north of Australia.[99] The mine, located near the Ok Tedi River, was primarily owned and controlled by BHP Billiton, one of the largest mining companies in the world. Through 1984 to 2013, discharge of mining waste breached into the environment, causing significant environmental damage. A group of local landowners filed a class action lawsuit against BHP and its Papua New Guinea subsidiary in Australian court in order to seek compensation for the long-term environmental contamination and its subsequent disruption to their way of life. In 2006, it was estimated that the mine discharged 80 million tons of contaminated mining waste for each year of operation. Further, the surrounding contamination left behind approximately 30 square kilometers of dead forest.[100]

On account of the flexible application of *forum non conveniens* adopted from the *Oceanic Sun*, *Voth* and *Regie Nationale* cases, the corporate defendants did not raise the issue of *forum non conveniens*. Instead, the defendants argued that the court should reject many of the claims on the grounds of the Mozambique rule, which essentially states that a court does not have jurisdiction to entertain an action concerning foreign land.[101] While the defendants were successful in having a portion of the claim struck given the Mozambique rule, the court allowed the claim for public nuisance and negligence to proceed. The class action was eventually settled for an estimated $28.6 million. As part of the settlement, a dredging operation was put in place and approximately $350–450 million was spent in an effort to rehabilitate the site around the mine.[102] It has been suggested that the financial compensation component of the settlement may have been even higher, at $40 million.[103] Some commentators believe that the settlement package was even more lucrative, and that the benefits from a ten per cent equity share in the mines were also given to the province in which the mine operates. One approximation was that the settlement was closer to $125 million.[104]

[99] *Dagi, Shackles, Ambetu and Maun v Broken Hill Proprietary Co and Ok Tedi Mining Ltd* [1997] 1 VR 428.

[100] S Kirsch, 'Cleaning up Ok Tedi: Settlement Favors Yonggom People' (1996) 4 *Journal of the International Institute*, hdl.handle.net/2027/spo.4750978.0004.104.

[101] *British South Africa Co v Companhia de Moçambique* [1893] AC 602 (HL); *Dagi* (n 99) 443.

[102] Amount cited is in US currency. O Webb, 'Kiobel, the Alien Tort Statute and the Common Law: Human Rights Litigation in This "Present, Imperfect World"' (2013) 20 *Australian International Law Journal* 131, 158.

[103] Amount cited is in Australian currency. L Enneking, *Foreign Direct Liability and Beyond: Exploring the Role of Tort Law in Promoting Corporate Social Responsibility and Accountability* (The Hague, Eleven International Publishing, 2012) 89.

[104] The commentator did not specify which currency is cited in this approximation. The commentator wrote that '[t]he Ok Tedi settlement package established a 90 million dollar trust fund for the people of the Fly River and another 35 million dollars for the communities in the most heavily impacted area of the lower Ok Tedi River'. Kirsch, 'Cleaning up Ok Tedi'.

More recently, a 2018 shareholder class action lawsuit has commenced in the Federal Court of Australia against BHP Billiton relating to the collapse of a dam at a mine in Brazil. This resulted in a 20 per cent fall in BHP Billiton shares that followed the 2015 disaster.[105] The company settled a similar lawsuit filed by US shareholders for $67 million. Previously, the company had agreed to a settlement with Brazilian authorities of over $5.3 billion for cleanup costs as well as a separate undisclosed amount paid as damages for the victims in Brazil.[106] No other actions have commenced in Australia relating to this incident. However, over 240,000 plaintiffs, including Brazilian municipalities and indigenous communities, filed a lawsuit in the UK against BHP Billiton seeking compensation for damages caused by the dam collapse.[107]

Altogether, these cases demonstrate that Australia has a lenient approach to exercising jurisdiction over extraterritorial matters. For this reason, it is somewhat surprising that Australian courts have not become the forum for more cases like *Dagi* involving extraterritorial litigation involving the extractive sector. The noted cases above appear to invite this type of litigation given the flexible application of *forum non conveniens* by Australian courts.

IV. Assessment of the Case Law

As explored in the previous chapter, US courts have permitted some claims arising from overseas activity to proceed, while others had been dismissed. The grounds used for allowing or dismissing claims vary from *forum non conveniens*, international comity and limitation of jurisdiction.

Of the reviewed federal cases decided based on *forum non conveniens*, only *Bhopal* and *Aguinda* were dismissed. In terms of international comity, *Talisman* and *Wiwa* proceeded in US court because both were of a commercial nature and did not interfere with the sovereign authority of the country where the disputed events took place. This is a very generous view in terms of what the federal court may consider when it comes to extraterritorial conduct. However, in *Daimler*, the most recent US Supreme Court case, general jurisdiction was denied.

Additionally, the application of the nationality principle in US case law does not confer the nationality of a parent corporation on its foreign subsidiaries. As such, US legislation does not apply extraterritorially to regulate foreign subsidiary corporations concerning human rights or environmental violations.

[105] Nine.com.au, 'Single BHP Samarco Class Action to Proceed' (18 December 2018), finance.nine.com.au/2018/12/18/14/03/single-bhp-samarco-class-action-to-proceed.

[106] The amounts cited are in US currency. Business & Human Rights Resource Centre, 'BHP Billiton & Vale Lawsuit (Re Dam Collapse in Brazil), www.business-humanrights.org/en/bhp-billiton-vale-lawsuit-re-dam-collapse-in-brazil.

[107] *Ibid.*

Further, the US Alien Tort Statute 1789 (ATS)[108] had been used by impacted individuals against multinationals to litigate alleged extraterritorial human rights violations. However, in a 2013 case the Supreme Court severely limited the statute on procedural grounds. That case was dismissed because of a lack of sufficient connection to the United States.

It appears that the case law is split when it comes to the question of whether foreign plaintiffs have the ability to bring claims in US courts concerning extraterritorial conduct. Adherence to the rules of civil procedure dominates the reasoning in these cases and is critical to the holdings. This is in contrast to a focus on favourable results for deserving plaintiffs and fairness as expressed in the legal systems of the UK and Australia. For these reasons, these US cases have generally not been decided in an explicit effort to promote socially desirable ends.

In Canada, the case law demonstrates that it is difficult for a foreign national to pursue a lawsuit in court against an extractive sector corporation for activities that occur abroad. Some recent cases such as *Hudbay*, *Tahoe* and *Nevsun* may suggest a growing promise that Canadian courts will provide a forum for redress to foreign claimants. However, none of these cases have been judicially tested on the merits, as they have simply passed procedural hurdles.

Canadian courts have traditionally been restrictive in their approach towards extending extraterritorial jurisdiction over the foreign activities of an extractive sector corporation. For instance, *Cambior*, *Anvil Mining Ltd* and *Piedra* are cases where the Court denied the ability to foreign claimants to bring claims for extraterritorial violations caused by the extractive sector.

In terms of the *Yaiguaje* decision on the recognition of foreign judgments, the Supreme Court ruled that the enforcement hearing of an Ecuadorian judgment may continue against a Canadian subsidiary of the energy giant Chevron. However, in the end the proceedings were halted because the Canadian subsidiary is a separate entity from its parent corporation. As such, Canadian courts refused to enforce the Ecuadorian judgment.

Enforcement of judgments is an important concern because it speaks to receiving a remedy as a consequence of a meritorious lawsuit. This is the crucial third pillar of the UN Guiding Principles.[109] In the case of environmental damage, it is about ensuring that defendants actually complete the required reclamation and remediation. Given the length and expense of litigation, winning a claim that cannot be enforced results in a pyrrhic victory of sorts.

The UK case law tends towards favouring the ability of foreign nationals to hold extractive sector corporations to account in the UK judicial system.

[108] Alien Tort Statute 1789 (28 USC § 1350).

[109] Special Representative on Business and Human Rights (SRBHR), 'United Nations Guiding Principles on Business and Human Rights: Implementing the United Nations "Protect, Respect and Remedy" Framework' (United Nations, 2011), www.ohchr.org/documents/publications/guidingprinciplesbusinesshr_en.pdf.

The courts are concerned with the plaintiffs' ability to obtain a fair and expedient trial and to retain competent legal counsel. This suggests that a results-based approach is used in the UK judicial system as court decisions emphasise the consequences of denying the plaintiffs' applications. These decisions focus on the desirability of the outcome, promoting fairness and empowering individuals as opposed to a rigid method concentrated on rule implementation. A primary concern is that the plaintiffs be given a reasonable opportunity to receive an adequate hearing.

Plaintiffs' cases have been allowed to proceed consistently with examples that include *Connelly*, *Lubbe*, *Guerrero* and *Vedanta*. In addition, the UK courts have permitted class action lawsuits in these cases, which suggest a commitment to providing a remedy to the full complement of plaintiffs instead of only a representative few. It is also noteworthy that after the plaintiffs were granted the ability to proceed to trial in both *Lubbe* and *Guerrero*, a settlement was reached. While proceeding to a hearing is a benefit to plaintiffs, the achievement of consequential results such as a settlement suggests that there is utility in bringing legal claims arising from the extraterritorial conduct of the extractive sector. However, a settlement is a negotiated agreement as opposed to a judicially granted remedy. It does not ostensibly indicate that the plaintiffs have achieved their desired result. This raises the question of whether accessibility to the courts is sufficient for those impacted by the overseas conduct of the extractive sector.

In contrast, Australian courts have taken a very flexible approach in exercising jurisdiction over matters that occur overseas in the extractive sector. The case law demonstrates that it is possible to receive a remedy in Australian courts for violations in the extractive sector. This finding should be tempered with the consideration that only one such case, *Dagi*, has achieved this result. It is possible that more cases have not been brought for reasons outside the scope of this analysis such as access to legal aid and the availability of skilled counsel willing to take on this genre of claims.

It should be noted that the important question reviewed in the case law from these various countries is whether or not the court took jurisdiction over claims against parent corporations. In this way, the outcome and the rules the court applies, such as limitations of jurisdiction and *forum non conveniens*, were the focus of this analysis. There are other litigation factors, often external to a court's decision, including legal costs and access to counsel that impact the viability of lawsuits. These factors are not considered in this review as they are outside of the court's analysis and application of the law.

Some commentators suggest that the implementations of legal rules are meaningless in a practical sense if corporate defendants are able to evade compliance with judicial remedies.[110] In other words, effectiveness should be defined by

[110] For an example, see Amnesty International, 'Injustice Incorporated: Corporate Abuses and the Right to a Remedy' (7 March 2014) 196–97, www.amnesty.org/en/documents/POL30/001/2014/en.

economic, social and financial outcomes as opposed to a narrow emphasis on legal outcomes. While there is utility in this approach, the primary focus of this chapter was to determine whether these jurisdictions have courts that are permissible and accommodate claims raised by foreign communities impacted by the extractive sector. It is a question of willingness to adjudicate claims with plaintiff-friendly outcomes, rather than an assessment of how successful cases lead to implementation of desirable objectives such as protection of the environment and human rights.

While the UK and Australian case law appears promising for those desiring to access their legal systems for disputes that occur abroad, it should be noted that only a few cases have proceeded and subsequently been settled between the parties. Unlike a judicially decided remedy, a settlement does not necessarily indicate that the plaintiff has achieved their desired result. This raises the question of whether accessibility to the courts is sufficient for those impacted by the overseas conduct of the extractive sector.

Simply removing the procedural barriers that prevent foreign disputes from being heard in the United States and Canada is not an appealing option. The barriers are designed to prevent the clogging of judicial systems with cases that belong in other forums and do not impact the particular jurisdiction or its citizens in a way that justifies the expending of limited resources. Further, these procedural rules prevent plaintiffs from forum shopping by picking a judicial system merely to gain a perceived advantage. As a result, the case law suggests that a judicial approach in the home state of a parent corporation is not an optimal solution for those impacted by the overseas conduct of the extractive sector.

Despite a few of examples in Australia and the United Kingdom of cases that resulted in a settlement, domestic courts are replete with procedural rules that challenge the ability of plaintiffs to bring lawsuits concerning extraterritorial conduct in the home state of an extractive sector corporation. This is one reason plaintiffs may seek assistance from a non-judicial grievance mechanism in seeking a remedy.

6

Utilising State-based and Civil Society Sponsored Mechanisms

Using existing principles of law as a basis of liability in US, UK, Canadian and Australian courts has not provided an effective remedy to victims of extra-territorial conduct in the extractive sector. This is primarily on account of numerous procedural and substantive limitations that prevent home state courts from asserting jurisdiction over foreign matters.

An alternative solution to this problem is the enactment of regulation, such the creation of judicial or non-judicial grievance mechanisms that provide a remedy to those who are negatively impacted by the extractive sector. The enactment of regulation can be interpreted as the development of policies that implement special laws that cast domestic regulation for extraterritorial conduct.

The laws and mechanisms that will be reviewed in this chapter include legislative attempts in the US, UK, Canada and Australia aimed at curbing the overseas human rights and environmental violations by their extractive sectors. This includes regulation that has been implemented and mere attempts at regulation.

State-based and non-state-based grievance mechanisms can take on a variety of forms. For example, Australia had a civil society sponsored non-judicial process for holding corporations to account, referred to as the self-styled Oxfam Australia's Mining Ombudsman (AMO). In 2009, Canada statutorily created a state-based mechanism known as the Corporate Social Responsibility (CSR) Counsellor. In 2018, it was replaced by the office of the Canadian Ombudsperson for Responsible Enterprise (CORE).

In comparison to Australia and Canada, the UK and US have not seen the creation of quasi-judicial bodies for the consideration of claims against extractive sector corporations for extraterritorial conduct. Further, the UK does not have a statutory framework such as the US Alien Tort Statute 1789 (ATS).[1]

The purpose of Part II of the book is to explore various strands of home state regulation aimed at governing the extractive sector's international conduct.[2]

[1] Alien Tort Statute 1789 (28 USC § 1350).

[2] The UK and US do not have a specific non-judicial programme or office that is representative of home state regulation concerning the foreign conduct of multinationals. For this reason, these

The findings demonstrate that state-based grievance mechanisms have not provided an effective remedy in preventing abuses caused by the extractive sector. These findings serve as an indictment of the regulatory attempts in the US, UK, Canada and Australia. In each case, there has been consistent opposition to home state regulation concerning the extractive sector. However, at least one civil society sponsored mechanism, the AMO, has had mixed success in its attempts at facilitating a remedy for those impacted by the extractive sector.

Generally speaking, civil society groups support the regulation of corporations by states. The analysis highlights the prominent involvement of civil society actors in facilitating a remedy for communities and individuals impacted by the extraterritorial conduct of the extractive sector. This leads to the consideration of whether effective state-based regulation should include an expansive role for civil society actors in representing or mediating between impacted parties and the extractive sector. Further, these findings serve as guidance in the proposal for a non-judicial grievance mechanism that is outlined in chapter seven.

The analysis in the next two chapters relies heavily on secondary sources from state-based dispute resolution systems and civil society-run complaint mechanisms.[3] The various reports include information on the local communities' cultural understandings of these institutions. This is quite different from judicial decisions, which tend to ignore, or simply not report, information on social or cultural reactions to the court system.

Given the lack of available literature on these cases from state-based and civil society-run dispute resolution mechanisms, most of the information gathered comes directly from these organisations, and thus it may lack objective creditability. Nevertheless, it is important to look at these reports to generate theories and hypotheses about the way in which non-judicial mechanisms regulate the extractive sector.

As such, the analysis in this chapter employs what has been described as a form of qualitative comparative law in looking at civil society and state-based institution reports. This particular method allows for the inclusion of actors' social experiences and cultural understandings of institutions that engage in dispute resolution between impacted communities and the extractive sector.[4]

countries are not included as part of this analysis. There is a European Ombudsman which deals with complaints against EU administration, EU Member States and EU private entities such as corporations. However, to launch a complaint one must be an EU citizen. As such, it does not serve as a dispute resolution mechanism for those outside the EU to bring complaints against the extractive sector. The European Ombudsman website is accessible at www.ombudsman.europa.eu/en/home.

[3] I consider closing reports, interim reports and field visit reports from Canada's CSR Counsellor. I also look at reports from Oxfam Australia's Mining Ombudsman. I did not look at Oxfam cases which began before 2000 because they predate the ombudsman service.

[4] M Cohen, 'Ex Ante Versus Ex Post Deliberations: Two Models of Judicial Deliberations in Courts of Last Resort' (2014) 62 *The American Journal of Comparative Law* 401, 405.

I. Failing Solutions

Legislation directed at the regulation of extractive sector corporations has been attempted without success in the US, UK, Canada and Australia. For instance, a 2006 proposed bill in the United States would have forced companies operating overseas to implement a specified Corporate Code of Conduct regarding a safe and healthy workplace and internationally recognised environmental, human rights, worker rights and core labour standards.[5] The bill failed upon a referral to a committee of Congress. In 2003, a similar bill was developed in the UK that promoted corporate responsibility, however it was not approved.[6]

Bill C-300 was introduced in Canadian Parliament in 2009.[7] It would have made Canadian mining companies subject to withdrawal of government support if their environmental and human rights performance abroad violated international standards. Bill C-300 was not passed into law due in part to opposition by industry.[8]

There has also been proposed legislation that would permit non-Canadian citizens to litigate extraterritorial tort claims that arise from violations of international law in Canada's Federal Court.[9] The defendants to these lawsuits could be Canadian and non-Canadian corporations. The proponents of the bill expressly suggest that it is meant to mirror the US ATS.[10] In 2016, a private member's bill was introduced to this effect. In a parliamentary system, such bills rarely become law, as was this case when this bill was not adopted. In 2019, a revival of the bill was before the Parliament of Canada, but similar to its previous iteration, it did not pass into law.[11]

The Australian Senate also introduced legislation in 2001 that would have imposed standards on the conduct of Australian extractive sector corporations that undertake business activities in other countries.[12] However, the Government determined the bill was unnecessary and unworkable.[13]

[5] Corporate Code of Conduct Act HR 5377 109th Congress (2006).

[6] J Lux, SS Thorsen and A Meisling, 'The European Initiatives' in R Mullerat (ed), *Corporate Social Responsibility: The Corporate Governance of the 21st Century*, 2nd edn (Alphen aan den Rijn, Kluwer Law International, 2011) 346.

[7] Bill C-300, Corporate Accountability of Mining, Oil and Gas Corporations in Developing Countries Act, 40th Parliament, 3rd Session (2009).

[8] K Keenan, 'Commentary. Desperately Seeking Sanction: Canadian Extractive Companies and their Public Partners' (2013) 34 *Canadian Journal of Development Studies* 111.

[9] Bill C-323, An Act to Amend the Federal Courts Act (International Promotion and Protection of Human Rights) 41st Parliament, 1st Session (2011).

[10] N Milanovic, 'A Canadian Alien Tort Statute? A Brief History of the International Promotion and Protection of Human Rights Act' (Universal Jurisdiction and Canadian Civil Courts: Strategic Directions Conference, 2008).

[11] Bill C-331, An Act to amend the Federal Courts Act (international promotion and protection of human rights) 42nd Parliament, 1st Session (2019).

[12] M Schwartz, 'Legally Mandated Self-Regulation: The Potential of Sentencing Guidelines' in W Cragg (ed), *Ethics Codes, Corporations, and the Challenge of Globalization* (Cheltenham, Edward Elgar Publishing, 2005) 294.

[13] *Ibid.*

These initiatives demonstrate the difficulty in attempting to bring reform by proposing fresh legislative measures to govern the foreign conduct of the extractive sector. In short, it is not realistic to expect the adoption of legislation as a cure to the concern with abuses by multinationals. These multinationals have been described by one Canadian politician as 'some bad apples'.[14] Despite these failures of attempted state-based regulation, there have been examples of grievance mechanisms that provide limited success in holding multinationals to account for overseas conduct. For instance, Australia and Canada have utilised non-judicial processes for holding corporations to account.

The following is a review of these mechanisms to explore whether the various forms of regulation represent effective models for governing the foreign conduct of the extractive sector. A leading theme in the review is the involvement of civil society actors. The review will demonstrate that civil society groups have taken on various roles from representing plaintiffs, mediating disputes, to advocating for home state regulation over the extraterritorial conduct of the extractive sector.

II. Canada: Office of the CSR Counsellor

Plaintiffs have experienced tremendous difficulty in attempting to hold multinational corporations to account for extraterritorial conduct in Canadian courts. This may be one reason lawmakers in Canada have developed non-judicial processes to regulate the Canadian extractive sector for human rights and environmental concerns in overseas operations. For instance, a committee report of the House of Commons found that mining activities by Canadian corporations operating in some developing countries have had adverse effects on local communities and the environment.[15] The committee report suggested that these corporations should endorse 'internationally agreed-upon corporate social responsibility standards'.[16] The committee report called on the Government to establish clear legal norms to ensure that Canadian mining companies are held accountable for environmental and human rights violations.

In responding to the committee report, the Government argued against the use of binding arbitration or other legal processes for compelling CSR on Canadian extractive sector companies.

[14] Open Parliament, 'An Act to Amend the Federal Courts Act (International Promotion and Protection of Human Rights)' (5 October 2011), openparliament.ca/bills/41-2/C-323/.

[15] S Seck, 'Home State Responsibility and Local Communities: The Case of Global Mining' (2008) 11 *Yale Human Rights and Development Law Journal* 177, 177–80.

[16] The Standing Committee on Foreign Affairs and International Trade, 'Fourteenth Report: Mining in Developing Countries' Parliament of Canada (2005), www.parl.gc.ca/content/hoc/Committee/381/FAAE/Reports/RP1961949/FAAE_Rpt14/FAAE_Rpt14-e.pdf.

The Government's response rejected many of the findings in the committee report given that, in their view, CSR was still an inchoate concept.[17] The doctrine of *forum non conveniens* was cited in the Government's response to suggest that Canadian law should not interfere with activities that occur in other jurisdictions. Further, the Government favoured market-based incentives compared to prescriptive law reform concerning CSR. As a result, the Government endorsed non-binding mechanisms for resolving CSR disputes that would not involve Canadian courts.

One recommendation the Government adopted from the committee report was to have public consultations on the issue of Canadian extractive sector companies impacting foreign communities and the environment. Public hearings took place across the country in 2006. Participants from civil society organisations recommended that the Government use criminal and civil liability regulation to enforce compliance by foreign operations of Canadian extractive sector companies with CSR best practices. Other participants, notably from industry, suggested that voluntary guidelines were sufficient.[18] In 2007, the National Roundtables on Corporate Social Responsibility reported the findings of this consultation. They concluded that the Government should set standards of CSR for Canadian extractive sector companies operating abroad in line with the International Finance Corporation Standards of the World Bank and other frameworks.[19]

In 2009, the Government of Canada unveiled its CSR Strategy for the Canadian International Extractive Sector.[20] It was released in part as a reaction to the near passage of a private member's bill, Bill C-300, that would have made Canadian mining corporations operating in developing countries and benefiting from the financial support of the Canadian Government subject to withdrawal of funding if its environmental and human rights performance abroad violated international standards.[21] The International Finance Corporation of the World Bank and the Overseas Private Investment Corporation of the United States apply similar requirements.

[17] Government of Canada, 'Mining in Developing Countries – Corporate Social Responsibility: The Government's Response to the Report of the Standing Committee on Foreign Affairs and International Trade' (2005), www.parl.gc.ca/HousePublications/Publication.aspx?Mode=1&Language=E&DocId=2030362&File=0.

[18] S Seck, 'Canadian Mining Internationally and the UN Guiding Principles on Business and Human Rights' (2011) 49 *Canadian Yearbook of International Law* 51, 60–61.

[19] National Roundtables on Corporate Social Responsibility and the Canadian Extractive Industry in Developing Countries, 'Advisory Group Report' (2007), web.archive.org/web/20110706185530/http://www.mining.ca/www/media_lib/MAC_Documents/Publications/CSRENG.pdf.

[20] Foreign Affairs, Trade and Development Canada, 'Building the Canadian Advantage: A Corporate Social Responsibility (CSR) Strategy for the Canadian International Extractive Sector' (2009), www.international.gc.ca/trade-agreements-accords-commerciaux/topics-domaines/other-autre/csr-strat-rse-2009.aspx?lang=eng.

[21] R Janda, 'Note: Act Respecting Corporate Accountability for the Activities of Mining, Oil or Gas in Developing Countries [Bill C-300]: Anatomy of a Failed Initiative' (2010) 6 *McGill International Journal of Sustainable Development Law and Policy* 97.

As part of this CSR strategy, the office of the CSR Counsellor was established.[22] Marketa Evans held the position until she resigned in October 2013. In March 2015, Jeffrey Davidson was appointed as her replacement. The office closed in 2018 and was replaced by the CORE.

The CSR Counsellor was not Canada's first attempt to regulate the social and environmental actions of corporations operating abroad. There are two government-backed agencies that provide a venue for dispute resolution concerning foreign operations of Canadian companies: 1) Canada's National Contact Point (NCP) for the Organisation for Economic Co-operation and Development (OECD), and 2) the Export Development Compliance Officer.

The implementation of a NCP is compulsory for Member States of the OECD that adhere to the OECD Guidelines. The purpose of an NCP is to provide a process for dealing with complaints against multinational corporations from that particular Member State. In this way, NCPs are responsible for promoting and implementing the OECD Guidelines.

The utility of the OECD NCP in Canada has been questioned. For example, one commentator noted that it 'handles very few cases in number'.[23] To illustrate this point, Canada's NCP has operated for 24 years and has received 21 complaints, only seven of which have been concluded.[24]

Usually, sanctions are not imposed by Canada's NCP, with one notable exception. In 2014, the Canadian NCP levied sanctions against China Gold International Resources Corp Ltd, a subsidiary of a Chinese state-owned extractive company.

China Gold is incorporated in Canada with its head office in British Columbia. A Canadian civil society group, the Canada Tibet Committee, submitted the complaint on behalf of impacted communities in Tibet. It was alleged that China Gold's labour, health and safety practices were below the benchmarks set out in the OECD Guidelines.

Sanctions by Canada's NCP were issued on account of China Gold's refusal to participate in the NCP process.[25] The impact of the sanctions was that China Gold became ineligible for advocacy on behalf of the Canadian Government such as letters of support and participation in Canadian Government trade missions. The final statement that outlined the findings of Canada's NCP was also made public, possibly leading to reputational harm for China Gold.

[22] Order-in-Council, Privy Council Number: 2009-0422 (2009).

[23] M Kerr, C Pitts and R Janda, *Corporate Social Responsibility: A Legal Analysis* (Markham, LexisNexis Canada Inc, 2009) 450.

[24] M Torrance, 'Remedying Human Rights: From the International, Regional and Domestic Status Quo to Future Innovations' (Human Rights Law and the Extractive Industries, Rocky Mountain Mineral Law Foundation, February 2016) 7.

[25] Global Affairs Canada, 'Final Statement on the Request for Review Regarding the Operations of China Gold International Resources Corp. Ltd., at the Copper Polymetallic Mine at the Gyama Valley, Tibet Autonomous Region' (Government of Canada, 2015), www.international.gc.ca/trade-agreements-accords-commerciaux/ncp-pcn/statement-gyama-valley.aspx?lang=eng.

Some commentators have argued that because the parent company was a state-owned enterprise, it did not need any Canadian Government support and thus, the sanctions were hollow.[26] At the time of writing, this is the only decision where Canada's NCP has imposed consequences, although they have threatened to impose sanctions in an ongoing case if constructive engagement between the parties and Canada's NCP falters.[27]

Similarly, there are also indications that the Export Development Compliance Officer (EDC Officer) has not been effective in resolving disputes between Canadian corporations and adversely affected parties. Out of 23 complaints from 2002 to 2009, only six fell within the EDC Officer's mandate.[28] The ineffectiveness of Canada's NCP and the EDC Officer in dealing with Canadian companies and impacted communities was likely one of the reasons the Federal Government instituted the office of the CSR Counsellor.

In building the CSR Counsellor's complaint process, several other third-party conflict resolution mechanisms were examined, including the NCPs, the AMO in Australia and the World Bank Group's Compliance Advisor Ombudsman.[29]

The procedure for submitting a dispute to the CSR Counsellor was quite simple. An individual, group or community that is adversely affected by the activities of a Canadian extractive sector corporation in its operations outside Canada may submit complaints. Canadian extractive sector corporations that believe they have become the subject of unfounded allegations could also submit requests for review.[30] Once a complaint was submitted, the CSR Counsellor advised stakeholders on the implementation of the performance guidelines.

Prior to 2014, these performance guidelines included the Performance Standards of the World Bank, the Voluntary Principles, the Global Reporting Initiative (GRI) and the OECD Guidelines, all of which deal with CSR concerns.[31] As part of its 2014 CSR strategy, the Federal Government added the OECD Due Diligence Guidance on Responsible Supply Chains of Minerals from

[26] S Imai, L Gardner and S Weinberger, '"The Canada Brand": Violence and Canadian Mining Companies in Latin America' (2017) Osgoode Legal Studies Research Paper No 17/2017, 39, dx.doi.org/10.2139/ssrn.2886584.

[27] Global Affairs Canada, 'Final Statement of the Canadian National Contact Point – Banro Corporation and a Group of Former Employees' (Government of Canada, 2017), www.international.gc.ca/trade-agreements-accords-commerciaux/ncp-pcn/statement-banro.aspx?lang=eng.

[28] Export Development Canada, '2009 Compliance Officer's Annual Report on Third Party Complainants' (2009), www19.edc.ca/english/docs/compliance_officer_report_e.pdf.

[29] Global Affairs Canada, 'A Report on the Visit of the World Bank Group's Compliance Advisor Ombudsman (CAO) to Toronto' (Government of Canada, 2012), www.international.gc.ca/csr_counsellor-conseiller_rse/publications/cao_rep-rap_cao-2012-01.aspx?lang=eng.

[30] Global Affairs Canada, 'The Review Process' (Government of Canada, 2013), www.international.gc.ca/csr_counsellor-conseiller_rse/review_process-processus_examen.aspx?lang=eng.

[31] On Common Ground Consultants Inc, 'Report for the Mining Association of Canada's International Social Responsibility Committee' (January 2012) 20, oncommonground.ca/wp-content/uploads/2012/07/Final-MAC-Roundtables-Report-_December-21-2011_-_3_5.pdf.

Conflict-Affected and High-Risk Areas (OECD Minerals Policy) and the UN Guiding Principles to these performance guidelines.[32]

These guidelines purport to regulate multinational corporate conduct. They do not create any civil or criminal liability for an offending or uncooperative corporate respondent. Nevertheless, surveying these international guidelines is an important undertaking because they have been identified as the criteria by which the Federal Government determines whether a multinational corporation operating abroad is in compliance with its obligation towards impacted communities. Further, it is important to review the content of these performance guidelines, as under my proposal for reforming the office of the CORE, these guidelines will continue to form the basis for allegations of wrongdoing by extractive sector corporations. The main difference under my proposal is that these guidelines will be transformed from voluntary norms to baseline requirements. The CORE may utilise these guidelines for the purpose of assessing financial liability against offending corporations. The following is a review of these performance guidelines except for the UN Guiding Principles which are set out in detail at the beginning of chapter eight.

A. World Bank Group's Performance Standards

The World Bank provides financial backing for projects in developing nations through its private sector arms, the International Finance Corporation (IFC) and the Multinational Investment Guarantee Agency (MIGA).[33] The IFC affects access to capital by providing loans, equity partnerships and other financial instruments, whereas the MIGA provides insurance and guarantees for those investments. Beginning in the 1990s, IFC and MIGA-funded projects began facing increasing criticism for adverse human rights impacts. In response, the World Bank

[32] Global Affairs Canada, 'Doing Business the Canadian Way: A Strategy to Advance Corporate Social Responsibility in Canada's Extractive Sector Abroad' (Government of Canada, 2014), www.international.gc.ca/trade-agreements-accords-commerciaux/topics-domaines/other-autre/csr-strat-rse.aspx?lang=eng.

[33] Investment law as a nexus between global trade and social policy has been cited as a means to improve multinational corporation accountability. The World Bank, the International Monetary Fund and the World Trade Organization have developed strategies to combat corporate human rights abuses. The academic literature concerning these institutions is vast and extensive and merits a project in its own right. Although it would be necessary in other settings to consider the role of these institutions in regulating extractive sector corporations, I have restricted my analysis to the World Bank because it is actively engaged in financing extractive projects in developing nations and that leverage can be used to promote corporate accountability. G Uriz, 'The Application of the World Bank Standards to the Oil Industry: Can the World Bank Group Promote Corporate Responsibility?' (2002) 28 *Brooklyn Journal of International Law* 77, 80. Moreover, the World Bank has an ombudsman office that impacted communities can access for redress of alleged human rights abuses by multinational corporations that are backed by World Bank financing. The World Bank ombudsman office is a similar structure to Canada's CSR Counsellor. Thus, the World Bank ombudsman office is a fitting mechanism to contrast with the CSR Counsellor in regulating the human rights and environmental record of Canadian extractive sector corporations.

developed social and environmental safeguards that provided guidelines for environmental protection, proper treatment of Indigenous peoples and workplace health and safety. These requirements were placed on the borrower and there was little oversight by the IFC or MIGA. Further, these safeguards were also criticised for failing to adequately address human rights concerns in a comprehensive fashion.[34] In 2006, the IFC expanded upon the social and environmental safeguards by adopting the Performance Standards and the IFC Policy on Environmental and Social Sustainability (IFC Policy), which were both updated in 2012.[35] In order to obtain funding in these programmes, investors and their proposed projects are required to demonstrate compliance with the Performance Standards and the IFC Policy. It is recommended by the IFC that borrowers create environmental and social management systems to implement the Performance Standards. The Performance Standards are unique among international instruments in that they are backed up through formal contractual sanctions.[36] They have become the most widely recognised instrument for managing social and environmental risks in investment projects occurring in the developing world. For instance, following the Performance Standards is a requirement for banking institutions that adhere to the Equator Principles, which is a risk management framework for project financing.[37] Additionally, the Performance Standards have broad application, as the credit agencies of all OECD member countries endorse them.[38]

There are several topics covered by the Performance Standards, including environmental and social risks, labour and working conditions, resource efficiency, pollution prevention, community health, safety, security, involuntary resettlement, biodiversity and protection for Indigenous peoples. Similar to the UN Guiding Principles, the Performance Standards require borrowers to conduct social and environmental due diligence on their foreign projects. However, the Performance Standards and IFC Policy do not specifically mention the Guiding Principles or its due diligence process.[39]

Under the IFC Policy, extractive sector projects are required to be assessed for social and environmental risks compared to the expected benefits. If the risks outweigh the benefits, the IFC will not support the project. The IFC Policy

[34] Compliance Advisor Ombudsman, 'Extracting Sustainable Advantage? A Review of How Sustainability Issues Have Been Dealt with in Recent IFC & MIGA Extractive Industries Projects' (April 2003) 36, www.cao-ombudsman.org/howwework/advisor/documents/FINALExtractiveIndustriesReviewReport.pdf, 36.

[35] International Finance Corporation World Bank Group, 'IFC Performance Standards on Environmental and Social Sustainability – Effective January 1, 2012'; International Finance Corporation World Bank Group, 'International Finance Corporation's Policy on Environmental and Social Sustainability' (1 January 2012).

[36] P Simons and A Macklin, *The Governance Gap: Extractive Industries, Human Rights, and the Home State Advantage* (Toronto, Routledge, 2014) 130–31.

[37] 'The Equator Principles July 2020' (2020), www.equator-principles.com.

[38] Simons and Macklin, *The Governance Gap* 132.

[39] Simons and Macklin (n 36) 138.

promotes transparency concerning payments made by the extractive industry to host governments by requiring borrowers to publicly disclose royalties, taxes and government profit sharing agreements. The IFC Policy also requires disclosure of significant contracts related to the principal investment for which funds are to be used.[40]

Both the IFC Policy and the Performance Standards require projects that may adversely impact local communities to have culturally appropriate grievance mechanisms.[41] Despite this obligation, a 2010 advisory report by the World Bank ombudsman found that just over half of borrowers subject to this requirement actually maintained a site-level grievance mechanism.[42] Even where borrowers had a functioning grievance mechanism, the ombudsman found that local community members were 'unaware of the existence of a complaints system, how to use it, who to contact, and how to follow up'.[43] Moreover, in cases where the borrower does not comply with the IFC Policy and Performance Standards, the practice of the IFC is to negotiate with the borrower until they are back in compliance.[44] Withdrawal of funding is only considered if the borrower fails to re-establish compliance.[45] For these reasons among others, some commentators have argued that the primary purpose of the Performance Standards and the IFC Policy is not to be a comprehensive system to address corporate human rights abuse; rather, it is a risk management tool, designed for the purpose of avoiding legal liability.[46]

As a final critique, many extractive sector companies are financed by equity, not debt, thus the Performance Standards and IFC Policy does not apply to their activities. Of those investors and proposed projects that are required to demonstrate compliance, there is little oversight by the IFC or MIGA as they rely on information provided directly from the borrower.

B. Voluntary Principles on Security and Human Rights

Another performance guideline of the CSR Counsellor is the Voluntary Principles. The Voluntary Principles were established in 2000 as a multi-stakeholder initiative between governments, the extractive sector and civil society organisations.

40 'IFC, 'Policy on Environmental and Social Sustainability' (n 35) 11–12.

41 This is addressed at several areas of the Performance Standards and IFC Policy. For example, see 'IFC, 'Policy on Environmental and Social Sustainability' (n 35) 3, para 12.

42 Compliance Advisor Ombudsman, 'Review of IFC Social and Environmental Performance Standards on Disclosure of Information' (May 2010) 14.

43 *Ibid.*

44 'IFC, 'Policy on Environmental and Social Sustainability' (n 35) 9–10, para 45.

45 As stated in the IFC Policy: 'Persistent delays in meeting these requirements can lead to loss of financial support from IFC.' 'IFC, 'Policy on Environmental and Social Sustainability' (n 35) 5, para 22.

46 Simons and Macklin (n 36) 130.

They were the result of an 11-month dialogue between the UK Foreign and Commonwealth Office, the US Department of State, major corporations in the extractive industry and representatives of civil society.[47]

The aim of the Voluntary Principles is to provide best practices for extractive sector companies invested in developing countries where private and public security forces may not observe the rule of law in dealing with local communities and workers. It is unsurprising that local security workers in developing nationals are often young men, not literate or trained in weaponry. They are typically underpaid, and in the extreme even malnourished.[48] Given these conditions, armed individuals may use their power to intimidate local communities and commit crimes against them.

The Voluntary Principles call on its member companies to use highly trained contractors for security services. In particular, the Voluntary Principles are important for companies operating in active conflict zones where protecting human rights and public safety is most challenging. They require member companies to ensure only reasonable force is used in protecting overseas facilities and to respect the exercise of basic labour rights such as freedom of association, peaceful assembly and collective bargaining.

On account of the Voluntary Principles, security arrangements should be transparent and human rights training provided to security forces. Companies should convey the high ethical standards they expect to the local government. They should actively consult with local communities about security and human rights concerns. Where possible, foreign companies should seek to employ private security providers that are representative of the local communities. If there is a potential violation of the Voluntary Principles, companies should push for a credible and transparent investigation by the local government that results in appropriate action.

The administration of the Voluntary Principles operates with an annual plenary of members and a steering committee made up of two members from each core group of industry, government and civil society organisations. Currently, its membership includes mainly OECD participants, with Columbia and Ghana as the only non-OECD members, and predominately large extractive sector companies. They have the ability to admit new members. There is also an internal complaint process for addressing alleged violations between members, but it is not available to the public and the only consequence for violating the principles is expulsion from the group.[49]

There are reporting requirements for corporate members to provide their human rights records and security risk assessment procedures to the Secretariat

[47] The content of the Voluntary Principles can be accessed at www.voluntaryprinciples.org/what-are-the-voluntary-principles.

[48] See Barrick Beyond Borders, 'In Conversation with Gare Smith' (October 2013), https://foleyhoag.com/-/media/files/foley%20hoag/other/gare-smith-beyond-borders-barrick.ashx?la=en.

[49] For a critique of the Voluntary Principles see Simons and Macklin (n 36) 122–30.

on an annual basis. Normally, this information does not become publicly available unless released by the company on a voluntary basis.[50] The reliance on self-reporting has been a cause of friction with civil society members. For instance, Oxfam America withdrew support from the Voluntary Principles because of their frustration at the lack of meaningful progress in developing independent assurance of member companies' annual reports.[51]

The Voluntary Principles were developed partially by the US and UK governments in collaboration with civil societies and companies, which suggests that these countries prefer corporate self-regulation techniques compared to public extraterritorial regulation. The Voluntary Principles incorporate provisions of international law. For instance, corporate members agree to promote international enforcement principles such as the UN Code of Conduct for Law Enforcement Officials and the UN Basic Principles on the Use of Force and Firearms. Additionally, according to the US Department of State, the Voluntary Principles reflect the UN Guiding Principles.[52] However, the Voluntary Principles suggest that local laws of the host state take precedence over applicable international norms.[53] A critical improvement would be requiring companies to obtain a written commitment from the host state government that they adhere to the Voluntary Principles as a condition of investment.

There is not a publicly available complaint mechanism set out in the Voluntary Principles, as it is left with companies to develop their own system for reporting and investigating allegations of human rights abuses. Thus, it suffers from the same deficiencies as similar international instruments in terms of transparency, effectiveness and accountability for corporate wrongdoing.

Without some form of mandatory participation or independent complaint process available to the public, the Voluntary Principles are limited in terms of encouraging extractive sector companies to respect human rights. As one exception, the Voluntary Principles may be useful for Canadian corporations on account of the Government's updated CSR strategy as extractive sector companies that follow the Voluntary Principles will be eligible for enhanced economic diplomacy.

[50] See, eg, British Petroleum, 'BP Annual Report on the Voluntary Principles on Security and Human Rights January to December 2012' (2013), www.bp.com/content/dam/bp/business-sites/en/global/corporate/pdfs/sustainability/group-reports/bp-report-to-the-voluntary-principles-plenary-2017.pdf.

[51] Business & Human Rights Resource, 'Oxfam Leaves Voluntary Principles for Security and Human Rights Multi-Stakeholder Initiative' (16 April 2013), business-humanrights.org/en/oxfam-leaves-voluntary-principles-for-security-and-human-rights-multi-stakeholder-initiative.

[52] A fact sheet from the US Department of State reports that: '[w]hile the duty to protect human rights rests with governments, businesses have a responsibility to respect human rights as outlined in the UN Guiding Principles on Business and Human Rights'. See US Department of State Bureau of Democracy, Human Rights and Labor, 'Voluntary Principles on Security and Human Rights. Fact Sheet' (20 December 2012), https://2009-2017.state.gov/j/drl/rls/fs/2012/202314.htm.

[53] P Simons, 'Corporate Voluntarism and Human Rights: The Adequacy and Effectiveness of Voluntary Self-Regulation Regimes' (2004) 59 *Industrial Relations* 1.

C. Global Reporting Initiative

The GRI is another performance guideline of the CSR Counsellor. It is an internationally-recognised voluntary reporting standard for business enterprises to enhance transparency and encourage market-based rewards for good CSR performance.[54] They are an emerging phenomenon in corporate voluntary CSR reporting and are an attempt to streamline protocols and provide consistency in the reports of corporations that purport to adopt industry best practices.[55] Initially in 1997, the GRI project was spearheaded by the Coalition for Environmentally Responsible Economics and the UN Environment Programme with the goal of producing standards for reporting on corporate environmental and social impacts.

By 2008, 79 per cent of the world's largest companies disclosed social and environmental data and 77 per cent of those used the GRI, according to the findings of one study.[56] Typically, the disclosure of environmental and social data is communicated through a CSR report. A CSR report is a document that a corporation publicly discloses that includes measurements and indicators of environmental and social performance. The accuracy and reliability of a company's CSR report is integral to the company to ensure that the company will be trusted by investors and the public.

In 2013, the GRI evolved with the development of G4 Sustainability Reporting Guidelines. The updated G4 recommends that companies report economic and social performance in an in-depth manner on issues regarding labour, human rights, stakeholder engagement, ethics and employee training.[57]

International instruments such as the GRI are based on the assumption that corporate self-reporting generates critical information for corporate stakeholders such as shareholders, creditors, employees, governments and the public. In analysing this information, these stakeholders can determine whether the corporation is accountable to the communities in which they operate, or conversely, whether they are not acting in a socially responsible manner.[58]

[54] Global Reporting Initiative (GRI), 'G4 Sustainability Reporting Guidelines: Implementation Manual' (2013), www.respect.international/g4-sustainability-reporting-guidelines-implementation-manual/. Note that the GRI Standards superseded the G4 Guidelines as of 2018. The aim and scope of the GRI Standards is largely the same as the G4 Guidelines.

[55] The GRI website is accessible at www.globalreporting.org.

[56] KPMG Unit for Corporate Governance in Africa, 'Carrots and Sticks: Promoting Transparency and Sustainability: An Update on Trends in Voluntary and Mandatory Approaches to Sustainable Reporting' (2008) 4, www.globalreporting.org/resourcelibrary/Carrots-And-Sticks-Promoting-Transparency-And-Sustainbability.pdf.

[57] GRI, 'Implementation Manual' (n 54).

[58] These types of metrics are also applied against countries. The Yale Center for Environmental Law & Policy has a biannual Environmental Performance Index that ranks countries on environmental issues in two broad policy areas: protection of human health from environmental harm and protection of ecosystems. 'Environmental Performance Index' (Yale Center for Environmental Law & Policy, 2018), epi.envirocenter.yale.edu.

One major shortcoming of the GRI is that corporations determine the level of materiality in reporting any significant fines and non-monetary sanctions they have incurred.[59] Thus, there are no objective standards to ensure that companies disclose consistently across an industry. The problem is that without consistency in reporting CSR information, a corporation may freely use the report to facilitate positive marketing as opposed to seriously reviewing social and environmental performance. Some have called this 'greenwashing'. By greenwashing, a corporation might increase profits or boost its brand through environmental rhetoric, but at the same time either pollute the environment, decline to spend money on the environment, or otherwise not honour its commitments to other stakeholders.[60]

If CSR reports are merely veiled corporate advertisements, then investors may be led to believe such policies carry more import then they actually achieve. The danger is that a corporation may treat a CSR report as a convenient form of self-serving promotion that is not judiciously followed. Arguably, the motive for producing and releasing CSR reports is to increase the value of the company through the promotion of corporate sustainable practices, as some studies suggest a positive correlation between CSR and financial success.[61] The GRI does not prevent corporations from using CSR reporting as a greenwashing tool.

Finally, given that the GRI is recognised as a performance indicator in Canada's updated CSR strategy, companies that report social and environmental indicators in accordance with the GRI will be eligible for enhanced economic diplomacy from the Canadian Government. While there may be market incentives for a corporation to follow the GRI, those incentives are purely voluntary from a regulatory standpoint.

D. OECD Guidelines for Multinational Enterprises

Currently, several transnational organisations, most notably the UN and the OECD, maintain guidelines for recommended business conduct. The OECD was the first to develop such guidelines. In 1976, they released the OECD Guidelines, which contains voluntary recommendations for multinational corporations. They were developed jointly by all the government members of the OECD to target

[59] GRI, 'Implementation Manual' (n 54) 131.

[60] MA Cherry and JF Sneirson, 'Beyond Profit: Rethinking Corporate Social Responsibility and Greenwashing After the BP Oil Disaster' (2010) 85 *Tulane Law Review* 985.

[61] For an overview on the literature and empirical evidence surrounding this linkage between sustainability and financial performance, see S Schaltegger and M Wagner, *Managing and Measuring the Business Case for Sustainability: Capturing the Relationship between Sustainability Performance, Business Competitiveness and Economic Performance* (Sheffield, Green Leaf Publishing, 2006).

multinational corporations. A key aspect of the OECD Guidelines is that as they are voluntary, they are not legally enforceable.[62]

The OECD Guidelines provide best practices consistent with applicable laws and internationally-recognised standards. They begin with the delineation of general policies encouraging multinational corporations to contribute to economic, social and environmental progress, with the aim of achieving sustainable development while respecting the human rights of those affected by business activities.

The OECD Guidelines have been updated five times since they were first adopted and cover areas such as the protection of the environment, employment, industrial relations, bribery, competition, taxation and human rights. They were most recently reviewed and updated in 2011 to incorporate additional human rights provisions and other principles aligned with the Guiding Principles, such as due diligence measures and responsible supply chain management.[63] They now provide guidance on specific criteria for corporations to disclose in corporate social responsibility reports[64] and include strong provisions on workers' rights, such as robust occupational health standards, abolition of abusive child labour practices and the general ability to unionise. However, some commentators have argued that more focus should be placed on the protection of women, the disabled and Indigenous rights under the revised OECD Guidelines.[65]

While the OECD Guidelines do not provide for independent monitoring, they do establish a process for dealing with complaints against multinational corporations. The process involves NCPs, which are located within OECD Member States and assigned with the task of promoting and implementing the OECD Guidelines. NCPs were first introduced in 1991 and today all OECD countries have NCP bodies.[66] Primarily, the NCP's role is to receive and assess complaints against multinational companies incorporated in its jurisdiction. They can consist of a single government official or be structured as an interdepartmental government group. They may also include representatives from other interested parties such as the private sector, unions and other members of civil society.[67]

The NCP acts in a gatekeeper capacity and has the discretion to decide whether a complaint requires further action or should be closed. If an NCP decides that the issue deserves further consideration, they may offer assistance to the parties in reaching a settlement.[68]

[62] OECD, 'The OECD Guidelines for Multinational Enterprises' (2011 edn) 17, www.oecd.org/dataoecd/56/36/1922428.pdf.

[63] This recommended human rights due diligence is similar, if not verbatim in many ways to the due diligence provisions of the UN Guiding Principles. JG Ruggie, *Just Business: Multinational Corporations and Human Rights* (New York, W. W. Norton & Company, 2013) 160–61.

[64] OECD, 'Guidelines for Multinational Enterprises' (n 62) 27.

[65] Simons and Macklin (n 36) 103.

[66] M Torrance, 'Remedying Human Rights' 7.

[67] OECD, 'Guidelines for Multinational Enterprises' (n 62) 33–35.

[68] B Choudhury, 'Beyond the Alien Tort Claims Act: Alternative Approaches to Attributing Liability to Corporations for Extraterritorial Abuses' (2005) 26 *Northwestern Journal International Law and Business* 41, 64.

There are no sanctions against multinational corporations for failing to obey the OECD Guidelines unless an individual state creates mandatory compliance provisions. At the time of writing, none of the OECD member countries have created mandatory provisions. However, as a step in this direction, as part of its 2014 CSR strategy, Canada has made cooperation with the country's NCP contingent upon receiving enhanced 'economic diplomacy' from the Canadian Government.[69] As another example, in the Netherlands, companies applying for financial support from the Dutch Government in their foreign operations must sign a declaration that they will adhere to the OECD Guidelines and accept recommendations from the Dutch NCP.[70]

There are several factors that detract from the effectiveness of the OECD Guidelines. First, corporate participation is entirely voluntary as there are no sanctions to levy against multinational corporations that fail to adhere to the OECD Guidelines or participate in an NCP complaint process. Second, all complaints are directed to a state-sponsored NCP. If the state is alleged to have participated, supported or overlooked the human rights violation, the NCP may have a conflict of interest in investigating its own government. Third, there are no appeal processes from the NCP. If the NCP cannot help the parties resolve their issue, the OECD Guidelines do not provide any further direction. Thus, if the NCP deems an issue to be meritless, victims have no further recourse under the OECD Guidelines. Fourth, there is inconsistency among NCPs in handling complaints. Part of this stems from the absence of a required timeframe for dealing with a dispute or central registry containing NCP cases.[71] The NCPs are also permitted to keep information exchanged through the complaint process confidential.[72] As such, the process is not transparent, as information pertaining to complaints may never be revealed to the public. It has been argued that with no public scrutiny, the 'procedure has little immediate impact on the behavior of specific companies'.[73]

As a result of the discussed issues, although the OECD Guidelines take a step forward in promoting corporate responsibility abroad, without some form of mandatory participation, appeal process, or independence of the NCP from that of the member government, the OECD Guidelines are limited from providing an effective model of regulating multinational corporations.

[69] Global Affairs Canada, 'Doing Business the Canadian Way' (n 32).

[70] Dutch Ministry of Foreign Affairs, 'Contribution by the Government of the Netherlands to the Renewed EU-Strategy for CSR' (2012) 2.

[71] On one hand, this offers the NCP flexibility in moving complaints forward. On the other, it allows some NCPs to proceed catatonically slow. P Feeney, 'Making Companies Accountable: An NGO Report on Implementation of the OECD Guidelines for Multinational Enterprises by National Contact Points' (October 2002) 2, www.oecd.org/dataoecd/16/37/2965489.pdf.

[72] OECD, 'Guidelines for Multinational Enterprises' (n 62) 27, 39 and 40.

[73] International Council on Human Rights Policy, 'Beyond Voluntarism: Human Rights and the Developing International Legal Obligations of Companies' (February 2002) 101, www.ichrp.org/files/reports/7/107_report_en.pdf.

Finally, the OECD has other policies applicable to multinational extractive sector corporations. The OECD Minerals Policy is a set of rules for how businesses are to prevent the sourcing of minerals where it may potentially lead to human rights abuses.[74] In particular, it is aimed at dealing with problems associated with certain minerals coming out of the Congo. It reflects aspects of businesses' responsibility to respect human rights as outlined in the Guiding Principles.[75]

In 2014, the OECD Minerals Policy was added as one of the listed performance guidelines that will be recognised by the CSR Counsellor's office. Thus, companies that follow the OECD Minerals Policy will be eligible for enhanced economic diplomacy according to the Canadian CSR strategy.[76] For those advocating that the OECD Minerals Policy is a positive development, adding it to the performance guidelines is desirable, as the Canadian Parliament has been unable to pass legislation aimed at implementing the directives of the OECD Minerals Policy.[77] Similar rules have also been developed for the US with Section 1502 of the US Dodd-Frank Act.[78] There were claims that this section may be repealed by legislation[79] or executive order.[80] However, legislative measures to this effect failed to pass through the US Senate.[81] At the time of writing, no action has been taken pursuant to an executive order. On could question whether the law is even being enforced as it has been suggested that the US Securities and Exchange Commission (SEC) appears to have ceased regulatory efforts on this front.

In sum, while some of the reviewed mechanisms, such as the World Bank and OECD Guidelines show some promise, on the whole, the international mechanisms do not exhibit any binding authority. For instance, a primary feature of the OECD and World Bank framework for resolving disputes is voluntary participation and the results are not legally enforceable against multinational corporations.

Thus, these various international mechanisms are voluntary and aspirational. Collectively, they do not create mandatory rules or provide sanctions for failure to

[74] The full name is the 'OECD Due Diligence Guidance on Responsible Supply Chains of Minerals from Conflict-Affected and High-Risk Areas'.

[75] Simons and Macklin (n 36) 101.

[76] Global Affairs Canada, 'Doing Business the Canadian Way' (n 32).

[77] Open Parliament, 'Bill C-486 (Historical) An Act respecting corporate practices relating to the extraction, processing, purchase, trade and use of conflict minerals from the Great Lakes Region of Africa', openparliament.ca/bills/41-2/C-486/.

[78] In 2012, the SEC recognised the OECD Minerals Policy as an appropriate guideline for corporations to follow in completing a conflict minerals report under section 1502 of the Dodd-Frank Wall Street Reform and Consumer Protection Act Pub L No 111-203, 124 Stat 1376 (2010).

[79] SP Boggs, 'Financial CHOICE Act Passes in the House – Would Repeal SEC Conflict Minerals Rule' *Lexology* (8 June 2017), www.lexology.com/library/detail.aspx?g=324964cb-19bc-4102-8bfa-63aaa27a620b.

[80] T Worstall, 'Trump's Executive Order to Repeal the Worst Law of the Year' *Forbes* (9 February 2017), www.forbes.com/sites/timworstall/2017/02/09/trumps-xo-to-repeal-the-worst-law-of-the-year-section-1502-of-dodd-frank-on-conflict-minerals/.

[81] M Butler, 'Why the Conflict Minerals Rule Refuses to Die' *Intelligize* (21 June 2018), www.intelligize.com/why-the-conflict-minerals-rule-refuses-to-die/.

abide by these voluntary measures. As such, they are not equipped to deal effectively with wrongdoing by extractive sector corporations operating in foreign countries.

The implementation of my proposal will operationalise these guidelines as instruments with legal effect. Under my proposal presented in Part III of this book, the CORE will be seized with the ability to financially penalise corporations that do not embrace these performance guidelines as part of their operations overseas.

III. History of Failure

The CSR Counsellor was not vested with any powers of enforcement. The office could not impose a remedy or issue a sanction against a party that fails to participate in its process and is entirely contingent on voluntary participation by both parties. A primary reason for this lack of authority was its reliance on international performance standards that are voluntary in approach.

From 2010 to 2013, almost all of the complaints filed with the CSR Counsellor ended with the corporate respondent refusing to participate in the process. Even those cases that proceeded failed to produce meaningful long-term results.

A telling example of the office's shortcomings was on display in the first case considered. In 2011, the CSR Counsellor received a request to review the operations of the Platosa mine, owned and operated by Excellon Resources Inc in Mexico. The complainants included Platosa workers represented by a Mexican trade union and a Mexican civil society organisation. According to the complainants, the company reported a potential theft of copper by its employees to the state police who, allegedly on the company's premises, beat several of the accused. None of the workers were charged in the theft. Further, it was alleged that workers who attempted to unionise were threatened, along with other various health and safety concerns. The complainants argued that these allegations were violations of the Voluntary Principles and the OECD Guidelines.[82]

As part of the review, the CSR Counsellor was permitted to visit the site and held numerous meetings with the mine's staff, local communities and company executives. After the CSR Counsellor received creditable evidence to support the claims of the complainants, the company decided against proceeding with the dispute resolution process, citing the best interest of the shareholders and company as a whole. As such, the file was closed. The closing report contains a forceful indictment by the CSR Counsellor against Excellon Resources for failing to

[82] Global Affairs Canada, 'Excellon was a mining company incorporated in British Columbia with a principal office in Toronto. 'File #2011-01-MEX: Office of the Extractive Sector CSR Counsellor's, Request for Review Closing Report' (Government of Canada, 2011), www.international.gc.ca/csr_counsellor-conseiller_rse/publications/2011-01-MEX_closing_rep-rap_final.aspx?lang=eng.

maintain a constructive dialogue with the CSR Counsellor and the complainants. In many ways, this case foreshadowed the fate of the CSR Counsellor's complaint process, as it became the norm for respondent companies to withdraw from review, thereby preventing the CSR Counsellor from investigating any further. It is also one of only a few cases where the CSR Counsellor was permitted to visit a project site and meet with staff and company officials as part of their review.

While some corporations have rejected mediation led by the CSR Counsellor for a variety of reasons as outlined below, others have embraced it. For instance, in the closing report concerning First Quantum Minerals, the CSR Counsellor wrote in a praising fashion that 'the company has consistently demonstrated its good faith efforts to deal with the issues'.[83] Local residents near the Guelb Moghrein copper-gold mine in Mauritania brought the complaint and alleged that the company used hazardous materials, engaged in excessive carbon emission, caused groundwater contamination and violated basic labour standards. This case was the only one to reach 'informal mediation' with the CSR Counsellor. However, Quantum Minerals had an existing internal grievance mechanism to receive complaints from the community that was aligned with International Finance Corporation best practice guidelines and had been used to settle other complaints. For this reason, the CSR Counsellor encouraged the complainants to first bring the matter to Quantum's internal grievance mechanism before a more formal review could proceed. The company also agreed to consider hiring an independent local convener to raise awareness about the site level grievance process in a culturally appropriate manner.

While little, if anything, was accomplished in the Quantum Minerals review, it proved to be a high-mark for the CSR Counsellor in terms of company participation and acknowledgment of the CSR Counsellor's role in dispute resolution. In the cases that followed, the CSR Counsellor did not receive the same level of cooperation from the corporate respondents. For instance, the CSR Counsellor received a request for review pertaining to alleged impacts on glaciers caused by a copper mining project in Argentina.[84] The company initially responded that these issues dealt directly with environmental law, which is exclusively a matter for the Argentinian Government to regulate. The CSR Counsellor clarified that their mandate was to deal with issues connected with the Performance Standards of the World Bank and not Argentinian law. Additionally, the company was incorporated in the United States and it was not clear if they could be subject to a review by the CSR Counsellor. On account of the company's identification of Toronto, Canada

[83] Global Affairs Canada, 'File #2011- 02-MAU: Office of the Extractive Sector CSR Counsellor's, Request for Review Closing Report' (Government of Canada, 2011), www.international.gc.ca/csr_counsellor-conseiller_rse/publications/2011-02-MAU_closing_report-rapport_final.aspx?lang=eng.

[84] Global Affairs Canada, 'Request for Review Closing Report File #2012-03-ARG' (Government of Canada, 2012), www.international.gc.ca/csr_counsellor-conseiller_rse/publications/2012-03-ARG_closing_report-rapport_final.aspx?lang=eng.

as the location of its head office, the CSR Counsellor found that the company had a sufficient Canadian interest for the purposes of its mandate.

The case is also unique because the complainants were two civil society organisations in their own right representing an environmental cause.[85] Nevertheless, the CSR Counsellor found that these organisations met the necessary requirements to bring a complaint. Arguably, this was a rather liberal interpretation of the CSR Counsellor's mandate given that the complainants were not groups or communities living close to an extractive sector project. The applicable law that created the CSR Counsellor specifies that it can accept requests for review from individuals, groups or communities that it reasonably believes is or may be adversely affected by a Canadian extractive sector corporation outside of Canada.[86] However, New Gold Inc rejected the notion that these non-governmental organisations (NGOs) were stakeholders of the company and for this reason, among others, they decided to withdraw from the process.

In 2013, the CSR Counsellor received another request from inhabitants of a small town in Mexico with the assistance of the Mexican/Canadian civil society group.[87] The request related to a mining project owned by New Gold. Representatives from the CSR Counsellor visited the site and met with New Gold management and staff, mine personnel, community members and other stakeholders. However, the CSR Counsellor failed to deliver a closing report and it is unclear if the review continued or resulted in any substantive action.

The next case brought to the CSR Counsellor also concerned a mining project in Argentina.[88] The complainants were representatives of several Indigenous communities living near an open-pit mine owned by Silver Standard Resources. Their primary concerns related to environmental impacts and community engagement. For instance, it was alleged that as a result of heavy rains and flooding, it was a common occurrence that the rivers flowing through the nearby communities became polluted with toxic run-off from the mine site and cause negative impacts to the local inhabitants downstream. It was claimed that when community representatives raised concerns with the company, they were not adequately addressed. As one example, it was claimed that water testing had been carried out after one such incident, but the results were not shared with the local residents. At the time of the complaint, the company initially cooperated with the CSR Counsellor and provided information to assist with the review. Subsequently, the company withdrew from the process.

[85] The complainants were the Centre for Human Rights and Environment and Fundacion Ciudadanos Independientes, which are two NGOs located in Argentina.

[86] Order-in-Council (n 22) s 6.

[87] Global Affairs Canada, 'Field Visit Report 2013-04-MEX:E the Office of the Extractive Sector CSR Counsellor' (Government of Canada, 2013), www.international.gc.ca/csr_counsellor-conseiller_rse/publications/2013-04-MEX_interim_rep_01-rap_provisoir_01.aspx?lang=eng.

[88] Global Affairs Canada, 'File # 2013-05-ARG: Office of the Extractive Sector CSR Counsellor's Closing Report Request for Review' (Government of Canada, 2013), www.international.gc.ca/csr_counsellor-conseiller_rse/publications/2013-05-ARG_closing_report-rapport_final.aspx?lang=eng.

Prior to the complaint, the company had established a stakeholder engagement process called the Liaison Table that met with representatives of the communities near the mine to share and exchange information. The company questioned why the CSR Counsellor's involvement was necessary in light of the forum provided by the Liaison Table. The CSR Counsellor responded that the requestors were not satisfied with this process, and therefore sought the involvement of a neutral third party.

Further, the impacted community was assisted by a Buenos Aires-based NGO in making their complaint. The company expressed concern about the NGO's involvement and suggested that the NGO's assistance was somehow inappropriate. This was not a concern for the CSR Counsellor as under its own guidelines, complainants are permitted to use the assistance of third party advisors such as lawyers, consultants and NGOs. The CSR Counsellor's office began planning for a visit to Argentina; however, the company declined to participate in the field visit and advised that they were withdrawing from the review process.[89]

This result is characteristic of the cases reviewed by the CSR Counsellor throughout the existence of the office. The former CSR Counsellor, Marketa Evans, quietly left her position in 2013.[90] Under her mandate none of the complainants in any case ever received a remedy as a result of utilising the CSR Counsellor. The lack of effective engagement was not likely the result of the CSR Counsellor's willingness to achieve meaningful outcomes, but reflective of the frail authority given to the office.

In 2014, the Government of Canada enhanced the CSR strategy by mimicking part of Bill C-300 with the use of economic diplomacy to encourage multinational corporations to align with best practices.[91] The Federal Government at the time became committed to withdrawing financial support to corporations that fail to follow best practices or as a result of a corporation's non-participation with the CSR Counsellor's dispute resolution mechanism or Canada's NCP.[92] In addition, the Government re-focused the role of the CSR Counsellor to 'prevent, identify and resolve disputes in the early stages'.[93] If the dispute required formal mediation, the CSR Counsellor would encourage the parties to request those services from Canada's NCP.

The 2014 update expanded the list of performance guidelines that would be recognised by the CSR Counsellor as eligible for 'enhanced Government of

[89] *Ibid.*

[90] C Coumans, 'Op-Ed: Canada Needs Effective Mining Oversight' (*Ottawa Citizen*, 31 October 2013).

[91] Global Affairs Canada, 'Doing Business the Canadian Way' (n 32).

[92] S Seck, 'Climate Change, Corporate Social Responsibility, and the Extractive Industries' (2018) 31 *Journal of Environmental Law and Practice* 276.

[93] Global Affairs Canada, 'Doing Business the Canadian Way' (n 32).

Canada economic diplomacy'.[94] The list included the OECD Guidelines, the UN Guiding Principles, the Voluntary Principles, the Performance Standards of the World Bank, the OECD Minerals Policy and the GRI.[95]

On a positive note for those seeking further accountability of corporate conduct abroad, the inclusion of economic diplomacy was a promising tool to enhance the human rights and environmental record of Canadian companies operating abroad and aligns with the original intent of the failed Bill C-300. This includes incorporating the policies used by the World Bank and the Overseas Private Investment Corporation of the United States.

As a critique, the 2014 update to Canada's CSR strategy significantly reduced the authority of the CSR Counsellor and instead promoted Canada's OECD NCP. The Government did not increase funding to support the operations of either office. The scope of the CSR Counsellor's role was effectively reduced to an intervener at an early stage and defers the authority over unsettled matters to Canada's OECD NCP. The 2014 update to Canada's CSR strategy made it clear that the CSR Counsellor's role would be reduced, not expanded. Some commentators began to speculate that given its constraints, the CSR Counsellor would not be able to provide an effective mechanism to regulate the foreign activities of the extractive sector.[96]

In 2015, the Canadian Government appointed a new CSR Counsellor after paying CND $180,000 to run the vacant office for more than a year. The appointment of Jeffrey Davidson, an academic at Queen's University, did not reflect a shift in the Government's approach to regulating the overseas activity of the extractive sector.

Subsequent to the 2014 CSR strategy, the CSR Counsellor did not see any increase in complaints. In fact, no complaints were brought between 2015 and 2018.[97] One commentator has speculated that this lack of complaints is due in part because civil society groups and impacted communities did not trust the CSR Counsellor's review process.[98]

The office of the CSR Counsellor during Mr Davidson's tenure was focused on early conflict resolution through informal mediation. A majority of the CSR staff's time was dedicated to public presentations and informal meetings with a

[94] This economic diplomacy includes: 'Government of Canada services include the issuance of letters of support, advocacy efforts in foreign markets and participation in Government of Canada trade missions.' Global Affairs Canada, 'Doing Business the Canadian Way' (n 32). Further, it may affect support from Export Development Canada.

[95] Global Affairs Canada, 'Doing Business the Canadian Way' (n 32).

[96] V Crystal, S Imai and B Maheandiran, 'Access to Justice and Corporate Accountability: A Legal Case Study of Hudbay in Guatemala' (2014) 35 *Canadian Journal of Development Studies* 286, 294.

[97] Global Affairs Canada, 'Registry of Requests for Review' (Government of Canada, 2017), www.international.gc.ca/csr_counsellor-conseiller_rse/Registry-web-enregistrement.aspx?lang=eng.

[98] C Kamphuis, 'Building the Case for a Home-State Grievance Mechanism: Law Reform Strategies in the Canadian Resource Justice Movement' in I Feichtner, M Krajewski and R Roesch (eds) *Human Rights in the Extractive Sector* (New York, Springer, 2019).

wide variety of mining companies, civil society organisations, academics, industry associations and consultants.[99]

There was some on-the-ground dispute resolution work. In 2016, Mr Davidson travelled to Honduras to mediate a dispute between Aura Minerals and a local impacted community.[100] In his report concerning this mediation effort, Mr Davidson described the concerns of various stakeholders respecting the impacts of mining in Honduras.[101]

At the end of the report, the Counsellor commented that certain civil society groups have contributed to the tense situation around mining activities in Honduras. He identified these groups as Mining Watch Canada and Rights Action. He asserted that these civil society groups define themselves as ideologically positioned against mining activities. According to the Counsellor, this results in confrontational and adversarial approaches when dealing with companies and governments. After chastising these groups, he went on to comment that a different approach will perhaps generate value for the communities they seek to represent.

In reaction, a letter was sent to the Canadian Minister of International Trade from a group of 24 Canadian civil society groups, unions and churches.[102] In their letter, these groups admonished the Counsellor for making sweeping and biased remarks against civil society. The impact of these remarks minimises their ability to be effective agents of change in countries like Honduras. The Government did not publicly respond to this letter.

On the whole, the report is a merit-based assessment of the situation between Aura Minerals, the impacted community and the Honduran Government. It may have been understandable on the part of the Counsellor to call out groups that are particularly unhelpful in resolving these matters. However, the report appears to be critical of the involvement of civil society as a whole. This position is unproductive. State-based dispute resolution mechanisms, such as the former office of the CSR Counsellor, require strong ties with civil society in order to be effective.

Civil society groups are the currency that state-based dispute resolution processes require to function. In questioning their legitimacy, the Counsellor eroded trust among key allies in confronting the negative impacts of the Canadian

[99] Global Affairs Canada, 'Annual Report to Parliament: May 2015 – May 2016 – The Office of the Extractive Sector Corporate Social Responsibility (CSR) Counsellor Government of Canada' (Government of Canada, 2016), international.gc.ca/csr_counsellor-conseiller_rse/publications/2016_annual_report-rapport_annuel_2016.aspx?lang=eng.

[100] P Mazereeuw, 'Liberals "Seriously" Considering Mining Ombudsperson, Says Federal Corporate Social Responsibility Adviser' *The Hill Times* (9 November 2016).

[101] Global Affairs Canada, 'Honduras Country Trip Overview: Office of the Extractive Sector Corporate Social Responsibility (CSR) Counsellor' (Government of Canada, 2016), www.international.gc.ca/csr_counsellor-conseiller_rse/trip_overview_Honduras-apercu_voyage_Honduras.aspx?lang=eng.

[102] Letter from Canadian civil society organisations to the Honourable François-Philippe Champagne, Minister of International Trade' (28 July 2017).

extractive sector abroad. These unsolicited comments of the CSR Counsellor serve as a reminder that questioning the role of civil society in these disputes leads to breakdown and discord among the stakeholders. This was an unfortunate act of the perishing office of the CSR Counsellor.

IV. The Canadian Ombudsperson for Responsible Enterprise

In 2018, the Federal Government announced the creation of the CORE. Some commentators had been advocating that the CSR Counsellor should be expanded into an ombudsperson service for some time.[103]

In 2019, Sheri Meyerhoffer was appointed as the first ombudsperson of the CORE. The CORE was specifically created in order to set aside the CSR Counsellor which formally closed in 2018. The CORE focuses on investigations, informal resolution of disputes and on making public recommendations. It may recommend compensation, an apology, cessation of certain activities or corporate policy changes.

The CORE's reach spreads far beyond the extractive industry. It is mandated to investigate human rights incidents involving Canadian companies operating in the mining, oil and gas as well as the garment sector. It is expected that the CORE will eventually be expanded to cover additional sectors in the future.[104] During the tenure of the CORE, Canada's NCP will continue to fulfill its mandate of dispute resolution for all sectors. The CORE may refer cases to Canada's NCP for formal mediation when the parties are in agreement.

In contrast to the CSR Counsellor, the Ombudsperson is appointed for a term of up to five years, whereas the CSR Counsellor served only a three-year term. Unlike the CSR Counsellor, the CORE may start an investigation without a formal complaint. It may also compel documents, witnesses and recommend remedies to be implemented by the Federal Government. This includes the withdrawal of government support and advocacy such as the assistance provided by Export Development Canada and Canadian Trade Commissioner Services.

To increase transparency, the CORE will make its reports publicly available at various stages of an investigation process and when monitoring recommendations. Comparatively, much of the CSR Counsellor's work was confidential. Further, the Minister of International Trade will table the CORE's annual reports in Parliament.[105]

[103] As one example, see Letter from Bishop Douglas Crosby, President of the Canadian Conference of Catholic Bishops to the Prime Minister of Canada (9 August 2017).

[104] Global Affairs Canada, 'Responsible Business Conduct Abroad – Questions and Answers' (Government of Canada, 2019), www.international.gc.ca/trade-agreements-accords-commerciaux/topics-domaines/other-autre/faq.aspx?lang=eng.

[105] Order-in-Council, Privy Council Number: 2019-299 (2019).

Simultaneously to the announcement on the CORE, the Government also revealed the creation of a Multi-Stakeholder Advisory Body of experts from business and civil society. This body supports the operation of the CORE and provides guidance to the Government on further regulation with respect to business and human rights. Additionally, the Federal Government reduced the list of internationally-recognised guidelines and standards of social and environmental performance compared to the previous practice of the CSR Counsellor.

The six performance guidelines as established in the 2014 CSR strategy included the OECD Guidelines, the UN Guiding Principles, the Voluntary Principles, the Performance Standards of the World Bank, the OECD Minerals Policy and the GRI.[106] Currently, the CORE focuses explicitly on promoting the implementation of the OECD Guidelines and the UN Guiding Principles. This is only two of the six performance guidelines. On account of this, the CORE is not promoting the criteria set out in the other four instruments. These instruments are useful guidelines for corporations operating in the mining sector. For instance, the Voluntary Principles provide best practices for extractive sector corporations that employ private and public security forces. The GRI enhances transparency and encourages market-based rewards for good CSR performance. I suggest that all six performance guidelines embraced in the 2014 CSR strategy should be utilised by the CORE as appropriate standards for business conduct. Together, the six standards provide clear rules for governing the activities of multinational corporations. Further, they have proven, tested and wide-ranging consensus on their application and use by industry.[107]

At the time of writing, the CORE has not yet considered or investigated any matters. The formal complaint process is set to be finalised in 2020, at which time the office will be able to effectively process outside complaints. The CORE will investigate allegations of human rights abuses that are internationally recognised. They define human rights abuses as those referred to in the Universal Declaration of Human Rights, the International Covenant on Civil and Political Rights and the International Covenant on Economic, Social and Cultural Rights.[108] These include various rights such as to be protected from torture, slavery and degrading treatment. There are also labour rights such as to reasonable limitation on working hours, as well as a right to education and a political and cultural life, among others.

In the CORE's Operating Procedures, it states that civil society organisations may be requested to provide submissions as part of the CORE's fact-finding process.[109] While the CORE considers civil society organisations as important

[106] Global Affairs Canada, 'Doing Business the Canadian Way' (n 32).

[107] Global Affairs Canada, 'Doing Business the Canadian Way' (n 32).

[108] Government of Canada, 'Operating Procedures of the Canadian Ombudsperson for Responsible Enterprise' (Government of Canada, 2020), core-ombuds.canada.ca/core_ombuds-ocre_ombuds/operating_procedures-procedures_exploitation.aspx.

[109] *Ibid* s 12.6.

stakeholders, it does not give them an express role as advocates on behalf of complainants or as potential mediators.

Some civil society groups have taken on more complicated roles beyond advocacy, such as legal representation. As addressed in chapter four, US civil society actors have represented plaintiffs in US federal court against corporations accused of wrongdoing in their foreign mining practices. Another avenue of involvement is mediation. For example, the AMO in Australia is a civil society sponsored office that has mediated complaints from local communities concerning environmental and human rights abuses by the Australian extractive sector.

V. Oxfam Australia's Mining Ombudsman

From the outset, it should be noted that the Australian model for dealing with extractive sector corporations that commit human rights abuses abroad provides a unique option that is outside of strict legal regulation. There are non-legal forums and processes available to seek recourse against the extractive sector. For instance, some Australian mining companies have established internal grievance mechanisms to deal with disputes arising from their operations and local communities, such as BHP's complaints process to address community concerns.[110] The effectiveness of BHP's internal complaint processes,[111] along with the processes of other companies has been questioned.[112]

Given the void of oversight concerning the extraterritorial conduct of the Australian extractive sector, civil society actors have stepped in to facilitate mediation between industry and negatively impacted communities. While this is not a form of state-based regulation, the involvement of civil society is included in this review because 1) civil society has lobbied for more government regulation;[113] and 2) their efforts in mediation has achieved limited success in some respects.

An alternative model that has been endorsed by the UN is the use of an external civil society organisation to act as an access point in local-level grievance mechanisms. For instance, the UN Guiding Principles suggest that civil society

[110] BHP, 'Respecting Human Rights' (2018), www.bhp.com/our-approach/our-company/our-code-of-conduct/caring-about-society/respecting-human-rights/.

[111] Bench Marks Foundation, 'Policy Gap 9 South African Coal Mining: Corporate Grievance Mechanisms, Community Engagement Concerns and Mining Impacts' (2014), www.bench-marks.org.za/research/policy_gap_9.pdf.

[112] C Coumans, 'Inequality of Arms: A Summary of Concerns Raised by Victims of Violence by Private and Public Mine Security at Barrick Gold's North Mara Gold Mine in Tanzania Regarding the Mine's New Operation-Level Grievance Mechanism' (*MiningWatch Canada*, 4 September 2018), miningwatch.ca/sites/default/files/north_mara_final_brief_-_inequality_of_arms_september_2018_-_clean_0.pdf.

[113] Oxfam Australia, 'Community–Company Grievance Resolution: A Guide for the Australian Mining Industry' (2010) 6, www.oxfam.org.au/wp-content/uploads/2011/11/OAus-GrievanceMechanisms-0410.pdf.

groups may serve as a trusted and credible 'access point' between a company and impacted stakeholders in order to resolve disputes.[114]

This approach has been utilised in Australia and proved rather effective. The AMO predates the UN Guiding Principles, as a civil society sponsored office that considered complaints from local communities concerning environmental and human rights abuses by the extractive sector. In 2000, Oxfam Community Aid Abroad (now Oxfam Australia) created the AMO to assist local and Indigenous communities whose human rights were threatened by the operations of Australian-based mining companies. A secondary purpose was to demonstrate the need for an official complaint mechanism within Australia that would in turn motivate the Australian Government to create a state-based complaint process.

The AMO received complaints through Oxfam Community Aid Abroad networks in Asia, the Pacific, Africa and the Americas and proceeded with investigations by conducting extensive interviews with local community members, civil society organisations and, where possible, company officials. If the company failed to respond or dismissed the validity of the grievances, the AMO would undertake further research and launch a public campaign to promote the particular grievances. If the company responded constructively, the AMO would facilitate a dialogue process between the communities and the company. In either case, the AMO published the community complaints and, where possible, the mining company's response in Case Reports and the Mining Ombudsman Annual Report, which were reviewed for the purpose of preparing the summary of AMO activities.[115] Grievances commonly expressed by communities impacted by mining activities in these reports include inadequate consultation and negotiation with local people, including women and Indigenous communities, minimal disclosure about proposed mining activities, forced evictions, adverse environmental, health and social impacts, harassment of community members and retaliation against anti-mine protesters.[116]

A. Achievement of Limited Success

The AMO operated from 2000 to 2009 without financial or statutory support from the Australian Government. Consequently, its primary function was to generate public concern for wrongful corporate conduct, which motivated extractive sector

[114] United Nations Special Representative on Business and Human Rights, 'The Corporate Responsibility to Respect Human Rights: An Interpretative Guide' (2011) 72, www.ohchr.org/Documents/Publications/HR.PUB.12.2_En.pdf.

[115] It should be noted that given the lack of available literature on these cases, most of the information came directly from the AMO, and thus it may lack objective creditability.

[116] These listed grievances were compiled by Oxfam Australia based on a review of complaints made to NCPs under the OECD Guidelines. Oxfam Australia also reviewed complaints made to the Compliance Advisor/Ombudsman for the IFC and MIGA. Oxfam, 'Grievance Resolution' (n 113) 8.

companies to action in several incidences. The work of the AMO was predicated on what it called a rights-based approach. This approach reflects the view that poverty results from the violation of human rights and through systems that are based on injustice, inequality and discrimination.[117]

Initially, the AMO took on several cases from 2000 to 2003, with its caseload eventually diminishing until finally closing in 2009. In 2000, the AMO began reviewing a complaint brought by local community representatives in Peru near the Tintaya mine. There had been a long history of community complaints against the various mine owners at the Tintaya mine. In the 1980s, the Peruvian Government took more than 2,000 hectares of land to develop the mine, resulting in the displacement of hundreds of people. The mine was subsequently privatised and sold to BHP and was eventually purchased by Xstrata. The communities affected by the mine allege that the Government failed to gain their informed consent for expropriating the land or to adequately compensate the displaced individuals. Other community members reported that water and air pollution from the mine had caused death and illness of people and livestock.[118] The AMO facilitated a productive dialogue between BHP and representatives from impacted communities and the dialogue continued when Xstrata purchased the mine.[119]

At first the local communities were reticent to negotiate with the mine owners. According to the AMO, some community members lacked the capacity to effectively participate and had an expectation that various civil society organisations would always defend their interest, rather than acting as a mediator in assisting the communities and the mine owners in reaching a fair and equitable resolution. On account of the mediation efforts by the AMO, the mine owners acquired an understanding of the culturally unique methods of seeking community approval.[120] The grievance resolution processes established by the AMO continued after it withdrew as a mediator.

In another one of the early cases, the AMO received a request for review from a group of students regarding a proposed BHP mining project on Gag Island, Indonesia. BHP was accused of failing to adequately consult the community about resettlement issues and the disposal of mine tailings. Partly in response to the AMO's investigation, BHP decided against using a controversial method of disposing of mine tailings and hired a liaison officer to provide the local communities with opportunities for input into the future development of the project.[121]

[117] Oxfam Australia, 'Tolukuma Gold Mine: Mining Ombudsman Case Report' (2004) 6, www.mpiasia.net/component/booklibrary/2/view_bl/88/154/mining-ombudsman-case-report-tolukuma-gold-mine.html?Itemid=2.

[118] Oxfam Australia, '2004 Mining Ombudsman Annual Report' (2005) 6, www.eldis.org/document/A16608.

[119] The AMO facilitated the establishment of the *Mesa de Diàlogo* (known as a dialogue table), with representatives from local communities, the mine owners and civil society. Oxfam, 'Grievance Resolution' (n 113) 12.

[120] Oxfam, 'Grievance Resolution' (n 113) 12–14.

[121] Oxfam, '2004 Annual Report' (n 118) 9.

The same year, the AMO received a complaint from local community members impacted by a gold mine in Papua New Guinea owned and operated by Durban Roodepoort Deep. The request concerned an incident in 2000 where a helicopter accidentally released cyanide while in transit to the mine. Partly due to repeated follow up by the AMO, the company acknowledged its accountability for the incident in a public statement addressed to the local communities of the mine, the Papua New Guinea Government and shareholders. The company made some effort to engage with local communities, civil society organisations and the AMO.[122]

Subsequent to the initial investigation, Emperor Mines merged with Durban Roodepoort Deep. The AMO met with the company's executives to continue resolving ongoing disputes surrounding the mine. Those disputes included the company's use of a tailings disposal system that is considered by some to be no longer acceptable. For instance, the World Bank does not fund projects using this technology. Additionally, a community of a few hundred people lived close to the mine in what was known as 'tent city'.[123] There was no electricity or sanitation facilities in this area and the AMO believed that the company should provide these utilities. Ultimately, the AMO helped achieve a commitment from Emperor Mines to undertake a study of the water quality downstream from the mine and recommend alternative sources of clean drinking water.[124] A grievance resolution process for local communities that was established by the AMO continued operating after they ceased to have any involvement with the mine.

In 2002, the AMO responded to a complaint by local communities living near the Didipio mine in the Philippines, which was being constructed by Climax Mining. The community members raised several concerns, including potential environmental damage associated with the mine and fear that they would be displaced from their lands. Additionally, it was alleged that the company did not receive the community members' free and informed consent prior to pursuing the mine project, as agents of the company had used intimidation and pressure tactics to elicit consent from local community members. Part of the problem was that the local population was divided on the mine, and it was alleged the company took advantage of that by allowing its agents to use 'strong armed tactics such as the forceful takings of land'.[125] Filipino law, international law and good business practice mandates obtaining free and informed consent before a mining project may begin.

The AMO attempted to raise these grievances with the company, but they did not receive a response for several years. Eventually, Climax Mining increased its communication with local communities by hiring a prominent Filipino person to

[122] Oxfam, 'Tolukuma Case Report' (n 117) 9.

[123] Oxfam, 'Tolukuma Case Report' (n 117) 20.

[124] Oxfam, 'Grievance Resolution' (n 113) 14.

[125] Oxfam Australia, 'Didipio Mining Projects: Mining Ombudsman Case Report' (2007) 4, www.mpiasia.net/component/booklibrary/2/view_bl/88/157/mining-ombudsman-case-report-didipio-gold-and-copper-mine.html?Itemid=2.

act on its behalf. Nevertheless, the company did not address the grievances relating to the issues of informed consent and potential environmental damage. The AMO found in its Case Report that the company had indeed failed to obtain free and informed consent.

In 2006, OceanaGold Corporation merged with Climax Mining and become the owners of the Didipio mine that had yet to begin production. At that time, OceanaGold negotiated a new agreement with representatives of the local communities before proceeding with the development of the mine. There have been reports that since the mine has been developed, OceanGold has largely been a responsible operator in terms of the environment and human rights.[126] However, other commentators have suggested that the company has caused human rights violations and environmental destruction.[127]

In another case from the Philippines, the AMO received a request from community members to investigate concerns with the Marcopper mines that they had been polluting the environment over a 20-year period.[128] The mining activities in question were located on Marinduque, a small island in the central Philippines. This is the same case considered by the Nevada District Court and the Nevada Supreme Court as outlined in chapter four on US law. Those cases were ultimately dismissed on the basis of *forum non conveniens*.[129]

The mines had previously been co-owned by Placer Dome and the former president of the Philippines until 1987, when the president was overthrown and Placer Dome continued to operate the mine solely. In the 1990s, a mine tailings dam collapsed and the resulting rush of water destroyed homes and livestock. Additionally, a drainage tunnel burst resulting in toxins being released into a nearby river. Placer Dome accepted partial responsibility, however the local community was not satisfied with the environmental remediation that had been undertaken and many claimants were delayed in receiving compensation. The community members wanted help from the AMO to determine who may be responsible for further remediation.

In their report, the AMO called on Placer Dome to complete more environmental clean-up, adequately compensate affected communities and take steps to prevent future disasters, among other recommendations.[130] Despite the AMO's best efforts, Placer Dome continued to deny responsibility to perform further environmental rehabilitation or compensate Filipino communities living near

[126] M Holmes, 'OceanaGold Didipio Operation Named Most Environmentally and Socially Responsible Mining Operation in the Philippines' (*Junior Mining Network*, 2017).

[127] Environmental Justice, 'Didipio Gold and Copper Mine, Nueva Vizcaya, Philippines' (23 January 2017).

[128] Oxfam Australia, 'Marinduque Island: Mining Ombudsman Case Report' (2005) 3, www.mpiasia.net/component/booklibrary/2/view_bl/88/152/mining-ombudsman-case-report-marinduque-island.html?Itemid=2

[129] *Provincial Gov't of Marinduque v Placer Dome, Inc* [2015] 131 Nev Adv Op 63076.

[130] Oxfam, 'Marinduque Case Report' (n 128) 3.

the mine.[131] At the time of the AMO's investigation, Placer Dome was the world's sixth largest gold producer.[132] In 2006, the Canadian gold company Barrick Gold purchased Placer Dome, along with the potential legal liability associated with the Marcopper mine. As previously mentioned, so far Barrick Gold has been successful at warding off legal action against them in the United States. However, in 2016, the provincial government of Marinduque announced that they were considering bringing a claim against Barrack in Canada.[133]

In another case, the AMO received a request to investigate the working conditions at the Fijian Vatukoula gold mine owned by Emperor Mines. The request came from a local trade union and civil society organisation in Fiji. The AMO met with striking workers from an unresolved industrial dispute in the early 1990s. They allege that the 1991 strike was on account of low wages, unsafe working conditions, health concerns and poor housing. The management of Emperor Mines met with the AMO and expressed the view that the sole objective of the 1991 strike was to force the company to formally recognise the workers' trade union.[134] It does not appear that the AMO's involvement substantially changed the relationship between the mine operators, workers or local communities.

In one of the last cases reviewed, the AMO investigated the mining practices of Lafayette Mining on Rapu Rapu island. The company eventually became bankrupt as a result of heavy losses that left the community with several social and environmental problems.[135] The mining project had received significant financial support from a consortium of international banks including ANZ of Australia. According to the AMO, ANZ failed to respond when communities and their supporters made it clear that the mining project was having significant adverse environmental impacts. For instance, poor environmental safeguards contributed to at least two cyanide-laden tailings spills. After its investigation, the AMO released a report citing the failure of ANZ to properly monitor the mine and its operators to ensure necessary measures were in place to prevent events such as the tailings spills. ANZ had a responsibility to monitor the project given that it had signed the Equator Principles, a framework that financial institutions follow for managing environmental and social risks in projects they fund. This includes assessing standards for Indigenous peoples and consultation with other locally affected communities impacted by a financed project.[136] Additionally, once

[131] Oxfam, 'Grievance Resolution' (n 113) 8.

[132] Oxfam, 'Marinduque Case Report' (n 128) 2.

[133] A Singh, 'Mining Industry Crackdown Continues in Philippines' *Asian Pacific Post* (29 November 2016).

[134] Oxfam Australia, 'Vatukoula Gold Mine: Mining Ombudsman Case Report' (2004) 9, www.mpiasia.net/component/booklibrary/2/view_bl/88/155/mining-ombudsman-case-report-vatukoula-gold-mine.html?Itemid=2

[135] Oxfam Australia, 'Rapu Rapu Polymetallic Mine: Mining Ombudsman Case Report' (2008) 20, www.banktrack.org/download/mining_ombudsman_case_report_rapu_rapu_polymetallic_mine/rapurapucasereport.pdf.

[136] 'The Equator Principles' (n 37).

Lafayette Mining was clearly in financial trouble, ANZ sold its debt associated with the mine without attempting to ensure that steps would be taken to deal with the social and environmental fall-out caused by the spills.[137] The publicity generated by the AMO report likely contributed to greater awareness about creditors' responsibilities under the Equator Principles.

In 2008, Oxfam lobbied the Australian Government to introduce an independent complaint mechanism for extractive sector corporations operating abroad.[138] The Australian Government did not act on these efforts. In 2009, Oxfam shed the 'ombudsman' moniker and began to focus on the development of community-company supported grievance mechanisms.[139]

Subsequent to the AMO ceasing operations, Oxfam Australia has been focusing on providing guidance to mining companies as they develop or strengthen their own complaint processes.[140] Oxfam bases its proposals on the UN Protect, Respect and Remedy Framework of John Ruggie. Oxfam suggests that a corporation can fulfill its responsibility to respect human rights by ensuring that communities affected by its operations have access to remedies through a dispute resolution process. Oxfam is continuing to encourage the Australian Government to create an 'independent third-party grievance mechanism, when company-level mechanisms either don't exist or fail to deliver a satisfactory outcome'.[141]

The AMO was not a judicial office with powers of remedy or enforcement. Despite this, the AMO operated effectively and achieved lasting results. The AMO had a track record of generating dialogue between extractive sector companies and the members of the community in which the company operated. It is not the type of legal power that some believe an impacted community should have in holding extractive sector corporations to account. Nevertheless, it is a mechanism that increases the ability of impacted communities to protect their rights and the environment in which they live. For this reason, it deserves further study.

It appears from this work of the AMO that civil society actors, if properly engaged, may have an influence in promoting the effectiveness of non-judicial

[137] Oxfam, 'Rapu Rapu Case Report' (n 135) 2.

[138] 'Ombudsman Needed to Monitor Australian Corporate Practice in Pacific' (*AustraliaPlus*, 6 June 2008).

[139] The reason for the change has not been widely documented. As stated by Chris Madden, Mining Advocacy Coordinator for Oxfam Australia on 24 January 2015 after an inquiry by the author: 'Oxfam conducted a major evaluation of the mining advocacy program in 2009, which concluded that it was time to renew the program and to focus it in a new direction. This led to the decision to discontinue the … [AMO] and place greater emphasis on helping communities speak on their own behalf and supporting affected women, men and Indigenous peoples affected by Extractive Industries have greater capacity to claim their rights. As you say, operating an ombudsman service is not really the role of an organisation such as Oxfam and the decision to discontinue this involved deciding how we could best focus our efforts to achieve the change that we want to see. The change also meant aligning more closely with Oxfam's approach of supporting active citizenship.'

[140] Oxfam, 'Grievance Resolution' (n 113) 4.

[141] Oxfam, 'Grievance Resolution' (n 113) 6.

grievance mechanisms. In this way, they can provide an integral role in resolving disputes between negatively impacted communities and the extractive sector.

In conclusion, the analysis in this chapter demonstrates three relevant findings. First, legislative attempts in the US, UK, Canada and Australia aimed at curbing the overseas human rights and environmental violations by their extractive sectors have failed. Second, statutes and state-based grievance mechanisms have not provided an effective remedy in preventing abuses caused by the extractive sector. Third, civil society actors have undertaken a prominent role in these jurisdictions by leading litigation using special statutes, and facilitating mediation that has led to tangible results between the extractive sector and those impacted by their extra-territorial conduct. These findings suggest that effective state-based regulation should include an expansive role for civil society actors in representing or mediating between impacted parties and the extractive sector.

PART III

Proposal

7

A New Policy Direction

To date, judicial systems, home state statutes and non-judicial grievance mechanisms have not produced an effective remedy for those negatively impacted by the extraterritorial conduct of the extractive sector. This chapter proposes the framework for a non-judicial grievance mechanism between home state extractive sector corporations and those they impact abroad. My proposal builds largely on the Canadian state-based office of the Canadian Ombudsperson for Responsible Enterprise (CORE).

The CORE is the office that replaced the Corporate Social Responsibility (CSR) Counsellor as Canada's voluntary dispute mechanism between some Canadian businesses and those that they impact outside of Canada. While the CORE also has jurisdiction over Canadian companies in the garment sector, this proposal focuses specifically on the CORE's application to the extractive sector.

In this book, Canada's political and legal system is utilised as a case study for implementing the proposal, but it is designed to be broadly applicable in other countries that are considering adopting a home state grievance mechanism. In particular, the proposal will be of assistance for other common law jurisdictions seeking compliance with the UN Guiding Principles.[1]

I propose a new system that augments and supersedes the existing powers of the CORE. These new processes will ensure the CORE becomes an effective agency with appropriate regulatory jurisdiction over disputes between the extractive sector and foreign communities. Such authority does not exist under the current mandate of the CORE.

This proposal is premised on the assertion that the involvement of civil society is beneficial in resolving disputes, and that enforcement, accountability, compliance and judicial review must feature prominently in a state-based grievance mechanism. The next section provides an overview of key terms used in this proposal.

[1] Special Representative on Business and Human Rights (SRBHR), 'United Nations Guiding Principles on Business and Human Rights: Implementing the United Nations "Protect, Respect and Remedy" Framework' (United Nations, 2011), www.ohchr.org/documents/publications/guidingprinciplesbusinesshr_en.pdf.

I. Key Terms

In this section, I attempt to establish workable definitions for the terms and principles employed in my proposal. This is an opportunity to ascribe meaning to broad principles, such as grievance mechanisms and performance guidelines within the context of my recommendations for reforming the office of the CORE:

- 'Arbitration' means a dispute resolution process in which a third party person, known as an arbitrator, renders a binding decision at the conclusion of the process.
- 'Canadian extractive sector' means oil, gas or mining companies that have been incorporated in Canada or that have their head offices in Canada.
- 'Complainant' means an individual (or representative) of a community impacted by the extractive sector activities of a Canadian mining company outside of Canada. The proposal will contemplate complainants raising concerns to both site-based and state-based complaint processes.
- 'Complaint' means the submission of a complaint against a respondent corporation to the CORE.
- 'Home state' refers to the government of a country in which a multinational extractive sector corporation is domiciled.
- 'Host state' refers to the jurisdiction in which the extractive sector corporation operates.
- 'Mediation' means a dispute resolution process in which a neutral person, known as a mediator, helps the parties reach an agreement.
- 'NCP' means the Canadian National Contact Point relating to the Organisation for Economic Co-operation and Development (OECD) Guidelines for Multinational Enterprises.
- 'Penalty or Bounty' means a monetary sanction assessed by the CSR Counsellor and paid by a respondent company in compensation for breaches of the Performance Guidelines directly to complainants.
- 'Performance Guideline(s)' means the OECD Guidelines, the UN Guiding Principles, the Voluntary Principles, the Performance Standards of the World Bank, the OECD Minerals Policy and the Global Reporting Initiative (GRI).
- 'Representative' means an advocate on behalf of a party before a contested hearing or during some form of negotiation.
- 'Respondent Corporation, Company or Party' means an extractive sector entity that is the subject of an allegation by a complainant.
- 'Review Process' means the process facilitated by the CORE pursuant to a complaint.
- 'Site-level Grievance Mechanism' means a company-sponsored and financed process that allows impacted communities and individuals to raise concerns directly with a company. They can also be referred to as site-based, community-level or operational-level grievance mechanisms.

II. Canada's Approach

The two main Canadian government offices responsible for holding the extractive sector to account are the CORE and Canada's NCP. The CORE replaced the CSR Counsellor, which closed in 2018. As of the time of writing, the CORE has not considered any disputes. This is because the CORE's formal complaint process is set to be finalised sometime in 2020, at which time the office will be able to effectively process outside complaints.

Neither the CSR Counsellor or Canada's NCP conducted investigations, nor did they have the power to levy fines against industry players or compensate victims. The CORE has the power to conduct investigations without a complaint. Along with Canada's NCP, it also has the power to sanction businesses by recommending the withdrawal of Canadian government embassy support and financial assistance such as in the form of export development credits.

The process utilised by the CSR Counsellor prior to 2013 did not produce any tangible results. Further, their records indicate that despite not closing until 2018, they had not acted on a formal complaint since 2013.[2] In 2016, the CSR Counsellor said that he personally helped to facilitate a peaceful resolution to a dispute between an extractive sector company and a community near that company's mining operation in Honduras. Though there is no formal record available of this facilitation from the CSR Counsellor, other evidence confirms that he assisted in mediation efforts between the parties.[3] This is one limited achievement in a long line of failed interventions by the CSR Counsellor.[4]

In 2014, updates to the Government of Canada's CSR strategy minimised the capacity of the CSR Counsellor to sanction or otherwise enforce non-participating respondent companies accused of wrongdoing. Currently, it is a mechanism that lacks incentive for the extractive sector to take it seriously. The same can also be said of the Canadian NCP, which has levied only one sanction in the five cases it has considered between 2011 and 2017.[5] From 2017 to the time of this writing, Canada's NCP has considered an additional seven cases that have not resulted in any sanctions.[6]

The 2015 election of the Liberal Party of Canada at the Federal Government level was a strong signal that the future of the CSR Counsellor was in question.

[2] The CSR Counsellor registry of reviewed files shows they have been inactive since 2013. Global Affairs Canada, 'Registry of Requests for Review' (Government of Canada, 2017), www.international.gc.ca/csr_counsellor-conseiller_rse/Registry-web-enregistrement.aspx?lang=eng.

[3] P Mazereeuw, 'Liberals "Seriously" Considering Mining Ombudsperson, Says Federal Corporate Social Responsibility Adviser' *The Hill Times* (9 November 2016).

[4] For a review of cases by the CSR Counsellor that failed to produce results for local communities impacted by the Canadian extractive sector, see chapter six.

[5] S Imai, L Gardner and S Weinberger, '"The Canada Brand": Violence and Canadian Mining Companies in Latin America' (2017) Osgoode Legal Studies Research Paper No 17/2017, 6 dx.doi.org/10.2139/ssrn.2886584.

[6] Global Affairs Canada, 'Closed National Contact Point Specific Instances' (Government of Canada, 2019), www.international.gc.ca/trade-agreements-accords-commerciaux/ncp-pcn/specific-specifique.aspx?lang=eng.

In a pre-election policy platform, the Liberals suggested that the voluntary nature of the former Federal Government's CSR strategy should be replaced by a more binding process.[7] In 2018, the Minister of International Trade announced the creation of the CORE.

The CORE is somewhat of an improvement in comparison to the powers of the CSR Counsellor. Unlike the CSR Counsellor, the CORE can compel parties to serve as witnesses and release documents. They can issue independent reports and recommend the withdrawal of government services. However, they can only recommend the withdrawal of government services. The CORE cannot unilaterally take such actions. On top of this, the recommendation for denial of government services affects very few public agencies. It has no effect on provincial governments or on the prodigious capital invested by the Canada Pension Plan Investment Board. This leaves the inherent powers of the CORE rather deficient.

My proposal focuses specifically on changes to the office of the CORE so that it may become a pragmatic grievance mechanism that addresses the concerns created by the overseas operations of Canadian mining companies. However, the proposal will be of assistance for other common law countries such as the US, UK and Australia if they choose to implement a non-judicial grievance mechanism to deal with the foreign conduct of their extractive sector.

The remainder of this chapter is organised thematically, addressing the framework of my proposed regime, including the involvement of civil society, enforcement, accountability and compliance, procedural fairness and judicial review. In my proposal, I incorporate key definitions, frame the scope of regulation, promote implementation and compliance, provide recourse to site-level dispute resolution, facilitate extractive sector cooperation, and attempt to carve out a role for external stakeholders such as civil society. I also attempt to balance pro-development of the extractive sector abroad with the necessary protection of the environment and human rights concerning the communities that their operations impact.

The focus of the proposal is three-fold: 1) protect the environment and human rights for the communities impacted by the extractive sector; 2) carve out regulation that only nominally impacts extractive sector corporations that meet their obligations under the UN Guiding Principles; and 3) minimise the costs and other burdens on the government and judicial system in regulating the operations of the extractive sector abroad. My intention for this proposal is to be functional, pragmatic and effective.

Several features of the proposal are meant to be operationalised in the creation of a new set of 'Operating Procedures' for the CORE.[8] These procedures are meant to dictate how the CORE will deal with a complaint from its initial submission to when its review is complete. In the Appendix of the book, I have set out new

[7] J Cumming, 'What the Liberals, Greens and NDP Have to Say on Mining in Canada' *Huffington Post* (10 April 2015), www.huffingtonpost.ca/john-cumming/mining-canada-federal-election_b_8235824.html.

[8] Government of Canada, 'Operating Procedures of the Canadian Ombudsperson for Responsible Enterprise' (Government of Canada, 2020), core-ombuds.canada.ca/core_ombuds-ocre_ombuds/operating_procedures-procedures_exploitation.aspx.

draft Operating Procedures, which contain provisions to embed many of these proposed reforms into the current structure of the CORE.

As a preliminary matter, a key component of this proposal is to bolster the use of sanctions and enforcement by the CORE in the event of non-participation or non-compliance by extractive sector industry members accused of wrongdoing. The lack of necessary tools to enforce participation and compliance has led to several of the key failures regarding the former CSR Counsellor process.

Further, dispute resolution before the CORE should involve the express inclusion of civil society organisations. A new approach must recognise, at the outset, that more effective compliance and monitoring is required; and the involvement of civil society will assist the CORE in achieving these ends.

III. Proposal: Framework for Reforming the Office of the CORE

Figure 1 Flowchart of Proposed New Process of the CORE

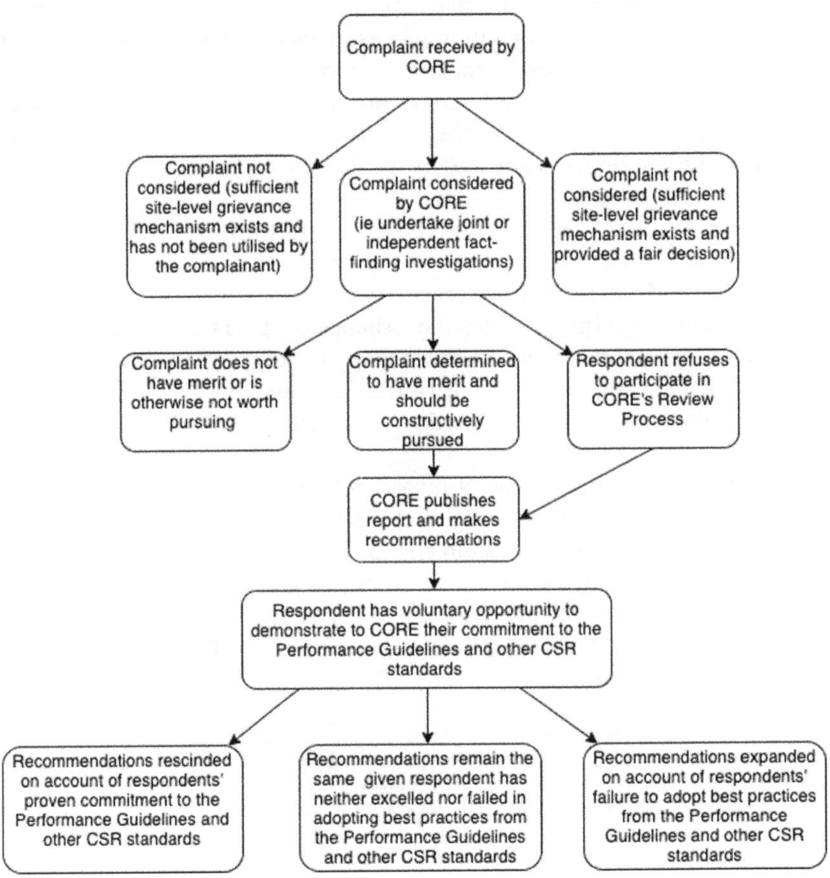

In reforming the powers of the CORE, I suggest that they require an enforcement mechanism to compel companies to take human rights issues seriously by introducing sanctions. These new powers must go above and beyond what is already in the purview of the CORE, such as the withdrawal of economic diplomacy from the Government of Canada. I suggest that proper sanctions should include the ability of the CORE to order a financial penalty to be paid in compensation for breaches of human rights and environmental norms directly to victims of the extractive sector.

The human rights and environmental norms I mention include the six pertinent Performance Guidelines embraced in the 2014 CSR strategy as standards of social and environmental performance. These Performance Guidelines include the OECD Guidelines, the UN Guiding Principles, the Voluntary Principles, the Performance Standards of the World Bank, the OECD Minerals Policy and the GRI.

Essentially, I suggest that the Government of Canada weaponise the CORE with the power to issue sanctions and enforce such orders. This is a civil penalty, as opposed to a fine, because the penalty is paid directly to the impacted individuals and not to the Government of Canada.[9] Additionally, the CORE will be empowered to levy a similar financial penalty against companies that fail to participate in the CORE's dispute resolution process. I also suggest that the CORE have the power to order respondent companies to pay legal and other associated costs to successful complainants, and in some cases, pay a public fine to the Federal Government as well as compensate their victims. This would only occur in specific cases where the respondent company has misled the CORE or otherwise harmed public interests in Canada.

Moreover, I would keep some of the framework from the 2014 CSR strategy update from the Government of Canada. For instance, businesses that adopt the Performance Guidelines into their practices should still be eligible for enhanced economic diplomacy. This includes the issuance of letters of support, advocacy efforts in foreign markets and participation in Government of Canada trade missions. Further, embracing the Performance Guidelines will also influence whether Export Development Canada will consider financially supporting a business.

In my proposal, I incorporate a pivotal role for site-level grievance mechanisms. As a continuing feature from the existing office of the CORE, complainants will be permitted to raise disputes directly to the CORE. One allowable exception would be if the company has an internal site-level grievance mechanism that the complainant has not utilised in pursuing a remedy to their claim. In these circumstances, the CORE could refuse to hear the case until the matter has been exhausted at the site-level process. If the site-level grievance mechanism is exhausted, the

[9] I adopt the type of penalty contemplated under the Canadian Energy Regulator Act which establishes the Canada Energy Regulator that states: 'penalty means an administrative monetary penalty imposed under this Act for a violation'. Canadian Energy Regulator Act SC 2019 c 28 s 10. Violations would be specifically defined as breaches of the six Performance Guidelines endorsed by the CORE.

complainant may bring an application for review to the CORE. However, this review is not automatic, and instead the CORE has discretion to dismiss the claim if they find that the site-level grievance process provided by the company has sufficiently dealt with the matter, or is capable of doing so.

As a final nuanced piece to this approach, I suggest that the extractive sector industry should be incentivised to incorporate the Performance Guidelines and other CSR standards into their management and operation practices. This includes the establishment of a fair and efficient site-level grievances mechanism. To this end, I recommend that the CORE have an atypical consideration in assessing penalties against offending corporations. Figure 2 represents this framework for how an assessed penalty would be reduced or increased based on these factors.

Figure 2 CORE Process for Assessing Penalties

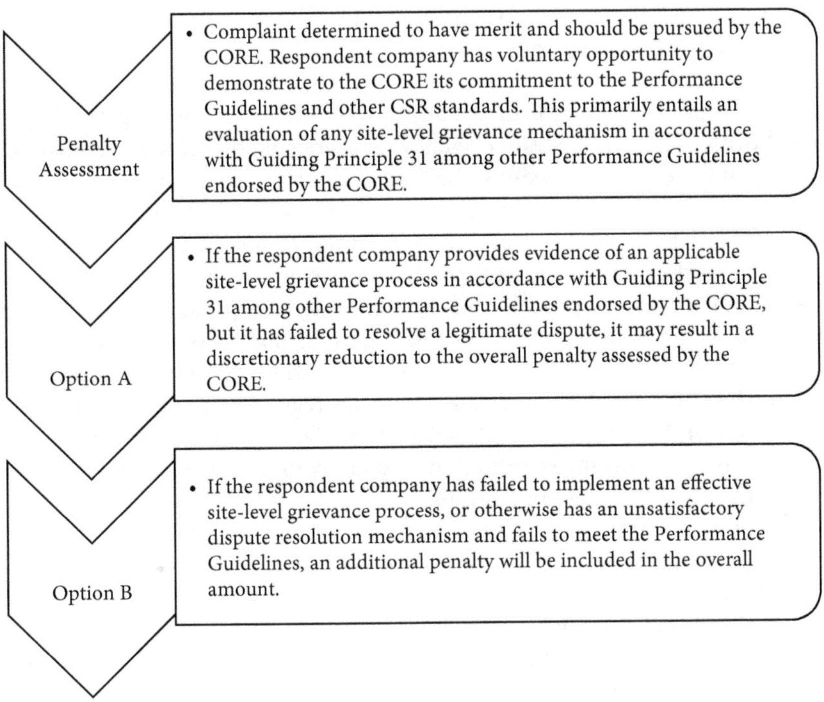

In order to provide predictability to this structure, the CORE must set out objective and transparent criteria for what constitutes a sufficient site-level grievance process and how it can be effectively implemented and delivered by the extractive sector.

Beyond setting out a framework for individual companies to establish site-level grievance mechanisms, it must be clear that failure to do so will carry significant legal and monetary risk. For this proposal to function in a practical sense, the penalties awarded by the CORE must be somewhat significant. If they are relatively minor, companies might proceed with a sense that they are mere licences to continue operating if the cost-benefit is greater to simply ignore effectively participating in a dispute resolution process and instead continue the offending activity.

I also suggest that it would also be appropriate to give the CORE capabilities to prevent potential human rights abuses or environmental damage in the time between when a complaint is submitted and when they have concluded their review. One option is to empower the CORE with an injunctive tool to utilise in the event that the CORE determines that it is necessary to suspend the foreign operations or the development of those operations by the respondent corporation pending the outcome of the review process.

I suggest informal injunction-like tools because attempting to give the CORE formal power to issue injunctions on the extraterritorial activities of the Canadian extractive sector is highly problematic. For one, it raises concerns of international comity and *forum non conveniens*, given that this would involve an attempt to regulate conduct outside of Canada. Second, the CORE is arguably overstepping the authority of an administrative agency by exercising this type of remedy. Such action would likely be successfully challenged in Canadian court.

The injunction-like tools that I suggest represent a less blunt option for the CORE in order to pressure corporations into compliance. For example, in the event that the CORE recommends the suspension of operations pending the outcome of their review process and the respondent corporation fails to comply, the CORE would issue press releases to highlight their dissatisfaction with the respondent corporation. If the respondent corporation is a publicly traded entity, the CORE would also alert applicable securities regulators to determine whether the corporation has properly disclosed material facts related to the dispute. This would put pressure on the corporation to comply or at the very least respond to the CORE's request to cease operations.

A recommendation by the CORE to suspend operations should only be given when there is a serious exigent threat of ongoing harm to human rights or the environment where this extractive sector operates. In these extreme circumstances, the CORE may refer the matter to the Attorney General of Canada to investigate, consider bringing criminal charges and potentially seek a court injunction against the corporation, its officers, directors or individual employees. It should be stressed that this should only be used in unique circumstances that warrant a severe response. It is hoped that such a manoeuvre will never have to be employed by the CORE against a Canadian extractive sector corporation or its leaders. It should be noted that under its current mandate, the CORE can provide evidence of criminal wrongdoing to appropriate law enforcement entities, including the Royal Canadian Mounted Police.

Additionally, the CORE should be mindful in executing their responsibilities that not all host states will require intervention. Certainly, there are underdeveloped legal systems or states in distress that for various reasons fail to protect their citizens or the environment from the extractive sector. However, for reasons already identified in this book, such as international comity and others, intervention in the affairs of other states is only warranted when the state has clearly failed to act on a pressing and obvious grievance caused by the foreign extractive sector. This should be considered delicately by the CORE on a case by case basis. Further, if a complainant has launched a legal action in Canadian court based on the same facts at issue before the CORE, the ombudsperson will not conduct an investigation while litigation is pending. This will prevent collateral attacks in court as well as by the CORE and is a common practice when it comes to the functioning of a typical ombudsperson office.[10] Currently, under the CORE's Operating Procedures, the Ombudsperson has the ability to decline to review a complaint if it is being reviewed or has been reviewed in another forum.[11] A useful addition to the Operating Procedures would be further guidance on what constitutes a robust enough process from an outside forum that would cause the Ombudsperson to exercise their authority to terminate the review of a complaint.

The involvement of civil society is another aspect at the core of my proposal. I argue that the involvement of civil society in grievance mechanisms between the extractive sector and impacted communities will support the process in achieving a fair resolution. I advance the notion that the involvement of civil society organisations in dispute resolution processes may lead to the facilitation of social licence on behalf of the extractive sector.

Currently, the CORE's Operating Procedures state that civil society organisations may be requested to provide submissions as part of the CORE's fact-finding process.[12] However, it is not contemplated that civil society actors may serve as advocates on behalf of complainants or as potential mediators under the CORE's dispute resolution process. In my proposal, civil society groups will have an express role to this effect under the revised Operating Procedures, as set out in the Appendix.

It should be noted that a similar type of proposal for dispute resolution, which is incorporated into my proposed framework, has been endorsed in the UN Guiding Principles in that they recommend business enterprises seek advice from credible external civil society organisations, among other independent stakeholders.[13] While the UN Guiding Principles do not specifically address the nature of civil society's role in these processes, I explore what, specifically, this role could be in terms of the CORE. I advocate that it can involve representing

[10] L Reif, *The Ombudsman, Good Governance and the International Human Rights System* (Leiden, Martinus Nijhoff Publishers, 2004) 16.

[11] Canada, 'Operating Procedures' (n 8) ss 6.1.4, 6.2 and 14.1.2.

[12] Canada, 'Operating Procedures' (n 8) s 12.6.

[13] United Nations Special Representative on Business and Human Rights, 'The Corporate Responsibility to Respect Human Rights: An Interpretative Guide' (2011) 51–55, www.ohchr.org/Documents/Publications/HR.PUB.12.2_En.pdf.

impacted individuals and communities before a grievance mechanism or serving as a mediator. In cases with consent of all parties, they may even serve in the role of an arbitrator with the authority to make a binding decision. However, it is unlikely that extractive sector corporations will find this acceptable. Nevertheless, various alternatives for involving civil society in site-level and state-based grievance mechanisms are set out in this chapter.

Finally, it is worth noting that in framing the role of the CORE, I have deliberately chosen to avoid language such as 'substantiated' or 'unsubstantiated' in the context of complaints, for example. Instead, I utilise language such as 'with or without merit'. The reason behind this choice is that often these matters are complex and do not result in straightforward findings of wrongdoing by one party. Misunderstandings or failure to live up to voluntary measures, such as commitments to build local schools or infrastructure for drinking water, are often central to the disputes between the extractive sector and impacted communities. As such, in most of the proceedings before the CORE, they will not seek to find liability or fault, as is the case with most judicial proceedings where laws have been contravened. Instead, the CORE will make determinations on whether the complaint has potential to be constructively resolved through a dispute resolution process.

The next section provides an overview of the Performance Guidelines, which outline the social and economic standards that the CORE will expect Canadian corporations to meet while operating abroad. As part of my proposal, these six guidelines will form the basis for allegations of wrongdoing by extractive sector corporations.

A. Implementation of the Performance Guidelines

The former office of the CSR Counsellor had a mandate to implement six Performance Guidelines that were endorsed by the Government of Canada.[14] On their own, these Performance Guidelines do not create legal liability as they are aspirational and voluntary. However, under my proposal these guidelines will be operationalised with legal import as the CORE will be able to levy financial penalties against corporations that do not abide by these Performance Guidelines.

I argue these Performance Guidelines provide excellent standards for the CORE to consider as the focus of any complaint. They are well-developed and pervasively used. Take, for example, the Performance Standards of the World Bank.[15] They are one of the most widely recognised instruments for mitigating

[14] Global Affairs Canada, 'Role of the Office of the Corporate Social Responsibility Counsellor' (Government of Canada, 2017), www.international.gc.ca/csr_counsellor-conseiller_rse/Our_Role-Notre_Role.aspx?lang=eng.

[15] International Finance Corporation World Bank Group, 'IFC Performance Standards on Environmental and Social Sustainability – Effective January 1, 2012'.

social and environmental risks in site-level development projects.[16] They are also very comprehensive, covering topics such as working conditions, resource efficiency, pollution prevention, community health, safety, security, involuntary resettlement, biodiversity and protection for Indigenous peoples. There are even disclosure requirements on industry as the International Finance Corporation (IFC) Policy promotes transparency by requiring industry to publicly disclose royalties, taxes and government profit-sharing agreements.[17]

The Voluntary Principles are also an important component in the Performance Guidelines, in particular for extractive sector companies operating in active conflict zones. They require industry to ensure that only reasonable force is used in protecting overseas facilities and to respect the exercise of basic labour rights.[18] In a Canadian context, this is relevant when considering legal cases such as *Hudbay*[19] which involve allegations that, if proven, violate the Voluntary Principles.

One of the shortcomings of the Voluntary Principles is the lack of a publicly available complaint mechanism. My proposal corrects this concern as the CORE serves as a publicly available complaint mechanism that will be empowered to sanction extractive sector companies for non-compliance with the Voluntary Principles.

The OECD Guidelines is another Performance Guideline of the CORE that contains voluntary recommendations that encourage multinational corporations to respect human rights. The OECD Guidelines are not legally enforceable.[20] In the same way as the Voluntary Principles, my proposal overcomes this hurdle by creating legal, financial and reputational liability for extractive sector companies that fail to implement the standards set out in OECD Guidelines.[21]

Another Performance Guideline of the CORE is the GRI, which is an internationally-recognised voluntary reporting standard for business enterprises.[22]

[16] See S Herz et al. 'The International Finance Corporation's Performance Standards and the Equator Principles: Respecting Human Rights and Remedying Violations' (Center for Environmental Law, Bank Information Center, BankTrack, Oxfam Australia and World Resources Institute, 2008) 1, www.ciel.org/wp-content/uploads/2015/06/Ruggie_Submission.pdf.

[17] International Finance Corporation World Bank Group, 'International Finance Corporation's Policy on Environmental and Social Sustainability' (1 January 2012) 11–12.

[18] The content of the Voluntary Principles can be accessed at www.voluntaryprinciples.org/what-are-the-voluntary-principles.

[19] *Angelica Choc et al v Hudbay Minerals Inc et al* 2013 ONSC 414.

[20] OECD, 'The OECD Guidelines for Multinational Enterprises' (2011) 17, www.oecd.org/dataoecd/56/36/1922428.pdf.

[21] Technically, Canada's NCP has authority to hear complaints against Canadian companies based on non-compliance with the OECD Guidelines. My proposal does not call on the CORE to interfere or otherwise supplement that process in terms of non-extractive sector companies. Instead, I recommend the possibility for complainants with a grievance against the extractive sector to choose whether to bring their concern to either the CORE or Canada's NCP when the allegations allege a violation of the OECD Guidelines.

[22] The GRI website is accessible at www.globalreporting.org. For a comprehensive review of the GRI see P Simons and A Macklin, *The Governance Gap: Extractive Industries, Human Rights, and the Home State Advantage* (Toronto, Routledge, 2014) 158–75.

The GRI guides businesses to enhance transparency and encourage market-based rewards for effective CSR performance. Currently, while there may be market incentives for a corporation to follow the GRI, those incentives are purely voluntary. My proposal would create potential liability for corporations that fail to engage in a sufficient level of disclosure concerning their CSR practices as set out by the GRI.

The UN Guiding Principles is also a Performance Guideline of the CORE. As previously addressed throughout this book, the UN Guiding Principles create obligations on businesses to respect human rights and to develop effective site-level grievance mechanisms to deal with disputes caused by their operations. My proposal incorporates these obligations and incentivises the extractive sector to follow the instructions of the UN Guiding Principles, given that they can avoid the CORE's dispute process if they perform adequately in this regard.

Besides the UN Guiding Principles, the final Performance Guideline of the CORE is the OECD Minerals Policy. The OECD Minerals Policy is a set of rules for how businesses are to prevent the sourcing of minerals where it may potentially lead to human rights abuses.[23] Canada has been unable to pass the directive of the OECD Minerals Policy into legislation.[24] There is significant uncertainty in the US where rules have been implemented but the US Securities and Exchange Commission (SEC) appears to have effectively ceased enforcement actions.[25] Thus, it would be appropriate to operationalise the OECD Minerals Policy by allowing the CORE to penalise those who breach it. My proposal achieves this result and provides a mechanism for Canada to enforce this OECD rule, which as a member country, Canada has a responsibility to take seriously.

There are several potential examples of how the CORE can incorporate the Performance Guidelines into my proposed framework. For instance, imagine Company A is accused of employing security officials at a foreign mine who commit acts of unnecessary violence against local protestors. Further, imagine a complaint is filed with the CORE and it is found to have merit. If a penalty is assessed against Company A, after a set amount of time has passed to address the complaint, the company may request a reduced penalty on account of a number of factors. They can argue that despite this incident, their security protocols are designed to align with the Voluntary Principles. They could do so by demonstrating that their security programme is actively monitored and superior training is provided to ensure only reasonable force is used in protecting overseas facilities.

[23] OECD, 'OECD Due Diligence Guidance on Responsible Supply Chains of Minerals from Conflict-Affected and High-Risk Areas: Second Edition' (2013), www.oecd.org/corporate/mne/GuidanceEdition2.pdf.

[24] Open Parliament, 'Bill C-486 (Historical) An Act respecting corporate practices relating to the extraction, processing, purchase, trade and use of conflict minerals from the Great Lakes Region of Africa', openparliament.ca/bills/41-2/C-486/.

[25] M Butler, 'Why the Conflict Minerals Rule Refuses to Die' *Intelligize* (21 June 2018), www.intelligize.com/why-the-conflict-minerals-rule-refuses-to-die/.

Company A can also argue the same in demonstrating how they meet the objectives set out in the World Bank's IFC Policy and Environmental and Social Sustainability Performance Standards. They can even point to their CSR disclosure programmes and suggest that they exceed legally required disclosure in accordance with the GRI, which can also be considered by the CORE in reducing the assessed penalty. Conversely, the CORE can increase the penalty for failure to engage in compliance with the Performance Guidelines.

Currently, the CORE focuses on promoting only the implementation of the OECD Guidelines and the UN Guiding Principles.[26] For the reasons cited above, I suggest that the CORE should impose the standards of the six Performance Guidelines embraced in the Federal Government's 2014 CSR strategy, as all six provide clear standards for basing claims against the extractive sector.

In sum, the Performance Guidelines are effective and appropriate tools for the CSR Counsellor to use in regulating the activities of multinational extractive sector companies. For the most part, they have been developed by intergovernmental organisations and civil society groups and contain clear standards for business.

Before further examining the details of my recommendations for reform, it should also be mentioned that by design, this proposal resembles elements of the whistleblower provisions of the Dodd-Frank Act and its corollary the SEC rules.[27] These SEC rules precipitated the establishment of the SEC Office of the Whistleblower in 2012. A similar regime was subsequently instituted in Canada with the Ontario Securities Commission Office of the Whistleblower. Additionally, the proposal for reducing penalties based on maintaining effective site-level grievance mechanisms is analogous to the process currently utilised by the US Federal Sentencing Guidelines.[28] The following section provides an overview of the comparisons between these regimes and my proposal for reforming the powers of the CORE.

B. The Development of a Bounty Programme

The best way to promote the development of fair and transparent site-level grievance mechanisms is to provide the CORE the ability to award punitive measures against companies that fail to have a robust site-level grievance process in place. In this conception, when companies fail to operate an effective grievance mechanism or operate in the complete absence of a grievance mechanism; the CORE may order additional punitive measures towards the high end of the spectrum of penalties they have authority to award. As such, the complainants would receive a

[26] Order-in-Council, Privy Council Number: 2019-299 (2019).

[27] SEC Press Release, 'SEC Adopts Rules to Establish Whistleblower Program' (25 May 2011), www.sec.gov/news/press/2011/2011-116.htm.

[28] United States Sentencing Commission, 'USSC Guideline Manual' (2018) Ch 8, www.ussc.gov/guidelines/2018-guidelines-manual/2018-chapter-8.

larger financial award. I call this a 'bounty' programme for the purpose of compelling the extractive industry to develop and operate site-level grievance processes. Further, it would serve as a mechanism to root out and discourage the development of site-level grievance processes that do not meet the objectives set out in the frameworks endorsed by the CORE on what constitutes an effective site-level grievance mechanism.

This method of regulation is modelled on the SEC Office of the Whistleblower. The creation of the office was the result of the 2010 Dodd-Frank Act, which expands upon existing whistleblower laws to include 'bounty' for whistleblowers that expose previously unknown securities fraud to the SEC.[29] In implementing these provisions, the SEC rules created a 10 to 30 per cent bounty programme to reward whistleblowers who raise concerns that lead to a successful enforcement.[30] This means whistleblowers receive a portion of the fine that is levied against those who commit securities fraud. As part of this programme, the SEC purposely gave whistleblowers the ability to bypass existing corporate compliance programmes and report directly to the SEC. Further, the SEC may provide any information received through the Office of the Whistleblower to the accused company in appropriate circumstances.[31]

Whistleblowers also receive protection against retaliation, such as discipline or termination, if the whistleblower raises concerns about potential wrongdoing by their employer. However, in order to qualify for protection against retaliation, the whistleblower must report directly to the SEC, as opposed to an internal corporate compliance programme.[32]

Corporate compliance programmes are systems that are designed to detect and prevent violations of law by the agents, employees, officers and directors of a corporation. The 2002 Sarbanes-Oxley Act[33] effectively requires corporations to create internal compliance programmes to allow employees, among others, to report company misconduct.[34] The programmes are also encouraged under the New York Stock Exchange listing requirements.[35] Further, the Federal Criminal Sentencing Guidelines potentially mitigates sanctions against offending corporations when they have robust compliance programmes in place.[36]

The comparison in my proposal is that the CORE's power would equate to the SEC Office of the Whistleblower in that it can grant penalties against Canadian

[29] See Securities Whistleblower Incentives and Protections 76 Fed Reg 34300 (13 June 2011).

[30] SEC Press Release, 'Whistleblower Program' (n 27).

[31] Proposed Rules for Implementation of the Whistleblower Provisions of Section 21F of the Securities Exchange Act of 1934 Fed Reg 70488 70496 (12August 2011).

[32] *Digital Realty Trust v Somers* (2018) 583 (USC).

[33] Sarbanes Oxley Act (US), 15 USC s 7264, codified at 17 CFR, ss 307 and 806.

[34] L Hartman, 'Comment, Whistle While You Work: The Fairytale-Like Whistleblower Provisions of the Dodd-Frank Act and the Emergence of "Greedy," the Eighth Dwarf' (2011) 62 *Mercer Law Review* 1279, 1285.

[35] New York Stock Exchange Listed Company Manual s 303A.10 and Marketplace Rule 4350(n).

[36] United States Sentencing Commission, 'USSC Guideline' (n 28).

extractive sector corporations that breach the standards set out in the Performance Guidelines. The existence of a site-based, company-run grievance process would be the equivalent of a compliance programme under the SEC's bounty system. Compliance programmes are similar to site-level grievance mechanisms in the sense that they are designed, implemented and operated at the company level and are not obligatory in nature.

It should be noted that in the Interpretative Guide to the UN Guiding Principles it expressly states that site-level grievance mechanisms are distinct from compliance or whistleblower programmes. In contrast, site-level grievance mechanisms are specifically a channel for individuals, internal and external to the corporation to raise concerns about impacts on themselves. Importantly, they do not require the individual to show a breach of a corporate code or policy. However, the Interpretative Guide goes on to suggest that compliance programmes and site-level grievance mechanisms do not necessarily need to be separate.[37]

To be clear, my proposal is not advocating for the merging of corporate compliance programmes with site-level grievance mechanisms. Rather, I merely make the comparison that they are similar for the purposes of contrasting the SEC regulations on securities fraud with what I propose for regulating the foreign activities of the Canadian extractive sector. I instead advocate for the development of a site-level grievance process specifically designed for impacted communities and civil society to rectify concerns about potential human rights and environmental abuses, among other matters.

The following section is an overview of site-level grievance processes and how they can be effectively implemented into my overall proposal for holding Canada's foreign extractive sector to account.

C. Untapped Potential: Site-Level Grievance Mechanisms

A site-level grievance mechanism is a company sponsored and financed process that allows impacted communities and individuals to raise concerns directly with a company. Site-level grievance mechanisms assist companies in addressing disputes in a non-judicial manner. They are broadly defined as 'a process or a set of processes for receiving, evaluating and addressing grievances from affected communities, in a timely and consistent manner at the site or operational level'.[38]

Several benefits of implementing a site-level grievance mechanism have been suggested. For instance, some commentators have identified a business case for promoting them, as they tend to mitigate the costs of conflict with affected

[37] United Nations, 'Interpretative Guide' (n 13) 69.

[38] E Wilson and E Blackmore (eds), *Dispute or Dialogue: Community Perspectives on Company-Led Grievance Mechanisms* (London, International Institute for Environment and Development, 2013) 10.

stakeholders and local communities.[39] Further, they help resolve disputes before they escalate and potentially reduce the risk of actions such as protests, blockades and similar activities. Site-level grievance mechanisms may also provide early warning to potential project concerns and strengthen relations between extractive sector operators and impacted communities. Arguably, they facilitate a learning culture that fosters the prevention of repeat grievances. In this way, they potentially provide benefits to both companies and communities. Site-level grievance mechanisms can also assist the extractive sector to be more socially, culturally and environmentally responsive to the local communities and other individuals that their operations impact.[40]

There have been certain concerns raised about company-run, site-level grievance mechanisms. For instance, many of them are established in an ad hoc manner and lack transparency.[41] Further, in the absence of a strong corporate policy and management framework regarding operating site-level grievance mechanisms, the results can be incoherent and inconsistent.[42] Finally, lack of meaningful consultation by industry with impacted communities about their grievance process has also been raised as a concern.[43]

Many extractive sector corporations have developed grievance mechanisms for individuals and communities affected by their presence in the foreign countries that they operate within. Given that these mechanisms are designed to address local community issues, the procedure of receiving, investigating and resolving grievances often differs between companies and even from location to location within the same company.[44]

The former office of the CSR Counsellor developed a CSR Standards Navigation tool in 2017 for companies to use to evaluate their social and environmental performance, including a review of corporate governance and labour issues.[45] This tool was aimed at fostering compliance with the six listed Performance Guidelines and does not specifically address the implementation of a site-level grievance programme.

[39] R Davis and D Franks, 'The Cost of Conflict with Local Communities in the Extractive Industry' (SR Mining, October 2011) 9, www.csrm.uq.edu.au/publications/the-costs-of-conflict-with-local-communities-in-the-extractive-industry.

[40] *Ibid.*

[41] MiningWatch Canada, 'Privatized Remedy and Human Rights: Re-Thinking Project-Level Grievance Mechanisms' (2014) 7, miningwatch.ca/publications/2014/12/1/privatized-remedy-and-human-rights-re-thinking-project-level-grievance.

[42] International Petroleum Industry Environmental Conservation Association (IPIECA), 'Community Grievance Mechanisms in the Oil and Gas Industry. A Manual for Implementing Operational-Level Grievance Mechanisms and Designing Corporate Frameworks' (2015) 63, www.ipieca.org/resources/good-practice/community-grievance-mechanisms-in-the-oil-and-gas-industry-a-manual-for-implementing-operational-level-grievance-mechanisms-and-designing-corporate-frameworks.

[43] MiningWatch Canada, 'Privatized Remedy' (n 41) 6.

[44] IPIECA, 'Community Grievance Mechanisms' (n 42) 42.

[45] Global Affairs Canada, 'Corporate Social Responsibility Standards Navigation Tool' (Government of Canada, 2018), www.international.gc.ca/csr_counsellor-conseiller_rse/csrsnt-gnrse.aspx?lang=eng.

As a shift beyond this tool utilised by the CSR Counsellor, I recommend that the CORE adopt a more concrete framework for corporations to handle disputes through an effective, fair and transparent site-level grievance process. Design and implementation manuals for site-level grievance mechanisms have been created by international organisations, notably the International Finance Corporation[46] and International Council on Mining & Metals.[47] The International Petroleum Industry Environmental Conservation Association (IPIECA) has also developed a manual for extractive sector companies to implement and design a site-level grievance mechanism. According to the standards recommended by the IPIECA, an effective site-level grievance mechanism will have sufficient resources, clarity on roles, systems to monitor and assess performance and commitment from management to meaningfully address complaints.[48] At least one Canadian mining industry group has also created an implementation guide for site-level grievance mechanisms.[49] Ideally, the CORE should study these manuals and formally adopt one or several of these approaches, or develop their own. There is also guidance available from the OECD specifically for the extractive sector on meaningful stakeholder engagement that the CORE may endorse when it comes to local consultation on the design and function of a site-level grievance mechanism.[50]

In sum, I propose the utilisation of industry-run, site-level grievance mechanisms as the primary function for resolving complaints from impacted individuals. However, it is recognised there are potential shortcomings with this recommendation. While understanding the potential that site-level grievance mechanisms possess, some commentators have suggested that they are not a panacea in the absence of a higher-level dispute resolution process.[51] For example, site-level grievance mechanisms typically lack any oversight by a third-party dispute resolution process to ensure that a fair remedy has been provided when warranted. This has been cited as a critical gap in ensuring effective remedies at the site-level and runs counter to several of the effectiveness criteria in Guiding Principle 31.[52]

[46] International Finance Corporation World Bank Group, 'Good Practice Note: Addressing Grievances from Project-Affected Communities – Guidance for Projects and Companies on Designing Grievance Mechanisms' (Washington, 2009).

[47] International Council on Mining & Metals, 'Human Rights in the Mining & Metals Industry: Handling and Resolving Local Level Concerns & Grievances' (2009).

[48] IPIECA, 'Community Grievance Mechanisms' (n 42) 28.

[49] The Mining Association of Canada, 'Site-Level Grievance and Community Response Mechanisms: A Practical Design and Implementation Guide for the Resource Development Industry' (2015), mining.ca/site-level-grievance-mechanisms-guide.

[50] OECD, 'OECD Due Diligence Guidance for Meaningful Stakeholder Engagement in the Extractive Sector' (Paris, OECD Publishing, 2017), doi.org/10.1787/9789264252462-en.

[51] M Torrance, 'Remedying Human Rights: From the International, Regional and Domestic Status Quo to Future Innovations' (Human Rights Law and the Extractive Industries, Rocky Mountain Mineral Law Foundation, February 2016) 22.

[52] D Kemp and CJ Bond, 'Mining Industry Perspectives on Handling Community Grievances: Summary and Analysis of Industry Interviews' (Centre for Social Responsibility in Mining, the University of Queensland, April 2009) 21–22, www.csrm.uq.edu.au/media/docs/260/mining_industry_perspectives_on_handling_community_grievances_summary.pdf.

The question remains then how such gaps may be closed. In my proposal, I attempt to harness the CORE as a dispute resolution forum that can monitor site-level grievance mechanisms to ensure that fair remedies have been provided. Oversight comes in the form of the ability of industry-run, site-level grievance processes and any findings they reach to be reviewed directly by the CORE. This will ensure that a fair remedy is achieved because complainants will have the ability to raise concerns directly with the CORE if they have not been provided proper redress from an industry-run, site-level grievance mechanism.

I maintain that it is important for complainants to first attempt resolution of a dispute with the extractive sector corporation, preferably at the site-level rather than bringing a complaint directly to the CORE. The convenience of site-level grievance mechanisms is predicated on the idea that complainants will be able to access a more readily available remedy as opposed to filing a complaint with the state-based office of the CORE in Canada. Barriers to filing a complaint in Canada include presuming that the individual raising the complaint is aware of this foreign office, one that is likely at a considerable distance from their location, and language proficiency issues. I suggest that these potential downsides to site-based and state-based grievance mechanisms may be adequately addressed by fostering a role for civil society.

D. Civil Society within the Regulatory Regimes of the Global Extractive Sector

The players in resolving extractive sector disputes have expanded beyond the traditional Westphalian model, which recognises states as the only legitimate actors, to now include a number of civil society organisations such as Oxfam and Amnesty international.[53] Although these actors play an important role in the lawmaking process, they do not possess the legal rights and obligations of states.

One of the goals of this book is to determine whether civil society organisations have a quasi-regulatory role concerning the human rights performance of extractive sector corporations. In this chapter, I make the case that they do, as these disputes between seemingly disparate groups require some sort of third party intervention. I suggest that civil society organisations can fulfill the role of mediator, arbitrator or act as a representative of complainants for the purposes of site-level grievance mechanisms.

As a starting point, some definitions are required for mediators, arbitrators and representatives. A representative simply advocates on behalf of a party before a contested hearing or during some form of negotiation.[54] In contrast, mediation is

[53] AC Cutler, *Private Power and Global Authority: Transnational Merchant Law in the Global Political Economy* (Cambridge, Cambridge University Press, 2003) 247–49.

[54] M McInnes, I Kerr and A VanDuzer, *Managing the Law: The Legal Aspects of Doing Business*, 5th edn (Boston, Pearson Education, 2017) 33.

a process in which a neutral person, known as a mediator, helps the parties reach an agreement.[55] Finally, arbitration is a process with a neutral third party or a series of individuals, known as arbitrator(s), whom impose a binding decision.[56]

In mediation, the parties can select the mediator and control the outcome, as any recommendation of the mediator is non-binding. Parties can also control an arbitration process by consenting to the selection of the arbitrator(s). Arbitration and mediation have both been characterised as processes that allow the parties to maintain an ongoing and workable relationship.[57] Further, in contrast to a judicial hearing, both processes are often confidential. The primary difference between mediation and arbitration is that an arbitrator renders a binding decision, whereas in mediation, the parties must consent to any recommendations of the mediator. Thus, the parties do not control the outcome in arbitration in the same way they do with mediation.

As previously set out, site-level grievance mechanisms carry potential shortcomings such as they may amount to mere negotiation between unequal parties. As an example, the extractive sector has been accused of not fairly engaging in meaningful consultation with impacted communities during grievance processes.[58] A potential reason for this is the lack of transparency concerning discussions in a private site-level grievance process. Further, given that a company controls its own site-level mechanism and cannot be compelled to act by effective government oversight, there is no guarantee of a fair remedy.

I posit that if extractive sector companies agree to have civil society organisations act as a mediator, arbitrator or representative of the complainant, then these shortcomings may be resolved. For instance, the involvement of civil society in a site-level grievance mechanism may assure transparency given that the civil society group could draw public and government attention to ineffective dispute resolution processes. Similarly, civil society could raise concerns if a company offers insufficient remedies or in the event that the complainant is simply stonewalled by the company.

Enabling trusted civil society organisations to act as an access point between industry and impacted local communities is an approach that has been endorsed by the UN.[59] It is also suggested in the Interpretative Guide on the UN Guiding Principles that funding for the involvement of civil society in site-level grievance processes should be provided by industry, as long as this does not damage the credibility of the civil society group on account of their participation.[60]

Moreover, there has been a consistent track record of support from civil society groups in attempting to remedy disputes between impacted communities and the extractive sector. Civil society groups have proven to be formidable

[55] *Ibid* 37.
[56] *Ibid* 54.
[57] *Ibid* 55.
[58] MiningWatch Canada, 'Privatized Remedy' (n 41) 6.
[59] United Nations, 'Interpretative Guide' (n 13) 72
[60] United Nations, 'Interpretative Guide' (n 13) 72.

at organising legal challenges against the extractive sector in judicial procedures using the US Alien Tort Statute 1789 (ATS)[61] and in mediating disputes between local communities and the extractive sector in non-judicial settings. For example, the disputes before the former office of the CSR Counsellor in Canada and Australia's Mining Ombudsman (AMO) illustrate that civil society has been highly active as an advocate and mediator in this area.[62] Thus, the ATS cases and the non-judicial proceedings before the former office of the CSR Counsellor and the AMO illustrate the great potential that civil society groups could bring to the issue of resolving grievances between the extractive sector and impacted communities.

Civil society may also play a pivotal part in elevating site-level grievance mechanisms in a way that manifests a social licence to operate. Social licence represents a merging of legal regulations with standards of suitable business conduct.[63] It is not conferred through formal legal authority. Rather, it is granted by groups such as civil society organisations.[64] Extractive sector companies that utilise civil society groups in their site-level grievance mechanisms may be praised by the CORE in a way that achieves a sense of social licence.

The necessity of attaining social licence as an emerging business model has elevated the role of civil society organisations in setting informal standards of corporate accountability. These less tangible factors, such as the CORE contributing to the positive reputation of responsible business corporations, are also effective in an overall approach to improving the extraterritorial performance of the Canadian extractive sector.

For these reasons, I envision civil society groups serving in the capacity as representatives of impacted communities before industry-run, site-level grievance mechanisms and before the CORE. Alternatively, in cases where they do not serve as a representative, I foresee civil society acting as a mediator in a site-level grievance process, in the same capacity as the AMO.

In the role of a representative, I suggest that civil society can draw on its expertise in advocating for the best interests of impacted communities. As one example, savvy and experienced civil society groups will have the nuanced understanding to request remedies and outcomes based on their knowledge of best practices for the extractive sector around the world. This knowledge of how to resolve grievances between the extractive sector and impacted communities is based in part on

[61] Alien Tort Statute 1789 (28 USC § 1350); J Davis, *Justice Across Borders: The Struggle for Human Rights in U.S. Courts* (Cambridge, Cambridge University Press, 2008) 18, 52, 274–75.

[62] For examples, see the overview on the work of the Canadian CSR Counsellor and the Oxfam Mining Ombudsman in Australia provided in chapter six.

[63] L Edelman, 'The Endogeneity of Legal Regulation: Grievance Procedures as Rational Myth' (1999) 105 *American Journal of Sociology* 406.

[64] See, eg, HH Koh, 'The 1994 Roscoe Pound Lecture: Transnational Legal Process' (1996) 75 *Nebraska Law Review* 181; HH Koh, 'The 1998 Frankel Lecturer: Bringing International Human Rights Home' (1998) 35 *Houston Law Review* 647; LC Backer, 'The Structure of Global Law: Fracture, Fluidity, Permeability, and Polycentricity' (2012) 17 *Tilburg Law Review* 177.

their experience advocating on behalf of plaintiffs using the ATS and in other non-judicial proceedings before the former office of the CSR Counsellor and the AMO. Without this assistance, it is unlikely that individuals impacted by the extractive sector will know what expectations they should have of extractive sector operators in their local community.

I suggest that the same experience will come to bear when a civil society group serves in the role of a mediator in terms of facilitating a fair conclusion to a dispute between the extractive sector and impacted individuals. Although it is worth considering, I am skeptical of whether civil society serving as arbitrators between the extractive sector and impacted communities is a viable alternative for dispute resolution.

While an interesting concept, it is a somewhat dubious notion to assume that the extractive industry would agree to allow civil society organisations to make a final binding decision in a site-level grievance process. Given their track record in advocating on behalf of plaintiffs,[65] civil society is often partial to the protection of human rights and the environment and is likely to be seen as an adverse party to industry. However, civil society organisations fulfilling a role akin to a mediator or representative would not render the same partiality. A mediator only facilitates the decision-making process, as opposed to exercising any actual decision-making authority. Equally, a representative for a complainant is not in a position to prejudice an extractive sector company, as the company can have their own representative as part of the grievance process. However, for the reasons cited above, the extractive sector may be incredulous to the idea that civil society mediators will be impartial. In order to convince companies and complainants alike that civil society actors can be unbiased in these processes, I recommend that the CORE reach out to develop working relationships with reputable civil society organisations located in areas where Canadian extractive sector companies operate. The CORE should extensively evaluate these organisations for impartiality based on their objectives, allegiances and mandates. The CORE will communicate to companies and the complainants that they have completed this process so that they know they can rely on these organisations' impartiality.

As a next step, the CORE should develop a publicly available roster of vetted civil society organisations that they can point complainants and extractive sector corporations to in order to deal with various questions or disputes. These civil society groups could serve in the capacity of representatives, mediators or arbitrators in a site-level grievance mechanism or even as part of the CORE's dispute resolution process.

The CORE should develop criteria for determining whether a civil society group qualifies to be listed on this roster. The criteria used in determining eligibility could include the objectives, independence, size, location and mandate of the civil society organisation. The primary focus in vetting these organisations should

[65] Davis, *Justice Across Borders* 18, 52, 274–75.

be whether they are reputable and knowledgeable in resolving specialised disputes between the extractive sector and impacted communities. This roster should be visited annually by the CORE to ensure that the listed civil society groups remain eligible.

I further suggest that civil society organisations can perform the necessary groundwork of communicating with local communities to make them aware of the services offered from industry-run, site-level grievance mechanisms as well as the CORE. Extractive sector companies should also reach out to civil society groups to assist in a formal capacity in their site-level grievance mechanisms. Extractive sector corporations can be incentivised to do so if the involvement of civil society is regarded by the CORE as a best practice and highly encouraged. As part of my proposal, extractive sector corporations would be given credit for involving civil society groups that are listed on the CORE's roster in their site-level grievance processes. This would provide a mitigating factor in the event that a penalty is assessed against the corporation. Moreover, this would serve as a positive factor in the event that the CORE, upon receiving a complaint, is; 1) considering whether to default to a previous decision of the company's site-level grievance process; or 2) whether the company's grievance process is effective and capable of rendering a fair and impartial decision prior to the dispute being considered by the CORE. This incentive will cause extractive sector corporations to adopt the practice of involving civil society groups so as to insulate themselves from review, and possible enforcement action by the CORE.

Similarly, I recommend that civil society may serve an important role in state-based grievance mechanisms such as with the CORE. The former office of the CSR Counsellor permitted a role for civil society, and these groups had extensively participated in the past. For instance, there are several examples where the CSR Counsellor considered complaints brought by civil society organisations on behalf of individuals, groups or communities.[66] In one particular case involving a copper mine in Argentina operated by McEwen Mining, two civil society organisations brought a complaint to the CSR Counsellor in their own right representing an environmental cause without the veneer that the representation was on behalf of a local community. In determining whether these civil society groups had standing in the McEwen Mining case, the CSR Counsellor found that they met the necessary requirements to bring a complaint.[67]

My proposal follows the CSR Counsellor's guidance in the McEwen Mining case and expressly assigns civil society formal representative status to advocate on behalf of impacted individuals under the revised Operating Procedures in the Appendix. Further, I suggest that the CORE utilise an alternative to their own dispute resolution process by referring complainants and respondent corporations

[66] Torrance, 'Remedying Human Rights' 30.

[67] Global Affairs Canada, 'Request for Review Closing Report File #2012-03-ARG' (Government of Canada, 2012), www.international.gc.ca/csr_counsellor-conseiller_rse/publications/2012-03-ARG_closing_report-rapport_final.aspx?lang=eng.

to a civil society mediator near the location of the dispute. These civil society mediators can be drawn from the roster of civil society organisations that have been vetted by the CORE as reputable and knowledgeable in resolving specialised disputes involving the extractive sector and local communities. In unique cases with a request of one of the parties, the CORE may even serve as an intervenor in the mediation process in order to assist in facilitating a settlement. It is anticipated this may occur in cases where the CORE has material information or expertise that will assist the assigned mediator in resolving that particular matter.

This reliance on mediation would reserve the CORE's formal dispute resolution process to matters where a civil society mediator at the local level is not an option. Accordingly, this would help to preserve the resources of the CORE as a state-based, tax-payer funded institution to perform only dispute resolution services in matters where it becomes absolutely necessary. Under the CORE's current Operating Procedures, they do set out a process for mediation, but they do not expressly create a role for civil society actors in the dispute process.[68]

In my proposed Operating Procedures, I further specify that extractive sector corporations should fund the involvement of civil society groups to act as a mediator or representative of the complainants in their site-level grievance process. These civil society groups should be jointly chosen by the corporation and complainant, and ideally drawn from the roster of qualified civil society organisations as established by the CORE. Finally, the proposed Operating Procedures recommend the development of a fee schedule to set out the reasonable costs that civil society groups will likely incur by acting in the role of representative, arbitrator or mediator. This will help guide both the extractive sector and civil society groups in determining which costs and what amount is appropriate for industry to fund in conducting these dispute resolution activities. As mentioned above, in unique cases where the CORE serves as an intervenor in a mediation process, their reasonable costs may also be reimbursed by the respondent corporation pursuant to the fee schedule.

I do not set out provisions in the proposed Operating Procedures for any prohibition on civil society groups acting formally as a representative of the extractive sector, nor do I anticipate this occurring. Civil society groups are understandably perceived as focusing on the protection of human rights and the environment, as this is often the point of contention between them and the interests of the extractive sector. This is demonstrated by civil societies' long-standing involvement representing victims of alleged human rights abuses, as opposed to aligning with industry.[69]

As a final note on this point, I suggest that the CORE should encourage local civil society organisations to participate in dispute resolution processes between the extractive industry and impacted individuals, as opposed to

[68] Canada, 'Operating Procedures' (n 8) ss 8.1, 9.2 and 9.4–9.10.
[69] Davis (n 61) 18, 52, 274–5.

global organisations. Some have suggested that large-scale, global civil society actors may be more aligned with the interests of states rather than local groups that are actually impacted by the extractive sector.[70] Further, local civil society organisations have different perspectives; modes of operation and communication sources that make them uniquely suited to resolve local disputes.[71]

For these reasons, civil society groups located near the origin of an extractive sector dispute will likely provide a niche service by focusing on the particular issues at hand and knowing the key players involved. This is in contrast to global civil society that has different interests and perspectives and is likely distracted by concurrently tackling several issues in many various locations. Thus, the global groups arguably lack the specialisation, focus and perhaps even passion to drive for an adequate remedy in comparison to local civil society groups.

The CORE and those who operate industry-run grievance processes should be cognizant of this trend and ensure that they elevate local civil society groups in the role of mediator, arbitrator or representative of impacted communities when it comes to dispute resolution within the extractive sector. This can be achieved by carving out in the CORE's Operating Procedures an emphasis on industry engaging local civil society groups as part of their site-level grievance process. Further, according to the draft Operating Procedures, any dispute reviewed by the CORE will, in the regular course, seek out local civil society to be a part of the review process in some capacity whether as a representative, mediator or arbitrator.

The following section is an overview of the enforcement, accountability and compliance features embedded in my proposal. These elements are a key reason that the proposal, if implemented, stands to be effective in resolving disputes between the extractive sector and impacted communities.

E. Enforcement, Accountability and Compliance

The proposed new capacity of assessing administrative penalties would provide the CORE with a tool of enforcement against extractive industry members who are unwilling to develop their own internal site-level grievance programmes, or against those who utilise programmes with inadequate processes. As previously suggested, further guidance should be provided by the CORE in terms of defining effective benchmarks of a site-level grievance programme.

In focusing on resolving these disputes in a company-run, site-level grievance programme, there is a peripheral benefit to Canadian tax payers, who would not have to fund either court challenges by overseas plaintiffs or dispute resolutions

[70] LC Backer, 'An Institutional Role for Civil Society Within the U.N. Guiding Principles?: Comments on César Rodríguez-Garavito and Tatiana Andia "Business and Human Rights: Beyond the End of the Beginning"' (Workshop on Implementing the UN's Guiding Principles on Business and Human Rights: A South-Initiated North-South Dialogue, Brown University, February 2014) 8.

[71] *Ibid.*

before the CORE. Those costs would instead be borne by industry. As such, the extractive sector would be held primarily accountable for resolving these disputes, as opposed to a government regulator such as the CORE.

Even though a primary focus of this proposal is the development of remedy processes funded by industry, I suggest that my proposal does not come up short in terms of providing tangible results for victims of the foreign Canadian extractive sector. New powers to award penalties vested with the CORE would provide effective oversight to ensure fair remedies, though the CORE would continue to exercise the power of holding its own dispute resolution process in Canada if it became necessary. The aim of this proposal is to make cases where the CORE actually convenes a dispute process an aberration as opposed to the norm.

In terms of conducting investigations, I suggest granting various powers to the CORE that include capabilities analogous to those of the Canada Energy Regulator (CER). For example, the CER is a court of record and its decisions are judicially noticed.[72] It has the power to compel the attendance of, swearing and examination of witnesses. It can demand the production and inspection of documents and can seek entry onto property.[73] In short, its powers, rights and privileges are equivalent to those vested in a Canadian superior court, and their decisions are binding.

The proposed new powers set out above would allow the CORE to conduct thorough investigations and assign penalties to companies that fail to comply with the six Performance Guidelines endorsed by the CORE. Crucially, they could also assign penalties against companies that fail to participate in their dispute process. Such administrative penalties would carry the same weight as judicial pronouncements and would be enforceable through processes similar to those used by Canadian administrative agencies such as the CER. All of these factors would necessarily compel extractive sector compliance.

Another option of dispute resolution is arbitration. While I am doubtful that the extractive sector will allow civil society organisations to serve as arbitrators for the purpose of rendering a binding decision, I do accept that arbitration can be a flexible and efficient dispute resolution process. My concern with allowing unfettered arbitration is that these processes are often confidential, informal and do not always adhere to procedural rules that guarantee fairness or effective oversight. With that said, a primary concern of the UN Guiding Principles is assuring access to a remedy in cases where wrongdoing has been found.[74]

In my draft Operating Procedures, I set out the possibility for parties to select binding arbitration as one form of dispute resolution. The draft rules also encourage the involvement of civil society groups in representing complainants or potentially serving in the capacity of arbitrators. Further, the draft Operating Procedures require that these arbitrations be conducted pursuant to private international arbitration legislation in Canada.

[72] Canadian Energy Regulator Act SC 2019 c 28 s 10, s 31(1).
[73] *Ibid* s 31(2).
[74] SRBHR, 'United Nations Guiding Principles' (n 1) 27.

Canada has vigorous laws for private international arbitrations, as it was the first country to formally adopt the United Nations Commission on International Trade Law Model Law on International Commercial Arbitration (Model Law).[75] The Model Law covers all aspects of the arbitral process, such as requiring a written arbitration agreement or contract, the composition and jurisdiction of an arbitral tribunal, the extent of court intervention through to the recognition and enforcement of arbitral awards.[76] It reflects international consensus on best practices for private international arbitration.

Every province and territory in Canada has specific legislation incorporating the Model Law for circumstances where one or more of the parties reside outside of Canada,[77] whereas the Federal Government does not.[78] The lack of federal authority over private arbitrations is explainable given that it has traditionally been understood that the Canadian Constitution confers arbitral jurisdiction with the provinces and territories.[79]

In operationalising the Model Law, the provincial and territorial statutes provide for the recognition and enforcement of arbitral awards and require a written arbitration agreement that sets out the terms of arbitration. These statutes are uniformly equivalent across the provinces and territories given that their purpose is to incorporate the Model Law. In my proposal, the applicable legislation for arbitration will be the province or territory where the respondent party is incorporated or where they acknowledge that they are governed by that jurisdiction. Providing rules to ensure that arbitrations are conducted pursuant to best practices and that resulting awards will be strictly enforced promotes compliance and accountability of the extractive sector in these disputes.

It should be noted that the current Operating Procedures of the CORE do allow for referral to outside arbitration if all parties agree.[80] My proposal goes beyond

[75] C Thomson and A Finn, 'International Commercial Arbitration: A Canadian Perspective' (2002) 18 *Arbitration International* 206.

[76] United Nations, 'UNCITRAL Model Law on International Commercial Arbitration (1985), with Amendments as Adopted in 2006' (2006), www.uncitral.org/pdf/english/texts/arbitration/arb-rules/MLARB-english_revised%2006.pdf.

[77] International Commercial Arbitration Act SA 2000 c I-5 (Alberta); International Commercial Arbitration Act RSBC 1996, c 233 (British Columbia); International Commercial Arbitration Act CCSM c C151 (Manitoba); International Commercial Arbitration Act RSNB 2011 c 176 (New Brunswick); International Commercial Arbitration Act RSNL 1990 c I-I5 (Newfoundland and Labrador); International Commercial Arbitration Act RSNWT 1988 c I-6 (Northwest Territories); International Commercial Arbitration Act RSNS 1989 c 234 (Nova Scotia); International Commercial Arbitration Act RSPEl 1988 c I-5 (Prince Edward Island); International Commercial Arbitration Act SS 1988 9 c 1-10.2 (Saskatchewan); International Commercial Arbitration Act SO 2017 c 2 Sch 5 (Ontario); International Commercial Arbitration Act RSY 2002 c 123 (Yukon); An Act to Amend the Civil Code and the Code of Civil Procedure in Respect of Arbitration SQ 1986 c 73 (Quebec); and International Commercial Arbitration Act RSNWT 1988 c I-6 (Nunavut).

[78] The Federal Government does have the Commercial Arbitration Act which adopts the Model Law. However, it is limited to maritime or admiralty arbitrations or those disputes that involve the Federal Government. Thus, it does not apply to circumstances between the Canadian extractive sector and impacted individuals abroad. Commercial Arbitration Act RSC 1985 c 17.

[79] Thomson and Finn, 'International Commercial Arbitration' 206.

[80] Canada, 'Operating Procedures' (n 8) s 18.

this process and seeks to ensure that if arbitration is chosen for dispute resolution by the involved parties, those parties will be afforded the opportunity to receive successful arbitral awards through a fair process.

F. Procedural Fairness and Judicial Review

The Supreme Court of Canada has defined procedural fairness as the right of individuals to have an opportunity to present their case fully and fairly, and have decisions affecting their rights, interests or privileges decided using a fair, impartial and open process.[81] Procedural fairness is crucial because it has the effect of persuading parties to accept outcomes that might initially appear to conflict with their interests.[82] It also furthers the element of legitimacy in Guiding Principle 31 as a necessary hallmark of an effective dispute process by ensuring an independent judicial review of the dispute resolution process for basic principles of procedural fairness.[83]

As one example of ensuring procedural fairness, I incorporate in the draft Operating Procedures in the Appendix a requirement that the CORE will release written decisions at the conclusion of its dispute resolution process in a timely manner. These written decisions may praise extractive sector companies that meet or exceed the Performance Guidelines. Alternatively, they may condemn companies that fail to provide sufficient site-level grievance mechanisms. In either case, providing reasons for a decision is in keeping with the rules of procedural fairness.[84]

Further, I include in the draft Operating Procedures a requirement during the review process for complainants and respondent corporations to disclose material information that they intend to rely on before the CORE. My draft Operating Procedures also state that all hearings before the CORE will be open to the public unless a legitimate request for confidentiality is made by one of the parties and approved by the CORE. This is similar to the current rules regarding confidentiality before the CORE.[85]

Complainants and respondent corporations will also have participatory rights, including a meaningful opportunity to present their cases fairly and fully. Finally, through maintaining independence and impartiality, the CORE must ensure that their decisions are perceived to be free from any reasonable apprehension of bias.[86] These features are the primary trademarks of procedural fairness.[87]

[81] *Baker v Canada (Minister of Citizenship and Immigration)* (1999) 2 817 (SCC), para 28.

[82] D Szablowski, *Transnational Law and Local Struggles: Mining, Communities and the World Bank* (Oxford, Hart Publishing, 2007) 12, 17 and 20.

[83] Torrance (n 51) 31.

[84] A Dodek et al (eds), *Public Law: Cases, Commentary, and Analysis*, 3rd edn (Toronto, Edmond Montgomery, 2015) 572.

[85] Canada, 'Operating Procedures' (n 8) ss 5.3 and 20.

[86] Dodek et al, *Public Law* 574.

[87] Dodek et al (n 84) 568.

I also address the critical issue of judicial review of the CORE's decisions. In my proposal, the CORE may grant a remedy that is binding on the parties, and therefore has the ability to definitively resolve disputes, subject only to judicial review in the Canadian Federal Court system. I suggest that this would be the appropriate court to begin the judicial review process in accordance with Canadian administrative agencies that are similarly placed and comparable to the CORE. For instance, requests for judicial review from the Office of the Privacy Commissioner of Canada are directed to the Federal Court.[88] The CER and the Canadian International Trade Tribunal, among several other Canadian administrative agencies, direct any judicial review applications to the Federal Court of Appeal.[89] I would recommend the same process be implemented regarding the decisions of the CORE to either the Federal Court or Federal Court of Appeal.[90] This would be an improvement over the current system that does not afford a right for judicial review except for referral to Canada's NCP, where there is no judicial review afforded from those outcomes.

Providing unsatisfied parties, both impacted communities and industry, the right to judicial review furthers principles such as legitimacy and procedural fairness and is highly desirable for those seeking better accountability over the foreign operations of the Canadian extractive sector. The following section will provide a discussion of potential critiques of my proposal.

G. Critique of the Proposal

The proposal that I have put forth has potential shortcomings. For instance, it is possible that irresponsible companies will not develop effective site-level grievance mechanisms, assuming that impacted communities will always elect to report externally to the CORE in order to be eligible for a bounty on any levied penalty. This would potentially mean that impacted communities would not enjoy the benefits of a strong site-based complaint process, further risking the kind of human rights and environmental harm that the CORE is meant to prevent.

In response to this critique, I would point out that under my proposal, the CORE would have the power to consider if a site-level grievance mechanism exists and whether it has been utilised before formally reviewing a complaint. As such, they could order the complainant to exhaust that opportunity before the CORE would take any action. Further, extractive sector companies would be properly incentivised to operate site-level mechanisms to maintain control over disputes to begin with. If the company resolves the matter internally they may proceed

[88] Personal Information Protection Act SA 2003, c P-6.5, ss 14 and 15.

[89] Federal Courts Act RSC 1985, c F-7, s 28(1).

[90] Note that in the draft Operating Procedures (Appendix), I have set the Federal Court of Appeal as the entity to hear these appeal matters.

with their operations in a peaceful fashion with minimal impact to profitability, as opposed to the possibility of discontinuing the project during the course of the review process by the CORE. The proposal also incentivises the extractive sector to develop these programmes to serve as a mitigating factor if a penalty is ever assessed. In this way, developing effective site-level grievance mechanisms and otherwise adopting CSR practices based on the Performance Guidelines creates a strategic advantage for extractive sector companies, with or without a formal review process by the CORE.

There is also a concern that a bounty programme may produce meritless complaints to the CORE with strongly biased, less reliable information in the hope that the complainant will be awarded a significant bounty. This could result in the CORE expending their limited resources on voluminous claims that are ultimately found to be without merit.

As a counter-argument, the involvement of civil society groups in representing and mediating the claims before the CORE will be helpful in ensuring that such claims are legitimate grievances. This can be relied upon given that civil society groups will not be eligible for any bounty programme under the draft Operating Procedures. Further, I suggest that legitimate civil society organisations that have been approved by the CORE and placed on its official roster will not spend their resources on claims that are groundless.

A valid point should be made in that this process gives the CORE the discretion to decline to hear matters if an effective site-level grievance process is in place. As such, the CORE would likely only review complaints where the respondent corporations have not provided effective site-level grievance mechanisms concerning their foreign operations. Thus, it is meaningless to suggest that the CORE will consider a case where a complaint is found to have merit and then subsequently award a reduced penalty based upon evidence of an effective site-level grievance programme. Under my proposal, the CORE will only award penalties that result in an increased punitive award where a site-level grievance mechanism is not in place or is insufficient.

I am aware of this irony embedded within the proposal, and it is entirely the point. By design, the CORE's dispute resolution process will only become necessary when respondent corporations that are the subject of a complaint have not established effective grievances mechanisms or otherwise have not taken their obligations under the Performance Guidelines seriously. The message is clear to industry that they must deal with these matters through their own site-level grievance mechanisms and do so fairly, efficiency and transparently in accordance with the Performance Guidelines.

To date, the approach of the Canadian judiciary has failed to provide a remedy to foreign communities seeking redress against the Canadian extractive sector when one is warranted. One potential solution is the reformation of the CORE's process to focus on site-level grievance decisions and to ensure consistency, fairness and a remedy when warranted. This is essentially what my proposal puts forth.

If the CORE considers a matter after review has occurred in a site-level grievance mechanism, the company can use its dispute resolution process and adherence to the Performance Guidelines as a defence to allegations against it from complainants. As such, industry is incentivised to have effective site-level grievance mechanisms in an effort to protect against future liability brought about by complaints to the CORE. These efforts would be a form of due diligence to stave off risk and liability.

Salient themes within this proposal include the involvement of civil society in dispute resolution, enforcement, accountability, compliance, procedural fairness and judicial review. I suggest that these concepts must be prominent features in a state-based grievance mechanism such as the CORE.

I advocate for the development of company-run, site-level grievance programmes specifically designed for the public, whistleblowers, civil society and others to raise concerns about human rights and environmental issues, among other matters. These site-level grievance mechanisms should be developed and implemented from established frameworks that set out goals and benchmarks for dispute resolution processes. Several manuals already exist pertaining to site-level grievance mechanisms and could be drawn from, such as the IFC Performance Standards.[91] Further, industry groups such as the IPIECA,[92] the International Council on Mining & Metals,[93] and the Mining Association of Canada[94] have generated similar guidance documents.

I suggest that this proposal empowers the office of the CORE, harnesses the strategic advantage of site-level grievance mechanisms, mandates the participation of industry and encourages support by civil society. These measures will provide lasting solutions to the inexorable problem of the extractive sector causing adverse human rights and environmental impacts abroad. In particular, I argue that the involvement of civil society in dispute resolution processes between the extractive sector and impacted communities is one path to create a social licence to operate.

[91] International Finance Corporation, 'Good Practice Note' (n 46).
[92] IPIECA, 'Community Grievance Mechanisms' (n 42).
[93] Mining & Metals, 'Human Rights in the Mining & Metals Industry' (n 47).
[94] Mining Association of Canada, 'Site-Level Grievance' (n 49).

8

Accountability, Effectiveness and Contrast

Proper accountability requires that foreign citizens seeking legal recourse against extractive sector corporations have the ability to access a legitimate complaint process. The decision-makers in this process should have the authority to levy adequate sanctions against corporations for failing to uphold internationally-recognised standards of human rights and environmental protection. The decision-makers must be neutral, independent and apolitical in their assessment of complaints. Further, a legitimate process entails that the complainants receive procedural fairness, dignity, respect and substantive justice in the particular forum of dispute resolution.

I measure effectiveness in accordance with the UN Guiding Principles. Specifically, I use the UN Guiding Principles key performance indicators (KPIs) for measuring effectiveness of non-judicial grievance mechanisms. The UN Guiding Principles are the result of the work of John Ruggie, who was given a mandate in 2005 from what is now the Human Rights Council, to explore the impacts of business on human rights. Ruggie was charged with identifying international human rights standards that apply to corporate conduct, as opposed to states and individuals, and describe what responsibilities are placed on states and multinational corporations respectively in safeguarding these rights under international law. In 2008, Ruggie developed the 'Protect, Respect, Remedy' Framework which involves three pillars: 1) the state duty to protect human rights; 2) the businesses' responsibility to respect human rights; and 3) access to remedy for victims of business-related abuses.[1] Ruggie's team was given a further mandate to develop the framework, which cumulated in the UN Guiding Principles. The Human Rights Council unanimously endorsed the UN Guiding Principles in 2011, making it the first corporate human rights responsibility initiative to be endorsed by the United Nations.

The UN Guiding Principles are a promising instrument to have states and transnational organisations regulate multinational corporations for human

[1] Special Representative on Business and Human Rights (SRBHR), 'United Nations Guiding Principles on Business and Human Rights: Implementing the United Nations "Protect, Respect and Remedy" Framework' (United Nations, 2011), www.ohchr.org/documents/publications/guidingprinciplesbusinesshr_en.pdf.

rights abuses. Canada, among other nations, regards the UN Guiding Principles as a key policy driver in promoting access to a remedy for human rights abuses that occur abroad.[2] The Organisation for Economic Co-operation and Development (OECD), the International Standards Organization, the International Finance Corporation and the European Union, among others, have adopted them.[3] Several countries, including the United States, United Kingdom, Ireland, Chile, Poland, Spain, Columbia, Norway and many others have produced national action plans.[4]

The extractive sector is also responding with plans to implement the UN Guiding Principles.[5] For these reasons, the UN Guiding Principles are a reliable and authoritative source for the purpose of designing an effective non-judicial grievance mechanism.

A state-based complainant system for the remedy of business-related human rights abuse is recommended under the UN Guiding Principles.[6] The UN Guiding Principles also suggest that business enterprises should establish or participate in effective operational-level grievance mechanisms for individuals and communities that may be adversely impacted.[7]

Local-level grievance mechanisms might, for example, provide compensation to displaced residents or injured employees. They are meant to provide an efficient and user-friendly dispute resolution process, and may serve to prevent disputes from escalating into full-blown human rights litigation.

It should be noted that UN Guiding Principle 31 is directed at non-judicial grievance mechanisms. UN Guiding Principle 25 refers to state-based and operational-level mechanisms that can be judicial or non-judicial in nature. Additional guidance that establishes criteria for the effectiveness of judicial mechanisms is not provided. However, Principle 25 states that a judicial mechanism may be supplemented or enhanced with regard to UN Guiding Principles 26 to 31.

[2] M Torrance, 'Remedying Human Rights: From the International, Regional and Domestic Status Quo to Future Innovations' (Human Rights Law and the Extractive Industries, Rocky Mountain Mineral Law Foundation, February 2016) 3.

[3] JG Ruggie, *Just Business: Multinational Corporations and Human Rights* (New York, W. W. Norton & Company, 2013) xx–xxi.

[4] UN Office of the High Commissioner on Human Rights, 'State National Action Plans on Business and Human Rights' (2020), www.ohchr.org/en/issues/business/pages/nationalactionplans.aspx.

[5] As one example of the extractive sector's response to the UN Guiding Principles, the International Petroleum Industry Environmental Conservation Association (IPIECA) created a manual on implementing operational-level community grievance mechanisms. See IPIECA, 'Community Grievance Mechanisms in the Oil and Gas Industry. A Manual for Implementing Operational-Level Grievance Mechanisms and Designing Corporate Frameworks' (January 2015), www.ipieca.org/resources/good-practice/community-grievance-mechanisms-in-the-oil-and-gas-industry-a-manual-for-implementing-operational-level-grievance-mechanisms-and-designing-corporate-frameworks.

[6] As stated in an implementation guide concerning the UN Guiding Principles, 'States should provide effective and appropriate non-judicial grievance mechanisms, alongside judicial mechanisms, as part of a comprehensive state-based system for the remedy of business-related human rights abuse.' SRBHR, 'United Nations Guiding Principles (n 1) 30.

[7] SRBHR, 'United Nations Guiding Principles (n 1) 31.

Principle 26 refers to the effectiveness of domestic judicial mechanisms when addressing business-related human rights abuses without providing further clarifying information. It simply suggests that states should not erect barriers to prevent cases from being brought before the courts concerning extraterritorial human rights abuses.[8]

These barriers include procedural limitations that prevent domestic courts from considering extraterritorial claims. Examples include the doctrine of *forum non conveniens*, international comity and limitations of jurisdiction that restricts the ability of domestic courts to adjudicate on matters that primarily occur elsewhere. The separate personality of corporations also prevents multinational business enterprises from being held accountable for the liabilities of their foreign subsidiaries. Conversely, the UN Guiding Principles do not expressly suggest that states have a positive obligation to create opportunities for foreign citizens to bring claims concerning extraterritorial human rights abuses in domestic courts or other forums.

The KPIs that outline effectiveness in the context of a non-judicial grievance mechanism are contained in UN Guiding Principle 31. This provision stipulates that grievance mechanisms, both state-based and non-state-based, should be legitimate, accessible, predictable, equitable, transparent, rights-compatible, a source of continuous learning and based on engagement and dialogue.[9] I use the KPIs outlined in UN Guiding Principle 31, otherwise known as the effectiveness criterion, for measuring the effectiveness of this proposal regarding a grievance mechanism process for Canada. These are explored next.

I. Testing Effectiveness of the Proposal under UN Guiding Principle 31

In the previous chapter, I proposed the development of a state-based grievance process that provides a remedy to those who are negatively impacted by the Canadian international extractive sector. Criterion that defines effectiveness in the context of a state-based grievance process is set out in the UN Guiding Principles.[10] In this section, I analyse my proposal to determine if it is consistent with the effectiveness criterion set out in UN Guiding Principle 31. While this criterion is directed at site-level grievance mechanisms, I suggest that it is equally applicable

[8] Commentary in the implementation guide concerning UN Guiding Principle 26 explains that:

> Effective judicial mechanisms are at the core of ensuring access to remedy … States should ensure that they do not erect barriers to prevent legitimate cases from being brought before the courts in situations where judicial recourse is an essential part of accessing remedy or alternative sources of effective remedy are unavailable. *Ibid* 28.

[9] SRBHR, 'The Corporate Responsibility to Respect Human Rights: An Interpretative Guide' (United Nations, 2011) 73–74, www.ohchr.org/Documents/Publications/HR.PUB.12.2_En.pdf.

[10] *Ibid.*

for state-based grievance processes such as the Canadian Ombudsperson for Responsible Enterprise (CORE). This exercise is not intended to be exhaustive. I only aim to demonstrate that my proposal is a practical approach that meets the effectiveness criterion set out in the UN Guiding Principles.

In this section, I focus in particular on my proposed Operating Procedures for the CORE that contain elements which reflect UN Guiding Principle 31. These draft procedures are contained in the Appendix of this book.

A. Legitimate

'Legitimate' is defined in the UN Guiding Principles to mean enabling trust from the stakeholder groups for whose use they are intended, and being accountable for the fair conduct of grievance processes.[11]

I suggest that the former office of the Canadian Corporate Social Responsibility (CSR) Counsellor was not legitimate because its process was built on voluntary cooperation by industry. This deficiency potentially explains why almost all of the complaints prior to 2013 were closed by the CSR Counsellor without a remedy on account of the withdrawal of the respondent company. It perhaps also explains the lack of any formal hearings before the CSR Counsellor from 2015 to 2018 when it was shuttered. As such, the legitimacy of that hearing process was corroded.

My proposal changes this by furnishing the CORE with the power to award monetary sanctions and enforce their orders, as well as compel industry participation. A site-level grievance mechanism on its own will not effectively promote legitimacy, as the process will be operated and controlled entirely by a private profit-driven extractive company. However, giving the power to award monetary sanctions to the CORE will harness a non-mandatory approach in crafting efficient and fair site-level grievance processes. In this way, the CORE can give input on the structure and function of these dispute processes and penalise corporations that are non-compliant or fail to implement a grievance mechanism. All of these features of my proposal will facilitate accountability and generate fair and legitimate dispute resolution processes.

B. Accessible

'Accessible' is defined in the UN Guiding Principles as being known to all stakeholders for whose use they are intended, and providing adequate assistance for those who may face particular barriers to access.[12] In this way, accessibility under the UN Guiding Principles means that a remedial path is known to all stakeholder groups for whose use they are intended.

[11] SRBHR, 'United Nations Guiding Principles (n 1) 33.
[12] SRBHR, 'United Nations Guiding Principles (n 1) 33.

For a dispute resolution process to be accessible, it must be readily available to consider complaints soon after they are raised. This is why I suggest that the extractive sector should be incentivised to develop, implement and operate robust and effective site-level grievance mechanisms that can consider matters early and in the location where the complainants live and the extractive sector operates. Unlike state-based mechanisms such as the CORE, a site-level grievance mechanism does not have to wait until an issue amounts to an alleged human rights abuse or a breach of other standards before it can be addressed.[13] Additionally, a site-level process will likely be faster, less formalised and a less expensive alternative to litigation.

Accessibility will also be accomplished by the CORE endorsing particular frameworks that industry can use in designing, implementing and operating site-level grievance mechanisms in a user-friendly manner. This will take initiative and the expense of some resources by the CORE. For instance, the CORE should visit the location of Canadian extractive sector grievance mechanisms regularly to audit, inspect and oversee operations to gauge their level of accessibility. Beyond looking at accessibility, the CORE should perform even more comprehensive site-level audits to ensure compliance with the six international Performance Guidelines. This is appropriate given the proposed new powers of the CORE to sanction operators that fail to comply with these requirements. Thus, a site-level audit and inspection programme is beneficial for the purpose of ensuring accessibility as well as other compliance concerns.

C. Predictable

'Predictable' under the UN Guiding Principles entails providing clear and known procedures with a proposed time frame for each stage, and clarity on the types of processes and outcomes that are available.[14]

Acquiring more clarity and predictability of the processes before the CORE as well as industry-run, site-level grievance mechanisms is one reason I advocate for an expansion of the Operating Procedures. For example, I set out strict timelines for the review process in the draft Operating Procedures for the CORE. They go beyond the current timelines provided by the CORE, which only cover the processing of an initial complaint.[15] Further, these draft rules formally require the CORE to be guided by their previous decisions when deciding subsequent cases with similar issues or facts. This follows in the same way as common law precedent. Common law legal systems place value on deciding cases in a consistent

[13] SRBHR, 'Interpretative Guide' (n 9) 68.

[14] SRBHR, 'United Nations Guiding Principles (n 1) 33.

[15] Government of Canada, 'Operating Procedures of the Canadian Ombudsperson for Responsible Enterprise' (2020) s 4.6, core-ombuds.canada.ca/core_ombuds-ocre_ombuds/operating_procedures-procedures_exploitation.aspx.

fashion so that subsequent cases with similar facts and issues will yield predictable outcomes.[16] Observing precedent is the mechanism by which this objective is achieved. According to the draft Operating Procedures, similar fact patterns would provide guidance on finding fault and assessing penalties in future cases. I suggest that this approach will benefit the CORE's process in terms of establishing predictability.

I also call for the development of timelines for industry-run, site-level grievance mechanisms as a key feature of an effective process. Incentivising corporations to create robust and effective site-level grievance mechanisms will encourage the development of faster and less expensive dispute resolution processes in contrast to court systems or state-based grievance mechanisms.

D. Equitable

'Equitable' under the UN Guiding Principles means ensuring that aggrieved parties have reasonable access to sources of information, advice and expertise necessary to engage in a grievance process on fair, informed and respectful terms.[17]

One key feature in my proposal that encourages this type of equity is the involvement of civil society organisations in dispute resolution processes between industry and impacted communities, which I address in the draft Operating Procedures. I suggest that civil society may serve in the role of representative, mediator or arbitrator in industry-run, site-level grievance mechanisms. I further propose that civil society may be involved in a similar capacity in the CORE's dispute process.

I also adopt the idea from the Interpretative Guide on the UN Guiding Principles which suggests that participation by civil society in site-level and state-based grievance mechanisms may be funded by industry.[18] For instance, the draft Operating Procedures call for the development of a fee schedule for respondent corporations to compensate the reasonable costs of civil societies' involvement in dispute resolution processes.

The presence of civil society in dispute resolution processes is equitable because its involvement will advance the interests of both the extractive sector and impacted communities. In the case of a representative, the involvement of civil society organisations in grievance mechanisms will assist complainants by allowing them to have a knowledgeable advocate. In the case of a mediator or arbitrator, it will assist complainants by giving them access to a resourceful third party facilitator or decision-maker. In terms of advancing the interest of the extractive sector, civil society's involvement can lead to the facilitation of social licence on behalf

[16] *Black's Law Dictionary*, 5th edn (Saint Paul, West Publishing Co, 1979) 1059.
[17] SRBHR, 'United Nations Guiding Principles (n 1) 33.
[18] SRBHR, 'Interpretative Guide' (n 9) 72.

of the extractive sector, on account of its independence and perceived legitimacy. The involvement of civil society in dispute resolution processes between the extractive sector and impacted communities is one path to create a social licence to operate, as social licence is granted by groups such as civil society organisations.[19] Thus, extractive sector corporations that employ civil society groups in their site-level dispute resolution processes will attain a sense of social licence.

Finally, I suggest that smaller civil society groups should be given formal representative status under the draft Operating Procedures to advocate on behalf of impacted individuals, and to serve as mediators and arbitrators. I suggest smaller civil society groups because presumably their interests are closely aligned with the local communities they advocate on behalf of, compared to global civil society groups which may be more affiliated with the interests of states.[20] While funding may be a concern for smaller groups, they will be able to participate in most cases if the costs associated with participating are sourced from industry.

E. Transparent

'Transparent' means keeping parties in a grievance process informed about its progress.[21] This includes the requirement to disclose information between the parties, have open hearings unless a legitimate request for confidentiality is made and the formal public release of decisions. Transparency in decision-making should be a goal of any dispute process. My draft Operating Procedures for the CORE incorporates these requirements for transparency.

The draft Operating Procedures attempt to balance the need to encourage transparency in terms of disclosing evidence, while at the same time protecting various interests of the parties. For example, the proposed rules grant protection from disclosing certain financial, commercial, scientific or technical information that is confidential in nature or deemed to be under forms of legal privilege. Without such protection, extractive sector companies may potentially be concerned about maintaining sensitive commercial information. This concern is recognised in the UN Guiding Principles, which affirms that disclosure in a grievance process should not eliminate rights to protect confidential information.[22]

[19] See, eg, HH Koh, 'The 1994 Roscoe Pound Lecture: Transnational Legal Process' (1996) 75 *Nebraska Law Review* 181; HH Koh, 'The 1998 Frankel Lecturer: Bringing International Human Rights Home' (1998) 35 *Houston Law Review* 647; LC Backer, 'The Structure of Global Law: Fracture, Fluidity, Permeability, and Polycentricity' (2012) 17 *Tilburg Law Review* 177.

[20] LC Backer, 'An Institutional Role for Civil Society Within the U.N. Guiding Principles?: Comments on César Rodríguez-Garavito and Tatiana Andia "Business and Human Rights: Beyond the End of the Beginning"' (Workshop on Implementing the UN's Guiding Principles on Business and Human Rights: A South-Initiated North-South Dialogue, Brown University, February 2014) 8.

[21] SRBHR, 'United Nations Guiding Principles (n 1) 33.

[22] SRBHR, 'United Nations Guiding Principles (n 1) 23.

Some commentators have argued that this may allow corporations to use legal privilege to cover material information regarding potential human rights or environmental violations.[23] However, even if corporations have a right to assert these protections regarding human rights violations, the UN Guiding Principles still require those corporations to be candid and open about these problems and take responsibility in dealing with impacted communities.[24] This position of expecting candid and open discussions of potential wrongdoing is the one I advocate for the CORE to take regarding confidential and privileged information. While I suggest that the CORE should respect these protections, this should not prevent the Ombudsperson from admonishing corporations that are not candid with it, for example, by unfairly concealing information. For instance, the CORE may fine respondent corporations if they claim privilege or confidentiality in bad faith.

As a comparison to other administrative agencies, the Privacy Commissioner of Canada recognises the protection of solicitor-client and litigation privilege.[25] Additionally, the Canada Energy Regulator has statutory protection regarding legal privilege and confidential information.[26] I have pointed to these agencies as models for the CORE to follow throughout my proposal, and I do the same regarding the concept of preserving confidential information and legal privilege, the latter of which is a fundamental common law right in Canada.[27]

F. Rights-compatible

The notion of 'rights-compatible' under the UN Guiding Principles suggests that any outcomes or remedies granted by a dispute resolution process must accord with internationally recognised human rights standards.[28]

Rights-compatibility was included in Canada's 2014 CSR strategy which embraced international Performance Guidelines such as the OECD Guidelines, the UN Guiding Principles, the Voluntary Principles, the Performance Standards of the World Bank, the OECD Minerals Policy and the Global Reporting Initiative (GRI).[29]

Abiding by these instruments helps to ensure that businesses have access to enhanced economic diplomacy such as the issuance of letters of support, and

[23] JF Sherman, 'The UN Guiding Principles: Practical Implications for Business Lawyers' (2012) *In-House Defense Quarterly* 55.

[24] *Ibid* 56.

[25] Personal Information Protection Act SA 2003, c P-6.5 ss 3(a) & (b); Privacy Act RSC 1985, c P-21 s 27.

[26] Canadian Energy Regulator Act SC 2019, c 28, s 10, ss 61–62, 111, 113(2) and 161(c).

[27] *Lizotte v Aviva Insurance Company of Canada* 2016 SCC 52.

[28] SRBHR, 'United Nations Guiding Principles (n 1) 34.

[29] Global Affairs Canada, 'Doing Business the Canadian Way: A Strategy to Advance Corporate Social Responsibility in Canada's Extractive Sector Abroad' (Government of Canada, 2014), www.international.gc.ca/trade-agreements-accords-commerciaux/topics-domaines/other-autre/csr-strat-rse.aspx?lang=eng.

it may affect support from Export Development Canada. My proposal goes a step further to suggest that the CORE should have the authority to order financial penalties be paid in compensation to impacted communities when businesses breach these Performance Guidelines. This would further promote rights-compatibility as defined in the UN Guiding Principles.

G. A Source of Continuous Learning

'A source of continuous learning' under the UN Guiding Principles focuses upon drawing relevant measures to identify lessons for improving grievance mechanisms and preventing future harm.[30]

In furtherance of continuous learning, I suggest the formal public release of written decisions by the CORE. A 2013 review by the CSR Counsellor of the practices of a Canadian mining company operating in Mexico helps explains why decisions should be publicly and formally released.[31] In this case, the CSR Counsellor visited the mine site in Mexico and met with company representatives, community members and other stakeholders. However, the CSR Counsellor failed to deliver a closing report and it is unclear if the review continued or resulted in anything substantive. Thus, the results, if any, were not transparently disclosed and cannot be used in furtherance of continuous learning regarding future projects.

My draft Operating Procedures also go a step beyond continuous learning in suggesting that the CORE's decisions should form a system of non-binding precedent to inform the reasoning of future complaints involving similar issues and concerns.

H. Based on Engagement and Dialogue

Finally, the UN Guiding Principles recommend that grievance mechanisms be 'based on engagement and dialogue', which includes consulting with stakeholders and focusing on dialogue as the means of addressing and resolving grievances.[32]

This is another opportunity where civil society can effectively serve as a conduit between industry and impacted communities in a grievance mechanism and increase the measure of the mechanism's effectiveness. Civil society is directly mentioned in the Interpretative Guide to the UN Guiding Principles in suggesting that civil society groups acting as stakeholders have valuable insights to provide in

[30] SRBHR, 'United Nations Guiding Principles (n 1) 34.
[31] Global Affairs Canada, 'Field Visit Report 2013-04-MEX:E the Office of the Extractive Sector CSR Counsellor' (Government of Canada, 2013), www.international.gc.ca/csr_counsellor-conseiller_rse/publications/2013-04-MEX_interim_rep_01-rap_provisoir_01.aspx?lang=eng.
[32] SRBHR, 'United Nations Guiding Principles (n 1) 34.

grievance mechanisms.[33] I suggest that the involvement of civil society in dispute resolution processes will promote engagement and dialogue between industry and impacted communities. In particular, its presence will be helpful during dispute processes where civil society is utilised as a third party mediator. Civil society groups can also assist in practical matters such as the translation of languages or explaining differences in cultural understandings.

II. Role for Civil Society Actors and Corporate Self-Governance

Civil society, if properly engaged, may have an influence in promoting the effectiveness of non-judicial grievance mechanisms when it comes to implementing all of the KPIs. As such, it can provide an integral role in resolving disputes between negatively impacted communities and the extractive sector.

Civil society actors could promote legitimacy as a representative of the party or as a mediator if they are seen to be neutral and impartial. In the same way, a civil society actor can aid in ensuring that a grievance process is accessible, predictable, transparent, rights-compatible, a source of continuous learning and based on engagement and dialogue. However, this is based on the assumption that civil society will not have its own agenda in either representing or mediating a dispute between industry and those whom they negatively impact. It is also assumed that it will be competent in resolving these often complicated disputes.

A proposal for dispute resolution that has been endorsed in the UN Guiding Principles is the use of an external civil society organisation to act as a mediator.[34] Despite this endorsement, some commentators suggest that the UN Guiding Principles do not go far enough in recognising the importance of civil society actors as a nexus between business and human rights.[35] Others commentators have alluded to the fact that the UN Guiding Principles suggest that the role of a mediator in disputes between local communities and industry should be delegated to civil society actors as the norm.[36] The involvement of civil society in regulating corporate conduct is a salient theme in terms of attempting to hold the extractive sector to account.

Effective accountability of the foreign extractive sector requires that impacted individuals and communities seeking legal recourse have the ability to access a

[33] SRBHR, 'Interpretative Guide' (n 9) 55.

[34] SRBHR, 'Interpretative Guide' (n 9) 51–55.

[35] T Melish and E Meidinger, 'Protect, Respect, Remedy and Participate: "New Governance" Lessons for the Ruggie Framework' in R Mares (ed), *The UN Guiding Principles on Business and Human Rights* (Leiden, Martinus Nijhoff, 2012).

[36] LC Backer, 'From Guiding Principles to Interpretive Organizations: Developing a Framework for Applying the UNGPs to Disputes That Institutionalizes the Advocacy Role of Civil Society' in C Rodriguez-Garavito (ed), *Business and Human Rights: Beyond the End of the Beginning* (Cambridge, Cambridge University Press, 2017).

legitimate complaint process. I suggest that a legitimate process requires that the complainants receive procedural fairness, dignity, respect and substantive justice. Further, I support the findings of a report from a UN Working Group on the UN Guiding Principles that found that accountability must be central to business-related remedy mechanisms.[37]

In assessing effectiveness of a complaint mechanism, I have chosen the KPIs set out in Principle 31. These KPIs suggest that grievance mechanisms, both state-based and non-state-based, should be legitimate, accessible, predictable, transparent, rights-compatible, a source of continuous learning and based on engagement and dialogue.

A state-based complaint system for the remedy of business-related human rights abuses is recommended under the UN Guiding Principles.[38] Company run, site-level grievance mechanisms are also recommended, as they arguably provide an efficient and user-friendly dispute resolution process and serve to prevent grievances from escalating into protracted litigation.[39] In this way, the UN Guiding Principles create obligations for the private sector.

As such, the UN Guiding Principles suggest that businesses should lead the development of site-level grievance processes. However, the commentary to the UN Guiding Principles does not further elaborate on best practices for developing such a programme. This perceived lack of direction for businesses seeking to comply with the UN Guiding Principles has been criticised by at least one observer.[40]

Another alternative put forward in the UN Guiding Principles is the fusion of international and domestic law institutions and site-level mechanisms.[41] This can include the involvement of a state-based mechanism, backed up by the power of government sanctions, which oversees site-level processes, paid for and directed by an extractive sector organisation. It can also entail the significant involvement of civil society. This is precisely the foundation of my proposal for reform.

Commentators who advocate for corporate self-governance argue that these programmes are effective and efficient in achieving desired outcomes.[42] Others have suggested that corporations will seek to follow best practices on account of 'enlightened self-interest',[43] and that corporations are creating a new

[37] United Nations General Assembly, 'Report of the Working Group on the Issue of Human Rights and Transnational Corporations and Other Business Enterprises' (28 April 2015) para 59, www.refworld.org/pdfid/5583f3144.pdf.

[38] SRBHR, 'United Nations Guiding Principles (n 1) 30.

[39] SRBHR, 'United Nations Guiding Principles (n 1) 31.

[40] T Thabane, 'Weak Extraterritorial Remedies: The Achilles Heel of Ruggie's "Protect, Respect, Remedy" Framework and Guiding Principles' (2014) 14 *African Human Rights Law Journal* 43, 57.

[41] SRBHR, 'United Nations Guiding Principles (n 1) 31.

[42] S Rose-Ackerman, 'Comment: Consensus Versus Incentives: A Skeptical Look at Regulatory Negotiation' (1994) 43 *Duke Law Journal* 1206, 1220.

[43] A Crane and D Matten, *Business Ethics: Managing Corporate Citizenship and Sustainability in the Age of Globalization*, 2nd edn (Oxford, Oxford University Press, 2007) 47.

'customary global law' as opposed to a voluntary regime.[44] My proposal is in congruence with these aspects of corporate self-regulation, but does not go as far.

The feature of my proposal that most clearly draws on corporate self-regulation is that the extractive sector is not legally compelled to develop site-level grievance programmes. The impetus comes from the consequences of not doing so, as under my proposal the CORE will have new powers to administer monetary penalties for the failure to establish effective grievance programmes.

A corporate self-governance approach towards developing site-level grievance programmes is flexible in allowing companies to develop mechanisms that suit their unique needs, along with those of the communities located near their operations. The way I have invoked corporate self-regulation does not amount to a global law, as my emphasis on developing effective site-level grievance mechanisms remains voluntary and self-driven. Thus, the proposal does not strictly mandate that the extractive sector must develop and fund these processes.

In sum, an analysis of my proposed reforms with the UN Guiding Principles demonstrates that my recommendations satisfy all of the effectiveness criteria in UN Guiding Principle 31. The effectiveness criterion suggests that grievance mechanisms should be legitimate, accessible, predictable, equitable, transparent, rights-compatible, a source of continuous learning and based on engagement and dialogue.

Civil society, if properly engaged, will have an influence in promoting the effectiveness of industry-run, site-level and state-based grievance mechanisms when it comes to implementing all of the effectiveness criteria. Civil society actors can promote legitimacy as representatives of a complainant; or as mediators or arbitrators in a grievance process. In the same way, a civil society group can aid in ensuring that a grievance process is accessible, predictable, transparent, rights-compatible, a source of continuous learning and based on engagement and dialogue. Finally, the proposal draws on various strands of corporate self-regulation to encourage businesses to establish effective site-level grievance processes on their own accord. In this way, they will avoid liability as a result of any potential investigation by the CORE.

III. Contrast and Approach

In arguing for the merits of my proposal, it is appropriate to contrast its design and functionality with similar proposals that have been developed by other commentators conversant in these issues. Their ideas have contributed to the development of my recommendations. I have endeavoured to learn from the strengths and avoid the shortcomings of their proposals in reforming the global activities of

[44] C Pitts, 'Business, Human Rights, and the Environment: The Role of the Lawyer in CSR & Ethical Globalization' (2008) 26 *Berkeley Journal of International Law* 479, 488.

the Canadian extractive industry. In this exercise, I aim to demonstrate that my proposal is sound and practical compared to various alternatives.

There is a paucity of well-developed plans for reforming the global activities of the Canadian extractive industry. Standing among the more comprehensive works on the subject is Penelope Simons and Audrey Macklin's *The Governance Gap: Extractive Industries, Human Rights, and the Home State Advantage*.[45] Both Simons and Macklin are Canadian legal scholars with academic positions in Ontario law schools. Their book explores what the authors characterise as a 'governance gap' with respect to extractive sector corporations operating in zones of weak governance. This gap is due, according to the authors, to the failure of corporate self-regulation, host state protection and international mechanisms to prevent wrongdoing by the extractive sector.

The authors question what the development of domestic and international regulation would look like if governments took seriously the duty to protect human rights from the activities of extractive sector corporations. While a valuable contribution for researchers on the extraterritorial activities of the extractive sector, certain aspects of the authors' proposal are impracticable and not the best alternative for addressing the problem of extraterritorial wrongdoing by the extractive sector. A 2017 critique of the proposal cited the assertion that home states have a 'moral responsibility' to regulate extraterritorial corporate conduct as a weak argument.[46] My critique is different in that I suggest that a more comprehensive analysis of private law strategies would have benefited the readers in communicating a thorough account of this fundamentally important issue of legal regulation.

In this chapter, I focus extensively on Simons and Macklin's book, as it is one of the more thorough and recent works on the subject of the human rights track record of the extractive sector abroad.

IV. Simons and Macklin's Proposal to Correct the 'Governance Gap'

In their book, the authors propose several forms of regulation through public law enforcement mechanisms. The various propositions put forward by the authors

[45] P Simons and A Macklin, *The Governance Gap: Extractive Industries, Human Rights, and the Home State Advantage* (Toronto, Routledge, 2014). Note that some of the analysis incorporated in this chapter on Simons and Macklin's book was previously published in J Bone, 'Book Review: The Governance Gap: Extractive Industries, Human Rights, and the Home State Advantage' (2015) 11 *McGill International Journal of Sustainable Development Law & Policy* 2.

[46] GA Sarfaty, 'Review Essay of The Governance Gap: Extractive Industries, Human Rights, and the Home State Advantage, Penelope Simons & Audrey Macklin' (2017) 67 *University of Toronto Law Journal* 655, 663.

include a combination of incentives based on home state fiscal and political support,[47] the creation of a public CSR agency[48] and statutory remedies.

Simons and Macklin's proposals are based on the premise that home states should take the duty to protect human rights seriously. Their strategy for home state regulation is a multifaceted and nuanced approach. However, I argue that certain aspects of the authors' proposals are unrealistic and not the best alternative for addressing the problem of extraterritorial wrongdoing by the extractive sector.

My analysis will address four features of the authors' proposals for regulating the overseas conduct of the extractive sector: 1) the application of the nationality and territorial principles; 2) the development of a home state CSR agency; 3) the feasibility of labeling countries as 'weak governance zones'; and 4) assumptions embedded in the proposal concerning whether civil society actors and extractive sector corporations will be receptive to a home state CSR agency.

First, the authors' proposal includes a very innovative application of the nationality and territorial principles to regulate parent and subsidiary corporations' overseas conduct. In suggesting that legislation may apply extraterritorially, the authors cite the nationality principle, which deems that a corporation effectively has citizenship of the home state. Thus, the nationality of a corporation, and applicable law, is generally considered to be that of the state of their incorporation. It can be used as the basis of jurisdiction to regulate conduct that occurs in part or fully outside of that jurisdiction.[49] The authors also consider the territorial principle, which suggests that a home state has jurisdiction over activity that largely takes place within its territory.[50] Whether these concepts would work in some countries is unclear. Take the United States as one example where, under the US Restatement, a foreign subsidiary does not acquire the nationality of the parent corporation.[51] The Restatement suggests that US legislation may have extraterritorial application that applies to the parent corporation and foreign subsidiaries for very limited purposes. However, the Restatement also suggests that the regulation of a foreign subsidiary should not interfere with local activities, such as it would impact employment law, health and safety or conservation of the local environment.[52] These local activities are precisely related to human rights. As such, they are outside the purview of what may be regulated under the Restatement.

The Restatement does not support the view that US legislation applies in regulating extraterritorially human rights impacts of US foreign subsidiaries.

[47] The first premise of the proposal is that the home state government will not provide public financial, fiscal or political support to a 'corporate citizen for investment projects in weak governance zones where that corporate citizen, directly or indirectly, intentionally or negligently, engages in, or is complicit in, actions that are likely to cause, or have caused, stipulated forms of serious harm'. Simons and Macklin, *The Governance Gap* 278.

[48] Simons and Macklin (n 45) 273 and 278.

[49] Simons and Macklin (n 45) 300–301.

[50] *American Banana Co v United Fruit Co* [1909] 29 S Ct 511.

[51] *Sumitomo Shoji Am Inc Avagliano* [1982] 457 US 176.

[52] Restatement (Third) of the Foreign Relations Law of the United States (Philadelphia, American Law Institute, 1987) s 414.

This finding conflicts with the authors' proposal concerning the nationality and territorial principles applying in the US to combat overseas human rights abuse by the extractive sector. Arguably, if a host state has investment-friendly laws that are harmful to the local environment or do not protect the human rights of its citizens, this alone does not justify the extraterritorial application of US law.

On the other hand, different sources of US law are more promising in the use of extraterritorial regulation. For instance, the authors cite the Cardin-Lugar provisions in the US Dodd-Frank Act[53] that require extractive sector corporations listed on US stock exchanges to disclose payments made to foreign governments.[54] Additionally, they consider the US Foreign Corrupt Practices Act 1977 (FCPA) that uses the territorial principle to claim jurisdiction over nearly any act by any corporation in the world, so long as it is an act in furtherance of a bribery that takes place in the United States.[55] Thus, some examples using the application of the nationality and territorial principle in the US suggest that the authors' proposal is workable, while other precedents, such as those found within the Restatement, do not support the authors' proposal. Given these conflicting precedents, it appears that the US is willing to apply extraterritorial application to legislation concerning financial markets and corruption, although it is unwilling to give extraterritorial effect to legislation aimed at local concerns of foreign states, such as labour law, health and safety or the preservation of the local environment, as reflected in the Restatement.

Further, the Restatement is potentially outdated, as its last revision was in 1987. Moreover, its purpose is to provide interpretation and guidance on US law and, as such, it is not mandatory. One could reasonably suggest that the substantially broad jurisdiction granted under the FCPA may represent the evolution of a modern form of regulation, and that the rules under the Restatement have become obsolete. The authors do not make this argument in the book, nor do they directly address the Restatement, although they do point to the FCPA as a potential model for the kind of regulation they are proposing.[56]

I also suggest that the authors' proposal regarding the territorial and nationality principle is not realistic for Canada. For one, consider the principle of international comity, which asserts that courts should be hesitant to declare jurisdiction over matters that take place primarily in other countries. International comity was cited as an important factor in the 2012 Supreme Court of Canada's *Van Breda* decision.[57] The case outlines the issues Canadian courts should consider before taking jurisdiction concerning foreign matters. In *Van Breda*, the Court further cautioned against placing too much weight on assuming that another

[53] Dodd-Frank Wall Street Reform and Consumer Protection Act Pub L No 111-203, 124 Stat 1376 (2010) s 1504.

[54] Simons and Macklin (n 45) 275.

[55] Foreign Corrupt Practices Act (1977) as amended, 15 USC ss 78dd-1, et seq.

[56] Simons and Macklin (n 45) 308.

[57] *Club Resorts Ltd v Van Breda* [2012] 1 SCR 572, para 92.

legal system is inadequate where it differs from Canadian law, as doing so would be inconsistent with international comity.[58] Thus, Canada is rather restrictive in its approach towards extending extraterritorial jurisdiction over the foreign activities of Canadian corporations.

Another proposition put forward in the book is the development of a home state CSR agency that engages in monitoring and dispute resolution concerning extractive sector corporations.[59] The CSR agency would also determine whether a particular extractive sector corporation has undertaken appropriate due diligence in accordance with the voluntary measures of the UN Guiding Principles. In this way, the CSR agency would play an active role in the human rights due diligence process of business.

Much like the CORE, the authors' proposed CSR agency would be implemented at the national level and operate at arm's length from government. This agency, as contemplated by the authors, would provide '[territorial] state auditing' and 'independent surveillance'.[60] Its primary function would be to assess, monitor and evaluate the impact of extractive sector corporations in zones of weak governance. In doing so, a CSR agency would have the mandate to determine which states are considered weak governance zones. This determination would directly impact the ability of foreign plaintiffs to seek civil liability against multinational corporations in home state courts. For example, in the case that a state is held to be a zone of weak governance by the CSR agency, the authors propose an alternative implementation of the *forum non conveniens* doctrine where the home state of a parent corporation will be considered the preferable forum for litigation.[61] Similarly, the authors propose the creation of a cause of action targeting corporations that are responsible for human rights abuses in zones of weak governance.

There are at least two concerns with this approach. First, it is not clear by what method this *forum non conveniens* test would be implemented or whether it is the most practical solution for promoting human rights overseas. Second, the definition of weak governance zones is a fairly malleable and subjective standard. In practice, classifying sovereign states in such a fashion is unrealistic, and perhaps inappropriate. In terms of the first concern, it is not clear how this modification of the *forum non conveniens* test would be implemented. For instance, it could be left to judges acting within the parameters of a case before them to adapt the common law doctrine of *forum non conveniens* in order to align with the authors' proposal that the home state of a parent corporation will be considered the preferable forum for litigation.

[58] *Ibid* para 112.

[59] Simons and Macklin (n 45) 329. According to the authors, a CSR agency would provide a market incentive for responsible human rights practices, as the various assessments, audits, and reports will enhance the basis upon which investors, shareholders and consumers make economic decisions concerning the extractive sector.

[60] Simons and Macklin (n 45) 316 and 346.

[61] The presumption is rebuttable if the host state is no longer a weak governance zone at the time of the litigation. Simons and Macklin (n 45) 286.

Alternatively, it might be achieved through a legislative directive from a government in order to clarify new requirements in the *forum non conveniens* test. The authors do not address these particular methods for implementation and both options present unique challenges that suggest that they are impracticable solutions. As such, a workable solution for implementing the proposed changes to the *forum non conveniens* test is difficult to conceive and the authors do not provide a means to this end.

Further, common law courts have adopted less prescriptive versions of the *forum non conveniens* test that do not exclusively target entities that operate overseas in so-called weak governance zones. For instance, the High Court of Australia devised a *forum non conveniens* test in which a claim will only be dismissed if the plaintiff is using the forum 'vexatiously, oppressively or in abuse of process'.[62] Thus, only a claim brought to Australian court for abusive or oppressive reasons would be dismissed on the grounds of *forum non conveniens*. In the same way, US states such as Texas have a limited version of *forum non conveniens*.[63] These jurisdictions have a rather lenient approach to exercising jurisdiction over extraterritorial matters. For those advocating for stronger pressure on extractive sector corporations concerning their overseas human rights track records, the Australian and Texan application of *forum non conveniens* is likely preferable to the authors' recommendations. These approaches allow plaintiffs to overcome the procedural doctrine of *forum non conveniens* and bring claims in the home state without limiting their ability to impact only communities in a subjectively declared zone of weak governance.

This leads on to the second concern with the authors' proposal regarding the CSR agency. Using the concept of a weak governance zone elevates a rather nebulous and potentially inconsistent standard to be used in determining the *forum non conveniens* test or civil liability in general. The authors counter this assertion with a reliance on transparent and impartial data in determining if a state is a weak governance zone. For instance, as reported by the authors, the UN Development Programme defines weak governance zones as places with 'extremely low "human development" indicators' such as infant mortality, literacy, life expectancy and various measures of material standard of living.[64] Although numeric indicators can potentially identify weak governance zones, there is a deep and abiding concern when a country in the developed world attempts to influence the internal affairs of a country in the developing world. On this point, Professor Sara Seck observes that host state regulation could amount to a neo-colonial incursion.[65]

[62] *Oceanic Sun Line Special Shipping Co v Fay* [1988] 165 CLR 197, para 24.

[63] LE Teitz, *Transnational Litigation* (Charlottesville, Michie, 1996) 27 and 35.

[64] Simons and Macklin (n 45) 291. Further, the authors contend that the impartiality and independence of the CSR agency will act as a buffer from political interference.

[65] S Seck, 'Conceptualizing the Home State Duty to Protect Human Rights' in M Morsing and L Roseberry (eds), *Corporate Social and Human Rights Responsibilities: Global Legal and Management Perspectives* (London, Palgrave Macmillan, 2011) 25.

Beyond a concern of appearing imperialistic, this policy would erode important legal principles such as international comity and limitations of jurisdiction.[66] As pointed out by the authors, another notable critic of this approach is John Ruggie, primary developer of the UN Guiding Principles, who described the concept of labeling a state a weak governance zone as 'inherently political'.[67]

While there is a compelling argument that more interference by developed states would be beneficial in ameliorating the adverse impacts of the extractive sector, I am skeptical that labelling states in this way is an appropriately tailored and overall productive strategy to achieve that result. My preference would be to follow the Australian model of *forum non conveniens* that does not limit the ability of plaintiffs to bring claims concerning only corporate activity in a subjectively declared 'weak governance zone'. However, as pointed out above, it would be difficult to promote such a change either legislatively or through common law intervention by the courts.

A final concern is that different CSR agencies from around the world may come to different conclusions on whether the same state is a weak governance zone, which could have consequential economic and human rights implications. For instance, if three large extractive sector economies, such as the United Kingdom, Canada, and Australia treat a particular state as a weak governance zone, the extractive sector companies from those countries will likely avoid investment in that host state, given the additional regulatory requirements imposed on them there. However, imagine another large extractive sector economy, such as Russia, that does not declare the host state a weak governance zone or does not maintain a CSR agency for this purpose. Effectively, Russian corporations in this scenario would operate as a monopoly in the host state, which would potentially reduce the standards of human rights even further because of a lack of competition and oversight.

I note two other concerns with labelling a country a weak governance zone. First, if a host state is labelled by a home state's CSR agency as a weak governance zone, it might reject investment from that home state in order to avoid being transparent about the human rights and environmental conditions of its extractive sector. Conversely, a host state may manipulate the circumstances of their classification by a CSR agency in order to gain perceived benefits from the status of 'weak governance zone'. For example, a developing country may release unreliable statistics for the express purpose of being labelled a 'weak governance zone'. This would allow their citizens to seek civil liability against foreign multinational corporations in home state courts. Furthering this possibility, lawsuits could be launched in other jurisdictions, utilising the cause of action proposed by the authors which

[66] *Hilton v Guyot* [1895] 159 US 113, 16 S Ct 139, paras 163–64.
[67] Simons and Macklin (n 45) 292.

target corporations that are responsible for human rights abuses in zones of weak governance.

Moving on from these criticisms, there are certain assumptions embedded in the proposal concerning whether civil society actors and extractive sector corporations will be receptive to a CSR agency. For instance, the authors suggest that recruiting civil society participation 'may prove challenging' because it will be seen to compromise the advocacy mandate of civil society actors.[68] The authors further suggest that corporations, which have experienced reputational damage through campaigns by civil society actors, 'may grasp more readily the comparative advantage of scrutiny by a body that is embedded within a home state architecture of public accountability'.[69] The assumption is that civil society actors will not be inclined to actively participate, whereas corporations will be motivated to engage with an independent CSR agency rather than face the public scrutiny and shaming of a civil society actor. However, the experience of the former office of the CSR Counsellor suggests otherwise. Similar to the proposal of the authors, the CSR Counsellor was a body that is embedded within Canada's 'architecture of public accountability' at the national level.[70] Almost all of the complaints filed with the CSR Counsellor ended with the corporate respondent refusing to participate in the process. In many cases, civil society actors were assisting impacted communities in bringing claims to the CSR Counsellor, and in one case the complainants were two civil society organisations in their own right representing an environmental cause.[71] The involvement of the CSR Counsellor provided the companies with an opportunity to elect to have the matter scrutinised by a public institution as opposed to campaigns by civil society actors that tend to view the extractive sector in a negative light. However, in most cases, the companies refused the intervention of the Counsellor.

Thus, it does not appear that Canada's extractive sector prefers public institutions to review disputes with overseas communities in contrast to the more predictable attention paid by civil society organisations. Comparatively, the involvement of various non-governmental organisations in preparing complaints to the former office of the CSR Counsellor suggests that civil society actors are highly motivated to participate in reviews by public institutions.

In sum, I suggest that certain aspects of the authors' proposal are impracticable and lack sufficient rigor to be implemented in an effective fashion. For this reason, the proposal in its current form is not the best alternative for addressing the problem of extraterritorial wrongdoing by the extractive sector.

[68] Simons and Macklin (n 45) 317.
[69] Simons and Macklin (n 45) 316–17.
[70] Simons and Macklin (n 45) 316–17.
[71] Global Affairs Canada, 'File # 2013-05-ARG: Office of the Extractive Sector CSR Counsellor's Closing Report Request for Review' (Government of Canada, 2013), www.international.gc.ca/csr_counsellor-conseiller_rse/publications/2013-05-ARG_closing_report-rapport_final.aspx?lang=eng.

V. Torrance's Proposal

While Simons and Macklin's book proposes the most comprehensive model for reforming the international practices of the extractive sector, it is not the only conception that has been proffered in recent years. This section provides a review of Michael Torrance's proposal that was put forward in a 2016 conference paper.

Michael Torrance, a practicing lawyer with experience in the mining sector, has developed a proposal of a territorial-state oriented mechanism to address human rights disputes. It is an innovative private law proposal that encourages the use of arbitration that would be akin to the model of labour arbitration currently utilised in Canada.[72]

As described by Torrance, labour arbitration is a method of private dispute resolution between union organisations and companies, usually backed by judicial processes to ensure procedural fairness. Torrance argues that labour arbitration is a suitable model for human rights dispute resolution for several reasons. For one, the arbitrators are typically selected jointly or by consent of the parties. Additionally, there are clear rules on who has standing to bring complaints. A key feature of Torrance's proposal is that once an arbitration has concluded, parties are prohibited from suing in the courts on the same issues. However, the decisions of arbitrators would be reviewable by courts if they are flawed on the basis of procedural fairness.[73]

Looking at the historical developments of labour arbitration in Canada and the United States, Torrance draws a comparison to extraterritorial human rights concerns in the extractive sector. He suggests that initial voluntary approaches towards labour disputes failed before paving the way to mandatory labour arbitration in the twentieth century. Comparatively, Torrance suggests that human rights and CSR dispute processes will develop similarly in the sense that voluntary grievance mechanisms will be replaced with mandatory arbitration processes.[74]

This analogy between labour arbitration and extraterritorial human rights disputes is not as convenient as Torrance asserts. The field of labour law does not equate easily to the situations of foreign communities impacted by the extractive sector. For one, the scope of determining which individuals are protected under labour law is quite clear; they are simply those employed by the employer. That relationship signifies an affiliation beyond legal contract. The employer-employee rapport intrinsically has an economic dynamic as both parties rely on each other in order to be successful. As an example, poor employee performance can result in lost profit for the employer; whereas strong employee performance will likely increase profits for the employer. In contrast, I would suggest that those who oppose development and operations by an extractive sector corporation will not

[72] Torrance, 'Remedying Human Rights' 24.
[73] Torrance (n 2) 27.
[74] Torrance (n 2) 28.

have mutual interests in the same way as employers-employees. The extractive sector does not need to rely on local communities in order to be profitable. For instance, if the interests of those communities are to increase salaries for local workers and maximise environmental protection, this may hinder profit for the extractive sector. Thus, resolving disputes will prove challenging given that the interests of these parties are inherently opposed.

Moreover, it is not clear which individuals or representatives will have the ability to raise a complaint for arbitration. Torrance does not address this factor, but my concern is that industry would attempt to limit its exposure by reducing the amount and type of complaints that are eligible for arbitration. For example, one logical method for determining which individuals have the ability to raise a complaint leading to arbitration is based on proximity to the extractive sector site. However, this potential would leave out other individuals with a legitimate grievance who are not directly proximate to the site-level operations.

For examples of grievances that may arise from individuals not directly proximate to an extractive site, consider the Canadian mining company Sherritt International, which in 2012 received several complaints about its operations in Madagascar from residents close to the facilities as well as from residents in nearby cities. The latter group complained that their daughters became engaged in prostitution because of the lucrative market created by mine workers.[75] Further, they reported that the same influx of workers made food in their location unaffordable due to increased demand. The company knew that food had become scarce in the country and decided to import more from South Africa exclusively for its workforce without making it available to local residents.[76]

Beyond these specific examples of social and economic ills brought about in Madagascar by Sherritt, I suggest that it is possible that every resident of a country could be impacted by one extractive sector project. Consider the potential that an extractive sector corporation supports corrupt or totalitarian governments, such as in the claims made against *Talisman*[77] in its operation in Sudan, or in the Canadian case of *Nevsun*[78] concerning a mine in Eritrea. Under Torrance's proposal, these grievances may not be eligible for arbitration if companies view the complainant's lack of proximity to the extractive site as a legitimate reason to refuse to participate in an arbitral process.

Torrance's proposal also does not address the matter of jurisdiction. For instance, I question whether an away or home state will recognise a private arbitrator's decision in a dispute resolution process between industry and impacted communities. It is unclear where the validity and authority would draw from to

[75] J Kuyek, 'Another Mining Horror Story? Sherritt International Corporation's Ambatovy Project in Madagascar' (*MiningWatch Canada*, 10 April 2012), miningwatch.ca/blog/2012/4/10/another-mining-horror-story-sherritt-international-corporation-s-ambatovy-project.

[76] *Ibid.*

[77] *Presbyterian Church of Sudan v Talisman Energy Inc* [2003] 244 FSupp2d 289.

[78] *Nevsun Resources Ltd v Araya* 2020 SCC 5.

ensure that the decisions of these proposed arbitrators are judicially recognised or otherwise backed with legal weight.

There are constructive elements in this proposal. For example, Torrance's approach incorporates private law norms in a more fulsome and blended way than Simons and Macklin's proposal. I suggest that this is useful given that public law remedies have proven more difficult to implement, both through legislation and in judicial process.[79] As previously stated, legislation aimed at regulating extractive sector corporations has been attempted without success in the US, UK, Canada and Australia.[80]

I agree with some of Torrance's observations, including that the effectiveness of non-judicial mechanisms like the CORE are questionable given the apparent hesitancy of policy-makers to inject legal content into these mechanisms. As cited by Torrance, these bodies such as Canada's national contact point (NCP) lack procedural fairness and the ability to make final determinations accompanied by impactful sanctions.[81] Torrance's proposal does attempt to address these shortcomings. However, his proposal, while appealing, relies on extractive sector businesses to introduce, finance and operate effective arbitration processes that settle disputes between individuals and their business interests. This framework is unlikely to produce impartial and fair results given that the control of this grievance mechanism is firmly with the extractive sector, without oversight by any government authority. Further, it is built into the proposal that these arbitrations can only be reviewed judicially in the event of procedural failings, and not on the merits of the claim. Thus, it is a weak proposal for those seeking a substantial and compelling opportunity to provide a remedy to those impacted by the foreign extractive sector.

In sum, Torrance's approach incorporates private law norms in terms of elevating the use of arbitration as a method of dispute resolution borrowed from labour law principles. However, this approach relies heavily on the extractive sector operating effective arbitration processes, and for that reason it is unlikely to produce impartial and fair results. Additionally, the proposal does not expressly give the Government or any court the authority to review these arbitrations on their merits. Thus, the proposal is not adequate in providing a remedy to those impacted abroad by Canadian extractive sector operations.

[79] See generally K Keenan, 'Commentary. Desperately Seeking Sanction: Canadian Extractive Companies and their Public Partners' (2013) 34 *Canadian Journal of Development Studies* 111.

[80] For examples, US: Corporate Code of Conduct Act HR 5377 109th Congress (2006); UK: J Lux, SS Thorsen and Meisling, 'The European Initiatives' in R Mullerat (ed), *Corporate Social Responsibility: The Corporate Governance of the 21st Century*, 2nd edn (Alphen aan den Rijn, Kluwer Law International, 2011) 346; Canada: Bill C-300, Corporate Accountability of Mining, Oil and Gas Corporations in Developing Countries Act, 40th Parliament, 3rd Session (2009); Australia: M Schwartz, 'Legally Mandated Self-Regulation: The Potential of Sentencing Guidelines' in W Cragg (ed), *Ethics Codes, Corporations, and the Challenge of Globalization* (Cheltenham, Edward Elgar Publishing, 2005) 294.

[81] Torrance (n 2) 21.

VI. Proposal Set Out by the Canadian Network on Corporate Accountability

The Canadian Network on Corporate Accountability (CNCA) has advocated for the creation of an ombudsperson's office that will have the authority to investigate the foreign activities of the Canadian extractive sector. In 2017, the CNCA drafted model legislation that would create this ombudsperson role. It has been noted by at least one commentator that the CORE adopts many of the features proposed in this draft legislation.[82]

This model legislation focuses on a non-judicial grievance process for investigating allegations of harm associated with overseas Canadian mining projects. This includes potential failures by industry to respect international human rights and environmental standards.[83]

Under the proposal, complaints can be made by any person, organisation or group.[84] The ombudsperson can decline to investigate a complaint if it is being effectively dealt with in another proceeding such as an internal grievance mechanism.[85] The ombudsperson may also refer the matter for mediation.[86]

As part of the investigation process, the ombudsperson may request disclosure of evidence with timelines for producing the disclosure for both the complainant and respondent.[87] That information may be kept confidential by request of one of the parties.[88] A Canadian judge can assist the ombudsperson in compelling disclosure and can order a search of property when it is relevant and justified.[89]

To a limited extent, the proposal calls for the activities of the ombudsperson to be publicly reported, and there are procedures for measuring and monitoring the implementation of any recommendations made by the ombudsperson.[90] As part of a recommendation, the ombudsperson may propose the withdrawal of economic and diplomatic support from the Government of Canada to an offending extractive sector company.[91] The CORE and Canada's NCP hold the same powers;

[82] C Kamphuis, 'Building the Case for a Home-State Grievance Mechanism: Law Reform Strategies in the Canadian Resource Justice Movement' in I Feichtner, M Krajewski and R Roesch (eds), *Human Rights in the Extractive Sector* (New York, Springer, 2019).

[83] Canadian Network on Corporate Accountability (CNCA), 'Executive Summary: Draft Model Legislation to Create a Human Rights Ombudsperson for the International Extractive-Sector in Canada' (2016), cnca-rcrce.ca/wp-content/uploads/2016/03/Executive-Summary-Global-Leadership-in-Business-and-Human-Rights-Draft-Extractive-Sector-Ombudsperson-Model-Legislation-11022016.pdf.

[84] CNCA, 'The Global Leadership in Business and Human Rights Act: An Act to Create an Independent Human Rights Ombudsperson for the International Extractive Sector Draft Model Legislation' (2 November 2016) pt 4, cnca-rcrce.ca/wp-content/uploads/2019/04/The-Global-Leadership-in-Business-and-Human-Rights-Act.pdf.

[85] *Ibid* pt 6.4.

[86] *Ibid* pt 11.

[87] *Ibid* pt 8.4.

[88] *Ibid* pts 8.5 and 10.

[89] *Ibid* pts 8.9–8.15.

[90] *Ibid* pts 13.1 and 13.4.

[91] *Ibid* pt 14.

they can both recommend the withdrawal of economic and diplomatic support to extractive sector companies. However, CNCA's proposal goes further. The recommendations of the ombudsperson must be implemented by the Government of Canada unless justifiable reasons are provided for not implementing them. This feature has not been adopted in the current mandate of the CORE.

Under CNCA's proposal, the Federal Court of Canada may be asked to judicially review the reasonableness of any government agency or department's reasons for non-implementation of the ombudsperson's recommendation, should that occur.[92] However, the CNCA's draft legislation does not provide a similar opportunity for judicial review by multinational companies that are subject to a recommendation calling for the withdrawal of government support.

Further, the CNCA ombudsperson office would be conferred status as an Officer of Parliament within the Government of Canada.[93] In my view, this is not a logical choice. Officers of Parliament in Canada include the Office of the Auditor General, the Chief Electoral Officer, the Conflict of Interest and Ethics Commissioner, the Official Languages Commissioner, among others. These Officers of Parliament carry out duties assigned by statute, and report to one or both of the Canadian Senate and House of Commons, but are seen as independent of government influence.[94] In this way, they serve as overseers of government activity. Given that the purpose of the proposed ombudsperson office is to regulate foreign activities of private Canadian companies, not government action, it is unclear why the ombudsperson should be considered an Officer of Parliament. In my view, the ombudsperson's office should simply be an administrative agency operating within the Federal Government.

Finally, in forming their recommendations, the ombudsperson may look at international norms on human rights and corporate accountability that include the six Performance Guidelines that were considered by the former office of the Canadian CSR Counsellor.[95] However, beyond these Performance Guidelines, the ombudsperson is required to investigate all complaints that allege harm based on 21 other 'core human rights treaties'.[96] The methodology for determining how these human rights treatises were chosen to be included on this list is not set out and little is mentioned about them in this proposal.

VII. Other Proposals

Beyond the potential solutions proffered by Macklin, Simons, Torrance and the CNCA, there are other proposals for reform that have been set out, with

[92] *Ibid* pts 14.4–14.5.
[93] *Ibid* pt 3.2.
[94] Parliament of Canada, 'Officers and Officials of Parliament' lop.parl.ca/sites/ParlInfo/default/en_CA/Parliament/OfficersParliament.
[95] CNCA, 'Business and Human Rights Act' (n 84) pts 13.2 and 13.3.
[96] CNCA, 'Business and Human Rights Act' (n 84) Sch 1.

insufficient details to warrant their inclusion in this analysis. For instance, a former Supreme Court of Canada Justice has advocated for increasing accessibility to litigation in Canada.[97] However, on account of *forum non conveniens* and other procedural barriers, it is unlikely that courts will be the venue by which a remedy is achieved for victims of abuses caused by the extraterritorial activities of the Canadian extractive sector.

Industry groups have also been making proposals for reform. In 2017, the Mining Association of Canada recommended the creation of a new dispute resolution process with a 'joint fact-finding' mandate to help solve disputes involving Canadian mining companies overseas.[98] The industry group defines joint fact-finding as a methodology where industry and the complainant conduct their own separate investigations and bring those findings together for discussion. They argue that this is more effective than a unilateral investigative process. However, they fail to cite any rationale for this belief beyond their 'experience'.[99] The greatest weakness in this proposal is that participation would be voluntarily in this joint fact-finding process. As such, this would not address one of the most critical shortcomings with the former CSR Counsellor given that respondent companies consistently refused to participate in dispute resolution when given the opportunity to decline without any sanction.

VIII. Contrast of the Various Proposals

The advantage of my proposal over Simons and Macklin's is that the home state judicial and non-judicial systems are not intended to be the initial mechanism for resolving disputes between impacted communities and the foreign activities of the extractive sector. This is because, under my proposal, the CORE would have discretion to take carriage of complaints in select cases where there is merit and the respondent company does not have a sufficient site-level grievance process.

The primary responsibility for resolving disputes would remain with individual companies that are incentivised to develop and pay for their own effective site-level grievance mechanisms. Site-level grievance mechanisms are preferable to state-level grievance mechanisms because they tend to mitigate the costs of conflict and help resolve disputes before they escalate. Further, they can also assist the respondent corporation in understanding how to be more socially, culturally and environmentally responsive to the complainant going forward.[100]

[97] I Binnie, 'Legal Redress for Corporate Participation in International Human Rights Abuses' (2009) 38 *The Brief* 44.

[98] P Gratton, 'If Human Rights Ombudsman Is Created, Learn from Experience' *The Hill Times* (22 March 2017) 17.

[99] *Ibid.*

[100] R Davis and D Franks, 'The Cost of Conflict with Local Communities in the Extractive Industry' (SR Mining, October 2011) 9, www.csrm.uq.edu.au/publications/the-costs-of-conflict-with-local-communities-in-the-extractive-industry.

In contrast to Simons and Macklin's proposal, the implementation of my plan will not burden the Government with the costs of regulating the activities of companies that have developed their own effective system for resolving disputes concerning their foreign extractive sector operations. Companies will also be incentivised to develop their own programmes to reduce any potential penalty awarded by the CORE in a review process. The primary method for companies to avoid oversight by the CORE will be to demonstrate that they have a robust site-level grievance process.

Torrance's recommendations for reforming the regulation of the Canadian international extractive sector lies in contrast to that of Macklin and Simons. For example, the use of public law tools such as statutory and judicial regulation to compel corporations to respect human rights was a dominant theme in the proposal raised by Macklin and Simons. Torrance's recommendations instead incorporate private law norms such as the use of mandatory arbitration processes as a method of dispute resolution, inspired by Canadian and US labour laws.

Torrance's private law approach relies heavily on the extractive sector operating effective arbitration processes. For this reason, I suggest that it is unlikely to produce impartial and fair results. The concern is that much of the control over the arbitration process is in favour of the extractive sector. For instance, it appears under Torrance's proposal that corporations which choose to implement these arbitral processes will be responsible for their design and operation with little oversight. The proposal does not specify any designated government agency to monitor or review these arbitration processes or the merits of the complaints they considered. It does provide for judicial review in limited circumstances where decisions are flawed on the basis of procedural fairness.[101] However, in practice, arbitrations are difficult to overturn in the judiciary. In most legal systems, including Canada, there are very limited avenues for appeal of an arbitral award.[102]

Torrance's proposal has a targeted scope in exclusively promoting arbitration as the sole means for dispute resolution. Complainants do not have the opportunity to attempt mediation or another method of dispute resolution under this model. In contrast, Simons and Macklin's proposal relies heavily on public law tools such as judicial and other regulatory oversight, including a CSR agency that closely monitors and regulates the Canadian extractive industry. This includes the responsibility to investigate host state countries to consider whether they are a weak governance zone. The authors also propose the application of the nationality and territorial principles in regulating parent and subsidiary corporations' overseas conduct. I question the effectiveness of this proposal, as enforcing extraterritorial jurisdiction has proved challenging on account of issues such as international comity and limitations of jurisdiction.

[101] Torrance (n 2) 27.

[102] *Sattva Capital Corp v Creston Moly Corp* 2014 SCC 53.

One additional concern with this model is that the Government is the primary actor with a responsibility to fund institutions such as the courts to regulate the activities of the extractive sector. One of the goals of my proposal is to minimise the costs and other burdens on the government and judicial system. This is why I propose a model that blends private and public law tools as the best approach. To this end, I advocate the use of soft law measures to compel the extractive sector to develop and operate effective site-level grievance mechanisms. The soft law measures include the proposed bounty programme that will increase any potential penalty from the CORE for companies that fail to operate, or even implement, a sufficient site-level grievance process. Conversely, the penalty may be reduced, or more importantly, not even reviewed by the CORE where the site-level grievance mechanism is adequate in terms of providing a fair process.

The advantage in my proposal over Torrance's model is that the complainants would have the option to avoid arbitration and instead utilise the CORE's review process or an alternative such as mediation. Under my proposal, the parties may still choose arbitration, however it is one of many possibilities for engaging in dispute resolution. Torrance calls for arbitration to take place in a similar context to labour arbitration, which is a unique form of arbitration with specific legislation and protocols.[103] In my view, the type of arbitration that would take place between impacted communities and the extractive sector is commercial arbitration, which is also governed by particular legislation.[104] In my proposal, I set out a framework for using Canadian commercial arbitration legislation to ensure that arbitrations are conducted pursuant to best practices, and that resulting awards will be enforced. In contrast, Torrance does not address any framework for implementing his proposal. Next, I compare and contrast the proposal put forward by the CNCA with my proposal.

As with my proposal, the ombudsperson's office proposed by the CNCA can decline to investigate a complaint if it is being effectively dealt with in another proceeding, such as an internal grievance mechanism.[105] The CNCA proposal also provides an option for mediation. Further, the ombudsperson may request disclosure of evidence, with timelines, for the complainant and respondent. That information may be kept confidential. However, the CNCA's proposal differs from my proposal in several respects.

First, the ombudsperson would be required to get a justice of a Canadian court to approve an order compelling disclosure.[106] In my proposal, the CORE can order the production of disclosure without judicial support. Further, the CORE may use their powers pursuant to their Operating Procedures to award penalties, fines and costs as they see fit in order to enforce proper disclosure. Under the CNCA's

[103] Torrance (n 2) 26.

[104] C Thomson and A Finn, 'International Commercial Arbitration: A Canadian Perspective' (2002) 18 *Arbitration International* 206.

[105] CNCA, 'Business and Human Rights Act' (n 84) pt 6.4.

[106] CNCA, 'Business and Human Rights Act' (n 84) pt 10.

model, this extra layer of requiring judicial support to compel disclosure will likely slow the process. One of the benefits of administrative processes is to avoid delays that may come with the judicial system. The authors of the CNCA proposal even acknowledge that similar offices such as the Canadian Privacy Commissioner have the authority to compel the production of documents without needing to seek a court order to that effect. The authors of the CNCA's model legislation suggest that requiring the involvement of the courts in ordering disclosure is a way of enhancing the procedural protections afforded to companies that are subject to a complaint.[107] Beyond this explanation, it is unclear what the authors believe is the downside to extending the same powers vested with the Privacy Commissioner to this proposed ombudsperson. Whether the reason is that they believe this will satisfy the concerns of the extractive sector opposed to such an office or process is unclear.

Second, in contrast to my proposal, the CNCA's draft model legislation does not include the ability of the ombudsperson to levy a monetary penalty as a form of sanction. Instead, the ombudsperson will merely form an opinion on whether companies are causing or contributing to alleged harm purported by complainants. The ombudsperson would then make public 'recommendations' of actions that could be taken by companies or the Canadian Government to provide remedy to victims or prevent future harm.[108] As such, the ombudsperson will not make findings of guilt or liability. The proposed ombudsperson can recommend the withdrawal of support from the Government of Canada. However, this is essentially the same power as Canada's NCP. Thus, this proposal does not offer an extension in terms of remedy compared to the current framework for sanctioning non-compliant corporations under Canada's NCP.

Third, the proposed new ombudsperson office would be conferred status as an Officer of Parliament. As noted in the previous section, Officers of Parliament typically serve as watchdogs on government activity as opposed to regulating the private sector. Further, unlike in administrative and judicial proceedings, Officers of Parliament may engage in express policy making.[109] However, I caution against expanding the role of an extractive sector ombudsperson into the formation and implementation of foreign policy. My proposal is rooted in the need to provide a dispute resolution process regarding specific extractive sector operations; it is not about resolving broader claims that transcend the scope of a particular project. In my view, any exercise or creation of foreign policy concerning the extractive sector should remain where it belongs, with Parliament.

Fourth, the extent of international human rights and environmental standards that are considered in the CNCA's proposal are much more extensive than the six

[107] CNCA, 'Executive Summary' 3.

[108] CNCA (n 83) 4.

[109] N Craik et al (eds), *Public Law: Cases, Materials and Commentary*, 2nd edn (Toronto, Edmond Montgomery, 2011) 288; *Cloverdale Shopping Centre Ltd v Etobicoke (Township)* [1966] 2 OR 439 (CA).

listed Performance Guidelines set out in my proposal. The CNCA's proposal does not justify the inclusion of such a wide variety of international standards. I suggest that the six Performance Guidelines on their own provide clear norms to base a claim.

Finally, unlike those put forward by the CNCA, Torrance or Simons and Macklin, my proposal expressly recommends the inclusion of civil society as representatives, or even to function as mediators in these grievance processes. One reason I advocate for the involvement of civil society organisations in dispute resolution processes between businesses and impacted communities is because this has been endorsed in the UN Guiding Principles. For all of these reasons, I suggest that my proposal is more practical than the recommendations offered by the CNCA, Torrance, Macklin and Simons.

Statutes and judicial mechanisms have also failed to provide meaningful remedies to individuals impacted by the foreign extractive sector. I suggest that in contrast to statutes and judicial mechanisms, an industry-run, state-based grievance process will be more pragmatic for those seeking legal recourse for wrongdoing by multinational corporations. This is a key feature regarding my proposal for holding the extractive sector to account for human rights abuses and environmental violations abroad.

In my proposal, site-level grievance mechanisms are not required in a prescriptive manner. Instead, I suggest that extractive sector corporations with robust site-level grievance processes will be acknowledged for conscientious efforts to mitigate their impacts on local communities and the environment. In the event that a complaint is raised to the CORE, companies that resolve disputes fairly, effectively and internally will not be compelled to a hearing on the merits of a dispute. Conversely, companies that fail to develop effective grievance mechanisms will face the prospect of increased monetary sanctions if a penalty is assessed.

Moreover, I suggest that the CORE should encourage widespread support from civil society in resolving disputes. For these reasons, I argue that this part of the proposal aligns with at least two measures of the UN Guiding Principles, as it strongly encourages extractive sector companies to develop internal grievance mechanisms and utilise credible stakeholders, such as civil society, in resolving disputes.

I suggest that the extractive sector will be supportive of this proposal at best, or at worst find it tolerable. In demonstrating its favourability, I have contrasted my proposal with previously outlined frameworks for reforming the foreign activities of the Canadian extractive sector. I suggest that my proposal is more practical than those previously offered by various commentators including the CNCA, Macklin, Simons and Torrance. For instance, through the use of incentives, as opposed to mandatory requirements, my proposal balances pro-development of the extractive sector abroad with the necessary protections for the environment and human rights. In contrast, Macklin and Simons offer a public law approach that requires burdensome government expense and involvement. Torrance offers a purely self-governance approach, which does not provide an adequate mechanism to effectively regulate the foreign conduct of the extractive sector. In contrast, my proposed model, which blends private and public law, is a better approach, as it does provide an adequate mechanism for effective regulation.

In contrast to the proposal put forward by the CNCA, my proposal is more effective because it creates an enforcement mechanism by providing the CORE with the power to issue monetary penalties. The CNCA's proposal does not provide any additional powers beyond those currently utilised by Canada's NCP.

An effective remedy is possible for those impacted by the overseas activities of the extractive sector because the proposal, if implemented, establishes an incentive scheme that provides an economic benefit for voluntary compliance, and a potential penalty for lack of adherence. For instance, the proposal rewards socially responsible actions such as the development of internal site-level grievance processes in the absence of an express legal requirement to do so.

IX. Concluding Thoughts

The judicial systems in the US, UK, Canada and Australia have been the forum for lawsuits concerning the extraterritorial conduct of the extractive sector. The claims have often been brought against the parent corporations in their countries of domicile, and consequently run into several procedural barriers. This suggests that using a judicial system in the home state of a parent corporation is not an optimal solution for those impacted by their overseas activities.

Partly as a result of these failed litigation attempts, civil society organisations and human rights groups have pressed governments to take action. Civil society organisations have utilised a variety of different strategies for holding extractive sector corporations to account for human rights abuses around the world. These strategies are wide-ranging, from lobbying governments to mediation efforts between communities and industry.

One potential solution is the development of an effective non-judicial grievance mechanism that provides a remedy to those who are negatively impacted by the extractive sector. Two examples of grievance mechanisms aimed at regulating the social and environmental actions of corporations operating abroad were in Australia with the Australia Mining Ombudsman (AMO) and Canada's CSR Counsellor. None of the complainants who raised concerns with Canada's CSR Counsellor received a remedy as a result of utilising that mechanism. As such, the CSR Counsellor's process did not manifest a preferred approach.

Both the AMO and CSR Counsellor utilised non-binding approaches as participation by corporations in their dispute resolution processes was voluntary. Voluntary participation by industry is evocative of corporate self-governance, and is tied to notions of corporate social responsibility. There is historical support for the effectiveness of initiatives such as the *Lex Mercatoria* that demonstrates the nimbleness of corporate self-governance.[110] It has even been suggested that by following best practices through self-governance, corporations may be creating a new customary global law.[111]

Using the example of the CSR Counsellor, it appears that multinational corporations may elect to voluntarily follow best practices, but this does not amount to the tangible creation of a new customary global law. An effective regulatory system requires some mandatory compliance in order to enforce corporate responsibility for actions aboard.

In contrast, despite corporations not being required to engage with the AMO, the AMO had a track record of opening dialogue between extractive sector companies and impacted communities. As a critique, the AMO could not legally compel corporations to participate in its process or enforce a remedy. Nevertheless, it was a mediation service that increased the ability of impacted communities to protect their interests.

A main difference between the CSR Counsellor and the AMO is that the latter was a civil society-run mechanism that was guided by principles of fairness and equity. The fact that the AMO was able to achieve some desirable and lasting outcomes for impacted communities suggests that engaging civil society groups in resolving these disputes is advisable.

With the erosion of public control, civil society organisations have attempted to fill the governance gap by entering the international regulatory sphere as dominant players. This involvement has been a prominent theme in attempting to hold the multinational extractive sector to account. A primary thrust of this book is that civil society groups can assist in resolving intractable disputes between mining enterprises and impacted communities because they foster a currency of legitimacy and transparency. However, civil society organisations concerned with corporate conduct abroad have not unilaterally produced effective models for regulating multinational enterprises.

In 2018, the Federal Government announced the creation of the CORE to replace the CSR Counsellor. The CORE is certainly a unique creature given similar offices do not exist elsewhere. Despite this, it lacks the power to affect consequential sanctions against businesses that commit wrongdoing. The only power the CORE has is to recommend the withdrawal of government advocacy and financial support. These proposed powers are banal and prosaic.

Setting out a proposal to further strengthen the authority of the CORE using realistic, industry-palatable and effective means is a primary motivation behind this book. While the proposal used Canada as a case study for implementation, the findings of the book are also applicable towards the design of similarly purposed dispute resolution mechanisms in other countries. Specifically, the proposal is applicable to other common law jurisdictions that seek to regulate the foreign

[110] See generally R Steinhardt, 'The New Lex Mercatoria' in P Alston (ed), *Non-State Actors and Human Rights* (Oxford, Oxford University Press, 2005).
[111] Pitts, 'The Role of the Lawyer' 488.

conduct of the extractive sector, such as the United States, United Kingdom and Australia.

I envision the CORE as a quasi-judicial institution that can review complaints and conduct hearings. This is in contrast to the rather stagnant function of a typical ombudsperson office that prepares long, drawn out reports that fail to result in substantive change. Under my proposal, the CORE has the powers, rights and privileges as vested in a superior court of record in Canada. This includes the powers to examine parties and evidence, to inspect property and to assess monetary financial penalties and issue costs.

With the implementation of my proposed changes, the CORE will harness the power of industry-sponsored dispute mechanisms and civil society for efficiency and practicality in achieving a fair result for those impacted abroad by Canadian enterprises.

A primary responsibility of corporations that operate internationally under my proposal is to develop and operate robust site-level grievance mechanisms. A best practice for businesses to ensure or exceed compliance is to include a role for civil society as part of the grievance process and to fund their services commensurately. In my view, Canadian businesses will welcome this proposal, as the primary control for preventing legal, financial and reputational liability is to follow the guidance of the CORE. This becomes, in effect, their main regulator in terms of foreign conduct. I suggest that this is what success looks like when it comes to providing a remedy for victims of the foreign operations of Canadian businesses. This can be accomplished without extensive new funding or expansion of the office, mandate or structure of the CORE. Rather, this can occur by simply empowering the CORE with tools to compel businesses to comply with the Performance Guidelines and develop, implement and operate sound site-level grievance mechanisms.

Criterion that defines effectiveness in the context of non-judicial grievance mechanisms is set out in the UN Guiding Principles. These KPIs in UN Guiding Principle 31 stipulate that grievance mechanisms should be legitimate, accessible, equitable, predictable, transparent, rights-compatible, a source of continuous learning and based on engagement and dialogue.

My proposal embraced all of the KPIs to demonstrate the merits of the proposal in regulating the foreign conduct of Canadian businesses. My proposed involvement of civil society is also key for assisting Canada, through the CORE, in meeting the requirements of an effective dispute resolution process as set out in the UN Guiding Principles.

In sum, what I propose is a nimble regulatory approach, given that companies are not mandated to create any particular form of site-level grievance mechanism. Rather, they have flexibility in choosing among several options. They may proceed with the creation and operation of an internal site-level resolution process, or utilise civil society as a third-party mediator. Further, to their own disadvantage, companies may choose not to have a grievance mechanism at all. In any event, the effectiveness of site-level grievance mechanisms, or lack thereof, will be judged in accordance with the UN Guiding Principles.

Under this proposal, companies will face legal, financial and operational risk based on the performance of their dispute resolution processes. One primary consequence of my proposal is that operators will face penalties from the CORE if they are found to have violated the Performance Guidelines. These penalties will be steeper if the site-level grievance process is found not to be in compliance with the standards endorsed by the CORE. In this way, strict participation in the CORE's process is not inescapably mandatory. It is only if the CORE receives a complaint that they would question whether respondent corporations have internal site-level grievance mechanisms.

A site level-grievance mechanism is preferable to a state-based process such as the CORE because they potentially help resolve disputes before they escalate. They also mitigate the risk of actions such as protests and blockades that an extractive sector company or government may take aggressive action to prevent. In cases where an effective site-level-grievance mechanism exists, the CORE may exercise discretion in declining to review the complaint. If companies fail to implement a site-level grievance mechanism, the CORE will review complaints against the respondent company. If such complaints are found to have merit, the offender will be penalised to a greater extent than if they had a site-level grievance process in place.

The instructions for Canadian businesses in my proposal are apparent and obvious. If companies prefer to insulate themselves from scrutiny from the CORE, they may exercise their prerogative by creating a robust site-level grievance mechanism. This will obviate any need or ability for a complainant to avail themselves of the CORE's review process. In this proposal, I am not suggesting the dismantling of the CORE or replacing it with a new entity. Rather, I am suggesting an overhaul of the CORE's Operating Procedures and the formal power of the CORE to levy administrative monetary sanctions in achieving its mandate. This would further include the uncoupling of the CORE with Canada's NCP, given the failure of these mechanisms to produce tangible results.

The implementation of this proposal will compel businesses to operate effective site-level grievance processes without onerous government support. Businesses are encouraged to utilise civil society as representatives or even to serve as mediators in their dispute resolution mechanisms. In this way, there is a pressing argument in favour of requiring companies to self-regulate to a limited degree and to encourage the involvement of civil society in regulating the foreign conduct of companies.

It is anticipated that the implementation of these proposed reforms will enhance the processes of the CORE to become an agency for effective dispute resolution between foreign communities and Canadian industries. Further, it could make Canada a global leader in complying with its commitment to align with the UN Guiding Principles and restore its brand as a human rights champion and protector of the environment. If it is not embraced in Canada to begin with, the proposal may be adopted by other countries that are seeking alignment with international norms for business conduct such as the UN Guiding Principles.

This may include other common law jurisdictions with a significant international extractive sector like the United States, United Kingdom or Australia.

There is no panacea for ensuring effective corporate responsibility in overseas operations. I cannot commit to the reader that implementing the recommendations in my proposal will stop all wrongdoing by the extractive sector in its foreign operations. What can be pledged is that it will balance the need to regulate with a reliance on industry to regulate itself. It is a solution that will be met favourably by civil society, investors, industry and those they impact abroad.

Appendix: Draft Operating Procedures for the Canadian Ombudsperson for Responsible Enterprise

1. Mandate

1.1 The mandate of the Canadian Ombudsperson for Responsible Enterprise (CORE) is to review the practices of Canadian mining, oil and gas and garment sector companies operating outside Canada and to enforce the implementation of the endorsed performance guidelines (the Organisation for Economic Co-operation and Development (OECD) Guidelines for Multinational Enterprises, the UN Guiding Principles on Business and Human Rights, the Voluntary Principles on Security and Human Rights, the International Finance Corporation Performance Standards of the World Bank, the OECD Due Diligence Guidance on Responsible Supply Chains of Minerals from Conflict-Affected and High-Risk Areas and the Global Reporting Initiative).

1.2 In performing dispute resolution services between companies and impacted individuals, the CORE will aim to foster constructive collaboration and dialogue and encourage the utilisation of third parties, such as civil society groups, in fostering effective dispute resolution.

2. Definitions

In these Operating Procedures, these terms shall have the following meanings:

a) 'Arbitration' is a dispute resolution process in which a third-party person, known as an Arbitrator, renders a binding decision at the conclusion of the process.
b) 'Arbitrator' is the facilitator of an Arbitration and renders a binding decision at the conclusion of the process.
c) 'Assessed Penalty' is the amount of monetary award to be distributed directly to Complainants at the discretion of the CORE. These penalties are potentially assessed in cases where a Respondent Party has failed to participate or the Complaint has been determined to have merit at the conclusion of a Hearing. The amount of the Assessed Penalty and the

rational that they are based upon are set out in Final Reports issued by the CORE at the conclusion of the Review Process.

d) 'Bounty Programmes' means an increase or decrease to the Assessed Penalty at the discretion of the CORE. These increases or decreases are based on whether the Respondent Party has a sufficient Site-level Grievance Mechanism and whether the Respondent Party has otherwise implemented the Performance Guidelines.
e) 'Complainant' means an individual impacted by the mining, oil and gas and garment sector activities of a Canadian company outside of Canada who is issuing a formal Complaint with the CORE.
f) 'Complaint' means the submission of a grievance against a Respondent Party to the CORE.
g) 'CORE' means the Office of the Canadian Ombudsperson for Responsible Enterprise.
h) 'Disclosure' means the sharing of material information between the Participants prior to a Hearing as ordered under these Operating Procedures by the CORE.
i) 'Enabling Act' means The Canadian Mining Accountability Act.
j) 'Fee Schedule' sets out the reasonable costs that Roster Members and other parties will likely incur by acting in the role of representative, arbitrator or mediator.
k) 'Final Reports' are the reports that the CORE will prepare at the termination or completion of all Complaints, which will be publicly available on the Office's website.
l) 'Hearings' means the formal proceedings before the CORE on the merits of a dispute between a Complainant and Respondent Party.
m) 'Extraterritorial State' refers to the jurisdiction in which the Respondent Party operates.
n) 'Initial Assessment' means the process of determining the eligibility of a Complaint, as carried out by the CORE.
o) 'Interim Reports' means the reports that the CORE may prepare at relevant stages during the Review Process. Interim Reports may include information relating to the Complainant and Respondent Party, the issues raised in the Complaint, eligibility determinations, activities aimed at resolving the dispute between the Participants and commitments made by the Participants.
p) 'Mediation' is a dispute resolution process in which a neutral person, known as a Mediator, helps the parties reach an agreement.
q) 'Mediator' is a facilitator of a Mediation process.
r) 'Minister' means the Canadian Minister for International Trade.
s) 'NCP' means the Canadian National Contact Point relating to the Organisation for Economic Co-operation and Development Guidelines for Multinational Enterprises.
t) 'Office' means the office of the CORE.

u) 'Performance Guideline(s)' means the OECD Guidelines for Multinational Enterprises, the UN Guiding Principles on Business and Human Rights, the Voluntary Principles on Security and Human Rights, the International Finance Corporation Performance Standards of the World Bank, the OECD Due Diligence Guidance on Responsible Supply Chains of Minerals from Conflict-Affected and High-Risk Areas and the Global Reporting Initiative.
v) 'Participants' means the Complainant and the Respondent Party.
w) 'Representative' means an advocate on behalf of a Participant before a Hearing, Mediation or Arbitration or during some other form of negotiation.
x) 'Respondent Party' means an extractive sector entity that is the subject of an allegation by a Complainant.
y) 'Review Process' means the process facilitated by the CORE pursuant to a Complaint from Initial Assessment to completion.
z) 'Roster Member' means a civil society organisation or other party that has been formally endorsed by the CORE to serve in the capacity of a representative, mediator or arbitrator in both Site-level Grievance Mechanisms and as part of the CORE's Review Process.
aa) 'Site-level Grievance Mechanism' means a company-sponsored and financed process that allows impacted communities and individuals to raise concerns directly with a Canadian company.

3. Function of the CORE Pursuant to the Enabling Act

3.1 **Role:** In undertaking reviews, the CORE may:

a) refuse to deal with a Complaint;
b) exclusively deal with a portion or particular segments of a larger Complaint;
c) determine how a Review Process is to be conducted;
d) determine at what stage to conclude a Review Process; and
e) determine whether a Review Process should be terminated before completion.

3.2 **Limitation:** The CORE cannot accept Complaints that:

a) were previously submitted to the Office for which there is no new information available;
b) were submitted anonymously (with exceptions for requests for confidentiality); or
c) broadly understood, do not fall within the remit of the Performance Guidelines.

3.3 **Conflict of Interest:** The CORE does not have jurisdiction to hear any matter in which the CORE has or has had an interest.

3.4 **Staff:** In accordance with the *Public Service Employment Act* there may be appointed officers and employees required to conduct the business of the CORE.

3.5 **A Court of Record:** A Hearing before the CORE is a court of record.

3.6 **Official Seal:** The CORE shall have an official seal, which shall be judicially noticed.

3.7 **Powers of the CORE:** The CORE has, for the purpose of matters in the Review Process, powers:

a) of a commissioner under the Inquiries Act, RSC 1985, c I-11, as granted in the Enabling Act;
b) to administer oaths, take affidavits and statutory declarations, receive affirmations and examine parties and witnesses, as the CORE may direct;
c) with respect to the attendance, swearing and examination of witnesses, the production and inspection of documents, the enforcement of its orders, the entry on and inspection of property owned or controlled by a Canadian mining, oil and gas or garment sector company, and all such powers, rights and privileges as are vested in a superior court of record in Canada;
d) to assess monetary financial penalties, costs and fines against Participants up to a collective amount as set out in the Enabling Act and its regulations;
e) to make its own Procedures pursuant to the Enabling Act;
f) to decline to conduct an investigation while litigation in a Canadian court is pending by the same Participants based on substantially similar facts as determined by the CORE.

3.8 **Failure to Participate:** If a Respondent Party fails to respond to a Complaint or a request for participation from the CORE, or fails to appear on the date set for a Mediation or a Hearing in respect of a Complaint, the CORE may assess a penalty against the Respondent Party and may award further monetary damages and non-monetary sanctions within the legislative power of the Enabling Act as they see fit.

3.9 **Costs and Fees:** The CORE may:

a) award costs and other legal fees from Participants in respect of the decisions made by the CORE to other Participants and directly to the CORE;
b) govern the rates of fees and expenses payable to witnesses, interpreters or other parties involved;
c) prescribe fees payable for the filing or issuing of documents in respect of a Hearing before the CORE and provide for waiving the payment of those fees;
d) prescribe fees, expenses and other forms of remuneration payable to operators and transcribers of sound-recording machines for the purpose of preserving a record of one or several aspects of the Review Process;

e) prescribe fees, expenses and other forms of remuneration payable to Roster Members serving in the role of a Representative, Mediator or Arbitrator; and
f) prescribe fees and other expenses respecting the preparation and publication of Interim and Final Reports.

3.10 **Referral to the Attorney General:** The CORE may refer a Complaint to the Attorney General of Canada for a potential criminal investigation.

4. Procedures of the CORE

4.1 **Admissibility of Evidence:** For the purposes of a Hearing, the CORE:

a) is not bound by the laws of evidence applicable to judicial proceedings;
b) may admit any oral or written evidence that it, in its discretion, considers proper, whether admissible in a court of law or not; and
c) may not admit into evidence at a Hearing anything that would be inadmissible by reason of any privilege under the law of evidence in Canada, or that is inadmissible by any Act of Parliament.

4.2 **Confidential Information:** During the Review Process, the CORE may take any measures to ensure the confidentiality of any information that is financial, commercial, scientific or technical information as long as:

a) the information has been consistently treated as confidential information by a person or organisation directly affected by the Review Process; and
b) the CORE considers that the person or organisation's interest in confidentiality outweighs the public interest in disclosure during the Review Process.

4.3 **Rules of Court:** Where these Operating Procedures do not provide for a specific practice or procedure of the CORE that is necessary to ensure an expeditious and inexpensive resolution of a matter, the CORE may:

a) apply the Federal Courts Rules (SOR/98-106); and
b) modify the Federal Courts Rules (SOR/98-106), as needed.

4.4 **Adjournment:** The CORE may, at any time in the Review Process and on any conditions that it considers proper, grant adjournments.

4.5 **Precedent:** the CORE shall be guided by previous decisions when deciding subsequent Complaints with similar issues or facts.

4.6 **Stages of the Complaint Process:** The Review Process comprises the following stages: Submission of Complaint; Initial Assessment; Opportunity for Mediation or Arbitration; Disclosure; Hearing; Potential Assessment of Penalty; Responses to Potential Assessment of Penalty; and Reporting.

5. Submission of Complaint

5.1 **Who may Submit a Complaint:** A Complaint may be submitted by an individual, group, organisation or community that:

a) reasonably believes that it is being or may be adversely affected by the activities of a Canadian mining, oil and gas or garment sector entity regarding its operations outside Canada; and
b) believes that these activities are inconsistent with the Performance Guidelines.

5.2 **Representation of Participants:** Participants are entitled to a Representative in respect of any step in the Review Process before the CORE by:

a) a lawyer called to practice law in a province anywhere in Canada;
b) a Roster Member; or
c) an agent, upon consent of the CORE.

5.3 **Appointment of Roster Members:** In any Hearing or other proceeding before the CORE, a Roster Member may be appointed as Representative, Mediator or Arbitrator in accordance with Procedures 7.15–7.17.

5.4 **Submitting a Complaint to the Office:** Complaints must be received in writing, via electronic or regular mail, or by fax, to the Office at: The Canadian Ombudsperson for Responsible Enterprise X Front Street Toronto, Ontario XXX XXX CANADA Email: core@international.gc.ca

5.5 **Format of Complaint:** Complaints need not be in any particular format as long as they include the information listed in Procedure 5.6.

5.6 **Required Information:** The following information must be provided in the Complaint:

a) the basis on which the Complaint is submitted;
b) information which supports the assertions made along with dates, locations and other details;
c) pictures, documents and other supporting evidence;
d) the name of the Respondent Party, or information pertaining to the identity of the Respondent Party;
e) a statutory declaration that the Complainant swears the information to be true;
f) confirmation that the Complainant understands these Operating Procedures;
g) confirmation of the Complainant's willingness to engage in constructive collaboration and dialogue with the Respondent Party;
h) the measures the Complainant has taken to try to resolve the matter; and
i) the Complainant's desired outcome from the Review Process.

5.7 **Language:** Complaints must be made in one of Canada's official languages (English and French). With prior consent of the CORE, Complaints may be submitted in another language.

5.8 **Provision of Assistance by the Office:** The Office may be contacted to answer any questions regarding the Complaint submission process. The Office will not provide guidance if such guidance would compromise the impartiality of the Office. The CORE will provide a list of potential Roster Members near the location of the Complainant or otherwise may be able to assist the Complainant in submitting their Complaint if requested.

5.9 **Registration of Complaint:** Upon receipt, the Office will open an internal file and assign a file number to the Complaint.

5.10 **Acknowledgement of Receipt:** The Office will respond to the Complainant with an acknowledgement of receipt of the Complaint within ten (10) business days of the submission date.

5.11 **Transmittal to the Respondent Party:** The Office will transmit the Complaint to the Respondent Party at the time of acknowledgement of receipt of the Complaint.

5.12 **Information Published:** At any time following ten (10) business days of receiving a Complaint, the Office may publish the following information on its website:

a) the name of the Complainant (subject to approved requests for confidentiality);
b) the name of the Respondent Party;
c) the date that the Complaint was received by the Office; or
d) a brief summary of the Complaint, as appropriate.

6. Initial Assessment

6.1 **Purpose of the Initial Assessment:** The CORE will make a determination on the eligibility of the Complaint. The CORE will apply the screening criteria set forth in this section of the Operating Procedures.

6.2 **Nature of the Initial Assessment:** The nature and extent of the Initial Assessment will be determined by the CORE in its discretion based on the issues raised in the Complaint. The CORE may ask for additional information from the Participants at any time.

6.3 **Timeframe:** The Initial Assessment will be completed within 40 business days from the date of acknowledgement of the Complaint.

6.4 **Screening Criteria:** In determining whether the Complaint is eligible, and with a view to the effective use of the Office's resources, the CORE shall consider:

a) whether a sufficient Site-level Grievance Mechanism exists in the Extraterritorial State that has not been utilised by the complainant;
b) whether a sufficient Site-level Grievance Mechanism exists in the Extraterritorial State and has provided a fair decision;

c) the amount of time that has elapsed since the alleged activity occurred;
d) the amount of time that has elapsed since the Complainant became aware of the issue;
e) the nature and seriousness of the issue;
f) whether the Complaint was made in good faith;
g) the extent to which other redress mechanisms have been exhausted; and
h) whether the issue is substantiated.

6.5 **Results of the Initial Assessment:** If the Complaint is:

a) found ineligible, the Complainant will be notified in writing and provided with reasons accordingly. The Respondent Party will also be notified of the CORE's decision. The Review Process may be terminated by the CORE at this time; or
b) if found eligible, the Participants will be informed by the CORE in writing, and the Review Process will proceed to the next stage.

6.6 **Determination and Publication of Results:** The CORE will update the file based on the Initial Assessment and may publish the results on the Office's website. The CORE may issue and publish on the Office's website an Interim Report or other form of a public report at that time.

7. Opportunity for Mediation or Arbitration

7.1 **Purpose:** Mediation and Arbitration are intended to complement the efforts of the Participants and the CORE to resolve their dispute prior to a Complaint undergoing a formal Hearing.

7.2 **General Timeframes:** Mediation and Arbitration are meant to be flexible undertakings and therefore there are no specific limits or timeframes during which these processes must be completed.

7.3 **Determination and Publication of Results:** At the completion of any Mediation or Arbitration, or if one of the Participants exits the Review Process during this stage, the CORE will update the file, issue a Final Report listing the conclusions with an Assessed Penalty where appropriate and publish the Final Report on the Office's website.

Mediation

7.4 **Nature of Mediation:** The CORE, independent third parties and/or the Participants may conduct Mediation, which is carried out with a view to improving the understanding of the issues that are giving rise to the dispute between the

Participants. Mediation is also intended to clarify the issues under dispute, result in an improved understanding of how various stakeholders view the situation and help determine how the issues may be resolved through constructive collaboration and dialogue, including determining alternatives for resolving the issues of concern.

7.5 **Mediation Timeframes:** Mediation may take place at any point during the Review Process. At any time after a Complaint is submitted, the CORE, or a person authorised by the CORE to do so, may refer the action for Mediation with the express written consent of the Participants.

7.6 **Settlement Privilege:** Any settlement discussions in respect of a Complaint that take place during a Mediation are privileged and are not admissible in any Hearing before the CORE or in any other civil action.

7.7 **Mediation Privilege:** Neither the CORE nor a Mediator who conducts a Mediation is compellable to give evidence in any court or in any proceedings of a judicial nature concerning any proceeding, discussion or matter that takes place during or with respect to the Mediation.

7.8 **Mediation Immunity:** No action may be brought against a Mediator who conducts a Mediation for any act carried out or omitted in the execution of the Mediator's duty, or for any act carried out in respect of that Mediation unless it is proved that the Mediator acted maliciously and without reasonable and probable cause.

7.9 **Results of Mediation:** If the Participants:

a) do not agree to a resolution following Mediation, the Review Process may continue to the next stage or be terminated at the discretion of the CORE; or
b) if the Participants reach a written agreement on a set of commitments for resolving their dispute, the Review Process will be considered closed; and
c) the CORE may remain seized of the matter to ensure the implementation of the commitments made by the Participants as a result of the Mediation.

Arbitration

7.10 **Nature of Arbitration:** Arbitration is a process resulting in a binding decision upon the Participants to a Complaint. Formally submitting a Complaint to Arbitration is a voluntary action and all Participants must consent. The Participants must also consent to the appointment of particular Arbitrator(s) to hear the dispute. The CORE encourages the use of Roster Members or otherwise independent third-party Arbitrators be chosen to make binding decisions in resolving Complaints.

7.11 **Arbitration Timeframes:** Arbitration may take place at any point during the Review Process. At any time after a Complaint is submitted, the CORE, or a person authorised by the CORE to do so, may refer the action for Arbitration with the express written consent of the Participants.

7.12 **Arbitration Immunity:** No action may be brought against an Arbitrator who conducts an Arbitration for any act carried out or omitted in the execution of the Arbitrator's duty or for any act carried out in respect of that Arbitration, unless it is proved that the Arbitrator acted maliciously and without reasonable and probable cause.

7.13 **Recognising Arbitration:** If an Arbitration has been completed consistent with these Operating Procedures, the CORE will consider the Review Process closed. The CORE may remain seized of the matter to ensure the implementation of the commitments made by the Participants as a result of the Arbitration.

7.14 **Failing to Recognise Arbitration:** The CORE only recognises Arbitrations that are conducted in Canada, pursuant to international commercial arbitration legislation that require that a written Arbitration Agreement be set out and provide for the recognition and enforcement of Arbitral Awards. The applicable legislation will be the province or territory where the Respondent Party is incorporated or otherwise acknowledge in writing that they are governed by that jurisdiction. One of the following provincial or territorial statutes (or subsequent versions with amendments) must govern the Arbitration: International Commercial Arbitration Act, S.A. 2000, c. I- 5 (Alberta); International Commercial Arbitration Act, R.S.B.C. 1996, c. 233 (British Columbia); International Commercial Arbitration Act, CCSM c C151 (Manitoba), c. 32, Chap. 0151; International Commercial Arbitration Act, RSNB 2011, c 176 (New Brunswick); International Commercial Arbitration Act, R.S.N.L. 1990, c. I-I5 (Newfoundland and Labrador); International Commercial Arbitration Act, R.S.N.W.T. 1988, c. I-6 (Northwest Territories); International Commercial Arbitration Act, R.S.N.S. 1989, c. 234 (Nova Scotia); International Commercial Arbitration Act, R.S.P.E.l. 1988 (Prince Edward Island), c. I-5; International Commercial Arbitration Act, S.S. 1988 9, c. 1-10.2 (Saskatchewan); International Commercial Arbitration Act, SO 2017, c 2, Sch 5 (Ontario); International Commercial Arbitration Act, R.S.Y. 2002, c. 123 (Yukon); An Act to Amend the Civil Code and the Code of Civil Procedure in Respect of Arbitration, S.Q (Quebec); or the International Commercial Arbitration Act, RSNWT 1988, c I-6 (Nunavut).

Roster Members

7.15 **Involvement with Dispute Resolution:** In appropriate cases, the engagement of a Representative, Arbitrator or Mediator may assist the Participants in the resolution of their dispute. Pursuant to agreements made by the Participants, a process for Mediation or Arbitration will be established with the engagement of a Representative, Mediator or Arbitrator such as a Roster Member.

7.16 **Purpose and Implementation of the Roster:** In accordance with its Mandate, the CORE will develop a Roster prior to the implementation of these Operating Procedures. The Roster will list civil society organisations or other parties located in areas where the Canadian Extractive Sector operates that are qualified to act as a Representative, Arbitrators or Mediators. Further information on the purpose and implementation of the Roster include that:

a) the CORE makes the Roster publicly available so that Complainants and Canadian mining, oil and gas or garment sector companies may use the services of the Roster Members in order to answer various questions or deal with disputes;
b) these Roster Members have been endorsed by the CORE to serve in the capacity of a Representative, Mediator or Arbitrator in both Site-level Grievance Mechanisms and as part of the CORE's Review Process;
c) the criteria used by the CORE in determining eligibility for Roster Members include the objectives, independence, size, location and mandate of the civil society organisations or other potential Roster Members;
d) the Roster shall be reviewed annually by the CORE to ensure that the listed Roster Members remain eligible;
e) the CORE may refer Complainants and Respondent Parties to a Roster Member prior to the CORE initiating their own Review Process; and
f) any dispute reviewed by the CORE will, in the regular course, seek out Roster Members, local to the Extraterritorial State or otherwise, to be a part of the Review Process in some capacity whether as a Representative, Mediator or Arbitrator.

7.17 **Recommendations for Utilising Roster Members:** The CORE will consider the degree of adherence to the following recommendations in determining whether to consider a Complaint, in referring the matter to Mediation, in the assessment of a penalty or in the content of Interim and Final Reports. It is recommended that:

a) the Canadian mining, oil and gas and garment sector reach out to Roster Members to assist in a formal capacity in their Site-level Grievance Mechanisms;
b) Roster Members fulfill the role of Mediator, Arbitrator or act as a Representative of Complainants for the purposes of Site-level Grievance Mechanisms;
c) the Canadian mining, oil and gas and garment sector fund the involvement of Roster Members to act as a Mediator, Arbitrator or Representative of the Complainants in their Site-level Grievance Mechanism; and
d) Roster Members shall be compensated based on the CORE's Fee Schedule, which sets out the reasonable costs that these parties will likely incur by acting in the role of Representative, Arbitrator or Mediator.

Involvement of the CORE

7.18 **Assistance with Mediation or Arbitration:** The CORE may facilitate the arrangements of Mediation or Arbitration with an external Mediator or Arbitrator, such as a Roster Member or other party, with the consent of all Participants. The CORE will assist the Participants in determining a suitable Mediator or Arbitrator, based on the potential Mediator or Arbitrator's neutrality and independence, as well as the Mediator or Arbitrator's cultural and linguistic skills to work effectively with the Participants. Roster Members are assessed on this criteria at the time they are evaluated for eligibility to be included on the list of Roster Members.

7.19 **The CORE as an Intervenor:** Upon request of any of the Participants, the CORE may serve as an Intervenor in a Mediation or Arbitration process.

7.20 **The CORE as Mediator:** The CORE may conduct a Mediation with the consent of all parties. In these cases, the CORE will not subsequently conduct a Hearing or assess penalties against the Participants on the same matter.

8. Disclosure

8.1 **Purpose:** The CORE may compel Participants to share among the parties all material information that is in their possession, including those materials that they wish to rely on in a Hearing.

8.2 **Timeframes:** The CORE may set and enforce a timeframe with limitations for Participants to exchange material information, subject to Procedures 3.7(c) and 3.9.

8.3 **Enforcement:** The CORE may use its powers pursuant to Procedures 3.7(c) and 3.9 in awarding penalties, fine and costs as they see fit in order to enforce proper Disclosure among the Participants.

8.4 **Legal Privilege and Confidential Information:** Procedures 4.1(c) and 4.2 on legal privilege and confidential information will be observed by the CORE throughout the Review Process.

9. Hearings

9.1 **General:** The practices and procedures for Hearings before the CORE shall be as provided in these Operating Procedures and the Enabling Act. Procedures for Hearings such as submission of evidence, process for Participants to present their arguments before the CORE and location and scheduling of Hearings will be conducted in accordance with provisions set out in Procedures 4.1, 4.3 and 4.4.

9.2 **Written Submissions:** A party to any proceeding before the CORE who will not be present or represented at a Hearing held by the CORE may submit written submissions to the CORE and the other Participants no later than 14 days before the time fixed for the hearing. The written submission must be signed by the Participant filing it or by their Representative.

9.3 **Timeframes:** The CORE may set and enforce timeframes for Hearings subject to Procedures 3.7(c) and 3.9.

9.4 **Open to the Public:** Hearings will be open to the public, including the media, unless a request for confidentiality and a private hearing is submitted and approved in writing by the CORE.

9.5 **Prohibition on Recording Devices:** The use of private recording devices is prohibited during a Hearing unless a request to use such devices is submitted and approved in writing by the CORE.

10. Potential Assessment of a Penalty

10.1 **When a Penalty is Assessed:** An Assessed Penalty is the amount of monetary award to be distributed directly to Complainants at the discretion of the CORE. The assessment of a penalty may occur:

a) in cases where a Respondent Party has failed to participate in the Review Process;
b) if the CORE determines that a Complaint has merit at the conclusion of a Hearing or other step in the Review Process; or
c) if the CORE has determined that the Respondent Party has failed to meet one of the Performance Guidelines.

10.2 **Publication:** The amount of any Assessed Penalty and the rationale behind it will be set out in the Final Report issued by the CORE at the conclusion of a Review Process.

11. Responses to Potential Assessment of Penalty

11.1 **Purpose:** A Respondent Party shall have a formal opportunity to demonstrate to the CORE that they abide by the Performance Guidelines and have an effective Site-level Grievance Mechanism.

11.2 **Bounty Programme**: The Assessed Penalty may:

a) be reduced on account of a Respondent Party's demonstration that they have an effective Site-level Grievance Mechanism, or on account of other proven commitments to the Performance Guidelines, at the discretion of the CORE;

b) remain the same if, in the discretion of the CORE, it is determined that the Respondent Party has neither excelled nor failed in providing a Site-level Grievance Mechanism, or in adopting best practices from the Performance Guidelines; or

c) be increased if, in the discretion of the CORE, it is determined that the Respondent Party failed to demonstrate that they offer an effective Site-level Grievance Mechanism, or otherwise failed to adopt best practices from the Performance Guidelines.

11.3 **Publishing Best Practices for Site-level Grievance Mechanisms:** The CORE shall publicly display on its website criterion on best practices for developing, implementing and operating effective Site-level Grievance Mechanisms. This criterion will be publicly available prior to the implementation of these Operating Procedures.

12. Reporting

12.1 **Purpose:** Reporting provides for an accounting of the activities of the CORE and Participants in respect to a Complaint.

12.2 **Nature of Reporting:** The CORE may prepare Interim Reports at relevant stages during the Review Process, and will prepare a Final Report at the termination or completion of any Complaint. In addition to other information, Interim and Final Reports may include information relating to the Complainant and Respondent Party, the issues raised in the Complaint, eligibility determination, activities aimed at resolving the dispute between the Participants, commitments made by the Participants and other final outcomes.

12.3 **Publication of Interim and Final Reports:** The Reports issued by the CORE will be publicly available and will be published on the Office's website in accordance with the timeframe set out in Procedure 12.5.

12.4 **Notification and Distribution:** The CORE will send every Interim and Final Report it creates to all Participants involved in a Complainant.

12.5 **Timing of Publication of Interim and Final Reports:** Interim Reports issued by the CORE will be published within 60 days of determining that such a report shall be issued. Final Reports will be published within 120 days of the conclusion of a Complaint.

12.6 **Effective Date of Interim and Final Reports:** Interim and Final Reports issued by the CORE are effective on and after the date the report is signed by the CORE or delegate, unless otherwise specified by the CORE.

13. Appeals

13.1 **Appeal Process:** Any Participant may appeal a decision of the CORE to the Federal Court of Appeal, within 30 days after the Final Report is signed by the CORE or delegate, by:

a) filing in the Federal Court of Appeal, a notice of appeal setting out the grounds of appeal;
b) serving the notice of appeal to the other Participant, that being either the Complainant or the Respondent Party;
c) serving the notice of appeal to the CORE; and
d) serving the notice of appeal to any other party that the Federal Court of Appeal directs.

14. General

14.1 **Application of Procedures:** Concerning these Procedures:

a) all Participants must comply unless the CORE otherwise orders;
b) the CORE may exercise any power under these Procedures on its own initiative or on the application of a Participant; and
c) the CORE may waive or vary a requirement of these Procedures and may shorten or lengthen any time limits in these Procedures at its discretion.

14.2 **Procedure-Making Authority:** The CORE shall have direct control over the creation and administration of the Procedures and rules contained in these Operating Procedures, as per the delegation by Parliament of procedure and rule-making authority through the Enabling Act. These Operating Procedures are subject to approval, implementation and review by the Minister.

14.3 **Approval:** These Operating Procedures are subject to the approval of the Minister.

14.4 **Implementation Period:** These Operating Procedures shall be implemented on a date selected by the Minister.

14.5 **Review:** These Operating Procedures will be subject to review in a time period set by the Minister.

14.6 **Conflict between the Procedures, Acts and Regulations:** If any of these Procedures conflict with, or are inconsistent with, an Act or Regulation, the Act or Regulation prevails to the extent of the conflict or inconsistency.

BIBLIOGRAPHY

Academic References

Akurang-Parry, K, 'Making a Difference in Colonial Intervention in Gold Mining in Wassa Fiase, Gold Coast (Ghana): The Activism of Two Women, 1874–1893' in J Gier and L Mercer (eds), *Mining Women: Gender in the Development of a Global Industry, 1670 to the Present* (New York, St Martin's Press, 2006).

Allen, WT, 'Our Schizophrenic Conception of the Business Corporation' (1992) 14 *Cardozo Law Review* 280.

Ararat, M, Colpan, AM and Matten, D, 'Business Groups and Corporate Responsibility for the Public Good' (2018) 153 *Journal of Business Ethics* 911.

Austin, J, *The Province of Jurisprudence Determined, and the Uses of the Study of Jurisprudence* (London, Weidenfeld and Nicolson, 1832).

Ayres, I and Braithwaite, J, *Responsive Regulation: Transcending the Deregulation Debate* (Oxford, Oxford University Press, 1992).

Backer, LC, 'From Guiding Principles to Interpretive Organizations: Developing a Framework for Applying the UNGPs to Disputes That Institutionalizes the Advocacy Role of Civil Society' in C Rodriguez-Garavito (ed), *Business and Human Rights: Beyond the End of the Beginning* (Cambridge, Cambridge University Press, 2017).

—— 'The Structure of Global Law: Fracture, Fluidity, Permeability, and Polycentricity' (2012) 17 *Tilburg Law Review* 177.

Barrett, EL, 'The Doctrine of Forum Non Conveniens' (1947) 35 *California Law Review* 380.

Baughen, S, *Human Rights and Corporate Wrongs: Closing the Governance Gap* (Cheltenham, Edward Elgar Publishing, 2015).

Bebbington, A et al, 'Mining and Social Movements: Struggles Over Livelihood and Rural Territorial Development in the Andes' (2008) 36 *World Development* 2888.

Bellia, A and Clark, B, 'The Alien Tort Statute and the Law of Nations' (2011) 78 *University Chicago Law Review* 445.

Benedict, R, 'The Historical Position of the Rhodian Law' (1909) 18 *Yale Law Journal* 223.

Berger, PL and Luckmann, T, *The Social Construction of Reality: A Treatise in the Sociology of Knowledge* (New York, Doubleday, 1966).

Bethall, L, *The Abolition of the Brazilian Slave Trade* (Cambridge, Cambridge University Press, 1970).

Bilsky, L, 'The Judge and the Historian: Transnational Holocaust Litigation as the New Model' (2012) 24 *History & Memory* 117.

Binnie, I, 'Legal Redress for Corporate Participation in International Human Rights Abuses' (2009) 38 *The Brief* 44.

Black, V, Pitel, S and Sobkin, M, *Statutory Jurisdiction: An Analysis of the Court Jurisdiction and Proceedings Transfer Act* (Toronto, Carswell, 2012).

Blackstone, W, *Commentaries on the Laws of England* (Chicago, University of Chicago Press, 1979 edn, first published in 1765).

Blumberg, P, *The Multinational Challenge to Corporation Law: The Search for a New Corporate Personality* (Oxford, Oxford University Press, 1993).

—— 'The Transformation of Modem Corporation Law: The Law of Corporate Groups' (2005) 37 *Connecticut Law Review* 605.

Bone, J, 'Book Review: The Governance Gap: Extractive Industries, Human Rights, and the Home State Advantage' (2015) 11 *McGill International Journal of Sustainable Development Law & Policy* 2.

Boxer, CR, *The Golden Age of Brazil, 1695–1750: Growing Pains of a Colonial Society* (Berkeley, University of California Press, 1962).

Boyajian, JC, *Portuguese Bankers at the Court of Spain, 1626–1650* (New Brunswick, Rutgers University Press, 1983).

Braithwaite, J, 'Responsive Business Regulatory Institutions' in CAJ Coady and CJG Sampford (eds), *Business Ethics and the Law* (Leichardt, The Federation Press, 1993).

—— *Restorative Justice & Responsive Regulation* (Oxford, Oxford University Press, 2002).

Burger, R, *Chavin and the Origins of Andean Civilization* (London, Thames and Hudson, 1992) 127.

Butler, M, 'Lessons from Thor Chemicals' in L Bethlehem and M Goldblatt (eds), *The Bottom Line: Industry and the Environment in South Africa* (Cape Town, University of Cape Town Press, 1997).

Butler, P, *Colonial Extraction: Race and Canadian Mining in Contemporary Africa* (Toronto, University of Toronto Press, 2015).

Carley, S, Evans, TP and Konisky, DM, 'Adaptation, Culture, and the Energy Transition in American Coal Country' (2018) 37 *Energy Research and Social Science* 133.

Carpenter, RC, 'Setting the Advocacy Agenda: Theorizing Issue Emergence and Nonemergence in Transnational Advocacy' (2007) 51 *International Studies Quarterly* 99.

Carroll, A, 'A Three Dimensional Model of Corporate Social Performance' (1979) 4 *Academy of Management Review* 497.

—— 'The Pyramid of Corporate Social Responsibility: Toward the Moral Management of Organizational Stakeholders' (1991) 34 *Business Horizons* 39.

Casto, W, 'SOSA v. Alvarez-Machain and the End of History' (2012) 43 *Georgetown Journal of International Law* 1001.

Cherry, MA and Sneirson, JF, 'Beyond Profit: Rethinking Corporate Social Responsibility and Greenwashing After the BP Oil Disaster' (2010) 85 *Tulane Law Review* 985.

Choudhury, B, 'Beyond the Alien Tort Claims Act: Alternative Approaches to Attributing Liability to Corporations for Extraterritorial Abuses' (2005) 26 *Northwestern Journal of International Law and Business* 41.

Cleveland, T, *Diamonds in the Rough: Corporate Paternalism and the Mines of Colonial Angola, 1917–1975* (Athens, Ohio University Press, 2015).

Coffee, J, 'Racing Towards the Top?: The Impact of Cross-Listings and Stock Market Competition on International Corporate Governance' (2002) 102 *Columbia Law Review* 1757.

Coffee, J, 'The Future as History: The Prospects of Global Convergence in Corporate Governance and Its Implications' (1999) 93 *Northwestern University Law Review* 641.

Cohen, M, 'Ex Ante Versus Ex Post Deliberations: Two Models of Judicial Deliberations in Courts of Last Resort' (2014) 62 *The American Journal of Comparative Law* 401.

Cole, J, *The Potosí Mita, 1573–1700: Compulsory Indian Labor in the Andes* (Palo Alto, Stanford University Press, 1985).

Conrad, J, *Heart of Darkness* (Waiheke Island, The Floating Press, 2008).

Conway, M, 'A New Duty of Care? Tort Liability from Voluntary Human Rights Due Diligence in Global Supply Chains' (2015) 40 *Queen's Law Journal* 741.

Cook, ND, *Demographic Collapse, Indian Perú, 1520–1620* (Cambridge, Cambridge University Press, 1981).

Craik, N et al (eds), *Public Law: Cases, Materials and Commentary*, 2nd edn (Toronto, Edmond Montgomery, 2011).

Crane, A and Matten, D, *Business Ethics: Managing Corporate Citizenship and Sustainability in the Age of Globalization*, 4th edn (Oxford, Oxford University Press, 2007).

Crilly, D, Ni, N and Jiang, Y, 'Do-No-Harm Versus Do-Good Social Responsibility: Attributional Thinking and the Liability of Foreignness' (2016) 37 *Strategic Management Journal* 1316.

Crystal, V, Imai, S and Maheandiran, B 'Access to Justice and Corporate Accountability: A Legal Case Study of Hudbay in Guatemala' (2014) 35 *Canadian Journal of Development Studies* 286.

Cutler, AC, *Private Power and Global Authority: Transnational Merchant Law in the Global Political Economy* (Cambridge, Cambridge University Press, 2003).
D'Altroy, TN, *The Incas* (Oxford, Blackwell Publishing, 2003).
Davies, DB, *The Problem of Slavery in the Age of Revolution, 1770–1823* (Ithaca, Cornell University Press, 1975).
Davis, J, *Justice Across Borders: The Struggle for Human Rights in U.S. Courts* (Cambridge, Cambridge University Press, 2008).
Dewiel, B, 'A Conceptual History of Civil Society: From Greek Beginnings to the End of Marx' (1997) 6 *Past Imperfect* 3.
Dhir, A, 'Realigning the Corporate Building Blocks: Shareholder Proposals as a Vehicle for Achieving Corporate Social and Human Rights Accountability' (2006) 43 *American Business Law Journal* 365.
Diaz, ME, 'Mining Women, Royal Slave: Copper Mining in Colonial Cuba, 1670–1780' in L Mercer and J Gier (eds), *Mining Women: Gender in the Development of a Global Industry, 1670 to the Present* (New York, St Martin's Press, 2006).
Dignam, A and Lowry, J, *Company Law*, 7th edn (Oxford, Oxford University Press, 2012).
Dodek, A et al (eds), *Public Law: Cases, Commentary, and Analysis*, 3rd edn (Toronto, Edmond Montgomery, 2015).
Donnelly, J, 'Human Rights and International Organizations: States, Sovereignty, and the International Community' in F Kratochwil and E Mansfield (eds), *International Organization: A Reader* (New York, HarperCollins Publishers, 1994).
Eakin, MC, *British Enterprise in Brazil: The St, John d'el Rey Mining Company and the Morro Velho Gold Mine, 1830–1960* (Durham, Duke University Press, 1989).
Eckerman, I, *The Bhopal Saga – Causes and Consequences of the World's Largest Industrial Disaster* (Hyderabad, Universities Press, 2005).
Edelman, L, 'The Endogeneity of Legal Regulation: Grievance Procedures as Rational Myth' (1999) 105 *American Journal of Sociology* 406.
Edinger, E, 'Club Resorts Ltd. v. Van Breda: Extraterritoriality Revisited Papers from the 43rd Annual Workshop on Commercial and Consumer Law' (2014) 55 *Canadian Business Law Journal* 263.
Ehrenberg, J, *Civil Society: The Critical History of an Idea* (New York, New York University Press, 1999).
—— 'The History of Civil Society Ideas' in M Edwards (ed), *The Oxford Handbook of Civil Society* (Oxford, Oxford University Press, 2011).
Enneking, L, *Foreign Direct Liability and Beyond: Exploring the Role of Tort Law in Promoting Corporate Social Responsibility and Accountability* (The Hague, Eleven International Publishing, 2012).
Eroglu, M, *Multinational Enterprises and Tort Liabilities* (Cheltenham, Edward Elgar Publishing Limited, 2008).
Falk, R and Kim, S (eds), *Towards a Just World Order* (Boulder, Westview Press, 1982).
Fentiman, R, 'Jurisdiction, Discretion and the Brussels Convention' (1993) 26 *Cornell International Law Journal* 59, 73.
Fiesel, C, 'Fiduciary Duties of Directors, Corporate Governance and the End of Shareholder Primacy' in P Puri (ed), *Corporate Governance and Securities Regulation in the 21st Century* (Toronto, Butterworths, 2004).
Finnemore, M and Sikkink, K, 'International Norm Dynamics and Political Change' (1998) 52 *International Organization* 887.
Frank, C, 'Bhopal Blowup: Are Some Lawyers Vultures?' (1985) 71 *American Bar Association Journal* 17.
Freeman, RE, *Strategic Management. A Stakeholder Approach* (Cambridge, Cambridge University Press, 2010).
Frey, B, 'The Legal and Ethical Responsibilities of Transnational Corporations in the Protection of International Human Rights' (1997) 6 *Minnesota Journal of Global Trade* 153.
Friedman, M, 'The Social Responsibility of the Corporation Is to Increase Its Profits' (*New York Times Magazine*, 13 September 1970).
Fuller, L, 'Positivism and Fidelity to Law-A Reply to Professor Hart' (1957) 71 *Harvard Law Review* 630.

—— *The Morality of Law* (New Haven, Yale University Press, 1964).

Garvin, T et al, 'Community–Company Relations in Gold Mining in Ghana' (2009) 90 *Journal of Environmental Management* 571.

Goldhaber, M, 'Corporate Human Rights Litigation in Non-U.S. Courts: A Comparative Scorecard' (2013) 3 *UC Irvine Law Review* 127.

Grotius, H, *De Jure Beli Ac Pacis Libri* (translated by FW Kelsey) (Oxford, Clarendon Press, 1925 edn, first published 1625).

Habermas, J, *The Theory of Communicative Action Volume 2: System and Lifeworld* (Boston, Beacon Press, 1987).

Hansmann, H and Kraakman, R, 'The End of History for Corporate Law' (2001) 89 *Georgetown Law Journal* 439.

Hardt, M and Negri, A, *Empire* (Cambridge, Harvard University Press, 2000).

Hart, HLA, 'Positivism and the Separation of Law and Morals' (1957) 71 *Harvard Law Review* 593.

Hartley, TC, 'The Brussels Convention and Forum Non Conveniens' (1992) 17 *European Law Review* 6.

Hartman, L, 'Comment, Whistle While You Work: The Fairytale-Like Whistleblower Provisions of the Dodd-Frank Act and the Emergence of "Greedy," the Eighth Dwarf' (2011) 62 *Mercer Law Review* 1279.

Hawkins, K, 'Compliance Strategy, Prosecution Policy, and Aunt Sally: A Comment on Pearce and Tombs' (1990) 30 *British Journal of Criminology* 444.

Held, D et al, *Global Transformations: Politics, Economics, and Culture* (Redwood City, Stanford University Press, 1999).

Hemming, J, *The Conquest of the Incas* (London, Macmillan Publishers Ltd, 1993).

Hertel, S, *Tethered Fates: Companies, Communities, and Rights at Stake* (New York, Oxford University Press, 2019).

Hochschild, A, *King Lepold's Ghost: A Story of Greed, Terror, and Heroism in Colonial Africa* (Boston, Houghton Mifflin, 1998).

Howard-Grenville, J, Nash, J and Coglianese, C, 'Constructing the License to Operate: Internal Factors and Their Influence on Corporate Environmental Decisions' (2008) 30 *Law & Policy* 73.

Hudson, A, 'NGO's Transnational Advocacy Network: From Legitimacy to Political Responsibility?' (2002) 1 *Global Networks* 331.

Ignatieff, M, *The Ordinary Virtues: Moral Order in a Divided World* (Cambridge, Harvard University Press, 2017).

Imai, S, Gardner, L and Weinberger, S, '"The Canada Brand": Violence and Canadian Mining Companies in Latin America' (2017) Osgoode Legal Studies Research Paper No 17/2017, dx.doi.org/10.2139/ssrn.2886584.

Janda, R 'Note: Act Respecting Corporate Accountability for the Activities of Mining, Oil or Gas in Developing Countries [Bill C-300]: Anatomy of a Failed Initiative' (2010) 6 *McGill International Journal of Sustainable Development Law and Policy* 97.

Janis, MW, 'Individuals as Subjects of International Law' (1984) 17 *Cornell International Law Journal* 61.

—— 'The Doctrine of Forum Non Conveniens and the Bhopal Case' (1987) 34 *Netherlands International Law Review* 192.

Jeurissen, R, 'Institutional Conditions of Corporate Citizenship' (2004) 53 *Journal of Business Ethics* 87.

Kamphuis, C, 'Building the Case for a Home-State Grievance Mechanism: Law Reform Strategies in the Canadian Resource Justice Movement' in I Feichtner, M Krajewski and R Roesch (eds), *Human Rights in the Extractive Sector* (New York, Springer, 2019).

—— 'Foreign Investment and the Privatization of Coercion: A Case Study of the Forza Security Company in Peru' (2012) 37 *Brooklyn Journal of International Law* 529.

Keenan, K, 'Commentary. Desperately Seeking Sanction: Canadian Extractive Companies and their Public Partners' (2013) 34 *Canadian Journal of Development Studies* 111.

Kennett, W, 'Forum non conveniens in Europe' (1995) 54 *Cambridge Law Journal* 552.
Kerr, M, Pitts, C and Janda, R, *Corporate Social Responsibility: A Legal Analysis* (Markham, LexisNexis Canada Inc, 2009).
Khanna, P, *How to Run the World: Charting a Course to the Next Renaissance* (New York, Random House, 2011).
Kinley, D and Tadaki, J, 'From Talk to Walk: The Emergence of Human Rights Responsibilities of Transnational Corporations at International Law' (2004) 44 *Virginia Journal of International Law* 931.
Kirsch, S, 'Cleaning up Ok Tedi: Settlement Favors Yonggom People' (1996) 4 *Journal of the International Institute*, hdl.handle.net/2027/spo.4750978.0004.104.
Koebele, M, *Corporate Responsibility under the Alien Tort Statute: Enforcement of International Law through US Torts Law* (Leiden, Martinus Nijhoff Publishers, 2009).
Koh, HH, 'The 1998 Frankel Lecturer: Bringing International Human Rights Home' (1998) 35 *Houston Law Review* 647.
—— 'The 1994 Roscoe Pound Lecture: Transnational Legal Process' (1996) 75 *Nebraska Law Review* 181.
Kolakowski, L, *Main Currents of Marxism: The Founders, the Golden Age, the Breakdown* (New York, W. W. Norton & Company, 2005 edn, first published in 1978).
Korten, D, *When Corporations Rule the World*, 3rd edn (Oakland, Berrett-Koehler Publications, 2015).
Kramer, M and Porter, M, 'Creating Shared Value: Redefining Capitalism and the Role of the Corporation in Society' (2011) 89 *Harvard Business Review* 62.
Lahav, A, 'The Political Justification for Group Litigation' 81 *Fordham Law Review* 3193.
Lamer, M, Laudati, A and Clark, J, 'Neither War nor Peace in the Democratic Republic of Congo (DRC): Profiting and Coping amid Violence and Disorder' (2013) 40 *Review of African Political Economy* 1.
Lopez, J, 'The New Normal: Climate Change Victims in Post-Kiobel United States Federal Courts' (2013) 8 *Charleston Law Review* 113.
Lux, J, Thorsen, SS and Meisling, A, 'The European Initiatives' in R Mullerat (ed), *Corporate Social Responsibility: The Corporate Governance of the 21st Century*, 2nd edn (Alphen aan den Rijn, Kluwer Law International, 2011).
Maitland, FW, Select Pleas in Manorial and Other Seignorial Courts (London, B. Quaritch, 1889).
Masulis, RW and Reza, SW, 'Agency Problems of Corporate Philanthropy' (2015) 28 *Review of Financial Studies* 592.
Matheson, MJ and Bickler, S, 'The Fifty-Fifth Session of the International Law Commission' (2004) 98 *American Journal of International Law* 309.
Matten, D et al, 'Behind the Mask: Revealing the True Face of Corporate Citizenship' (2003) 45 *Journal of Business Ethics* 109.
McCoy, A, *In the Shadows of the American Century: The Rise and Decline of US Power* (Chicago, Haymarket Books, 2017).
McInnes, M, Kerr, I and VanDuzer, A, *Managing the Law: The Legal Aspects of Doing Business*, 5th edn (Boston, Pearson Education, 2017).
Means B and Yockey, J (eds), *The Cambridge Handbook of Social Enterprise Law* (Cambridge, Cambridge University Press, 2019).
Melish, T and Meidinger, E, 'Protect, Respect, Remedy and Participate: "New Governance" Lessons for the Ruggie Framework' in R Mares (ed), *The UN Guiding Principles on Business and Human Rights* (Leiden, Martinus Nijhoff, 2012).
Mickenberg, N and Cumming, P (eds), *Native Rights in Canada*, 2nd edn (Toronto, The Indian-Eskimo Association in Canada and General Publishing, 1970).
Miller, R et al, *Discovering Indigenous Lands: The Doctrine of Discovery in the English Colonies* (Oxford, Oxford University Press, 2010).
Milton, J, *Paradise Lost* (W Kerrigan, J Rumrich and SM Fallon, eds, 2008 edn, New York, The Modern Library, first published 1667).

Mitchell, W, *An Essay on the Early History of the Law Merchant* (Cambridge, Cambridge University Press, 1904).

Mitrany, D, *A Working Peace System* (London, Royal Institute of International Affairs, 1943).

Mocle, A 'Corporate Human Rights Risk' in L Rayman-Bacchus and P Walsh (eds), *Corporate Responsibility and Sustainable Development: Exploring the Nexus of Private and Public Interests* (New York, Routledge, 2016).

Muchlinski, P, 'Corporations in International Litigation: Problems of Jurisdiction and the United Kingdom Asbestos Cases' (2001) 50 *International & Comparative Law Quarterly* 1.

Oates, W, *The Economics of Environmental Regulation* (Cheltenham, Edward Elgar Publishing, 1996).

Ohmae, K, *The End of the Nation State* (New York, Simon and Schuster Inc, 1995).

Oshionebo, E, *Regulating Transnational Corporations in Domestic and International Regimes: An African Case Study* (Toronto, University of Toronto Press, 2009).

—— 'The U.N. Global Compact and Accountability of Transnational Corporations: Separating Myth from Realities' (2007) 19 *Florida Journal of International Law* 1.

Pearce, F and Tombs, S, 'Ideology, Hegemony and Empiricism: Compliance Theories of Regulation' (1990) 30 *British Journal of Criminology* 423.

Pitts, C, 'Business, Human Rights, and the Environment: The Role of the Lawyer in CSR & Ethical Globalization' (2008) 26 *Berkeley Journal of International Law* 479.

Posner, E, *Law and Social Norms* (Cambridge, Harvard University Press, 2000).

Putnam, R, *Bowling Alone: The Collapse and Revival of American Community* (New York, Simon & Schuster, 2000).

Rauxloh, RE, 'A Call for the End of Impunity for Multinational Corporations' (2008) 14 *Texas Wesleyan Law Review* 297.

Rehaag, S, 'The Hart-Fuller Debate in the Twenty-First Century' (2010) 48 *Osgoode Hall Law Journal* 691.

Reif, L, *The Ombudsman, Good Governance and the International Human Rights System* (Leiden, Martinus Nijhoff Publishers, 2004).

Restatement (Fourth) of the Foreign Relations Law of the United States Jurisdiction (Philadelphia, American Law Institute, 2017).

Restatement (Third) of the Foreign Relations Law of the United States (Philadelphia, American Law Institute, 1987).

Risse, T and Sikkink, K, 'The Socialization of International Human Rights Norms into Domestic Practices: Introduction' in S Ropp, K Sikkink and T Risse (eds), *The Power of Human Rights: International Norms and Domestic Change* (Cambridge, Cambridge University Press, 1999).

Rodríguez-Garavito, C, 'The Future of Human Rights: From Gatekeeping to Symbiosis' (2014) 11 *International Journal on Human Rights* 499.

Rose-Ackerman, S, 'Comment: Consensus Versus Incentives: A Skeptical Look at Regulatory Negotiation' (1994) 43 *Duke Law Journal* 1206, 1220.

Rowe, J, 'Inca Culture at the Time of the Spanish Conquest' in J Steward (ed), *Handbook of South American Indians* (Washington, Smithsonian Institution, 1946) 2nd Vol.

Ruggie, JG, *Just Business: Multinational Corporations and Human Rights* (New York, W. W. Norton & Company, 2013).

Sarfaty, GA, 'Review Essay of The Governance Gap: Extractive Industries, Human Rights, and the Home State Advantage, Penelope Simons & Audrey Macklin' (2017) 67 *University of Toronto Law Journal* 663.

Schaltegger, S and Wagner, M, *Managing and Measuring the Business Case for Sustainability: Capturing the Relationship between Sustainability Performance, Business Competitiveness and Economic Performance* (Sheffield, Green Leaf Publishing, 2006).

Scheffer, D, 'The Impact of War Crimes Tribunals on Corporate Liability for Atrocity Crimes under US Law' in C Walker-Said and JD Kelly (eds), *Corporate Social Responsibility? Human Rights in the New Global Economy* (Chicago, University of Chicago Press, 2015).

Schwartz, M, 'Legally Mandated Self-Regulation: The Potential of Sentencing Guidelines' in W Cragg (ed), *Ethics Codes, Corporations, and the Challenge of Globalization* (Cheltenham, Edward Elgar Publishing, 2005).
Seck, S, 'Canadian Mining Internationally and the UN Guiding Principles on Business and Human Rights' (2011) 49 *Canadian Yearbook of International Law* 51.
—— 'Climate Change, Corporate Social Responsibility, and the Extractive Industries' (2018) 31 *Journal of Environmental Law and Practice* 276.
—— 'Conceptualizing the Home State Duty to Protect Human Rights' in M Morsing and L Roseberry (eds), *Corporate Social and Human Rights Responsibilities: Global Legal and Management Perspectives* (London, Palgrave Macmillan, 2011).
—— 'Home State Responsibility and Local Communities: The Case of Global Mining' (2008) 11 *Yale Human Rights and Development Law Journal* 177.
Seck, S and Simons, P, 'Resource Extraction and the Human Rights of Women and Girls' (2019) 31 *Canadian Journal of Women and the Law* 1.
Sethi, S and Schepers, D, 'United Nations Global Compact: The Promise-Performance Gap' (2014) 122 *Journal of Business Ethics* 193.
Sherman, JF 'The UN Guiding Principles: Practical Implications for Business Lawyers' (2012) *In-House Defense Quarterly*.
Shiu, Y and Yang, S, 'Does Engagement in Corporate Social Responsibility Provide Strategic Insurance-like Effects' (2017) 38 *Strategic Management Journal* 455.
Simons, P, 'Corporate Voluntarism and Human Rights: The Adequacy and Effectiveness of Voluntary Self-Regulation Regimes' (2004) 59 *Industrial Relations* 1.
Simons, P and Macklin, A, *The Governance Gap: Extractive Industries, Human Rights, and the Home State Advantage* (Toronto, Routledge, 2014).
Simpson, LB, *Studies in the Administration of the Indians in New Spain* (Berkeley, University of California Press, 1940).
Smis, S and Van der Borght, K, 'Belgium: Act Concerning the Punishment of Grave Breaches of International Humanitarian Law: A Contested Law with Uncontested Objectives' (American Society of International Law, 2003).
Smith, A, *An Inquiry into the Nature and Causes of the Wealth of Nations* (New York, Modern Library, 1937 edn, first published 1776).
Steinhardt, R, 'Soft Law, Hard Markets: Competitive Responsibilities for Multinational Corporations' (2008) 33 *Brooklyn Journal of International Law* 933.
—— 'The New Lex Mercatoria' in P Alston (ed), *Non-State Actors and Human Rights* (Oxford, Oxford University Press, 2005).
Stephens, B, *International Human Rights Litigation in U.S. Courts*, 2nd edn (Leiden, Martinus Nijhoff Publishers, 2008).
Stone, I, 'British Direct and Portfolio Investment in Latin America Before 1914' (1977) 37 *Journal of Economic History* 690.
Studnicki-Gizbert, D, *A Nation upon the Ocean Sea: Portugal's Atlantic Diaspora and the Crisis of the Spanish Empire, 1492–1640* (Oxford, Oxford University Press, 2007).
Sweeney, JM, 'A Tort Only in Violation of the Law of Nations' (1995) 18 *Hastings International and Comparative Law Review* 445.
Szablowski, D, *Transnational Law and Local Struggles: Mining, Communities and the World Bank* (Oxford, Hart Publishing, 2007).
Tandeter, E, *Coercion and Market: Silver Mining in Colonial Potosi 1692–1826* (Albuquerque, University of New Mexico Press, 1992).
Teitz, LE, *Transnational Litigation* (Charlottesville, Michie, 1996).
Thabane, T, 'Weak Extraterritorial Remedies: The Achilles Heel of Ruggie's "Protect, Respect, Remedy" Framework and Guiding Principles' (2014) 14 *African Human Rights Law Journal* 43.
Thomson, C and Finn, A, 'International Commercial Arbitration: A Canadian Perspective' (2002) 18 *Arbitration International* 206.

Tocqueville, A, *Democracy in America* (Birmingham, The Legal Classics Library, 1988 edn, first published in 1838).
Uriz, G, 'The Application of the World Bank Standards to the Oil Industry: Can the World Bank Group Promote Corporate Responsibility?' (2002) 28 *Brooklyn Journal of International Law* 77.
Varma, R and Varma, D, 'The Bhopal Disaster of 1984' (2005) 25 *Bulletin of Science, Technology and Society* 37.
Viotti da Costa, E, *The Brazilian Empire: Myths and Histories* (Chicago, Chicago Dorsey Press, 1988).
Wagner, H and Parish, H, *The Life and Writings of Bartolomé de Las Casas* (Albuquerque, University of New Mexico Press, 1967).
Watson, B, 'John Marshall and Indian Land Rights: A Historical Rejoinder to the Claim of "Universal Recognition" of the Doctrine of Discovery' (2006) 36 *Seaton Hall Law Review* 481.
Watson, B, 'The Doctrine of Discovery and the Elusive Definition of Indian Title' (2012) 15 *Lewis & Clark Review* 995.
Webb, O, 'Kiobel, the Alien Tort Statute and the Common Law: Human Rights Litigation in This "Present, Imperfect World"' (2013) 20 *Australian International Law Journal* 131.
Weissbrodt, D and Kruger, M, 'Norms on the Responsibilities of Transnational Corporations and Other Business Enterprises with Regard to Human Rights' (2003) 97 *American Journal of International Law* 901.
West, R, *Colonial Placer Mining in Columbia* (Baton Rouge, Louisiana State University Press, 1952).
—— 'Early Silver Mining in New Spain, 1531–1555' in A Criag and R West (eds), *In Quest of Mineral Wealth: Aboriginal and Colonial Mining and Metallurgy in Spanish America* (Baton Rouge, Geoscience Publication, 1994).
Whellams, M, 'The Role of CSR in Development: A Case Study Involving the Mining Industry in South America' (Masters Theses, Saint Mary's University, 2007).
Williams, C, 'Corporate Compliance with the Law in the Era of Efficiency' (1998) 76 *North Carolina Law Review* 1265.
Wilson, E and Blackmore, E (eds), *Dispute or Dialogue: Community Perspectives on Company-Led Grievance Mechanisms* (London, International Institute for Environment and Development, 2013).
Wolf, P, 'International Organization and Attitude Change: A Re-examination of the Functionalist Approach' (1973) 27 *International Organization* 347.
Wood, S, 'Voluntary Environmental Codes and Sustainability' in B Richardson and S Wood (eds), *Environmental Law for Sustainability* (Oxford, Hart Publishing, 2006).
Worthen, K, 'Sword or Shield: The Past and Future Impact of Western Legal Thought on American Indian Sovereignty (Book Review)' (1991) 104 *Harvard Law Review* 1372.
Zavala, SA, *Libros de Asientos de La Gobernación de La Nueva España: Período Del Virrey Don Luis de Velasco, 1550–1552* (Mexico, Archivo General de la Nación, 1982).

Conference Papers

Backer, LC, 'An Institutional Role for Civil Society Within the U.N. Guiding Principles?: Comments on César Rodríguez-Garavito and Tatiana Andia "Business and Human Rights: Beyond the End of the Beginning"' (Workshop on Implementing the UN's Guiding Principles on Business and Human Rights: A South-Initiated North-South Dialogue, Brown University, February 2014).
Milanovic, N, 'A Canadian Alien Tort Statute? A Brief History of the International Promotion and Protection of Human Rights Act' (Universal Jurisdiction and Canadian Civil Courts: Strategic Directions Conference, 2008).
Pigrau, A, Borras, S and Cardesa-Salzmann, A, 'The Interplay of National, Transnational and International Litigation for Environmental Justice: Seeking Effective Means of Redress for Grave Environmental Damage' (ISEE Conference – Ecological Economics and Rio+ 20: Challenges and Contributions for a Green Economy, 2012), www.isecoeco.org/conferences/isee2012-versao3/pdf/p751.pdf.

Torrance, M, 'Remedying Human Rights: From the International, Regional and Domestic Status Quo to Future Innovations' (Human Rights Law and the Extractive Industries, Rocky Mountain Mineral Law Foundation, February 2016).

Government Documents

Export Development Canada, '2009 Compliance Officer's Annual Report on Third Party Complainants' (2009), www19.edc.ca/english/docs/compliance_officer_report_e.pdf.

Foreign Affairs, Trade and Development Canada, 'Building the Canadian Advantage: A Corporate Social Responsibility (CSR) Strategy for the Canadian International Extractive Sector' (2009), www.international.gc.ca/trade-agreements-accords-commerciaux/topics-domaines/other-autre/csr-strat-rse-2009.aspx?lang=eng.

Global Affairs Canada, 'Annual Report to Parliament: May 2015 – May 2016 – The Office of the Extractive Sector Corporate Social Responsibility (CSR) Counsellor Government of Canada' (Government of Canada, 2016), international.gc.ca/csr_counsellor-conseiller_rse/publications/2016_annual_report-rapport_annuel_2016.aspx?lang=eng.

—— 'A Report on the Visit of the World Bank Group's Compliance Advisor Ombudsman (CAO) to Toronto' (Government of Canada, 2012), www.international.gc.ca/csr_counsellor-conseiller_rse/publications/cao_rep-rap_cao-2012-01.aspx?lang=eng.

—— 'Closed National Contact Point Specific Instances' (Government of Canada, 2019), www.international.gc.ca/trade-agreements-accords-commerciaux/ncp-pcn/specific-specifique.aspx?lang=eng.

—— 'Corporate Social Responsibility Standards Navigation Tool' (Government of Canada, 2018), www.international.gc.ca/csr_counsellor-conseiller_rse/csrsnt-gnrse.aspx?lang=eng.

—— 'Doing Business the Canadian Way: A Strategy to Advance Corporate Social Responsibility in Canada's Extractive Sector Abroad' (Government of Canada, 2014), www.international.gc.ca/trade-agreements-accords-commerciaux/topics-domaines/other-autre/csr-strat-rse.aspx?lang=eng.

—— 'Excellon was a mining company incorporated in British Columbia with a principal office in Toronto. 'File #2011-01-MEX: Office of the Extractive Sector CSR Counsellor's, Request for Review Closing Report' (Government of Canada, 2011), www.international.gc.ca/csr_counsellor-conseiller_rse/publications/2011-01-MEX_closing_rep-rap_final.aspx?lang=eng.

—— 'Field Visit Report 2013-04-MEX:E the Office of the Extractive Sector CSR Counsellor' (Government of Canada, 2013), www.international.gc.ca/csr_counsellor-conseiller_rse/publications/2013-04-MEX_interim_rep_01-rap_provisoir_01.aspx?lang=eng.

—— 'File #2011- 02-MAU: Office of the Extractive Sector CSR Counsellor's, Request for Review Closing Report' (Government of Canada, 2011), www.international.gc.ca/csr_counsellor-conseiller_rse/publications/2011-02-MAU_closing_report-rapport_final.aspx?lang=eng.

—— 'File #2013-05-ARG: Office of the Extractive Sector CSR Counsellor's Closing Report Request for Review' (Government of Canada, 2013), www.international.gc.ca/csr_counsellor-conseiller_rse/publications/2013-05-ARG_closing_report-rapport_final.aspx?lang=eng.

—— 'Final Statement of the Canadian National Contact Point – Banro Corporation and a Group of Former Employees' (Government of Canada, 2017), www.international.gc.ca/trade-agreements-accords-commerciaux/ncp-pcn/statement-banro.aspx?lang=eng.

—— 'Final Statement on the Request for Review Regarding the Operations of China Gold International Resources Corp. Ltd., at the Copper Polymetallic Mine at the Gyama Valley, Tibet Autonomous Region' (Government of Canada, 2015), www.international.gc.ca/trade-agreements-accords-commerciaux/ncp-pcn/statement-gyama-valley.aspx?lang=eng.

—— 'Honduras Country Trip Overview: Office of the Extractive Sector Corporate Social Responsibility (CSR) Counsellor' (Government of Canada, 2016), www.international.gc.ca/csr_counsellor-conseiller_rse/trip_overview_Honduras-apercu_voyage_Honduras.aspx?lang=eng.

—— 'Registry of Requests for Review' (Government of Canada, 2017), www.international.gc.ca/csr_counsellor-conseiller_rse/Registry-web-enregistrement.aspx?lang=eng.
—— 'Request for Review Closing Report File #2012-03-ARG' (Government of Canada, 2012), www.international.gc.ca/csr_counsellor-conseiller_rse/publications/2012-03-ARG_closing_report-rapport_final.aspx?lang=eng.
—— 'Responsible Business Conduct Abroad – Questions and Answers' (Government of Canada, 2019) www.international.gc.ca/trade-agreements-accords-commerciaux/topics-domaines/other-autre/faq.aspx?lang=eng.
—— 'Role of the Office of the Corporate Social Responsibility Counsellor' (Government of Canada, 2017), www.international.gc.ca/csr_counsellor-conseiller_rse/Our_Role-Notre_Role.aspx?lang=eng.
—— 'The Review Process' (Government of Canada, 2013), www.international.gc.ca/csr_counsellor-conseiller_rse/review_process-processus_examen.aspx?lang=eng.
Government of Canada, 'Mining in Developing Countries – Corporate Social Responsibility: The Government's Response to the Report of the Standing Committee on Foreign Affairs and International Trade' (2005), www.parl.gc.ca/HousePublications/Publication.aspx?Mode=1&Language=E&DocId=2030362&File=0.
—— 'Office of the Canadian Ombudsperson for Responsible Enterprise' (2020), core-ombuds.canada.ca/core_ombuds-ocre_ombuds/index.aspx?lang=eng.
—— 'Operating Procedures of the Canadian Ombudsperson for Responsible Enterprise' (2020), core-ombuds.canada.ca/core_ombuds-ocre_ombuds/operating_procedures-procedures_exploitation.aspx.
Natural Resources Canada, 'Canadian Mining Assets' (Government of Canada, February 2019), www.nrcan.gc.ca/mining-materials/publications/19323.
National Roundtables on Corporate Social Responsibility and the Canadian Extractive Industry in Developing Countries, 'Advisory Group Report' (2007), web.archive.org/web/20110706185530/http://www.mining.ca/www/media_lib/MAC_Documents/Publications/CSRENG.pdf.
Open Parliament, 'An Act to Amend the Federal Courts Act (International Promotion and Protection of Human Rights)' (5 October 2011), openparliament.ca/bills/41-2/C-323/.
—— 'Bill C-486 (Historical) An Act respecting corporate practices relating to the extraction, processing, purchase, trade and use of conflict minerals from the Great Lakes Region of Africa', openparliament.ca/bills/41-2/C-486/.
The Standing Committee on Foreign Affairs and International Trade, 'Fourteenth Report: Mining in Developing Countries' Parliament of Canada (2005), www.parl.gc.ca/content/hoc/Committee/381/FAAE/Reports/RP1961949/FAAE_Rpt14/FAAE_Rpt14-e.pdf.

Newspaper Articles

Bermingham, F, 'Exclusive: 30 Years on from Bhopal Gas Tragedy, Dow Chemical Shareholders Demand Justice' *International Business Times* (19 November 2014), www.ibtimes.co.uk/exclusive-30-years-bhopal-gas-tragedy-thousands-victims-still-wait-justice-1475466.
Boggs, SP, 'Financial CHOICE Act Passes in the House – Would Repeal SEC Conflict Minerals Rule' *Lexology* (8 June 2017), www.lexology.com/library/detail.aspx?g=324964cb-19bc-4102-8bfa-63aaa27a620b.
Butler, M 'Why the Conflict Minerals Rule Refuses to Die' *Intelligize* (21 June 2018), www.intelligize.com/why-the-conflict-minerals-rule-refuses-to-die/.
Coletta, A, 'A Canadian Company Is Accused of Human Rights Abuses Overseas. Can It Be Sued in Canada?' *The Washington Post* (24 January 2019).
Coumans, C, 'Op-Ed: Canada Needs Effective Mining Oversight' *Ottawa Citizen* (31 October 2013).

Cumming, J, 'What the Liberals, Greens and NDP Have to Say on Mining in Canada' *Huffington Post* (10 April 2015).

Darimani, A, 'Canadian Company Plunders Ghana' *Modern Ghana* (8 April 2004), www.modernghana.com/news/62859/canadian-company-plunders-ghana.html.

Forget, A, 'Church's Knowledge of Doctrine of Discovery "Woefully Inadequate"' *Anglican Journal* (28 August 2015), www.anglicanjournal.com/articles/church-s-knowledge-of-doctrine-of-discovery-woefully-inadequate.

Goodard, E, 'Bhopal Disaster Victims May Never Get Compensation Following Dow-DuPont Merger, Fears UN Official' *Independent* (14 September 2017), www.independent.co.uk/news/business/news/bhopal-disaster-victims-dow-dupont-merger-un-india-official-gas-leak-chemical-industrial-a7946346.html.

Gratton, P, 'If Human Rights Ombudsman Is Created, Learn from Experience' *The Hill Times* (22 March 2017).

Gray, J 'Nevsun Resources Faces Lawsuit over "Forced Labour" in Eritrea' *The Globe and Mail* (20 November 2014).

Hecht, P, 'Andean Villagers Seek American Justice: Mercury Contamination near Peru Mine Leads to Legal Showdown in Denver Court' *Chronicle Foreign Service* (14 March 2015), www.sfgate.com/news/article/Andean-villagers-seek-American-justice-Mercury-2723416.php.

Imai, S, 'Will Canadian Companies Be Held Responsible for Their Actions Abroad?' *The Globe and Mail* (31 July 2013).

Kettle, J, 'Mining Sector Faces Energy Transition Conundrum' *Financial Times* (18 February 2020), www.ft.com/content/36ef7ab2-4f44-11ea-95a0-43d18ec715f5.

Koven, P, 'HudBay Case Raises Litigation Risk for Canadian Resource Companies' *Financial Post* (30 October 2013), https://financialpost.com/legal-post/hudbay-case-raises-class-action-risk-for-canadian-resource-companies.

Mazereeuw, P, 'Liberals "Seriously" Considering Mining Ombudsperson, Says Federal Corporate Social Responsibility Adviser' *The Hill Times* (9 November 2016).

Menchu, S 'Guatemala Court Confirms Suspension of Tahoe Mining Licenses' *Reuters* (6 July 2017), www.reuters.com/article/us-guatemala-mining/guatemala-court-confirms-suspension-of-tahoe-mining-licenses-idUSKCN1LK074.

Mouwad, J, 'Shell to Pay $15.5 Million to Settle Nigerian Case' *New York Times* (8 June 2009).

Perlez, J and Bergman, L, 'Tangled Strands in Fight Over Peru Gold Mine' *New York Times* (25 October 2005).

Ryan, M, 'Plight of Peru Town Dim after Mine's Mercury Spill' *Reuters* (3 July 2002) www.business-humanrights.org/en/plight-of-peru-town-dim-after-mines-mercury-spill.

Singh, A, 'Mining Industry Crackdown Continues in Philippines' *Asian Pacific Post* (29 November 2016).

'Uranium One to Delist Shares as Russia's State Nuclear Firm Takes Control' *Reuters* (19 October 2013), www.reuters.com/article/uranium-one-private-idUSL5N0I902T20131019.

Worstall, T, 'Trump's Executive Order to Repeal the Worst Law of the Year' *Forbes* (9 February 2017), www.forbes.com/sites/timworstall/2017/02/09/trumps-xo-to-repeal-the-worst-law-of-the-year-section-1502-of-dodd-frank-on-conflict-minerals/.

Websites

Bone, J, 'Do Mining Companies Adequately Value Corporate Social Responsibility?' (*Mining.com*, 4 March 2015), www.mining.com/web/mining-companies-adequately-value-corporate-social-responsibility/.

Business & Human Rights Resource Centre, 'BHP Billiton & Vale Lawsuit (Re Dam Collapse in Brazil), www.business-humanrights.org/en/bhp-billiton-vale-lawsuit-re-dam-collapse-in-brazil.

—— 'Oxfam Leaves Voluntary Principles for Security and Human Rights Multi-Stakeholder Initiative' (16 April 2013), business-humanrights.org/en/oxfam-leaves-voluntary-principles-for-security-and-human-rights-multi-stakeholder-initiative.

—— 'Shell Lawsuit (Re Oil Spills & Ogale & Bille Communities in Nigeria – Okpabi v Shell)' (2020), www.business-humanrights.org/en/shell-lawsuit-re-oil-spills-ogale-bille-communities-in-nigeria-okpabi-v-shell.

Cavendish, R, 'The Treaty of Westphalia' (1998) 48 *History Today*, www.historytoday.com/richard-cavendish/treaty-westphalia.

Coumans, C, 'Inequality of Arms: A Summary of Concerns Raised by Victims of Violence by Private and Public Mine Security at Barrick Gold's North Mara Gold Mine in Tanzania Regarding the Mine's New Operation-Level Grievance Mechanism' (*MiningWatch Canada*, 4 September 2018), miningwatch.ca/sites/default/files/north_mara_final_brief_-_inequality_of_arms_september_2018_-_clean_0.pdf.

—— 'Marinduque vs. Barrick Gold: The Province at a Crossroads. Handout to Facilitate Discussion of Options' (*MiningWatch Canada*, 13 August 2014).

Dizon, N, 'The Marcopper Disaster: A Tragedy that Continues in People's Veins' (*MiningWatch Canada*, 3 April 2019).

Earthworks 'Yanacocha' (2017), earthworksaction.org/stories/yanacocha/.

'Environmental Performance Index' (Yale Center for Environmental Law & Policy, 2018), epi.envirocenter.yale.edu.

Financial Times, 'FT Global 500' (2014), www.ft.com/content/988051be-fdee-11e3-bd0e-00144feab7de.

Gillis, C, 'Ecuador vs. Chevron-Texaco: A Brief History' (*Counterspill*, 27 April 2011).

Holmes, M, 'OceanaGold Didipio Operation Named Most Environmentally and Socially Responsible Mining Operation in the Philippines' (*Junior Mining Network*, 2017).

Nine.com.au, 'Single BHP Samarco Class Action to Proceed' (18 December 2018), finance.nine.com.au/2018/12/18/14/03/single-bhp-samarco-class-action-to-proceed.

Parliament of Canada, 'Officers and Officials of Parliament' lop.parl.ca/sites/ParlInfo/default/en_CA/Parliament/OfficersParliament.

The Gilder Lehrman Institute of American History, 'The Doctrine of Discovery, 1493' (2012) www.gilderlehrman.org/sites/default/files/inline-pdfs/04093_FPS.pdf.

Letters

Canadian civil society organisations to the Honourable François-Philippe Champagne, Minister of International Trade' (28 July 2017).

Crosby, D, President of the Canadian Conference of Catholic Bishops to the Prime Minister of Canada' (9 August 2017).

Hadunka, M, Governance and Community Liaison Officer at the Network for Community Resource Governance to Clive Newall, President of First Quantum Minerals (30 July 2018).

Justice and Corporate Accountability Project to the British Columbia Securities Commission (3 January 2019).

Other References

Africa Progress Panel, 'Equity in Extractives: Stewarding Africa's Natural Resources for All' (2013).

Amnesty International, 'Injustice Incorporated: Corporate Abuses and the Right to a Remedy' (7 March 2014), www.amnesty.org/en/documents/POL30/001/2014/en.

Canadian Centre for the Study of Resource Conflict, 'Corporate Social Responsibility: Movement and Footprints of Canadian Mining and Exploration Firms in the Developing World' (October 2009), caid.ca/CSRRep2009.pdf.

Barrick Beyond Borders, 'In Conversation with Gare Smith' (2013), https://foleyhoag.com/-/media/files/foley%20hoag/other/gare-smith-beyond-borders-barrick.ashx?la=en.

Bench Marks Foundation, 'Policy Gap 9 South African Coal Mining: Corporate Grievance Mechanisms, Community Engagement Concerns and Mining Impacts' (2014), www.bench-marks.org.za/research/policy_gap_9.pdf.

BHP, 'Respecting Human Rights' (2018), www.bhp.com/our-approach/our-company/our-code-of-conduct/caring-about-society/respecting-human-rights/.

British Petroleum, 'BP Annual Report on the Voluntary Principles on Security and Human Rights January to December 2012' (2013), www.bp.com/content/dam/bp/business-sites/en/global/corporate/pdfs/sustainability/group-reports/bp-report-to-the-voluntary-principles-plenary-2017.pdf.

Canadian Network on Corporate Accountability (CNCA), 'Executive Summary: Draft Model Legislation to Create a Human Rights Ombudsperson for the International Extractive-Sector in Canada' (2016), cnca-rcrce.ca/wp-content/uploads/2016/03/Executive-Summary-Global-Leadership-in-Business-and-Human-Rights-Draft-Extractive-Sector-Ombudsperson-Model-Legislation-11022016.pdf.

—— 'The Global Leadership in Business and Human Rights Act: An Act to Create an Independent Human Rights Ombudsperson for the International Extractive Sector Draft Model Legislation' (2 November 2016), cnca-rcrce.ca/wp-content/uploads/2019/04/The-Global-Leadership-in-Business-and-Human-Rights-Act.pdf.

Compliance Advisor Ombudsman, 'Extracting Sustainable Advantage? A Review of How Sustainability Issues Have Been Dealt with in Recent IFC & MIGA Extractive Industries Projects' (April 2003), www.cao-ombudsman.org/howwework/advisor/documents/FINALExtractiveIndustriesReviewReport.pdf.

—— 'Review of IFC Social and Environmental Performance Standards on Disclosure of Information' (May 2010).

Davis, R and Franks, D, 'The Cost of Conflict with Local Communities in the Extractive Industry' (SR Mining, October 2011), www.csrm.uq.edu.au/publications/the-costs-of-conflict-with-local-communities-in-the-extractive-industry.

Dutch Ministry of Foreign Affairs, 'Contribution by the Government of the Netherlands to the Renewed EU-Strategy for CSR' (2012).

EarthRights International, 'Peruvian Farmers Appeal in Fight to Hold Newmont Accountable in U.S. Court' (4 May 2018), earthrights.org/media/peruvian-farmers-appeal-fight-hold-newmont-accountable-u-s-court/.

Enodo Rights, 'Pillar III on the Ground: An Independent Assessment of the Porgera Remedy Framework' (2016), barrick.q4cdn.com/788666289/files/porgera/Enodo-Rights-Porgera-Remedy-Framework-Independent-Assessment.pdf.

Environmental Justice, 'Didipio Gold and Copper Mine, Nueva Vizcaya, Philippines' (23 January 2017).

Environmental Justice Organisations, Liabilities and Trade (EJOLT), 'The Yanacocha Mine Case' (5 August 2015), www.ejolt.org/wordpress/wp-content/uploads/2015/08/FS-43.pdf.

Fairley, S and Sumakova, A, 'Tort Liability at Home for Alleged Wrongs Abroad: The Common Law Goes Extraterritorial?' (*WeirFoulds LLP*, November 2014), www.mondaq.com/canada/international-trade-investment/357576/tort-liability-at-home-for-alleged-wrongs-abroad-the-common-law-goes-extraterritorial.

Feeney, P, 'Making Companies Accountable: An NGO Report on Implementation of the OECD Guidelines for Multinational Enterprises by National Contact Points' (October 2002), www.oecd.org/dataoecd/16/37/2965489.pdf.

German NGO Working Group on Deep Sea Mining, 'Position Paper of German Civil Society Organizations on Deep Sea Mining: Stop the Exploitation of the Deep Sea!' (April 2018), www.asienhaus.de/archiv/asienhaus/erklaerungen/Position_paper_on_Deep_Sea_Mining-web.pdf.

Global Reporting Initiative (GRI), 'G4 Sustainability Reporting Guidelines: Implementation Manual' (2013), www.respect.international/g4-sustainability-reporting-guidelines-implementation-manual/.

Herz, S, et al. 'The International Finance Corporation's Performance Standards and the Equator Principles: Respecting Human Rights and Remedying Violations' (Center for Environmental Law, Bank Information Center, BankTrack, Oxfam Australia and World Resources Institute, 2008), www.ciel.org/wp-content/uploads/2015/06/Ruggie_Submission.pdf.

Human Rights Clinic (Columbia Law School) & International Human Rights Clinic (Harvard Law School), 'Righting Wrongs? Barrick Gold's Remedy Mechanism for Sexual Violence in Papua New Guinea: Key Concerns and Lessons Learned' (2015).

Human Rights Watch, 'Human Rights Impacts of Papua New Guinea's Porgera Gold Mine' (February, 2011), www.hrw.org/report/2011/02/01/golds-costly-dividend/human-rights-impacts-papua-new-guineas-porgera-gold-mine.

ICIS Chemical Business, 'Thor Chemicals Settles out of Court for \$2.1m' (20 April 1997), www.icis.com/resources/news/1997/04/21/30350/thor-chemicals-settles-out-of-court-for-2-1m/.

International Council on Human Rights Policy, 'Beyond Voluntarism: Human Rights and the Developing International Legal Obligations of Companies' (February 2002), www.ichrp.org/files/reports/7/107_report_en.pdf.

International Council on Mining & Metals, 'Human Rights in the Mining & Metals Industry: Handling and Resolving Local Level Concerns & Grievances' (2009).

International Finance Corporation World Bank Group, 'Good Practice Note: Addressing Grievances from Project-Affected Communities – Guidance for Projects and Companies on Designing Grievance Mechanisms' (Washington, 2009).

—— 'IFC Performance Standards on Environmental and Social Sustainability – Effective January 1, 2012'

—— 'International Finance Corporation's Policy on Environmental and Social Sustainability' (1 January 2012).

International Petroleum Industry Environmental Conservation Association, 'Community Grievance Mechanisms in the Oil and Gas Industry. A Manual for Implementing Operational-Level Grievance Mechanisms and Designing Corporate Frameworks' (January 2015), www.ipieca.org/resources/good-practice/community-grievance-mechanisms-in-the-oil-and-gas-industry-a-manual-for-implementing-operational-level-grievance-mechanisms-and-designing-corporate-frameworks.

International Women and Mining Network 'Women from Mining Affected Communities Speak Out: Defending Land, Life & Dignity' (*Academia.edu*, 2010), www.academia.edu/4195877/Women_from_Mining_Affected_Communities_Speak_Out_Defending_Land_Life_and_Dignity.

Kemp, D and Bond, CJ, 'Mining Industry Perspectives on Handling Community Grievances: Summary and Analysis of Industry Interviews' (Centre for Social Responsibility in Mining, the University of Queensland, April 2009), www.csrm.uq.edu.au/media/docs/260/mining_industry_perspectives_on_handling_community_grievances_summary.pdf.

KPMG Unit for Corporate Governance in Africa, 'Carrots and Sticks: Promoting Transparency and Sustainability: An Update on Trends in Voluntary and Mandatory Approaches to Sustainable Reporting' (2008), www.globalreporting.org/resourcelibrary/Carrots-And-Sticks-Promoting-Transparency-And-Sustainbability.pdf.

Kuyek, J 'Another Mining Horror Story? Sherritt International Corporation's Ambatovy Project in Madagascar' *MiningWatch Canada* (10 April 2012), miningwatch.ca/blog/2012/4/10/another-mining-horror-story-sherritt-international-corporation-s-ambatovy-project.

Lee, J, 'Brief: Comparing NGO Influence in the EU and the U.S.' (September 2006), www.files.ethz.ch/isn/25102/ngoinfluenceinuandusa.pdf.

Luk, S, 'Ditching the Doctrine of Discovery (and What That Means for Canadian Law)' (*Olthuis Kleer Townshend LLP*, 30 November 2015), oktlaw.com/ditching-doctrine-discovery-means-canadian-law.

Macey, J, 'The Three Justifications for Piercing the Corporate Veil' *Harvard Law School Forum on Corporate Governance* (27 March 2014), corpgov.law.harvard.edu/2014/03/27/the-three-justifications-for-piercing-the-corporate-veil/.

Meeran, R, 'Liability of Multinational Corporations: A Critical Stage' (1999), www.labournet.net/images/cape/campanal.htm.
Mining Association of Canada, 'Site-Level Grievance and Community Response Mechanisms: A Practical Design and Implementation Guide for the Resource Development Industry' (2015), mining.ca/site-level-grievance-mechanisms-guide.
Mining Technology.com, 'Australian Mining Industry Forecast to 2015' (2011), www.mining-technology.com/features/featureaustralian-mining-industry-forecast-to-2015.
MiningWatch Canada, 'Can Slave Labour Charges Against Canadian Company Be Heard in Court in Canada? Supreme Court of Canada Hears Arguments Today' (23 January 2019).
—— 'Guatemala's Highest Court Orders Tahoe's Escobal Mine to Remain Suspended' (4 September 2018), https://miningwatch.ca/news/2018/9/4/guatemala-s-highest-court-orders-tahoe-s-escobal-mine-remain-suspended?.
—— 'Privatized Remedy and Human Rights: Re-Thinking Project-Level Grievance Mechanisms' (2014), miningwatch.ca/publications/2014/12/1/privatized-remedy-and-human-rights-re-thinking-project-level-grievance.
—— 'The Lawsuit (Tahoe on Trial)' (2019), tahoeontrial.net/the-lawsuit/.
Newman, S, 'Summary of Provincial Gov't of Marinduque v. Placer Dome, Inc., 131 Nev. Adv. Op. 63076 (11 June 2015) Paper 878' *Nevada Supreme Court Summaries* (2015), scholars.law.unlv.edu/nvscs/878.
OECD, 'OECD Due Diligence Guidance for Meaningful Stakeholder Engagement in the Extractive Sector' (Paris, OECD Publishing, 2017), doi.org/10.1787/9789264252462-en.
—— 'OECD Due Diligence Guidance on Responsible Supply Chains of Minerals from Conflict-Affected and High-Risk Areas: Second Edition' (2013), www.oecd.org/corporate/mne/GuidanceEdition2.pdf.
——, 'The OECD Guidelines for Multinational Enterprises' (2011), http:www.oecd.org/dataoecd/56/36/1922428.pdf.
Office of the Compliance Advisor/Ombudsman, 'Regarding Two Complaints Filed with the CAO in Relation to Minera Yanacocha, Cajamarca, Peru' (February 2006), www.cao-ombudsman.org/cases/document-links/documents/Exitreportenglish02-7-06-final.pdf.
'Ombudsman Needed to Monitor Australian Corporate Practice in Pacific' *AustraliaPlus* (6 June 2008).
On Common Ground Consultants Inc, 'Report for the Mining Association of Canada's International Social Responsibility Committee' (2012), oncommonground.ca/wp-content/uploads/2012/07/Final-MAC-Roundtables-Report-_December-21-2011_-_3_5.pdf.
Oxfam Australia, 'Community–Company Grievance Resolution: A Guide for the Australian Mining Industry' (2010), www.oxfam.org.au/wp-content/uploads/2011/11/OAus-Grievance Mechanisms-0410.pdf.
—— 'Didipio Mining Projects: Mining Ombudsman Case Report' (2007), www.mpiasia.net/component/booklibrary/2/view_bl/88/157/mining-ombudsman-case-report-didipio-gold-and-copper-mine.html?Itemid=2.
—— 'Marinduque Island: Mining Ombudsman Case Report' (2005), www.mpiasia.net/component/booklibrary/2/view_bl/88/152/mining-ombudsman-case-report-marinduque-island.html?Itemid=2.
—— 'Rapu Rapu Polymetallic Mine: Mining Ombudsman Case Report' (2008), www.banktrack.org/download/mining_ombudsman_case_report_rapu_rapu_polymetallic_mine/rapurapucasereport.pdf.
—— 'Tolukuma Gold Mine: Mining Ombudsman Case Report' (2004), www.mpiasia.net/component/booklibrary/2/view_bl/88/154/mining-ombudsman-case-report-tolukuma-gold-mine.html?Itemid=2.
—— 'Vatukoula Gold Mine: Mining Ombudsman Case Report' (2004), resources.oxfam.org.au/pages/view.php?ref=99.
—— '2004 Mining Ombudsman Annual Report' (2005), www.eldis.org/document/A16608.
Panel of Experts on the Democratic Republic of the Congo, 'Final Report of the Panel of Experts on Illegal Exploitation of Natural Resources and Other Forms of Wealth of the Democratic Republic of Congo' (2002), repositories.lib.utexas.edu/bitstream/handle/2152/5170/2477.pdf?sequence=1.

Pastrana, D, 'US Mining Company Demands $3.5 Billion Dollars from the Mexican Government for Stopping Project' (*stopesmining.org*, 24 September 2019), www.stopesmining.org/news/89-free-trade-agreements-news/576-us-mining-company-demands-3-5-billion-dollars-from-the-mexican-government-for-stopping-project.

Pertoldi, A and McIntosh, M, 'Brexit under the Withdrawal Agreement: The Implications for Disputes' *Herbert Smith Freehills LLP* (22 January 2020).

SEC, 'Division of Corporate Finance Letter' (18 March 2014), www.sec.gov/divisions/corpfin/cf-noaction/14a-8/2014/amnestyinternational031814-14a8.pdf.

SEC, 'Form 10-Q' (30 September 2009), www.sec.gov/Archives/edgar/data/1164727/000095012309054293/c91265e10vq.htm.

SEC Press Release, 'SEC Adopts Rules to Establish Whistleblower Program' (25 May 2011), www.sec.gov/news/press/2011/2011-116.htm.

Siskinds LLP, 'Siskinds LLP Announces Filing of Proposed Securities Class Action against Tahoe Resources Inc.' *CISION* (19 November 2018), www.newswire.ca/news-releases/siskinds-llp-announces-filing-of-proposed-securities-class-action-against-tahoe-resources-inc-700827921.html.

Skinner, G, McCorquodale, R and De Schutter, O, 'The Third Pillar: Access to Judicial Remedies for Human Rights Violations by Transnational Business' (The International Corporate Accountability Roundtable, 2013).

Special Representative on Business and Human Rights (SRBHR), 'United Nations Guiding Principles on Business and Human Rights: Implementing the United Nations "Protect, Respect and Remedy" Framework' (United Nations, 2011), www.ohchr.org/documents/publications/guidingprinciplesbusinesshr_en.pdf.

Stikeman Elliott, 'Global Mining Update: Québec Court Decides to Dismiss Proceedings: Tailings Dam Collapse to Be Litigated in Guyana' (1999).

Subcommission on the Promotion and Protection of Human Rights, 'Norms on the Responsibilities of Transnational Corporations and Other Business Enterprises with Regard to Human Rights' (*United Nations Digital Library*, 2003), digitallibrary.un.org/record/501576?ln=en.

United Nations, 'Paris Agreement' (2015), unfccc.int/files/essential_background/convention/application/pdf/english_paris_agreement.pdf.

—— 'Secretary-General Proposes Global Compact on Human Rights, Labour, Environment, in Address to World Economic Forum in Davos' (1999), www.un.org/press/en/1999/19990201.sgsm6881.html.

—— 'UNCITRAL Model Law on International Commercial Arbitration (1985), with Amendments as Adopted in 2006' (2006), www.uncitral.org/pdf/english/texts/arbitration/arb-rules/MLARB-english_revised%2006.pdf.

United Nations General Assembly, 'Report of the Working Group on the Issue of Human Rights and Transnational Corporations and Other Business Enterprises' (28 April 2015), www.refworld.org/pdfid/5583f3144.pdf.

United Nations Office of the High Commissioner on Human Rights, 'State National Action Plans on Business and Human Rights' (2020), www.ohchr.org/en/issues/business/pages/nationalactionplans.aspx.

United Nations Special Representative on Business and Human Rights, 'The Corporate Responsibility to Respect Human Rights: An Interpretative Guide' (United Nations, 2011), www.ohchr.org/Documents/Publications/HR.PUB.12.2_En.pdf.

—— 'United Nations Guiding Principles on Business and Human Rights: Implementing the United Nations "Protect, Respect and Remedy" Framework' (2011), www.ohchr.org/documents/publications/guidingprinciplesbusinesshr_en.pdf.

US Department of State Bureau of Democracy, Human Rights and Labor, 'Voluntary Principles on Security and Human Rights. Fact Sheet' (20 December 2012), https://2009-2017.state.gov/j/drl/rls/fs/2012/202314.htm.

Vergara, S and Gneiting, U, 'Why Did Goldcorp Really Pull out of Tahoe Resources's Troubled Guatemalan Mining Project?' (*Oxfam America*, 7 July 2015), https://politicsofpoverty.oxfamamerica.org/why-did-goldcorp-really-pull-out-of-tahoe-resourcess-troubled-guatemalan-mining-project/.

INDEX

www.ingramcontent.com/pod-product-compliance
Lightning Source LLC
Chambersburg PA
CBHW071259180926
51613CB00001B/77
* 9 7 8 1 5 0 9 9 4 1 8 7 2 *